Constitutional Democracy in Africa

Spectrum Law Series

Nigerian Legal System – *Obilade*

An Introduction to Equity in Nigeria – *Kodilinye*

Nigerian Law of Contract – *Sagay*

Criminal Law in Nigeria – *Okonkwo* and *Naish*

The Law of Evidence – *Aguda*

Nigerian Tax Law – *Ayua*

Introduction to International Law – *Umozurike*

History and Sources of Nigerian Criminal Law – *Karibi-Whyte*

Law of Judicial Immunities in Nigeria – *Olowofoyeku*

Military Rule and Constitutionalism in Nigeria – *Ben Nwabueze*

Military Rule and Social Justice in Nigeria – *Ben Nwabueze*

Democratisation – *Ben Nwabueze*

The Making of the 1989 Constitution of Nigeria – *Aniagolu*

Jurisprudence – *Elegido*

Sharia Law Reports of Nigeria Vol. 1 – *Mahmood*

A Compendium of Notable Pronouncements of our Jurists Through Cases – *Sanda*

Justice Delayed is Justice Denied – *Sanda*

Customary Law in Nigeria Through the Cases – *Kolajo*

Layman's Guide to Criminal Law and Anti-Corruption Law – *Kolajo*

Law for the Layman – *Kolajo*

Modern Digest of Case Law – *Aderemi*

Family Law – *Onokah*

All-Nigeria Judges' Conference 2001 – *National Judicial Institute*

Constitutional Democracy in Africa
Volume 1

Structures, Powers and Organising Principles of Government

Ben Nwabueze

Spectrum Books Limited
Ibadan
Abuja •Benin City •Lagos •Owerri

Spectrum titles can be purchased on line at
www.spectrumbooksonline.com

Published by
Spectrum Books Limited
Spectrum House
Ring Road
PMB 5612
Ibadan, Nigeria
e-mail: *admin1@spectrumbooksonline.com*

in association with
Safari Books (Export) Limited
1st Floor
17 Bond Street
St Helier
Jersey JE2 3NP
Channel Islands
United Kingdom.

Europe and USA Distributor
African Books Collective Ltd
The Jam Factory
27 Park End Street
Oxford OX1, 1HU, UK

© Ben Nwabueze

First published, 2003

ISBN: 978-029-432-5

Dalag Prints & Packaging Limited Ibadan

Foreword

This seven-volume work now being presented is the culmination of an ambitious project of an illustrious Nigerian jurist who has already made his mark in the field of constitutional law and jurisprudence. It comes at a most appropriate time when ethnic nationalism is tearing apart the superstructure of states even in the old Western world and now brutally in the Balkans. Exploring the evolution of the state system transplanted to Africa by European colonialism, the author analyses the nature of this sophisticated organism and the failure of African leaders since independence to domesticate it.

Professor Nwabueze argues that this **alien state** system had all but destroyed the mind, culture and personality of the African, eroded the indigenous bases of authority without establishing any roots in African culture, deconstructed the traditional African political institutions and offices and generated social violence, unrest and incompatibilities among the plural societies that make up each African state. He goes further to explore the differences between the more recent Western European colonial heritage with that of the ancient and medieval colonialism in North Africa and the subsequent Arab and Islamic religious and cultural colonialism in Africa, south of the Sahara. In the author's view, one of the most serious problems haunting the post independence African governments is the **national question,** that is, how to weld together harmoniously into one nation in each African territory, the peoples of different culture, language and sometimes even of race forcibly brought together by the colonial regimes.

Professor Nwabueze puts forward the thesis that a precondition for the evolution of true African states in the post colonial era, is the **decolonisation** of the African mind, culture, society and state in a conscious, slow but sympathetic effort. Without such a process of decolonisation, the endemic chaos that has set in everywhere cannot be dislodged nor can the plural societies forcibly patched together in the so-called post-colonial African states cohere for long.

Professor Nwabueze's book does not merely fill a gap or a void in the literature of African history, law, economy, politics and society; rather, it creates a novel and significant niche that will, for many years to come, serve as a quarry for scholars and researchers seeking the explanation for the disorder and trauma that have followed the nominal transfer of power from the old colonials to the naive inheritors.

In its sweep and its formidable scholarship, its historicism and its underlying jurisprudence, this study is comparable to two projects of a similar nature by UNESCO: **A Scientific and Cultural History of Mankind** and the companion volume, **General History of Africa.** Professor Nwabueze's work is at once magisterial and authoritative; it is learned and erudite without being pedantic, critical, incisive and perceptive without being carping, informative and comprehensive without being tedious. It will place the author securely in the gallery of Africa's great scholars.

These volumes are warmly recommended to all serious students of African politics, law, culture and society and to all those interested in restructuring African states into lasting and orderly societies and polities.

Julius K Nyerere

Julius Nyerere

Postscript: Since this Foreword was written by Julius Nyerere who died not long after writing it, the work has been re-structured into two sets of volumes under the titles **Colonialism in Africa** (two volumes of 831 pages and **Constitutional Democracy in Africa** (five volumes of more than 2,500 pages).

Preface

Statism and constitutional democracy may be said to be European colonialism's great, and seemingly enduring legacies to Africa. But what is the nature of these two complex and sophisticated notions brought to Africa by European colonialism? In the sophisticated form in which it was transplanted to Africa by European colonialism, the state, with its institutions, principles and processes, notably legislated law regularly enforced by courts with compulsive jurisdiction, was certainly unknown to the continent before colonisation and was, consequently, without roots in its culture, political system and way of life. So was constitutional democracy which is defined in the study as a government freely elected by the people on a universal adult franchise, (one person, one vote) and limited in its power by a written constitution (a written constitution was unknown in Africa before European colonization) having the force of a supreme law overriding all inconsistent legislative and executive acts of government and whose provisions are observed and respected **in practice** by the rulers and the ruled as the active, governing rules of government administration and of the game of politics generally. The question that arises is whether statism and constitutional democracy are a blessing or curse or a mixture of both. And what is the nature of colonialism itself? How did Africa come to be colonised by Europe? How did it regain its sovereignty seized from it during the period of colonisation? Apart from the alien state system and constitutional democracy, what are the other legacies of European colonialism to Africa?

These are the central issues examined in this seven volume work, **Colonialism in Africa: Ancient and Modern** in two volumes of 831 pages (a third volume is projected on the inheritance of social violence – civil wars and wars of secession) and **Constitutional Democracy in Africa** in five volumes of over 2,500 pages.

It has been an exciting, if exacting, task, which has left me thoroughly exhausted as well as broken healthwise. Studying the constitutions of African countries from independence to date, with the everfrequent changes, is a most daunting task indeed. But I am pleased to have accomplished it.

Acknowledgements

I wish now to acknowledge my heavy debt of gratitude to the following people – the late Julius Nyerere, former President of Tanzania, for writing the Foreword; the late Dr. Pius Okigbo, for writing the Introduction to both volumes of **Colonialism in Africa: Ancient and Modern;** Hon. Justice Mohammed Bello, former Chief Justice of Nigeria, Chief F.R.A Williams SAN, Hon. Justice Chukwudifu Oputa, former Justice of the Supreme Court of Nigeria, General (Dr) Yakubu Gowon, former Head of State of Nigeria, and Chief Emeka Anyaoku, former Secretary-General of the Commonwealth, for writing the Introductions to volumes 1, 2, 3, 4 and 5 respectively of **Constitutional Democracy in Africa.** My debt to them is all the heavier because of the enormous sacrifice of having to squeeze out the time amidst their extremely crowded programmes. My Secretary, Damian Obiefule, has been as untiring as ever in typing the manuscripts.

To my wife, Ngozi, and my sweet little daughter, Sarafina, I owe more than I can acknowledge for putting up perseveringly with the hell of life with me during the long years that I was working on the volumes. Only they know what it meant. I am by nature an irritable and hot-tempered person, but my work on the volumes had made me infinitely more so.

Ben Nwabueze
Lagos
April 2003

Contents

page

Foreword   *v*

Preface   *vii*

Acknowledgements   *ix*

Table of Cases   *xiii*

Table of Statutes   *xvii*

Introduction   *xxviii*

1.   The Concept of Constitutional Democracy   1

2.   Functions of a Constitution   36

3.   Federal-State Relations under the Constitution
     of Nigeria   59

4.   Fundamental Principles of Federalism and the
     Subversion of them and Other Aspects of the
     Constitution by a Federal Statute in Nigeria   90

5.   The Controversy over the Sharing of Money in
     the Federation Account among the Constituent
     Governments in Nigeria   119

6.   Local Government in a Federal and Presidential System   155

7.   Nature and Role of Legislation in Modern
     Government and the Struggle between Rival
     or Competing Interests for the Control of
     Legislative Power   181

8.   Nature and Extent of Executive Power   211

9.   Separation of Powers under the Constitution:
Its Merits and Demerits   241

10.   Limits of the Separation of Powers   258

11.   Consequences Flowing from the Separation of Powers   278

12.   Efficacy of Separation of Powers and Other
Constitutional Limitations on Power: The Question
of Enforcement and Remedies   312

13.   Fostering Partnership between the Legislature
and the Executive for Sustainable Democracy:
A Constitutionalist Perspective   337

14.   Limitations on Legislative and Executive
Powers Arising from Constitutional Protection
of the Liberty of the Individual   370

Index   405

Table of Cases

Page

Adeniji-Adele & Others *v.* Governor of Lagos State & Others (1982) 162
Adiukwu & Others *v.* Federal House of Representatives & Others (1982) 350
Allgeyer *v.* Louisiana (1897) 373
Anyah *v.* Attorney-General Borno State & Another (1982) 365
Archbishop Okogie *v.* Attorney-General of Lagos State, Suit
   No. FCA/L/74/80 .... 399, 403
————— & Others *v.* Attorney-General of Lagos State, Suit
   No. FHC/L/74/80 104
————— *v.* Attorney-General of Lagos State Suit No. ID/17M/80 403
Attorney-General *v.* Colonial Sugar Refining Co. Ltd, (1914) A.C. 237 at p. 253 61
————— for Ontario *v.* Attorney-General for the Dominion (1896)
   A.C. 348 (P.C.) 315
————— , Kaduna State *v.* Hassan (1983) 236
————— of Ogun State & Others *v.* Attorney-General of the Federation &
   Ors. (1982) 3
   NCLR 583 .... 92, 97, 100, 254
————— of Ondo State *v.* Attorney-General of the Federation & 35 Others
   SC 2000/2001 .... 92, 98, 101, 116
————— of Ontario *v.* Hamilton Street Ry (1903) A.C. 524 at p. 529 316
————— of Southern Nigeria *v.* John Holt (1915) A.C. 599 .... 123, 140

Balewa *v.* Doherty (1963) 108
Balogun *v.* Attorney-General of Lagos State (1980) 163
Bates *v.* Little Rock 361 U.S. 516 (1960) 378-379
Bribery Commission *v.* Ranasingbe (1965) A.C. 172 .... 193, 335-336, 380
Brown *v.* Board of Education, 347 U.S. 483 (1954) 324

Cohen *v.* Virginia 19 U.S. 264 at 404 (1821) 333-334
Communist Party *v.* Subversive Activities Control Board 351 U.S. 115
   (1956); 361 U.S. 1 (1961) 379
Cummings *v.* State of Missouri (1866) 294
Cunningham *v.* Neagle (1890) 215, 218-219

D'Emden *v.* Pedder (1904) 1 CLR, at p. 111 94

Eshugbayi Eleko *v.* Government of Nigeria (1931) 371

Federal Minister of Internal Affairs & Others *v.* Shugaba (1982) 3 N.C.L.R. 915 77

Fletcher *v.* Peck (1810) 382

Governor, Kaduna State *v.* House of Assembly, Kaduna State (1981) 227, 280, 346
Governor of Lagos State *v.* Chief Odumegwu Ojukwu (1986) 190

Harris *v.* Minister of the Interior (1952) (2) S.A. 428 329
Huddari, Parker & Co. Ltd. *v.* Moorehead (1909) 8 C.L.R. 330, per Griffith,
    C.J. of the High Court of Australia 43
Humphrey *v.* U.S. (1935) 282, 284, 291

Illinois C.R. Co. *v.* Interstate Commerce Commission (1906) 283

Kariapper *v.* Wijesinha (1965) 294
———— *v.* ———— (1967) 293
Konigsberg *v.* State Bar of California 366 U.S. 36 (1961) 379

Lakanmi *v.* Attorney-General (West) (1970) 292
Lawal *v.* Lagos State Electoral Commission (1980) 166-167
Liyange *v.* R. (1966) 293, 295
———— *v.* ———— (1967) 1 A. C. 259 .... 335, 382
———— (Appeal from Ceylon) 8
Lockner *v.* New York (1905) 387

Madras *v.* Champahan (1951) SCR 252 104
Maigida (Solicitor-General & Permanent Secretary; Ministry of Justice,
    Kaduna State) *v.* House of Assembly, Kaduna State & Another (1981) 256
Marbury *v.* Madison 1 Cranch 137 (1803) 28, 249, 313, 333
McCullock *v.* Maryland 4 Wheat 31 (1819) 94, 109
Melbourne Corporation *v.* Commonwealth (1947) 74 CLR 31, 82-83 95
Minister of the Interior *v.* Harris (1952) (4) S. A. 330
Momoh *v.* Senate of the National Assembly (1981) 350
Myers *v.* United States (1926) 215, 249, 255-256, 279, 283, 303, 354

National Association for the Advancement of Coloured People *v.* Alabama
    357 U.S. 449 (1958) 378
Ndlwana *v.* Hofmeyr (1937) A.D. 229 328
New York *v.* United States (1946) 326 U.S. 572 96
———— ex rel Bryant *v.* Zimmerman 278 U.S. 63 (1928) 379
Ngwenya *v.* Deputy Prime Minister (1973) 295
Nyadi Limited *v.* Attorney-General (1956) 1 Q.B. 1 at p. 15 137

Obeya Memorial Specialist Hospital *v.* Attorney-General of the Federation
    (1987) 190
Okitipupa Oil Palm Company Ltd. *v.* Jegede & Others (1982) 350
Olajire *v.* Superintendent-General of Local Government Services (1961)
    All N.L.R. 826 84

Panama Refining Co. *v.* Ryan (1935) 305

Pesikata *v.* State of Bombay (1955) 257

Plessy *v.* Ferguson 163 U.S. 537 (1996) 324

R. *v.* Commonwealth Court of Conciliation and Arbitration Ex Parte Victoria
(1942) 66 CLR 488 94

———— *v.* Earl of Crewe (1910) 2 K.B. 576 at p. 620 .... 136, 383

———— *v.* Keyn (1876) 2 Ex. D. 63 at p. 67 139

———— *v.* Kidman (1915) 107, 109-111

Railroad Company *v.* Brown, 17 Wall 445 (1873) 324

Re: Ownership of Offshore Mineral Rights (1968) 65 DLR (2nd) 353 142

Schechter Poultry Corp. *v.* United States 301-302, 305

Standard Oil Company *v.* United States (1930) 283

The State *v.* Akor & Others (1981) 238

———— *v.* Ilori & Others (1982) 239

State of Madras *v.* Champaham (1951) S.C.R. 252 399

Staub *v.* Baxley 335 U.S. 313 (1958)) 378

United States *v.* Evans 213 U.S. 297 pp. 300-1 (1909) 315

———— *v.* Ferreira 13 How: 40 (1851) 313

———— *v.* Lorell 328 U.S, 303, 314 313

———— *v.* Lovett (1945) 293

———— *v.* State of California 332 U.S. 19 143

Viereck *v.* United States (1943) 318 U.S. 236 379

Wall *v.* Parrot Silver & Copper Co. (1917) 256

Waterside Workers Federation of Australia *v.* J.W. Alexander Ltd. (1918) ... 297

West *v.* Commissioner of Taxation (1937) 56 C.L.R. 657 at p. 681 94

Williams *v.* Majekodunmi (1962) 303

———— *v.* United States (1932) 283

Yakus *v.* U.S. (1944) 306

Youngstown Sheet and Tube Co. *v.* Sawyer (1951) 216, 302, 371

Table of Statutes

Page

ACTS

Act of Congress, 1876 279
Acts of Parliament 71, 331
Allocation of Revenue (Federation Account, etc)
    Act Cap. 16 .... 126, 129, 175
    s. 4(A) (6) 127
Companies and Allied Matters Act, the Banks and Financial Institutions
    Decree 186
Constitution, 1960
    s. 70 69
    s. 124 267
    s. 134(6) 141, 147
Constitution, 1963
    s. 5 67
    s. 11 67-68
    s. 11(4) 75
    s. 11 (5) 75
    s. 71 67
    s. 99 97
    s. 100 97
    s. 105 (7) 84
    s. 130 267
    s. 140 (6) 141, 147
    s. 305 (3) 74
    s. 305 (4) 74
    s. 305 (5) 75
Constitution, 1979
    s. 2(2)(a) 148
    s. 4(2) 311
    s. 11 51
    s. 47 338
    s. 75 267
    s. 82 (1) 97
    s. 149 (2) 148
    s. 274 (1) 309
    s. 274 (2) 308-311, 344

s. 274 (4) 309
s. 315 (2) 311
s. 315 (4)(c) 311

Constitution, 1999

s. 1 .... 148, 255, 332
s. 1(1) 121, 335
s. 2 134
s. 2(2) 143-144
s. 2 (2) (a) 148
s. 3 134
s. 3 (1) 143-144
s. 3 (6) 164-165
s. 4 .... 25, 92, 100-102, 106, 183, 198, 258, 291
s. 4(A)(6) 148
s. 4(1) 306
s. 4(2) 117, 311
s. 4(3) 86
s. 4(7) 160, 171
s. 4(8) 105
s. 5 .... 75, 102, 236
s. 5(1) 215, 222, 287, 291-292, 373
s. 5(1)(b) 217, 254
s. 5(2) 160
s. 5(3) 66
s. 5(4)(a) 347
s. 5(4)(b) 348
s. 5(5) 171
s. 6 .... 102, 283, 341
s. 6(2) 347
s. 6(6) 75, 102
s. (6)(c) 105, 115-116
s. 6(d) 105
s. 7 .... 162, 283
s. 7(1) 160-161
s. 7(2) 162-163
s. 7(4) 168-169
s. 7(5) 170
s. 8 .... 99, 198, 217
s. 8(1)(d) 347
s. 8(2)(b) 348
s. 8(2)(b)(1) 347
s. 8(3) 165
s. 8(4) 165
s. 8(6) 165
s. 9 .... 78, 99, 198
s. 10 .... 66, 99, 367
s. 11 .... 67-68, 81, 99, 102, 107, 388
s. 11(4) 75

s. 11(5) 75
s. 12 99
s. 12(1) 217
s. 12(2) 132-133
s. 13 .... 102, 104, 112-113, 266
s. 14 113
s. 14 (1) 288
s. 14(3) 56
s. 14(4) 357
s. 15 113
s. 15(5) 100-104, 115, 117
s. 16 113
s. 16(4) 347
s. 18 403
s. 33 387
s. 34(1) (a) and (b) 387
s. 34(1) and (2) 387
s. 35 .... 383, 387
s. 35(1) (c) 387
s. 36 387
ss. 37-39 389
s. 40 .... 374, 389
s. 41 389
ss. 42-44 387
s. 45(1) 389
s. 45(2) 388-389
s. 50(2)(c) 347
s. 51 287
s. 54 299
s. 58 198
s. 58(1) 281
s. 58(4) 207
s. 58(5) 335
s. 59 .... 198, 210
s. 59 (4) 210
s. 61(3) 100
s. 64 274
s. 64(3) 274
s. 65(2)(a) 352
s. 67(1) 274
     (2) 348
s. 74 348
s. 77(2) 169
s. 80 .... 221, 226, 270
s. 80(4) 221
s. 81 .... 192, 266, 268-270
s. 81(1) 263
s. 81 (2) 263

s. 81 (3) 290
s. 86(1) 280
s. 88 .... 347, 349
s. 88(1) 349
s. 88(2) 349
s. 98 .... 111, 114
s. 100 198
s. 106 170
s. 107 170
s. 113 266
s. 117(2) 169
s. 130(1) 338
s. 131(d) 352
s. 135(3) 347
s. 140(1) 254
s. 143(2) 364
s. 143(3) 347
s. 143(4) 347
s. 143(9) 347
s. 143(11) 364
s. 146(3) 348
s. 147(1) 265
s. 147(2) 280
s. 148(2) 259
s. 148(5) 212
s. 149(2) 148, 175
s. 150 233
s. 150(1) 347
s. 151(2) 233
s. 152 .... 330, 332
s. 153 .... 228, 231
s. 153(1) 280
s. 154(2) 280
s. 157 228
s. 160(2) 236
s. 162(2) 119, 145-149, 154
s. 162(3) 129, 152-153, 175
s. 162(5) 175
s. 162(7) 175
s. 171 231
s. 171 (4) 280
s. 173(2) 357
s. 174(3) 233
s. 191 238
s. 191(2) 236
s. 214(1) 84
s. 214(2) 85
s. 214(2)(a) 85

s. 214(2)(b) 85
s. 215 .... 231-232, 292
s. 215(1) 87
s. 216(2) 87
s. 222 .... 374-375, 377
s. 223-226 376
s. 228 377
s. 251(1) 78
s. 274(1) 166
s. 274(2) 345
s. 305 358
s. 305(3) 74
s. 305(4) 74
s. 305 (5) 75
s. 305 (6) 347
s. 305(6)(d) 348
s. 308(1) 340-342
s. 308(1)(c) 341
s. 310 287
s. 313 126
s. 315 .... 105, 133, 311
s. 315(1) 166, 306
s. 315(1)(a) 306
s. 315(2) 310-311
s. 315(4)(c) 311
s. 318 .... 103, 287
s. 318(1) 171, 352
Corrupt Practices and Related Offences Act 2000 ..... 90, 92, 108, 111-112, 285
s. 2 113
s. 3(6) 90
s. 3(8) 90
s. 5(2) 90-91
s. 61(1) 91

Education Act 394
Electoral Act, 1977 167-168
Emergency Powers Act, 1961 .... 70-71, 302-303
s. 5 303
Exclusive Economic Zone Act Cap. 116 131
Federal Trade Commission Act, 1914 282
Fisheries Act
  Cap. 404 131-132
High Court of Parliament Act, 1952 330-331
Immigration Act, 1964 295-296
Independence Act, 1960
  s. 1(1) 138
Land Use Act, 1978 82
Natives Act 328

Nigeria Independence Act, 1963 63
Nigerian Enterprises Promotion Act, 1977 401
   – amendment of 1973, 1974, 1976 401
Parliament Act, 1952 330
Prevention Detention Act 300
Public Holidays Act
   s. 2(1) 306
Reconstruction Acts 355
Representation of Natives Act 329
Sea Fisheries Act 142
Senate Act, 1955 325
Separate Representation of Voters Act, 1951 329
South African Act 327
   Amendment Act, 1956 325
Tenure of Office Act, 1867 .... 254, 354
Territorial Sea and Fishing Zone Act, 1964 (Canada) 142
Territorial Waters Act
   Cap. 428 .... 121, 131, 142

BILLS
Appropriate Bill 263-269
Constitution Bill, 1964 205
National Assembly Service Commission Bill, 1980 .... 286, 289

CONSTITUTIONS
American Constitution, 1787 .... 49, 195
Constitution of
   – Australia
      s. 76 76
   – Burundi's Second Republic 197
   – Ceylon 336
   – Chad, 1962 208
   – former Soviet Union, 1936 4
         , 1977 4
   – France, 1958 .... 51, 192, 207, 259, 263, 274, 339
   – French Third Republic (1875) 314
   – French Fourth Republic (1946) 195
   – Ghana, 1960 .... 248, 253, 300
   – India, 1948 .... 54, 103
      s. 15(e) 54
      s. 16(4) 54
      s. 335 54
   – Italy, 1947 339
   – Papua New Guinea, 1975 52
   – USSR, 1977 5
Egyptian Constitution, 1964 39
Ethiopia's Socialist Constitution 197
French Constitution, 1946 51

, 1958 .... 274, 314
Guinean's Second Constitution, 1982 41
Italian Constitution 318
Liberia's Constitution, 1847 197
Madagascar's Socialist Constitution, 1975 4-5
Revolutionary Socialist Constitution of Russia, 1918 38
South Africa Constitution, 1983 197
Swiss Constitution, 1848 11
U.S. Constitution, 1787 .... 37, 43, 50, 245, 322, 342, 354, 364, 372, 384, 386, 394
Zambian Constitution, 1991 103

CONVENTION, LEGISLATURE AND RIGHTS

Ceylon Legislature, 1967 .... 294, 297
Declaration of Rights of Man, 1789 51
European Convention on Human Rights and Fundamental Freedoms
   (1954) 392
Geneva Convention on the Territorial Sea and the Contiguous Zone,
   1958 .... 121-122, 124, 131, 133, 139, 141
International Covenant on Civil and Political Rights (1966) 51
United Nations Universal Declaration of Human Rights, 1948 51

ETHIOPIAN LAWS

Supreme Law of the Land, 1987
   act. 188 3

LAWS OF THE FEDERATION OF NIGERIA

Allocation of Revenue (Federation Account etc)
   Act Cap. 16 .... 148, 175
   – amendment of 1992 148
   s. 4 A (6) 148
Appropriation Bill, 2000 192-193
Corrupt Practices Decree, 1975 114
Exchange Control Regulation 393
Finance (Control and Management) Act.
   Cap. 144 .... 266, 270
Kaduna State Appropriation Law, 1980 256
Lagos State Local Government Electoral Regulation, 1976 166
Local Government
   – (Basic Constitutional and Transitional Provisions) (Amendment)
     No. 3) Decree No. 23, 1991 179-180
   – Edict, 1976 165-166
     s. 20 168
   – Electoral Regulations, 1976 165
   – Police Law, 1959 84
Native Authority Ordinance, 1943 84
Police Act
   Cap. 359 232
Public Holidays Act,

Cap. 378 306
s. 2(1) 306
State's Electoral Regulations, 1976 167-168
Territorial Waters Act, 1967
Cap. 428 140-141

LEGISLATIVE LISTS
Exclusive Legislative List
Item 2 221
Item 3 221
Item 5 222
Item 6 221-222
Item 7 221
Item 10 222
Item 11 221
Item 12 222
Item 13 222
Item 15-16 222
Item 17 67
Item 18 221
Item 20 221
Item 23-25 222
Item 26 .... 132, 221
Item 29 221
Item 33 221
Item 37 108
Item 45 85
Item 51 306
Item 56 377
Item 60(a) 111-113, 115, 118
Item 67 116-117
Item 68 .... 108, 292

MODIFICATION ORDER
Local Government Edict (Modification) Order, 1979 310
Modification Order 344-345

NIGERIAN CONSTITUTIONS
1951 62
1958 51
1960 .... 69, 73, 80-81, 83, 141, 145, 147, 267, 303-304, 339
1963 .... 67, 74, 80-82, 84, 97, 141, 147, 267, 339
1979 .... 51, 56, 64, 67, 73, 80, 84-88, 92, 97, 103, 148, 156, 164, 267-268, 273, 308-311, 338-339, 344, 352
1999 .... 56, 64, 67, 73, 80, 84-88, 92, 97, 103, 164, 166, 259, 266-269, 273, 280, 289-290, 306, 338-339, 341, 345, 348, 352
Imperial Constitution, 1960 63

Independence Constitution 197
Pre-Independence Constitution 267
Republican Constitution, 1963 63

REVOLUTION
Glorious Revolution, 1688 27
, 1699 202
Instrument of Government, 1649 .... 27, 202

Introduction

It is a great pleasure to have been asked to write the Introduction to Volume 1 of Professor Ben Nwabueze's five-volume work on *Constitutional Democracy in Africa*. Written in the author's characteristically lucid and engaging style, the book is an embodiment of immense learning and scholarship. It bears all about it the mark of a master's handwork both in the insightful depth and the wide breadth of the author's thorough knowledge and grasp of the subject and the beauty of his craftsmanship, which makes the book a real delight to read. All the complex and teasing concepts with which the subject is replete are unravelled and explained in a manner that makes them easily understood by the general, non-specialist reader. The volume may quite justifiably be described as Constitutional Democracy Made Easy. It entrenches the author's already widely acknowledged reputation as a leading authority on the subject.

As an introductory volume to the study of Constitutional Democracy in Africa, the book focuses on a discussion of constitutional institutions, structures and devices of a general nature necessary for a proper understanding of the subject. The discussion begins with an analysis of the concept of constitutional democracy itself, which is defined in the book as a government freely elected by the people and limited in its powers by a written constitution having the force of a supreme law overriding all inconsistent legislative and executive acts of government and whose provisions are observed and respected **in practice** by the rulers and the ruled as the active, governing rules of government administration and the game of politics generally. In short, a government of laws, i.e. government according to law and by institutions established by the laws, rather than a government of men. Rules of law embodied in a supreme constitution are of little value if they are not the active instruments governing the conduct or actions of the rulers.

A government of men, or personal rule as it is called, says the learned author, is the antithesis of constitutional government. This is so because, under the former:

> persons take precedence over rules, the office holder is not effectively bound by his office and is able to change its authority and powers to suit his own personal or political needs. In such a system of personal rule, the rules do not effectively regulate political behaviour, and we therefore cannot predict or anticipate conduct from a knowledge of the rules.

Government in a regime of personal rule, the author further tells us:

> is uncertain and problematic because 'it is largely contingent upon men, upon their interests and ambitions, their desires and aversions, their hopes and fears, and all the other predispositions that the political animal is capable of exhibiting and projecting upon political life'; and further because it is restrained, to the extent that it is restrained at all, only by 'private and tacit agreements, prudential concerns and personal ties and dependencies rather than by public rules and institutions'. And it is dangerous because of its tendency to give rise to an assault, sometimes even a tyrannical assault, on human rights and to the privatisation of the state itself.

What emerges from the above exposition is that constitutional democracy is a combination of two distinct concepts – the concept of democratic government (i.e. a government freely elected by the people) and that of constitutional government (i.e. a government limited in its powers by the supreme, overriding law of a written constitution observed and respected in practice by the rulers and the ruled). A government need not be a democratic government to be constitutional nor need it be constitutional to be democratic. But it must be both to be a constitutional democracy. The term constitutionalism, which originally referred only to constitutional government, has nowadays, with the democratization of constitutional government, come to denote the combined concepts, i.e. constitutional democracy.

I have quoted at some length from the book to show how illuminating and insightful the author's definition of constitutional democracy is, a definition with which I entirely agree.

With its illuminating definition of constitutional democracy, the book goes on to identify and analyse the institutions, devices and mechanisms of the concept. The essential institutions and principles of democratic government are identified as free and fair elections on a universal adult franchise and the responsibility and accountability or answerability of the rulers to the people; the necessary devices for limiting government are a constitutional guarantee of the basic rights of the individual, separation of powers and federalism, amongst other forms of limitations, while the mechanisms for the exercise of power are legislation and executive action. These are then extensively examined and analysed in the book.

In the disputation about whether the doctrine of the separation of powers is really a necessary requirement of constitutional government, the author takes a firm stand with the school of thought which regards as inadequate any definition of constitutionalism that does not include the limitations implied by the doctrine, arguing that "the diffusion of authority among different centres of decision-making is the antithesis of totalitarianism or absolutism". He quotes in support, the well-known words of Justice Brandeis of the U.S. Supreme Court in a 1926 case, quoted and re-quoted in later cases, that:

> the doctrine of the separation of power was adopted by the Convention of 1787, not to promote efficiency but to preclude the exercise of arbitrary power. The purpose was, not to avoid friction, but, by means of the inevitable friction incident to the distribution of governmental powers among three departments, to save the people from autocracy.

The merits and demerits of the doctrine, its limits, the consequences flowing from it and its efficacy as a device for limiting power are examined in a penetrating and masterful expose (chapters 8 –11).

"Of all checks on democracy", says the learned author, quoting Professor John Dalberg-Acton (better known as Lord Acton), "federalism has been the most efficacious and the most congenial". The principles of federalism and its problems are discussed with remarkable insight, drawing from the application and operations of those principles in Nigeria (chapters 3 and 4). The problems of federalism have a certain linkage with local government, which is examined in chapter 5.

The emergence of legislation as a potent instrument of control and coercion of the individual and society is perhaps the most significant development in the evolution of the state and its government. Legislation, says the author, quoting the Nobel Laureate, Friedrich von Hayek, "has justly been described as among all inventions of man the one fraught with the gravest consequences, more far-reaching in its effects even than fire and gun-power". Hence the fierce struggle for its control between rival or competing interests in the state – the people versus the government, the executive versus the legislative assembly, the upper versus the lower house in a bicameral legislative assembly – and the necessity for a limitation on its use in the constitution. These and other vexed issues connected with legislation in modern government are the subject of an insightful and incisive discussion in chapter 6.

Perhaps, the most difficult and perplexing issue associated with constitutional democracy is the nature and extent of executive power. The discussion in chapter 7 of the different theories of the extent of executive power and of its varying extent under various constitutions is again masterful, studded with so much learning and scholarship.

I can testify to having learnt and profited a lot from reading this marvelous book, and I recommend it to all.

Mohammed Bello
Kaduna
May 2003

CHAPTER 1

The Concept of Constitutional Democracy

With the exception of the countries which at independence became socialist states (Algeria, Angola and Mozambique) or adopted socialist-oriented constitutions (Guinea-Bissau, Cape Verde, and Sao Tome and Principe), all African countries previously under colonial rule attained independent statehood under a system of constitutional democracy of one type or another, adapted or modified as deemed appropriate or expedient in the circumstances of the countries concerned, *viz,* the Westminster export model, the American system, the French system and other forms inspired by Belgian and Italian constitutions. The first three, with adaptations or modifications, were the systems applied at independence in the constitutions of former British and French colonies as well as in Liberia, and the last in the constitutions of the former Belgian and Italian colonies, [Congo (Leopoldville) 1960, Rwanda 1962, Burundi 1962, Libya 1951, and Somalia 1960].

In this chapter, we examine the basic elements that constitute and define constitutional democracy with a brief account of its historical origins and evolution. Also examined is the issue of whether indefinite eligibility for the highest office in the land, which until now characterised the system of government in the constitutions of most African countries, is compatible with constitutional democracy.

The Concept of Constitutional Government

Government is universally accepted to be a necessity, since man cannot fully realise himself – his creativity, his dignity and his whole personality – except within an ordered society. Yet the necessity for government creates its own problems for man, the problem of how to limit the arbitrariness inherent in government, and to ensure that its powers are used for the good of society. It is this limitation on the arbitrariness of political power that is expressed in the concept of constitutional government. Constitutional government recognises the necessity for government but insists upon a limitation being placed upon its powers. It connotes in essence therefore a "limitation on government; it is the antithesis of arbitrary rule; its opposite is despotic government, the government of will instead of law."[1] Arbitrary rule is government conducted not according to predetermined rules, but according to the momentary whims and caprices of the rulers; and an arbitrary government is no less so because it happens to be benevolent, since all unfettered power is by its very nature autocratic. A dictatorship, that is to say, a government of absolute, unlimited power, is thus clearly not a constitutional government, however benevolent it may be, and a totalitarian regime is even less so.

The concept of constitutional government involves three issues, which are here examined; these concern its relationship, first, with the constitution, and, secondly, with democratic government; and then the nature and types of limitations upon government it requires.

Relation to the Constitution

The term "constitutional government" is apt to give the impression of a government according to the terms of a constitution. That there

---

1   C.H. McIlwain, *Constitutionalism: Ancient and Modern* (1940), pp. 21-22;   also K.C. Wheare, *Modern Constitutions* (1966), p. 137; Cowen, *The Foundation of Freedom*, (1960).

is a formal written constitution according to whose provisions a government is conducted is not necessarily conclusive evidence that the government is a constitutional one. The determining factors are: Does the constitution have the force of a supreme, overriding law, does it impose limitations upon the powers of the government, and, if so, what is the nature and extent of the limitations; and, are the limitations observed in the actual conduct of government?

There are indeed many countries in the world today with written constitutions but without constitutional government. Normally, a constitution is a formal organic document having the force of a supreme, overriding law, by which a society organises a government for itself, defines and limits its powers, and prescribes the relations of its various organs *inter se*, and with the citizen. But a constitution may also be used for other purposes than as a legal restraint upon government.[2] It may consist to a large extent of nothing but lofty declarations of objectives and a description of the organs of government in terms that import no enforceable legal restraints. Far from imposing a brake upon government, such a constitution may indeed facilitate or even legitimise the assumption of dictatorial powers by the government.

Yet, strange as it may appear, the constitution has in fact been employed to grant and legitimise **total** power (i.e., power without limitations) in the socialist or former socialist states. This has been possible only because the socialist constitution does not have the character of law at all, not to say a supreme law that limits the powers of government and renders void inconsistent government acts, legislative and executive. (The Socialist Constitution of Ethiopia of 1987 declares itself in a preamble and in article 118, "the supreme law of the land", but how could Lt-Col. Mengistu Haile Mariam's murderous reign of terror have taken place under a so-called supreme constitution that purported to guarantee individual liberty?).[3]   There

---

2   William G. Andrews (ed.), *Constitutions and Constitutionalism*, 2nd ed., (1963), pp. 21-25.

3   Arts. 35-37; the guarantee must, however, be read subject to the provision in art. 58 to the effect that "the exercise of freedoms and rights ... shall be determined by law."

is a mutual antagonism between the communist conception of government and the notion of a constitution as a supreme, overriding law. In communist theory and practice, a constitution is conceived rather as essentially a political, social and economic charter consisting largely of declaration of objectives and directive principles of government as well as description of the organs of government in terms that import no enforceable legal restraints. A communist constitution has essentially a political existence, its provisions are political, serving mainly to exhort, to direct and to inspire governmental action, and to bestow upon it the stamp of legitimacy. Its contents are rooted in ideology, society, politics and economics. Thus, the earlier 1936 Constitution of the former Soviet Union and the earlier constitutions of the other communist countries modelled upon it read more like manifestoes of social, political, economic and ideological goals to be pursued by the state together with a description of the institutions and procedures for realising them. No doubt, the later generation of communist constitutions, e.g., the 1977 Constitution of the former Soviet Union, has tended to assume a somewhat normative character;[4] even so, they are only normative, not coercive. They command no coercive legal force, such as to render void any inconsistent governmental act.

The socialist constitution, by implication, sanctions total rule, because the objectives of the social order it establishes presuppose total rule, indeed they require it for their realisation. The elimination not only of the exploitation of the workers by the entrepreneurs but also the removal of "those obstacles of an economic and social order which limit equality among citizens,"[5] the division of society into classes, the replacement of class divisions by a classless society, and the enthronement of the dictatorship of the working people, with the communist party as their "vanguard and guiding force," are hardly possible except under a system of total rule. In the words of the

---

4   William Simon, ed. *The Constitutions of the Communist World* (1980), Introduction, p. xi.

5   Art. 12, Madagascar (1975).

USSR Constitution (1977), "the state is to promote the strengthening of the social homogeneousness of society, the effacement of class differences and of the essential differences between town and country, and between mental and physical labour, and the all-round development and rapprochement of the nations and nationalities" comprised in the country.[6]   All this seems to spell the virtual destruction of civil society as an autonomous entity capable of acting as a check on government.

In a socialist communist state, constitutionality is judged in terms of the performance of government in the "realisation of socialist democratism,"[7] of its ability to realise in practical terms the political, economic and social goals of the socialist order, and to this end everything else, including human rights, is subordinated. Madagascar's Socialist Constitution (1975) is quite unequivocal and emphatic on this. "Fundamental liberties and individual rights," it says, "shall be guaranteed within the framework of the Charter of the Socialist Revolution," and "shall be so guaranteed only to citizens who work within the guidelines of the Charter and who fight for the triumph of a socialist society."[8]   Not only is every citizen under a positive duty to respect the charter of the socialist revolution, but also "no right or liberty may be invoked by a citizen who has not fulfilled his duty" accordingly, nor may any right be "invoked to hinder the state in its work of establishing the socialist order;" and "any one who abuses constitutional or legal liberties to fight against the Revolution or to impede the coming of the Socialist State ... shall forfeit his rights and liberties."[9]   "The state shall punish with the greatest severity anyone who harms, by act or omission, the establishment of a socialist economy."[10]   Further, "freedom of speech, of the press and of assembly

---

6   Art. 19.

7   G. Antaliffy, "The Amendment of the Constitution of Hungary," Hungarian Law.

8   Arts. 13 & 15.

9   Arts. 14, 16 & 17.

10   Art. 36.

shall be guaranteed to all citizens if exercised in conformity with the objectives of the Revolution, the interests of the workers and of the community, and with the purpose of strengthening the new democracy for the coming of a socialist state."[11]

Apart from such clearly derogatory stipulations, the text of many of the so-called "guarantees" embodied in the socialist constitutions of African countries as well as those of former Soviet Union and communist countries of Eastern Europe seems clearly to indicate that whatever obligations they impose on the state are political only, and are not meant to create legal restraints enforceable by a court of law. Such, for example, is the provision that "any acts aimed at ... creating divisions or privileged positions based on colour, race, sex, ethnic origin, place of birth, religion, level of education, social position or occupation are punishable by law;"[12] that "the law shall guarantee to the citizens ... the inviolability of their homes and secrecy in their correspondence,"[13] that "the life, liberty, personal integrity, good name and repute of every citizen shall be protected by law;"[14] that "private ownership shall be guaranteed by law, which shall define the modes of acquisition and forfeiture, and the contents and limits of its enjoyment for the purpose of safeguarding its social functions;"[15] or that "the law shall ensure freedom of expression, assembly and association in the context of the achievement of the basic objectives of the People's Republic of Angola."[16] A provision that a fundamental right shall be protected or guaranteed by law is no more than a declaration of political objective, a directive to the state as to a purpose to which its law-making power should be applied. The obligation

---

11 Art. 28.

12 Arts. 26 & 29, Mozambique (1975).

13 Arts. 135 & 139, Benin (1974).

14 Angola (1975) Art. 17.

15 Art. 28, Somalia (1979).

16 Art. 22, Angola (1975).

thereby created is plainly political, and confers upon the individual no legal right to get or compel the legislative organ to make law for the purpose.

The paramount duty of all state institutions as indeed all social organisations is to "promote, with special diligence, the realisation of the aims set precisely in the constitution."[17] And all powers necessary for the accomplishment of the socio-economic objectives and goals of the socialist order are deemed to be granted by the constitution, and are therefore lawful and legitimate. A socialist constitution is considered to be faithfully implemented when the material conditions of socialism are fully realised.

Clearly, therefore, constitutional government connotes, not just government under a constitution, but rather government under a constitution which has the force of a supreme, overriding law, and which imposes limitations on it. The nature and types of limitation required for this purpose are examined below.

One important qualification needs, however, to be made with respect to countries where, although there is a constitution with the force of a supreme, overriding law but its binding, coercive force as law applies only to the executive and judicial branches of the government, not to the legislative. The notable case is England with its unwritten constitution whose force, as a supreme, overriding law, does not, because of the manner of its historical origin as an organic growth from immemorial custom, bind and limit the legislative organ (parliament), but only the executive and judicial branches. It binds and limits parliament only as a matter of convention, but not of law. As a matter of law, parliament is not bound to act conformably to the constitution, and if it does act contrary to it, its act, though it may provoke public outcry, is not illegal or unlawful. The sanction of public opinion is entirely extra-legal, and the true legal position

---

17   G. Antaliffy, *op.cit.*

recognises in parliament a legal sovereignty, indeed a supremacy, that is at once absolute and unlimited, a power to alter the constitution as and how it pleases; the supremacy of law means no more than the supremacy of the legislature. No legal limitation based upon the law of nature can be implied in such an unwritten constitution. Natural law can have no more than a moral force, providing merely "a basis of comparison ... an intellectual standard."[18] In a recent case the Judicial Committee of the Privy Council emphatically rejected the argument that a legislature is limited by the law of nature.[19]

The effectiveness of extra-legal, as compared with legal, sanctions is of course another matter. Given ideal conditions, it is possible perhaps for a conventional sanction to compel as much obedience on the part of the government as a legal sanction. No matter how effective a conventional sanction may be, however, the question is whether the absolute sovereignty of the legislature under an unwritten constitution is compatible with constitutionalism. Since "by definition, a constitutional democracy is one which does not grant all power to the majority,"[20] it has been argued that the absolute sovereignty of the legislature is "incompatible with constitutionalism." The example of England, with its unwritten constitution which accords to parliament a sovereignty unlimited in law, makes it difficult to maintain this viewpoint as an invariable rule. For England undoubtedly has the most constitutional of all constitutional governments.

Happily England stands almost alone today as a country without a formal constitutional code. From the eighteenth century onwards, as a result of armed rebellion against the arbitrariness of monarchical absolutism, inspired in many cases by the revolutionary teachings of doctrinaire philosophers, proclaiming the message of liberty, equality and fraternity, unwritten constitutions, with their corollary of absolute, unlimited sovereignty of the government, have become

---

18   C. H. McIlwain *op. cit.,* p. 35.

19   *Liyanage v. R.* [1967] 1 A.C. 259 (Appeal from Ceylon).

20   Carl J. Friedrich, *Constitutional Government and Democracy* (1950), p. 123.

discredited and have given place to written constitutions consciously framed by the people as a supreme law, creating, defining and limiting governments. "The precedent for these, first developed in North America, was naturalised in France and from there transmitted to most of the continent of Europe, from which it has spread in our own day to much of the Orient."[21] This development has been given a new boost by the emergence from colonialism of a host of new nations in Africa and Asia which needed written constitutions to launch them into their new, independent existence and to impose checks against majority power in the interest of tribal, racial or religious minorities. All the colonial territories in Africa attained independent statehood with this type of written constitution, and there are no African countries today without written constitutions.

Thus it is that constitutionalism has come by and large to presuppose a written constitution as a supreme overriding law. Government is a creation of the constitution. It is the constitution that creates the organs of government, clothes them with their powers, and in so doing delimits the scope within which they are to operate. A government operating under such a written constitution must act in accordance therewith; any exercise of power outside the constitution or which is unauthorised by it is invalid. The constitution operates therefore with a supreme, overriding authority.

The rationale for this supremacy has a rational basis: the constitution is (or is supposed to be) an **original** act of the people directly; an act of government is a derivative, and *ipso facto* a subordinate, act. "There is no position," writes Alexander Hamilton,

> which depends on clearer principles than that every act of a delegated authority, contrary to the tenor of the commission under which it is exercised, is void. No legislative act, therefore, contrary to the constitution can be valid. To deny this would be to affirm that the deputy is greater than his principal; that the servant is above his

---

21   C.H. McIlwain, *op.cit.*

master; that the representatives of the people are superior to the people themselves; that men acting by virtue of powers may do not only what their powers do not authorise, but what they forbid.[22]

No doubt the view of the constitution as law made directly by the people raises some conceptual difficulty. For it was generally thought that law-making was a function **only** of a political community, not of the people in their mass; in other words that only a people organised as a political community can enact law through the machinery of the state. On this hypothesis, while the power of the people in their mass to constitute themselves into a political community is admitted, any such constituent act by which a constitution is established is purely a **political** act, giving the constitution only a political, as distinct from legal, existence. If it is intended that the constitution should also be a law, then it is for the resultant political creation, the state, to enact it as such through its regular procedure for law-making. Thus the American Constitution, as a law "ordained and established" by the people, is said to have broken with "the dominant tradition."[23] Tradition is, however, sought to be reconciled by asserting that:

the agency by which constitutions are nowadays drawn up, namely constitutional conventions, had become such usual phenomena as to have been substantially assimilated to the machinery of organised government, so that one looking back to the state conventions that had in 1787 ratified the Constitution found it natural to regard them as organs of existing political societies, rather than as directly representative of the individuals back of these societies.[24]

The argument smacks of excessive formalism. If the state is a creation of the people by means of a constitution, and derives its power of law-making from them, it may be wondered why the people who constitute and grant this power cannot act directly, in a referendum

---

22   *Federalist* 78.

23   Edward S. Corwin, *The Doctrine of Judicial Review* (1963), p. 105.

24   Corwin, *loc.cit.*

or otherwise, to give the constitution the character and force of law. After all, the constitution being the starting-point of a country's legal order, its "lawness" should not depend upon its enactment through the law-making mechanism of the state, but rather upon its recognition as such by the people to be governed by it. It is today generally accepted that the American Constitution "obtains its entire force and efficacy, not from the fact that it was ratified by a pre-existent political community or communities — for it was not — but from the fact that it was established by the people to be governed by it." There can be no doubt that today a referendum or plebiscite is a legally accepted way of adopting a constitution, and giving it force of law, though adherence to formalism still sometimes requires that, after adoption by the people, the constitution should be **formally** promulgated by a pre-existing state authority, invariably the head of state. It is pertinent to emphasise, however, that a referendum or plebiscite lacks a genuine constituent and legitimising effect unless it is preceded, at the drafting stage or after, by serious discussion on as popular a platform as possible, of the constitutional proposals. This is exemplified by the process followed in America, where the constitution was drafted by a convention after thorough discussion, followed by even more mature and long deliberation in the ratifying conventions in the various states. An equally genuine process is adoption by a constituent assembly and ratification in a plebiscite as in the case of the Swiss Constitution of 1848.

But what is so supremely important in the concept of constitutional government as a system of rules is, not rules as abstract prescriptions in a constitution or other laws, but rather the observance of the rules in the actual conduct of government. Constitutional democracy is not defined merely by the existence of a constitution as a supreme law which establishes organs and institutions of government, defines their relations *inter se*, prescribes and limits their powers and the procedure for exercising powers, provides for the election of their primary functionaries, guarantees the fundamental rights of the individual, etc. It is defined more essentially by the actual observance of the rules in the practice of government. Rules are of little value if they are not the active instruments governing the conduct or actions of the rulers.

Government according to rules imply of course government by institutions established by the rules, i.e., institutional government. Rules and institutions are inextricably intertwined. Political institutions have been defined as:

> an impersonal system of rules and offices that effectively binds the conduct of individuals involved in them ... In an effectively institutionalised state, the rules are respected by all persons no matter how important they may be; indeed the rules in a well-established state with a strong institutional tradition appear entirely natural.[25]

Constitutional government is thus by definition institutional government, and personal rule is its very antithesis. This is so because under the latter:

> persons take precedence over rules, the office-holder is not effectively bound by his office and is able to change its authority and powers to suit his own personal or political needs. In such a system of personal rule, the rulers and other leaders take precedence over the formal rules of the political game; the rules do not effectively regulate political behaviour, and we therefore cannot predict or anticipate conduct from a knowledge of the rules. To put this in old-fashioned, comparative government terms, the state is a government of men and not of laws.[26]

Government in a regime of personal rule is uncertain and problematic because "it is largely contingent upon men, upon their interests and ambitions, their desires and aversions, their hopes and fears, and all the other predispositions that the political animal is capable of exhibiting and projecting upon political life;" and further because it is restrained, to the extent that it is restrained at all, only by

---

25   Jackson and Roseberg, *Personal Rule in Black Africa* (1982), p. 10.

26   Jackson and Roseberg, *loc.cit.*

27   *Ibid.* pp. x and 1.

"private and tacit agreements, prudential concerns and personal ties and dependencies rather than by public rules and institutions."[27] And it is dangerous because of its tendency to give rise to an assault, sometimes even a tyrannical assault, on human rights and to the privatisation of the state. The nature and character of African regimes of personal rule has been insightfully described by Robert Jackson and Carl Roseberg thus:

> Most African states have **abstract** constitutions and institutions ... but very few have them in fact; the formal rules of the political game do not effectively govern the conduct of rulers and other political leaders in most places most of the time. In so far as rules are followed by African rulers it is only after they have been changed by the ruler or oligarchy in question to suit his or their personal-political convenience. But rules of expediency are not, patently, rules of institutional government: They are better conceived ... as instruments of power and not as normative restraints on power. Being wholly instrumental to ruling power, they are the hallmarks of political authoritarianism, which is closely allied to personal rule. In institutionalised systems personal calculations are made, but in terms of the universally accepted rules and requirements of the political game; in personal systems such calculations are not mediated by reference to rules agreed to by all leaders and factions. Thus, for example, while a governing party and its rivals in a constitutional democracy will go to great lengths to win elections, they will not seek to abolish elections to stay in power or manipulate the electoral rules or their supervision to the point where they no longer are basically fair. By contrast, such manipulation is precisely what we should expect to see in personal, authoritarian regimes.[28]

It is indeed what obtained in actual practice in most African countries.

Relation to Democratic Government

Democratic government is a separate concept, and is not a necessary constituent element of constitutional government. It is, after all, a

---

28   *Ibid*, pp. 11-12.

development of the 19th and 20th centuries (i.e., democratic government of the representative type, as distinct from the direct democracy of ancient Greek city-states and Rome), whereas constitutional government had its origins in antiquity, more specifically in the republican era in Rome (508-27 B.C.).[29] A government need not be a democratic one to be constitutional, nor need it be constitutional to be democratic. For, as Sir Kenneth Wheare has pointedly observed:

> universal suffrage can create and support a tyranny of the majority or of a minority or of one man ... The absolutism of the twentieth century have usually been based upon universal suffrage – and a compulsory universal suffrage at that. Have not modern tyrannies been returned to power by majorities of over 90 percent?[30]

A government must be both constitutional and democratic to be a constitutional democracy. It is the combination of the two concepts that is called constitutional democracy. The term constitutionalism, which originally referred only to constitutional government has nowadays, with the democratisation of constitutional government, come to denote the combined concepts, i.e., constitutional democracy.

The concept of democratic government needs further elucidation and amplification of its meaning. The underlying idea is the popular basis of government, the idea that government rests upon the consent of the governed, given by means of elections at periodic intervals of time, in which the franchise is universal for all adult men and women and that it exists for their benefit. The distinction is thus between democratic government as against monarchical, aristocratic or oligarchical government.

The necessity for elections at frequent intervals arises from the fact that the outlook and needs of the people change with the times. The issues upon which the government won an election may have ceased to have relevance after, say, five years, while, on the other

---

29   C.H. McIlwain, *op.cit.*

30   K.C. Wheare, *Modern Constitutions* (1966), p. 137.

hand, the people may have developed a new outlook diametrically opposed to that upon which their earlier decision had been based. If government is to be representative of the changing outlook and needs of the people, it is necessary therefore that the people should be able at reasonably frequent intervals to give practical expression to their changing wishes upon government. An irremovable legislature or executive may thus rightly be regarded as a negation of democratic government.

The definition of democratic government as government elected by the people at periodic intervals of time on a universal adult franchise needs to be complemented by the principle, that the election must be a free and fair competition between candidates for political office sponsored for the most part by different political parties. The element of free and fair competition has the intrinsic value that contenders for political office are thereby subjected to institutionalised and regularised processes, procedures and rules of the political game accepted and respected as binding by all players.

By subjecting all political groups to competition, representative democracy deprives them of the ability to dictate *ex ante* or to reverse *ex post* outcomes of the political process adverse to their interests, and so leaves uncertain and indeterminate the interest of which group will triumph in the struggle for power. This, as Adam Przeworski pertinently observes, is what constitutes the decisive element of democratic rule, and which distinguishes it from authoritarian rule. The latter, he says, "has an effective capacity to prevent political outcomes that would be highly adverse to its interest." On the other hand in a democracy, competition ensures that:

> no one can be certain that their interests will ultimately triumph ... One's current position within the political system does not guarantee future victories; incumbency may be an advantage, but incumbents do lose. In a democracy all forces must struggle repeatedly for the realisation of their interests since no one is protected by virtue of their position.[31]

---

31 Adam Przeworski, "Democracy as a contingent outcome of conflicts," in Elster and Slagstad (eds), *Constitutionalism and Democracy* (1993), p. 62.

He accordingly defines democratisation as "a process of subjecting all interests to competition, of institutionalising uncertainty," of devolving power from "a group of people to a set of rules,"[32] with all the limitations which that implies.

Another element of democratic government is the political responsibility of the rulers to the people, which requires that public opinion should be one of the factors informing the actions of government. Indeed an extreme view of political responsibility postulates public opinion as the determinant of policy, since, as it is said, a responsible person is one whose "conduct responds to an outside determinant."[33] On this view, government should do nothing of which public opinion disapproves. This would be carrying the idea of responsibility too far, and it is both unrealistic and misconceived; unrealistic, because it attributes to the electorate a degree of ability, which it does not possess, to rationalise its wants in terms of detailed measures and of their conformity to technical requirements; it is misconceived because it is based on too narrow a conception of governmental responsibility, which is not just to interpret and follow public opinion but to lead it along more rational and desirable lines. It is necessary to take a longer term view of responsibility as being owed not only to the individuals who constitute the electorate at a given time but also to its future members. "Where the alternative lies between conducting the community along a popular path to disaster and trying to persuade it to adopt another and better one the statesman has to remember his responsibility to lead, as well as to interpret, opinion."[34]

The second element of political responsibility is the accountability or answerability of the rulers to the governed. This requires of the government to give an account of its actions to the people. Accountability should involve more than a periodic progress report

---

32   *Ibid*, at p. 63.

33   Carl J. Friedrich, *Man and Its Government* (1963), p. 310.

34   H.R.G. Greaves, *The British Constitution* (1958), p. 92.

via radio broadcast or an election campaign. It presupposes freedom on the part of the people at all times directly or through their elected representatives, to question or criticise the action of the government, a duty on the part of the government to explain and try to justify its conduct, and lastly the availability of sanctions for unsatisfactory or unjustifiable conduct, the ultimate sanction being that of the removability of the rulers by the people.

Nature and Types of Limitations upon Government Required by Constitutional Democracy

The term "limitations upon government" is apt to be understood as referring to limitations on the extent of governmental powers or limitations on the range of matters embraced within its powers. But its meaning and scope is far wider than that. It covers not only limitations on the extent of powers but also a whole gamut of restraints and checks on the exercise of power as limited in its extent as well as control and inhibiting mechanisms designed to make government responsive to the needs and wishes of the people.

According to a leading authority, Professor de Smith:

> A contemporary liberal democrat, if asked to lay down a set of minimum standards, may be very willing to concede that constitutionalism is practised in a country where the government is genuinely accountable to an entity or organ distinct from itself, where elections are freely held on a wide franchise at frequent intervals, where political groups are free to organise in opposition to the government in office and where there are effective legal guarantees of fundamental civil liberties enforced by an independent judiciary; and he may not easily be persuaded to identify constitutionalism in a country where any of these conditions is lacking.[35]

This definition is more or less the same as that of Professor McIlwain who maintains that all that is required is the ancient legal restraint of a guarantee of civil liberties enforceable by an independent

---

35   S.A. de Smith, *The New Commonwealth and Its Constitution* (1964), p. 106.

court and the modern concept of the full responsibility of government to the whole mass of the governed.[36] Professor McIlwain does not posit the limitation on power implied by a constitutional guarantee of human rights and elections as the **minimum** requirements of constitutionalism, as does Professor de Smith. He emphatically rejects separation of powers as a requirement of the concept. As he says, "among all the modern fallacies that have obscured the true teachings of constitutional history few are worse than the extreme doctrine of the separation of powers and the indiscriminate use of the phrase 'checks and balances'."[37]

Yet there is a school of thought that holds strongly that any definition of constitutionalism that does not include the limitations implied by the doctrine of the separation of powers is inadequate. It is argued that only by separating the function of execution from that of law-making, by insisting that every executive action must, in so far at any rate as it affects an individual, have the authority of some law, and by prescribing a different procedure for law-making, can the arbitrariness of executive action be effectively checked. The idea of procedure has an important controlling role. Where a procedure, separate from that involved in execution, is laid down for law-making, and must be complied with in order for the government to secure the necessary authority for measures it contemplates taking, then regularity in the conduct of affairs is ensured. It is usual in most countries to subject proposals for legislation to discussion and deliberation in a legislative assembly. The separation of functions, between execution and legislation, requiring separate procedures, is thus of the utmost importance, for even if government is regarded as a single, indivisible structure, the separation in procedure will necessarily operate as a limitation upon the incidence of arbitrariness. The conduct of affairs in accordance with predetermined rules is perhaps the best guarantee

---

36   C.H. McIlwain, *op.cit.*, pp. 141-6.

37   *Ibid*, p. 414.

of regularity, and restraint has little or no value in constitutionalising government unless it is regularised. Regularity enables the individual to know in advance how he stands with the government, and how far the latter can go in interfering with the course of his life and activities.

Separation in procedure carries with it, however, the idea of a separate agency or structure. For although it may be theoretically possible to prescribe different procedures for the two functions of execution and legislation while at the same time vesting them in the same agency, this hardly accords with common sense or experience. A separation of the agencies to be entrusted with these functions would seem, in the nature of things, to be inescapable if constitutionalism is to be maintained. As Vile has put it:

> we are not prepared to accept that government can become, on the ground of "efficiency", or for any other reason, a single undifferentiated monolithic structure, nor can we assume that government can be allowed to become simply an accidental agglomeration of purely pragmatic relationships. Some broad ideas about "structure" must guide us in determining what is a "desirable" organisation for government.[38]

It may be concluded that constitutionalism requires for its efficacy a differentiation of governmental functions and a separation of the agencies which exercise them. For "the diffusion of authority among different centres of decision-making is the antithesis of totalitarianism or absolutism."[39]

It must of course be admitted that, in the light of the practice and exigencies of modern government, governmental agencies are multifunctional; some overlapping in the functions of the various agencies is inevitable. Thus the executive agencies do make rules. Yet this fact is only a qualification upon, and not a negation of, the basic idea about a division of functions and of agencies, since in its ordinary application,

---

38 M.J.C. Vile, *Constitutionalism and the Separation of Powers* (1967), p. 10.

39 *Ibid*, pp. 15.

rule-making by the executive is subordinate to that of the legislature. This subordination accords with the concept of government as consisting of a "hierarchy of norms that will enable each of the decisions of an official to be tested against a higher rule."[40] This fact, as Vile pointed out, is further reinforced by the internal rules of behaviour by which, notwithstanding the considerable overlapping of functions, agencies recognise that particular functions are the primary responsibility of a given organ, and so refrain from unwarranted encroachment upon each others' primary function.

In orthodox theory, separation is extended beyond functions and agencies to the personnel of the agencies. It is insisted that the same person or group of persons should not be members of more than one agency. The most remarkable example of the application of this extreme separation is under the American Constitution, and the American application of the doctrine finds justification perhaps in its federal and presidential systems of government. But, whatever may be the objections to this extreme separation, it is no argument for complete fusion of personnel. Even the parliamentary executive of the Westminster system is not a complete fusion. Though members of the executive are also members of the legislature, separation is maintained by the fact that such members form a very small proportion of the total membership of the legislature, and, more important, by the existence, in its British prototype, of an effective organised opposition whose role makes the legislature more than a mere reflection of the executive.

Not many of even the sternest critics of the doctrine of separation of powers deny its necessity as regards the judicial functions. For the rule of law as an element of constitutionalism depends more upon how and by what procedure it is interpreted and enforced. The limitations which the law imposes upon executive and legislative actions cannot have much meaning or efficacy unless there is a separate procedure comprising a separate agency and personnel for an

---

40   Vile, *op.cit.,* p. 320.

authoritative interpretation and enforcement of these actions. This separate procedure is provided by the ordinary courts of law. The unique virtue of the separate procedure and personnel of the courts is that, being unaffected by the self-interest and consequent bias of the legislature or executive in upholding their actions, it can be expected to apply in their interpretation of the constitution or a statute an impartiality of mind which inhibits any inclination to vary the law to suit the whim or personal interest of either the judge or a party to a dispute, thus ensuring "stability and predictability of the rules which is the core of constitutionalism." Whilst admittedly judges may not be entirely devoid of self-interest in the subject-matter of a legislative act — for no human procedure is ever completely neutral — yet this impartiality serves at once as a safeguard against the possible danger of arbitrariness on the part of the judges in the discharge of their interpretative function, and is reinforced for this purpose by the doctrine of precedent and the tradition of judicial self-restraint. Furthermore, the process by which the courts exercise their function affording as it does, ample opportunity for full argument by the parties or their lawyers on the interpretation of the law in the context of the facts before the courts, ensures that the court's decision would reflect the reasonable or acceptable view of the meaning of the law.

There is thus implicit in the doctrine of the separation of powers, the conception of constitutionalism as requiring that government be conducted through constitutionally established institutions and impersonal bureaucratic procedures and processes, that is to say, an institutionalised and bureaucratised government, with all the restraints on the behaviour of rulers, which it implies, as opposed to personal rule.

Historical Origins and Evolution of Constitutional Democracy

The absolute monarchy had long established itself as the universal form of rule in nearly every part of the world. Its universality owed in large measure to the great appeal of its structural simplicity. "The idea is simple. It appeals to all orders of intellect. It can be understood by all. Around this centre all nationalism and patriotism are grouped. A nation comes to know the characteristics and nature of an individual."[41]

In Europe and its offspring, the Americas, we need go no farther back in time than to ancient Rome and its extensive empire (which embraced not only much the greater part of Europe and Britain but also Asia Minor and North Africa). Rome begain its life under an absolute monarchy, which lasted for some 245 years from the founding of the city-state in 753 B.C. to 508 B.C. when, following a revolt against the system, it was abolished, and death without trial was decreed for any one attempting to make himself king.

Absolute monarchy was replaced with constitutional government under a republic (508 B.C.-27 B.C.) in which severe limitations upon government and various checks and balances were instituted by law. These limitations and checks and balances took five main forms.

First, with the aim of checking the excesses and despotism of monarchy, state power was shared among three primary organs in a manner designed to maintain a certain balance of power among them, *viz,* two assemblies of the people (a Centurial Assembly and a Tribal Assembly), a senate and a magistracy. Most important of all, law-making was a joint responsibility: the magistracy proposed, the senate deliberated and might approve or disapprove, and the measure was then submitted to the Assemblies, which might pass or reject it (but without debate). The significant point to emphasise is that a legislative measure initiated by the magistracy and approved by the senate did not become law unless and until passed by the Centurial Assembly or the Tribal Assembly. We are told that by 200 B.C. the Tribal Assembly had become "the chief source of private law in Rome."[42]

The incorporation of the people into the established processes of government, as the body with power to pass into law, measures initiated by the magistracy and approved by the Senate, meant, as

---

41   Henry C. Lockwood, *The Abolition of the Presidency* (1884), pp. 191-2.

42   Will Durant, *The Story of Civilisation* vol. III, p. 27.

Charles McIlwain said, that the fundamental doctrine underlying the Roman state during the period was "constitutionalism, not absolutism."[43]   Thus was introduced to the world the form of government **limited by law**, otherwise known as constitutionalism.

The power of the Assemblies as the final legislative authority was, however, balanced by the right of the magistracy to convene them, to preside at their meetings and to determine the business to be transacted, and by the fact that they could not discuss any measure presented to them but could only pass or reject it by a Yes or No vote.

Secondly, executive and judicial powers were shared between the senate and the magistracy. The former, an aristocratic body drawn from the ranks of clan heads, ex-consuls, ex-censors, ex-tribunes and other persons of patrician or equestrian rank nominated by the censors, was the leading organ of the government, with exclusive authority over the conduct of foreign relations, the making of alliances and treaties, the waging of war, the government of the colonies and provinces, the management and distribution of public lands, the control of the treasury and its disbursement, the trial of crimes like treason, conspiracy or assassination, and the appointment from among its members, of judges in most major civil trials. Membership was for life, barring earlier removal for crime or serious moral offence. Its powers were balanced by the right of the magistracy to nominate its members, to convene it and to preside at its meetings.

The magistracy – the consuls, the censors, the praetors, the aediles and quaestors – had charge of all executive functions not reposed in the senate and the right to propose legislation. Its powers were balanced by the right of the Centurial Assembly to elect its functionaries and the right of the senate to remove them by impeachment for crime or serious moral offence.

Thirdly, within the magistracy, functions were not concentrated but rather distributed among various functionaries in a manner designed again to maintain a certain balance of power. The consuls,

---

43   C.H. McIlwain, *Constitutionalism: Ancient and Modern* (1940), p. 59.

the highest ranking (two in number), summoned and presided over the senate and the Assemblies, initiated legislation, administered justice, and in general executed the laws. In war they levied armies, raised funds, and commanded the legions. They led the state in the most solemn religious rites, which lent sanctity to the office.[44] To the censors, the next ranking (also two in number) was assigned the function, *inter alia*, of taking the quinquennial census of the citizens and assessing their property for political and military status and for taxation, examining the character and record of every candidate for office, collection or farming of taxes, the construction of public buildings, the letting of government property or contracts, and the proper cultivation of the land. They prepared and published a budget of state expenditure on a five-year plan.

Then there were the praetors (4) who in war led armies and in peace acted as judges and interpreters of the law; the aediles (4) charged with the care of buildings, aqueducts, streets, markets, theatres, brothels, saloons, police courts and public games; and the quaestors who, under the senate and the consuls, managed the expenditure of state funds, and assisted the praetors in preventing and investigating crimes.[45]

Fourthly, running through every political office in the magistracy was the principle of collegiality; each office was held by a **collegium** of two or more functionaries of equal power, with a veto over the other(s). Each office was held for one year only (except for the censorship which ran for eighteen months), and could not be held by the same person again until after an interval of ten years. A person leaving one office could not take on another one until after one year, and in the interval he could be prosecuted for malfeasance.[46]

Fifthly, the most significant of the safeguards was the office, comparable to our modern **ombudsman**, of the "tribune of the plebs"

---

44   Will Durant, *op.cit.*, p. 30.

45   Will Durant, *op.cit.*, pp. 28-29.

46   Will Durant, *loc.cit.*

(ten in number), appointed by the Tribal Assembly to act as watchdog for the plebs, and to protect them against the government. Each tribune was armed with a veto power by means of which he could, if he deemed it necessary, stop any act of the government.

> As a silent observer the tribune could attend meetings of the senate, report its deliberations to the people, and, by his veto, deprive the senate's decisions of all legal force. The door of his inviolable home remained open day and night to any citizen who sought his protection or aid, and this right of sanctuary or asylum provided the equivalent of *habeas corpus*. Seated on his **tribunal** he could act as a judge, and from his decision there was no appeal except to the assembly of the tribes. It was his duty to secure the accused a fair trial, and, when possible, to win some pardon for the condemned."[47]

Allowance was of course made for situations of national exigency necessitating the declaration of an emergency and the appointment of a dictator, with complete authority over all persons and property for a limited period of six months or a year. There had been not a few such dictatorships during the republican period. Incidentally, it was the appointment of Caesar as dictator for ten years in 46 B.C. and its extension for life in 44 B.C. in violation of the six to twelve months' limitation, that really drew the curtain on the era of the Republic, and marked the beginning of the march back to monarchy; for this and for his alleged monarchical ambition, he was brutally murdered in the same year (44 B.C.). The only other violation of the six to twelve months' limitation on the tenure of a dictator during an emergency was the two-year dictatorship of Sulla which ended in 80 B.C.

Together with the principle of conscious law-making by legislation as a systematic, regular instrument of government rather than as an occasional one, constitutional or limited government was Rome's most important legacy to the science and practice of government. And they provided the base from which she was able to reach out to the

---

47 Will Durant, *op.cit.*

world, conquer and rule it for several hundred years. Rome's system of constitutional or limited government was indeed an ingenious mixture of elements of monarchy, aristocracy, plutocracy, democracy and of checks and balances. The monarchical element was represented by the magistracy, the aristocratic by the senate, the plutocratic by the Centurial Assembly (because of the method by which decisions were taken) and the democratic by the Tribal Assembly and, to some extent, by the Centurial Assembly.

The democratic principle had features which limited its scope. It was partly direct democracy in that the two assemblies were assemblies of the whole people, and partly elective in that the executive functionaries were elected by the Centurial Assembly as an assembly of the whole people. But the democratic character of the Centurial Assembly was largely stultified because of the method by which decisions were taken. The population was divided into "centuries" (hundred each), ranked hierarchically, beginning with the patrician and equestrian classes followed by first, second, third, fourth, fifth, and sixth class citizens according to wealth, the vote of the various centuries (each century had one vote which was determined by a majority of its members present and voting) being heavily weighted in favour of the patrician, equestrian and wealthy classes, whose votes together therefore carried the day on every issue submitted for decision. The voting arrangement in the Tribal Assembly did not discriminate between the citizens on this basis of rank or wealth. The votes of the poor counted as much as those of the aristocracy and the rich.

The Roman government during the Republican era was thus essentially an aristocratic and plutocratic one. Not only was the principal organ of the government, the senate, an aristocratic body, but the higher magistracy, the consuls, the censors and even the tribunes of the plebs, were, for the most part, chosen from the aristocratic or wealthy classes. The Centurial Assembly, as just noted, was, because of the method by which its decisions were taken, essentially an aristocratic body too. Then there was the frequent incidence of wars, social disorders, pestilence and other situations of exigency necessitating the declaration of an emergency and the appointment of a dictator, with complete authority over all persons and property for a limited period of six months or a year.

From 27 B.C. Rome reverted again to monarchy, first under a so-called principate (27 B.C.-192 A.D.), described by Edward Gibbon as "absolute monarchy disguised in the form of a commonwealth," and later under undisguised absolute monarchy (192 A.D.-1453). The description of the principate as absolute monarchy in disguise was because the institutional restraints noted above except the senate had disappeared, leaving the prince/emperor as virtual absolute ruler. The assemblies had ceased to function as law-making bodies, the people having become too large in number to meet for that purpose. Their role as the body to give force of law to legislative measures had passed partly to the senate whose *senatus consulta*, while not strictly law, had now acquired by convention the effect of law and were treated as such, but **mostly** to the prince/emperor who was recognised as having power, invested in him by the people (so it was rationalised), to make laws. And by 192 A.D. the senate itself had ceased to play any role in legislation, and was reduced to merely ceremonial functions. After the collapse of the Roman Empire in Western Europe in 476 A.D. and in Eastern Europe and Asia Minor in 1453, the absolute monarchy still continued to hold the stage there for several centuries more..

England was the first to rise against monarchy and to shorn it of its absolutism in the course of a series of revolutions in the 17th century – the civil war which culminated in the establishment of the commonwealth under the Instrument of Government of 1649, followed by the Restoration of Charles II in 1660 upon certain terms, and finally the Glorious Revolution of 1688 by which the crown was bestowed on William of Orange and his wife, Mary, after the flight to France of Mary's father, James II. Included in the terms of the offer was what was termed a Bill of Rights, which contained thirteen stipulations, among which were the abolition of the power of the monarch to make or suspend laws, to take executive actions not authorised or backed by law, and to act as supreme judge of acts committed against the government.

The stipulations, known as the Bill of Rights, established constitutional government as a definite principle of government in England, although limited in their terms and application to the executive, as it was also limited in Rome. The principle, thus firmly established in England, later moved across the seas and was accepted in parts of Europe – France, Italy, Scandinavia, Poland and Hungary – and in North America.[48] It has been rightly described as England's "pre-eminent contribution to the history of Western freedom."[49]

It is necessary to emphasise that, up to this stage in its development, constitutional government only involved legal limitations upon the executive government through its subjection to law and the review of its actions by the courts to ensure their conformity with the law. Legal limitations upon the legislature itself, as distinct from merely conventional or political ones, were as yet unknown, and had to await the invention of the written constitution as a by-product of the revolution in America in the 18th century, which was itself a revolt against the notion of the unlimited and unlimitable sovereignty of the British Parliament, an invention described by Chief Justice John Marshal as "the greatest improvement on political institutions."[50] From the United States in 1787, the written constitution as a mechanism for imposing legal limitations and controls upon government, particularly its legislative organ, spread to, and was adopted by, Poland on 3 May 1791, France on 3 September 1791, Sweden 1809, Venezuela 1811, Ecuador 1812, Spain 1812, Norway 1814 (the second longest surviving written constitution in the world after that of the U.S.A.), Mexico 1824, Central American Federation 1825 and Argentina 1826. So much has this development encompassed the world that only six countries are today without written constitutions.

---

48   Treadgold, *Freedom: A History* (1990), p. 191.

49   Herbert J. Muller, *Freedom in the Western World: From the Dark Ages to the Rise of Democracy* (1963), p. 290.

50   *Marbury v Madison* 1 Cranch 137 (1803).

England again took the lead in the experimentation with democratic government in the sense of a government freely elected by universal suffrage (as contra-distinguished from the direct democracy of the ancient city-states of Greece and Rome), but the experimentation in this field did not even begin until the 19th century, and when it did, it took some 86 years to accomplish in England through a process of piece-meal extensions of the franchise in 1832, 1867, 1885 and 1918. Universal adult suffrage was not attained in Europe and the United States until later in the 20th century.

The revolt against absolute monarchy in Russia came in 1917, and resulted in its overthrow and in the establishment of a new form of government based on the dictatorship of the working people and the peasants (the proletariat) led by a single, exclusive party – state. It tries to integrate, regiment and control "so many aspects of human existence: family life, friendship, work, leisure, production, exchange, worship, art, manners, travel, dress – even that final assertion of human privacy, death."[51] It is a despotism with a vengeance. It simply "magnifies the elements of autocracy to their farthest limits."[52] From Russia, it has spread to parts of Africa, Asia and to Cuba in South America.

Indefinite Eligibility for Re-election to the Presidential Office and its Compatibility or otherwise with Constitutional Democracy

Until lately, indefinite eligibility for re-election to the office of president has been almost an invariable rule in Africa, being explicitly instituted in the constitutions of 15 countries, and (except in three cases only) recognised in all the others by implication from the absence of a constitutional limitation on the number of times a person may be re-elected to the office. (The three surviving hereditary monarchies, Lesotho, Morocco and Swaziland, are not counted for this purpose).

---

51   Harry Eckstein and David Apter, (eds), *Comparative Politics* (1965), p. 434.

52   Eckstein and Apter, *op.cit.*, p. 433.

In the three excepted cases, re-election was constitutionally limited to one consecutive term in Guinea (1958) and Congo (Leopoldville) (1964) and four successive terms in Rwanda (1962) – the term was seven, five· and four years respectively – but the restriction was later abolished in Guinea and Congo (Leopoldville).

The provision for re-election for an indefinite number of times in Liberia (1847) was so clumsily worded as to obscure its import somewhat. It reads:

> No president may be elected for two consecutive terms of eight years, but should a majority of the ballots cast at a second or any other succeeding election by all of the electors voting thereat elect him, his second or any other succeeding term of office shall be for four years.[53]

Thus, with the backing of constitutionally ordained eligibility for re-election indefinitely, rulership in Africa has tended to become a permanent appointment, much like appointments in the civil service. Felix Houphouet Boigny of Cote D'Ivoire died in office after 34 years as President, William Tubman of Liberia after 28 years, Sekou Toure of Guinea after 26 years, Abdel Nasser of Egypt after 16 years, Jomo Kenyatta of Kenya and Sir Seretse Khama of Botswana after 15 years. Mobutu Sese Seko of Zaire [Congo (Leopoldville)], Sir Dauda Jawara of The Gambia, Lebua Jonathan of Lesotho, Hamani Diori of Niger and Kwame Nkrumah of Ghana were in office for 32, 29, 20, 14 and 10 years respectively before being overthrown in military coups or armed revolt, and Kamuzu Banda of Malawi and Kenneth Kaunda of Zambia for 29 and 27 years respectively before they were voted out in a free multi-party democratic election. Habib Bourguiba of Tunisia was dismissed after 32 years in office on the ground of senility certified by a group of medical doctors. Julius Nyerere of Tanzania voluntarily retired after 27 years in office as did Leopold Senghor of Senegal after 21 years. Gnassingbe Eyadema of Togo, Omar Bongo of Gabon and Muammar Gaddafi of Libya are still in office (August 2001) after 30, 30 and 27 years respectively.

---

53   Art. 3, sec. 1.

Habib Bourguiba of Tunisia and Kamuzu Banda of Malawi had themselves proclaimed life president in the constitution as had Emperor Jean-Bedel Bokassa of the Central African Republic before his overthrow by the military in 1972. Other African presidents, like Kwame Nkrumah and Kenneth Kaunda, rejected offers of a life presidency, just as Banda did for some time before finally succumbing to the pressure and the temptation. But all have said they would stay in office for as long as the people wanted them, which, given the indefinite eligibility for re-election, means in effect for life, the only difference being that every four, five or so years they will have to submit themselves to the ritual of an election. It was the ritualistic nature of the exercise perhaps that finally induced Banda, with his characteristic aversion to hypocrisy, to accept the life presidency.

Now, a life president, or one who has held office for 20 years or 30 years, is a different kind of functionary from one who is limited to a maximum of two terms of four or five years each. His authority is bound to be greater; for after twenty or thirty years in office he is apt to become an institution himself, attracting loyalties of a personal nature.

This propensity to perpetuate rulership indefinitely is perhaps the most outstanding contrast between the politics of the emergent states and those of the established democracies, especially Britain and America. In Britain, politics has attained a happy equilibrium in which the alternation of government at not too distant intervals between two parties has become a political pattern.

This owes to the good sense not only of the electorate but of the politicians themselves. It is unthinkable that a party in office should want to rig an election in order to stay in power. But what is equally, if not more, remarkable is the frequent change in the personnel of the rulers within the governing party. A British politician would not normally want to remain prime minister for as long as his party continues to win elections. No law forbids him to do so, but there is a general acceptance that the talent for leadership is not the exclusive property of any one individual. Many would be satisfied with two terms, some indeed would prefer to retire before the expiration of their second term, as did Harold Macmillan; this may be due partly to health and other personal reasons, as well as desire to give others within the party a chance to succeed to the leadership. (Margaret Thatcher breached this principle and had to be forced out.) And from the point of view of the nation, a change in leadership may guarantee against sterility, complacency and the danger of the cult of personality. Change may enable a fresh vitality and a fresh approach to be brought to bear upon the problems of government. "An untried president may be better than a tired one; a fresh approach better than a stale one."[54] There is yet another striking feature of the system of rulership in Britain. It is not considered *infra dig* for a person who has once been prime minister to serve as an ordinary minister under another leader. Each party has its own system of choosing its leader, and a previous appointment as prime minister carried with it no title to the continued leadership of the party in the future. A former prime minister who has lost in the contest for the party leadership will not necessarily feel embarrassment in serving as minister under a new party leader as prime minister, as happened in the case of Sir Alec Douglas-Home. The prime minister enjoys prestige and power no doubt, but he does not consider himself as uniquely set apart from the rest of the community.

In the United States the problem of succession to the rulership has received an equally happy solution, as a result again of the good sense of successive presidents from the first downwards. Until 1951, the American Constitution imposed no restrictions on the eligibility of a president to seek re-election indefinitely. At the time of the Constitution's adoption, most Americans wished indeed that George Washington, the first president, would retain his office indefinitely, so profound was the confidence and love they had for him. As a matter of general political principle, quite apart from the personality of Washington, the question of indefinite eligibility had provoked a

---

54   E.S. Corwin, *The President: Office and Powers*, 4th ed., p. 37.

disagreement of views. Washington himself and Alexander Hamilton favoured it while Jefferson opposed it. Hamilton, in *The Federalist*, argued that a limitation on the number of terms permitted to a president would stifle zeal and make the president indifferent to his duty, that a president, knowing he would be barred from the office for ever after, might be tempted to exploit for personal advantage the opportunities of the office while they lasted; that an ambitious president might be tempted to try to prolong his term by pervert means; that it would deprive the community of the advantage of the president's previous experience in the office; and that it would lead to a lack of continuity in policy, and consequently to instability in administration.

Washington did, however, retire after two terms, much against the wishes and expectations of his countrymen. His example was followed by Jefferson, also against appeals from eight State Legislatures that he should continue in office. "If," he argued, "some termination to the services of the chief magistrate be not fixed by the Constitution, or supplied by practice, his office, normally four years, will in fact become for life, and history shows how easily that degenerates into an inheritance."[55] Since then the tradition has stuck that no person should be president for more than two terms. Until 1940, this tradition was consistently observed except when, taking advantage of the uncertainty as to whether two terms meant two consecutive terms, Theodore Roosevelt sought (but failed) to be elected in 1912 for a third term some years after his first two consecutive terms. Tradition was finally breached when Franklin D. Roosevelt was re-elected for a third consecutive term in 1940 and for a fourth in 1944. But those were periods of grave emergency, the period of the Second World War. It is such emergency situations that present the strongest argument in favour of indefinite eligibility. In such a situation the prestige and authority of the president's personality might be invaluable in saving the life of the nation. This was the consideration

---

55   Quoted in E.S. Corwin, *op.cit.*, p. 332.

underlying the break with tradition of Franklin Roosevelt's third and fourth consecutive re-elections. Roosevelt himself professed a desire to adhere to the tradition, and to relinquish office in 1941 to a successor if only he could do so with an assurance that:

> I am at the same time turning over to him as president a nation intact, a nation at peace, a nation prosperous, a nation clear in its knowledge of what powers it has to serve its own citizens, a nation that is in a position to use those powers to the full in order to move forward steadily to meet the modern needs of humanity, a nation which has thus proved that the democratic form and methods of national government can and will succeed.[56]

These are words which might be used by an African president to justify his rule in perpetuity, and it might even be more cogent and compelling in his case. As Corwin points out, this is just the "indispensable man" argument. To accept it, he says, "is next door to despairing of the country."[57] In a temporary emergency, like a war, it might perhaps be condoned, but in the context of the sort of emergency created by the development crisis in the emergent states it is a positive evil. For since the development crisis is a continuing "emergency," the argument tantamounts to making the presidency a life appointment. In any case, the Americans, after the Roosevelt experience, had to amend their constitution in 1951 to give force of law to the tradition limiting the presidential office to two full elective terms or one full elective term plus more than half of another term inherited from a previous president.[58] African countries must follow in the footstep. After eight or ten years in office as president, no one should, in justice to the country and to other citizens, want to continue, and no nation, with the right kind of ethic, should allow it. It is gratifying that, with the recrudescence of constitutional democracy in Africa since 1990, indefinite eligibility for re-election to the

---

56   Quoted in E.S. Corwin, *op.cit.*, p. 336.

57   *Ibid*, p. 337.

58   XX Amendment.

presidential office is now giving way in a growing number of African countries to a constitutional limitation to two terms of four or so years each. Africa is, happily, coming round to a realisation that indefinite eligibility so grievously undermines constitutional democracy as to be incompatible with it. (The present position since 1990 is examined in chapter 8 of vol.5.)

CHAPTER 2

Functions of a Constitution

A Constitution as the Foundation of the State and Government

If we imagine a collection of peoples inhabiting contiguous areas of territory but as yet not formed into one political community, then, a written constitution for them will serve four primary functions. These are, first, to constitute them into a polity or state; second, to institute a frame of government armed with powers and institutions necessary and adequate to the effective management of public affairs; third, to limit those powers in the interest of the protection of the liberty of the individual; and, fourth, to declare the ideals and objectives of the nation and the duties of the state to its subjects.

The first two functions flow from the definition of a constitution as meaning "the act of constituting (a state or government or both) as well as the law or rules of government that are constituted, be these embodied in written documents or, as in the case of the British Constitution, implied in institutions, customs, and precedents".[1] A constitution, defined as the act of constituting a state and its

---

1   Hannah Arendt, *On Revolution* (1962), p. 145.

government, is well exemplified in North America. Before the adoption of the U.S. Constitution in 1787, there were thirteen political communities occupying contiguous areas of territory in North America, but there was no common political organisation uniting them into one polity or state. The first function required of the 1787 Constitution was therefore to constitute the several political communities into one body politic, with one name – United States of America. And so was born a new state. The makers of the American Constitution became the founding fathers of the new state thus brought into existence by the constituent act of themselves and their fellow countrymen.

The new sovereign states created by European colonialism in Africa share with the United States of America a common origin as states constituted or brought into existence for the first time by a written constitution. But whereas the U.S. was created by a constitution adopted and enacted into law by the people in exercise of their revolutionary sovereignty, the African states were the creation of colonial constitutions made abroad by European imperial powers by virtue of sovereignty seized from colonised Africans. Lamentably, because of their origin in colonial constitutions made abroad by European colonisers, the new African states have no African founding fathers; they were the illegitimate offsprings of European colonialism without the rallying sentiment associated with the worship of founding fathers as national heroes. The nationalist leaders who led independence movements were certainly not the founding fathers, the state having come into being, albeit as a colonial state, before most of them were born. (The Nigerian state came into being in 1914 when the former protectorates of Southern and Northern Nigeria were amalgamated into one, just as the United States in 1787 was an amalgam of the former thirteen colonies which later became independent states.)

In the 20th century, there has emerged a new type of state, the party-state. The U.S. Constitution of 1787 made no mention at all of political parties, not because they were unknown at the time, but perhaps because they were not so central or even crucial in the organisation of society, the state and government to warrant a mention in the constitution. Since then, however, the political party had acquired in most countries of Eastern Europe, Asia and Africa a radically changed role and status as the focal institution integrating society, the state and/or government. Thus, between 1787 and the twentieth century, there has occurred a radically novel conception of the relation between the political party on the one hand and society, the economy, the state and government on the other.

For the constitution and its role, the implication of the change is also radical and overwhelming. If a new state, like the United States of America in 1787, is the creation of a constitution, then, the political party, conceived as the focal institution that integrates society, the state and/or government, has necessarily to be given a place in the constitution, and a central, dominating place for that matter. The state having become a party-state, the new type of state has also to be established and its organs and role enshrined, in the constitution, just as the new state born in 1787, the U.S.A., was the creation of a constitution.

And so, the Communist Party, its role and status, was enshrined in the 1918 Revolutionary Socialist Constitution of Russia, the preamble to which proclaimed as follows:

> The Great Socialist October Revolution carried out by the workers and peasants of Russia under the leadership of the Communist Party, headed by V.I. Lenin, overturned the power of the capitalists and land owners, broke the chains of oppression, established the dictatorship of the proletariat, and created the Soviet state – **a state of a new type**, the basic instrument to defend the revolutionary achievements and to build socialism and communism. The worldwide historical turning point of mankind from capitalism to socialism began. (emphasis supplied).

The Communist Party was proclaimed in the Socialist Constitution of 1918 as the "vanguard and guiding force" of the dictatorship of the working people thereby instituted.

The socialist party-state, with its established role and status, has been received for varying periods of time in eleven African states – Algeria, Angola, Benin, Congo (Brazzaville), Egypt, Ethiopia, Libya, Madagascar, Mozambique, Tanzania (since 1984), and Somalia.[2] In all eleven (except Egypt and Libya), as in Russia in 1918, a party of workers and peasants or the popular masses was established in the constitution as the sole party permitted to exist and function as a political party – the Popular Revolution Party of Benin (PRPB), the Workers' Party of Ethiopia (WPE), the MPLA-Workers' Party of Angola (MPLA is abbreviation for the Popular Movement for the Liberation of Angola), FRELIMO (Mozambique), the National Front for the Defence of the Revolution (Madagascar), the National Liberation Front (FLN) in Algeria, the Congolese Labour Party (Congo Brazzaville), and the Somali Revolutionary Socialist Party. The Egyptian Constitution of 1964 is strangely out of step in proclaiming the country "a socialist state based on the alliance of the forces of the working people being the farmers, workers, soldiers and intellectuals" (Arts. 1 and 3), but without establishing an exclusive party of the working people, and constituting the country a party state. The "Socialist People's Libyan Arab Jamahiriya" established in 1975 is avowedly a no-party state; according to Gaddafi, political parties are part of a "sham democracy" with its resultant dictatorship by a minority.

In the building of a socialist socio-economic order, the party in each of the 11 states was proclaimed in the constitution "the organised vanguard of the working people ... responsible for the political, economic and social leadership of the state in the effort to construct Socialist Society" (Angola); "the leading force of the State and Society", with responsibility to lay down the basic political orientation and the political line to guide the state, to "direct and supervise the work of state organs, in order to ensure that the state policy is in conformity with the people's interest" (Mozambique); "the guiding force of the state and the entire society", and the vanguard party to "serve the

---

2   The Saharawi Arab Republic (SADR) is left out of account whilst its fate still hangs in the balance.

working people and protect their interests" (Ethiopia); a "progressive party of the oppressed masses" – workers and poor peasants (Benin); the motivator, inspirator and guide of the activity of the state and the spirit of the revolution towards the establishment of socialism (Madagascar); the revolutionary movement of the popular masses, the only guiding political and ideological force, with responsibility to control the country, and to direct its policy towards the realisation, through the instrumentality of the state and its institutions, of a socialist society (Algeria); the supreme form of political and social organisation of the people, with the role of inspiring and directing the policy of the state towards the realisation of a socialist socio-economic order (Congo Brazzaville); the supreme authority of political and socio-economic leadership for the socialist construction of the country (Somalia). Thus, a truly party-state was constituted by the constitutions of these countries.

As distinct from the above-named 11 socialist states constituted as such in their respective constitutions, a party-state had also been constituted by the constitution in 34 other countries in Africa but without creating them as socialist state, with its accompanying socialist socio-economic order (a few pursued a certain amount of socialist economic strategy of development) and the socialist legal system associated with it – i.e., socialist legality. The common feature shared with the 11 socialist states was that only one political party was permitted under the constitution to exist and function. Without the underpinnings of the socialist socio-economic order and the socialist legal system, the **African** one-party state, as it became known, was essentially different in status from its counterpart in the socialist countries in that it did not integrate society and the economy. It did, however, integrate the government as much, if not more, than the Communist Party or the workers' party in the socialist state, which required therefore that it be enshrined in the constitution. And because it integrated the government, the state was as much a party-state. Indeed, in two of the countries, Zambia and Seychelles, the constitution of the party was scheduled to the state constitution.

The party-state under Guinea's Second Constitution of 1982 may be described as a kind of half-way house between the socialist state prototype and the African one-party state. The Democratic Party of Guinea (PDG) was proclaimed as embodying the popular masses, as integrating all social strata, and as the supreme instrument and the principal directing force of the action of the people whose pre-eminence and primacy as the source of all legitimacy and legality is explicitly recognised. Within the popular masses embodied by the party, however, the working people represent the "class power" and constitute the "people-class", which made the PDG the party of the people-class. As the creator of the Guinean state in the sense of being the architect of its independence from colonial domination, the PDG was further proclaimed the sole and exclusive directing force, with the right to control the state, which must therefore identify itself with the party. The party, as the sole and exclusive directing force, was pledged to the radical transformation of society through creative work aimed at the domination of nature by the appropriation of all knowledge and the eradication of exploitation of man by man. Thus, the new party-state in Guinea is conceived on the basis of a more or less total merger of the state with the party. Yet, the country did not thereby become a socialist state, having only moved, according to its leader, Sekou Toure, to the stage of "advanced popular democracy" which is only the fourth stage in the process leading to a "revolutionary popular government." (The name of the country had earlier been changed to the Popular Revolutionary Republic of Guinea.)

The disputation about whether or not the state antedates, and exists apart from, the constitution must therefore distinguish between states already formed and in existence before a written constitution was adopted and those (including states of the new type) brought into existence for the first time through a constitution. Undeniably, the latter owe their origin and creation, though perhaps not their continued existence, to a constitution. Interesting as it is, the question of whether the overthrow of the constitution in a *coup d'etat* also destroys the state or leaves its existence unaffected is outside our present concern.[3]

A Constitution as the Creator of Powers as well as Institutions and Principles of Government

The act of constituting a government necessarily implies arming it with powers and institutions needed for the effective conduct of public affairs. The constitution is thus the source of power wielded by government over the people. Under a written constitution as supreme law, government has no more powers than are granted to it, either expressly or impliedly, by the constitution, and any exercise by it of power not so granted or which is prohibited to it is unconstitutional and void. Effective conduct of public affairs demands that the powers granted to government by the constitution should be adequate. For, as Professor McIlwain says:

> a student of history may be warranted in thinking that in the past weakness has probably caused the fall of more governments than wickedness. An unjust ruler is hated by his subjects, but they usually tolerate him longer than one incapable of preventing injustice in others.[4]

In the Anglo-American system, certain formulas have been developed and accepted as apt to confer upon government, a full plenitude of executive, legislative and judicial powers. As regards legislative powers, the form of words employed is that the legislative body may make laws for "the peace, order and good government" of the country. The phrase "peace, order and good government" does not delimit the purpose for which the power is granted, in the sense that a law must be for peace, order or good government in order to be

---

3   On this, see B.O. Nwabueze, *Constitutionalism in the Emergent States* (1973), pp. 236-238.

4   C.H. McIlwain, *Constitutionalism and the Changing World* (1939), p. 276.

valid. It is simply, as the Judicia! Committee of the privy Council has held, a legal formula for expressing the widest plenitude of legislative power exercisable by a sovereign legislature, subject to limitations arising from the division of powers between a central and regional governments in a federal system, such as Nigeria. Thus, the legislative power of the National Assembly in Nigeria is not a power to make law for "peace, order and good government" **generally**, but a power to make law for "peace, order and good government" with respect **only** to matters specified in the Constitution. The formula, "peace, order and good government", which is also used by the Constitution to define the legislative power of the State Houses of Assembly, confers no **inherent** power on the National Assembly to legislate outside the matters so specified as being within its legislative competence.

The notion of judicial power connotes the power which every sovereign state of necessity possesses to decide justiciable disputes between its subjects, or between itself and its subjects.[5] The formula for conferring it is to empower the court to decide all such disputes arising under the constitution and under the laws of the country.[6]

The formula for conferring executive power in its fullest plenitude is to empower the executive authority, however designated, to execute and maintain the constitution, the ordinary laws of the land and other matters with respect to which the legislative body has power to make laws. A tremendous amount of power of an undefined extent and potency, can be derived from the execution and maintenance of the constitution. See Chapter 7 for further discussion.

A Constitution as a Charter of Freedom for the Individual and a Device for Limiting Power Generally

The third function, that of imposing limitations on government for

---

5   *Huddart, Parker & Co. Ltd. v. Moorehead* (1909) 8 C.L.R. 330, per Griffith C.J. of the High Court of Australia; for discussion of the nature of judicial power, see Nwabueze, *Judicialism in Commonwealth Africa* (1977), pp. 1-19.

6   See, e.g. Art. III of the U.S. Constitution.

the protection of the liberty of the individual, is as primary and basic as the first two. Indeed the singular importance of the emergence of the institution of a written constitution as law antecedent and superior to government lies, not so much in its function as a source of governmental power but rather in the consequence that it necessarily operates as a limitation upon government, a consequence that flows inexorably from the fact that in constituting a government and in granting and distributing power, a constitution cannot but limit it. A constitution as a supreme law which merely grants power in all its plenitude without limitations of any kind hardly merits to be so called. To justify the name, it must be "a constitution of liberty, a constitution that would protect the individual against all arbitrary coercion" on the part of the legislature as well as the other branches of government.[7]

The two methods of protection commonly employed and which are indispensable in the definition of a constitutional government are a constitutional guarantee of life, liberty and private property in justiciable form, otherwise known as a bill of rights, and the separation of powers, in particular the separation of judicial from legislative and executive power. The one protects and safeguards liberty by limiting the extent of governmental power as regards the subject-matter over which it may be exercised, and the other by avoiding its concentration in the same hands. The device of separation of legislative and executive powers as a constitutional means of protecting liberty, however, confronts the constitution-maker with the perennial problem of how to balance the competing objects of liberty and effective government to ensure that the acknowledged need for limitation on government in the interest of liberty does not result in government being so enfeebled to the point where it is rendered incapable of governing effectively. For feebleness has been among the chief causes of the collapse or overthrow of constitutionalism, as happened in nearly all European countries since the abolition of absolute monarchies after the First World War.[8]

---

7   F.A. Hayek, *The Constitution of Liberty* (1960), p. 182; also p. 178.

8   Hannah Arendt, *op.cit.,* pp. 145-146; also C.H. McIlwain, *ibid.*

In the light of the primary and basic nature of the constitution's function in limiting government, it may seem strange that a constitution should ever also be a source of total power or a means by which to legitimise the arrogation of it by government. But strange as it may appear, it has in fact, as shown in Chapter 1, been so employed in communist countries. This is possible, as there explained, only because the communist constitution is not conceived as a law, supreme over the government and endowed with a coercive force that overrides all inconsistent governmental acts.

A Constitution as a Medium for Declaring the Ideals and Fundamental Objectives of a Nation and Affirming the Duty of the State to the People

Just as the notion of government by the people is implemented in the constitution of a democratic government, so also, it is suggested, should that of the public welfare as the object of government be given constitutional force, by making a positive declaration in the constitution to that effect, coupled with a directive as to the broad lines of policy to be pursued by government in furtherance thereof. It should also give constitutional force to the notion of civic virtues by embodying the necessary civic virtues in a code of conduct for public servants. The effect of such a constitutional declaration of public welfare as the object of government, and of directive principles of state policy and a constitutional code for public servants will be to cast upon the legislative and executive functionaries of government a constitutional obligation to inform and guide their actions in accordance with such stipulations. They would also serve as a reminder to them that their position is one of trust involving powers as well as duties. A truly republican tradition and culture may thereby, hopefully, be nurtured among the leadership.

The appropriateness of the constitution directing the state as to its duties to the citizenry and the policies and actions called for on its part should perhaps be less grudgingly conceded. It is not enough to grant powers to government and to impose limitations upon them. For power is, by its nature, discretionary, and implies no obligation to exercise it at all or to exercise it in a particular direction. The legislature is under no duty to exercise its power to make law on any matter nor is the executive obliged to execute the law when it is made. Thus, although government has the constitutional power to do so, it is not legally obliged to provide medical, educational and other social amenities for the welfare of the people. Similarly, the limitation on power implied in a constitutional guarantee of individual liberties imposes no duty on the state positively to do anything to promote the material well-being of the people, but only a negative duty not to violate them.

A constitution should not stop with just affirming the duties of the state for the welfare of its citizens; it should also embody and affirm the ideals and fundamental objectives of the nation. By this, it would be playing more than a symbolic role in rallying the minds of the members of the society around those ideals, with a view to establishing them as part of the ethic of the nation. The constitution should indeed be the catalytic starting point in the process of creating a national acceptance of, and attachment to, those beliefs, ideas and objectives as national ideals, with the object that they might eventually strike firm roots as habits or traditions of respect for them. Enshrining an affirmation or declaration of a nation's common ideals and objectives in the constitution would make them appear less of a political slogan, and invest them with the character of constitutional, if non-justifiable, norms, thereby making it easier for the rulers and the ruled alike to develop the desired identification with them.

Happily, this view of the function of a constitution finds ample precedent in the constitutions of most European countries, the constitution of African countries derived from European tradition, and, to a limited extent, the Constitution of the United States of America. In contrast, the British tradition in the matter, which is reflected in the constitutions of African and other countries derived from it, is that a constitution is not an appropriate place for lofty but empty declaration of ideals and objectives. And that its proper concern is with the practical business of organising a government and powers. This is a misconception. The idea of a constitution is one that is familiar to all of us in our various capacities as members of clubs, trade or professional associations, village or town unions, and so on. Every such association is governed by a constitution which sets out the aims and objectives of the association and how its affairs are to be conducted and managed. It is the same idea that is applied to the association of all the people living within a given geographical area.

In this context, a constitution is the means by which a people organises a government for itself and defines the aims and objectives of the political association, the conditions of membership, the rights and obligations of membership, the organs and powers necessary for the conduct of the affairs of the association and the duties and responsibilities of those organs to the individual members. That is what the idea of a constitution for a nation is all about. It is the same simple idea to which our membership of clubs and trade or professional associations has familiarised us. Admittedly, the infinitely larger number of people involved in the association of a nation and its wider purposes call for a form of organisation and for a structure of powers, rights and relationships that gives to a national constitution a complexity which makes it appear as if it is something different in nature and character from the constitutions of other associations.

It is unheard of for the constitution of a club, trade or professional association, or village or town union not to state the aims and objectives of the association. That is the axiomatic starting point. A statement of objectives is necessary because it focuses attention on the reasons for the existence of the association. It is perhaps one of those great distortions in ideas that something so basic to the idea of a constitution should be regarded as out of place in a national constitution.

A national constitution should organise a government for the nation but it should also define the ideals of the national association and the organising ideas of the people. Consequently, a nation without a body of organised ideas reflecting its ideals is not worthy of the name. As Wole Soyinka has rightly said, there is no other definition of a nation than a unit of humanity bound together by a common ideology. And there is no more appropriate and effective medium for proclaiming and affirming a nation's ideals and organising ideas than the basic instrument of its association. A national constitution should not be simply a code of legally enforceable rules and regulations about powers and institutional structures.

These observations and those made earlier in support of a constitutional affirmation of the duty of the state for the welfare of its citizens apply with greater force in Africa where the state has a character significantly different from that of the state in Western Europe. Two important differences are here relevant. The state in Western Europe has become, since at least the end of the Second World War, a welfare state; there, the claims of the individual for social benefits and amenities have been fully accepted and are being implemented. The state in Western Europe is further characterised by certain beliefs, ideas, habits, traditions and moral values shared in common by the generality of the population. In Africa, on the other hand, the state has nothing of this character. The notion of the welfare state, of the welfare of the people as the object of government, is still a far cry in Africa. The consequence of this is to further widen the existing gap in living standards arising from the disparity in income and wealth between the various classes in the society – between

> the huge mass of family farmers, living very like the English peasant of the middle ages, illiterate, superstitious, handling very little money, their world bounded by the family or clan; the wage-earners and urban proletariat, living like their counterparts in nineteenth century Britain, semi-literate, under-paid, badly-housed, and the top professional and businessmen, whose material and often, professional standards equal or exceed those of the Western world.[9]

The African state is an example **par excellence** of a plural society.

---

9   Wraith and Simpkins, *Corruption in Developing Countries* (1963), p. 196.

Whilst they are characterised by a basic similarity in culture and way of life, the various social groups comprised within each state have no system of beliefs, ideals and objectives shared in common by all; the colonially-created state in Africa is a state with no national civil society, no united public opinion as a basis for common action, no common habits, beliefs, traditions and moral values. But, as Alexis de Tocqueville tells us, "without common belief no society ... can exist; for without ideas held in common, there is no common action, and without common action, there may still be men, but there is no social body".[10] The affirmation of ideals and objectives in the constitution can serve as a catalyst to rally the people around them as part of the nation's ethic.

The British tradition in this matter is becoming increasingly outdated since the world's first written constitution, the American Constitution (1787), whose preamble proclaims:

> We the People of the United States, in Order to form a more perfect Union, establish Justice, insure domestic Tranquility, provide for the common defence, promote the general Welfare, and secure the Blessings of Liberty to ourselves and our Posterity, do ordain and establish this Constitution for the United States of America.

The practice is today almost universally accepted for a constitution to begin with a preamble affirming the ideals and fundamental objectives of the nation. Of the 160-odd written constitutions in the world, all but 41 have a preambulary affirmation of ideals and objectives, and all, in varying forms, follow the U.S. in affirming the ideals and objectives of national unity, justice, liberty, peace and public welfare, which undoubtedly are the abiding and most fundamental desire of humankind everywhere.

Since 1787, the preambulary affirmation has undergone considerable enlargement in the range of ideals and objectives proclaimed. Obviously, the affirmation in the preamble to the U.S.

---

10   Alexis de Tocqueville, *Democracy in America* (1835), ed. Richard Heffner (1956), p. 146.

Constitution is somewhat limited in scope, especially judged in the light of the wider and more complex objects of today's society. As one obvious example, although justice is mentioned in the U.S. preamble, it seems clear from the context of the entire U. S. Constitution that the justice referred to is justice between person and person, i.e., (individual justice) and does not embrace social justice, but no affirmation of ideals and objectives in a constitution can today be considered adequate without a mention of social justice which, together with liberty, individual justice, peace (both domestic and international), and public welfare, is the paramount objective in all countries. The absence of any mention in the preamble to the U.S. Constitution, of equality is another omission made good in many modern constitutions. Equality is of course a principle of social justice, but deserves a specific mention on its own. Fraternity (or the more modern term brotherhood), the other ideal in the time-honoured trilogy, "Liberty, Equality and Fraternity" is also affirmed in many a preamble.

With liberty, justice (both individual and social), peace, public welfare and equality must be ranked the Rule of Law, an ideal whose paramountcy and centrality became underlined by the rise of fascism in Germany and Italy in the 1930s and the spread to Eastern Europe and other parts of the world in the 1940s and after, of communist-type totalitarianism. All the other ideals and objectives, liberty, justice, peace and public welfare, have meaning and reality only in so far as the state is one governed and permeated by the rule of law, a law-governed state as it is referred to in some of the newest constitutions. And so it is that the rule of law has come to feature in many of the preambulary affirmations. And democracy too, which is nowadays an ideal accepted by nearly every country of the world as the natural form of government.

Some of the other ideals and objectives featured in the preambles of the world's constitutions include allegiance to the constitution and laws of the country; social, cultural and economic progress; primacy of the individual as the subject and purpose of the social order, recognition of the family as the primary and fundamental basis of society's spiritual and moral values; eradication of ignorance, fear, disease and misery; total liberation from the vestiges of colonialism. The wide range of ideals and objectives affirmed in the preambles of some modern constitutions makes an interesting and instructive study indeed.

A belief in God or Allah and in the doctrines and principles of Islam is affirmed in the preamble to the constitutions of all Moslem countries – one goes so far as to incorporate the principles in the Quoran as part of the constitution. In the non-Moslem countries, God is mentioned in the preamble of 38 constitutions, some even affirming adherence to Christian principles. Considering the role of religion as a source of, or as a sanction for, morality, this is alright. It seems, however, something of a contradiction to affirm in a preamble, as is done in Nigeria, a firm and solemn resolve to "live in unity and harmony as one indivisible and indissoluble sovereign Nation under God" and at the same time to prohibit in a substantive provision the adoption of any religion as state religion,[11] if by this is meant the neutrality of the state on all matters of religion.

The preambulary statement has in some countries been transformed in character from a mere affirmation to a lengthy declaration of rights or of ideals and objectives. Thus, the preamble to the French Constitution of 1946 not only reaffirmed the historic 1789 Declaration of the Rights of Man, it also declared a long list of other rights. While they were not incorporated as part of the 1958 Constitution, the rights in the 1789 Declaration and in the 1946 Declaration were reaffirmed in the preamble to that Constitution, an example that has been followed in some of her former African colonies. Following also in the French example, some countries, including some former French African colonies, proclaim in a preamble, adherence to the United Nations Universal Declaration of Human Rights (1948).

The lengthy preambulary declaration of ideals and objectives in

---

11   S. 11, *Constitution of Nigeria 1979.*

the Constitution of Papua New Guinea 1975, which is also coupled with a declaration of rights (it runs to six full pages), is perhaps the most remarkable example. The method adopted is to declare certain broad goals – human development, equality of opportunity to participate in, and benefit from, the development of the country, economic independence and self-reliance, utilisation of natural resources for the common good and their replenishment for the benefit of future generations, and the evolution and use of Papua New Guinean forms of social, political and economic organisations as a basis for development – and then to spell out specific objectives to be pursued within the framework of the broad goals.

Affirmation of ideals and objectives in a preamble has, no doubt, great value, mainly symbolic, but it has no binding or coercive force, whereas their declaration in substantive provisions of the constitution legally binds the government and its agencies and functionaries to observe and conform to the ideals and objectives as a matter of peremptory duty, although the duty may expressly or impliedly be made non-justiciable in the courts of law. For example, the provisions in Chapter 11 of the Nigerian Constitution proclaim freedom, equality, participatory democracy and social justice as the ideals upon which the nation is founded.[12] This is amplified by the declaration that the welfare of the people shall be the primary purpose of government; that government shall be responsible and accountable to the people; that every citizen shall have equality of rights, obligations and opportunities before the law; that the sanctity of the human person shall be recognised and human dignity shall be maintained and enhanced; that government actions shall be humane; that human exploitation in any form whatsoever shall be prevented; and that the independence, impartiality, integrity and easy accessibility of the courts shall be secured and maintained. Unity and faith, peace and progress are proclaimed the national motto, and discipline, self-reliance and patriotism the national ethic.

---

12   Chap. 11.

The Romanian provisions proclaim Romania "a social and democratic state of law in which human dignity, the rights and liberties of citizens, the free development of the human personality, justice and political pluralism represent supreme values and are guaranteed;" that "national sovereignty belongs to the Romanian people who exercise it through their representative bodies and through referendums" and that "no group or individual may exercise sovereignty on his own behalf;" that "the state is based on the unity of the Romanian people" and "is the common and indivisible homeland of all its citizens regardless of race, ethnic origin, language, religion, sex, opinion, political allegiance, wealth or social origin;" that "the state recognises and guarantees for members of national minorities the right to preserve, develop, and express their ethnic, cultural, linguistic and religious identity;" that "Romania maintains and develops peaceful relations with all states and, in this framework, relations of good neighbourliness based on the principles and on the other generally accepted norms of international law;" and that the "Romanian state pledges to fulfill, to the letter and in good faith, its commitments under the treaties to which it is a party."[13]

The preambles to the constitutions of African countries adopted since 1990 have broken new grounds in this matter, as the discussions in chapters 3 and 8 of vol. 5 show.

Role of the Constitution in Ensuring Social Justice for Disadvantaged Ethnic, Racial or Religious Groups in a Plural Society

The state in Africa, as earlier stated, is an example **par excellence** of a plural society. Yet, having regard to its duty to treat equally all citizens whose circumstances are the same, the state is not competent to try to redress inequalities in wealth, income, standard of living or social status between racial or ethnic groups by means of preferential measures

---

13   Title arts. 1-11.

designed for the exclusive benefit of disadvantaged groups. But the constitution itself can, in order to secure or promote social justice, institute such measures directly or authorise the government to do so.

The Constitution of India affords an example of this. It provides that the guarantee of non-discrimination shall not "prevent the state from making any special provision for the advancement of any socially and educationally backward classes of citizens or for the scheduled castes and scheduled tribes" [S. 15(e)] or from "making any provision for the reservation of appointments or posts in favour of any backward class of citizens" [S. 16(4)]. In even more affirmative terms, it provides for the reservation of appointments for scheduled castes and scheduled tribes in the administrative services as well as in Parliament and the State Assemblies [S. 335]. We need not concern ourselves with the elaborate quota reservations in the Cyprus Constitution which simply caricature reason.

Preferential measures designed avowedly for the exclusive benefit of a disadvantaged group are open to objection because it is unjustifiable to give a benefit to an individual in preference to more deserving, more meritorious or more needy individuals, simply because he belongs to a disadvantaged group. Clearly, in the distribution of benefits, the depressed social and economic circumstances of a group should not be a justifiable basis for preferring an individual member thereof to someone else from a privileged group, even though the former, considered as an individual, may not personally be disadvantaged or otherwise deserve, merit or need such preferential treatment. Preferential treatment of an individual based on his membership of a disadvantaged group rather than on his individual desert, merit or need is objectionable because it sacrifices individual rights to group rights; it runs counter to the whole concept of a right as something inhering in, or pertaining to, a person, not a racial or ethnic group.

Fixed quota reservations are objectionable on other grounds. There is, first, the danger that acceptable minimum requirements in public appointments and admissions to universities and colleges might be abandoned. They are also over-laid with the notion of proportionality of representation. Once conceded, it should not, logically, stop short of being made to bear a statistical proportionality to the numerical strength of the group. For, since it implies that the group in question is under-represented, full redress demands proportionality of representation or at least a representation that bears an equitable relation to its numerical strength, not an arbitrary concessionary quota totally unrelated to its population. But once we begin to talk in terms of the reservation of statistically proportionate quota for a disadvantaged group(s), then, merit would have been compromised to an unacceptable extent.

The experience of India shows that the system of quota reservations is a veritable source of endless controversies about the criteria for choosing groups to be given preferences, the choice of groups in accordance with the criteria so determined and about the kinds of preferences to be provided. The years since the introduction of the system have witnessed a vast extension of groups covered by preferences and of preferences provided. The process seems a never-ending one as agitations by groups for inclusion continue to mount, marked by "struggles in the streets, at the polls, within the government bureaucracy and in state legislatures. Concessions granted to one group then become the basis for demands by another."[14]

Yet, while inherently objectionable for the reasons above stated, preferential measures are necessary for democracy and social justice in a multi-racial or multi-ethnic society. In such a society, a right to govern, or participate in government based solely on individual merit, is no less unacceptable than one based on birth or wealth. Participation by group representation in a plural society should not be confined to elective offices in the legislature and other bodies. Group representation must be carried to the non-elective offices in the executive council, civil service, the armed forces, police, parastatals, etc. The problem of

---

14   Myron Wefner, "The Pursuit of Ethnic Equality through Preferential Policies: A Comparative Public Policy Perspective," in Goldmann and Wilson, ed., *From Independence to Statehood* (1948), p. 76.

social justice and democracy in a multi-racial or multi-ethnic society is about how to give all the component groups the opportunity to participate in both the elective and non-elective organs, arms and agencies of government, since only thus can each feel that it is a full member of the nation, bound to the others by a common feeling of belonging together. "National loyalty," Professor Arthur Lewis has said, "cannot immediately supplant tribal loyalty; it has to be built on top of tribal loyalty by creating a system in which all the tribes feel that there is room for self-expression"[15] and participation in the government.

The provision in the Nigerian Constitution (1979 and 1999) seems quite apt to answer the need for constitutional protection. It avoids the inflexibility of fixed quota reservations and the dangers with which it is fraught. It simply says that:

> the composition of the Government of the Federation or any of its agencies and the conduct of its affairs shall be carried out in such manner as to reflect the federal character of Nigeria and the need to promote national unity, and also to command national loyalty thereby ensuring that there shall be no predominance of persons from a few states or from a few ethnic or other sectional groups in that government or in any of its agencies [S. 14(3)].

As articulated in this provision, the federal character principle is not a rigid formula, but only a broad guide for action. As a guide, it needs to be applied, not with the mathematical exactitude of fixed quota reservations, but only with a due sense of equitable balance. This requires that public appointments, in particular appointments in the strategic departments and functions of government, should be equitably distributed among the component groups, and to be equitable the distribution should reflect, in some **rough or approximate** way, the respective numerical strengths of the groups but without adhering rigidly to fixed quota reservations. Obviously, the application of such

---

15   Arthur Lewis, *Politics in West Africa* (1965), p. 68.

a broad guide calls for a high degree of statesmanship.

Properly applied, it should not require the appointment or promotion of anyone who does not possess the qualification prescribed for an office or the admission to a university or college of anyone who did not score the minimum pass mark in an entrance examination. All it does is to permit a person with the requisite qualification to be appointed or admitted to represent his group, although he may not be the best man available in a nation-wide competition. Admittedly, he may not perform as well as the best man. Yet, so long as acceptable standard determined by prescribed minimum qualification or experience are not lowered to unacceptable level simply to accommodate the disadvantaged groups, his appointment or admission to represent his group fulfills a higher societal need than that of the highest standards of performance which may be expected from the best man.

But it is not enough that the "federal character" of the country is reflected, in the way suggested, in the composition of the government and its agencies and in the conduct of their affairs unless the application of the principle results in "ensuring that there shall be no predominance of persons from a few states or from a few ethnic or other sectional groups in that government or in any of its agencies." It is not enough that each group is represented in the organs, councils and departments of the government if the government is permanently dominated by one group or a combination of the same groups. The prevention of domination, more than mere participation by representation, is 'the central objective of the federal character principle in the Nigerian Constitution.

Now, domination arises not so much from numbers as from control of the key positions where vital decisions regarding policy, financial disbursements, appointments, award of contracts, etc., are made, where, in short, the business of governing takes place. The messengers, artisans, clerks, the technicians, executive officers and the middle cadre officers are undoubtedly an indispensable part of the machinery for the administration of government. They all contribute vital inputs to the total material on which decisions about government are based. They are even more vital in the execution of decisions. Yet they are no more than supports with very little real power to affect the conduct of government. They cannot dominate, whatever their number. Domination is material at the level of the director-general and his deputy, minister and head of government. It is at these levels that the actual governing takes place. In terms of representational value, the director-general or minister counts for almost as much as the rest of the staff in a ministry put together. Indeed, under the presidential constitution of Nigeria, the president was, to all intents and purposes, the executive government. So is the Head of the Federal Military Government (FMG) in the military administration. It is such key positions particularly that the federal character principle requires not to be dominated by any one group.

The principle requires therefore, above all else, that the headship of the government should move round, and that **ordinarily** no two persons from the same group should hold it successively when the other groups have not held it. It is predicated upon the view of a multi-ethnic society as a house built on many pillars, which edifice will begin to wobble and its stability imperilled if the headship of the government is not made to move round the groups. That is the national question in all multi-ethnic societies. It is also the lesson of the break-up of the Czechoslovak Federation.[16] The question can be constitutionally resolved, either by a formula for rotating the office, or by a simple provision to the effect that no one ethnic group shall hold the office twice when other groups, qualified by a criterion or criteria prescribed in the constitution for the purpose, have not held it.

---

16   See the Editorial in *The Guardian*, Wednesday, August 5, 1992, p. 8.

CHAPTER 3

Federal-State Relations under the Constitution of Nigeria

A Unitary Constitution for a Federal System of Government

The sub-title of this chapter – A Unitary Constitution for a Federal System of Government – reflects great insight, and exposes a fundamental contradiction in our constitutional system. Few contradictions could be more self-evident than that of a unitary constitution for a federal system of government. For unitarism and federalism are mutually exclusive, logically opposing concepts.

Federalism is an arrangement whereby powers and resources within a country are shared between a national, countrywide government and a number of regionalised (i.e., territorially localised) governments in such a way that each exists as a government separately and independently from the others operating directly on persons and property within its territorial area, with a will of its own and its own apparatus for the conduct of its affairs, and with an authority in some matters exclusive of all the others. Federalism is thus essentially an arrangement between governments, a constitutional device by which powers and resources within a country are shared among two (or more) units of government. Government is thus the most significant concept in the definition of federalism.

Now, it is sheer contradiction to conceive of a government, whether in a federal or unitary system, without a constitution. There is just no such thing. The very notion of a government necessarily implies a constitution. Hence we speak of the constitution of a government.

In its original meaning, which was the meaning it bore in ancient Greece and Rome and throughout antiquity right down to the 18th century, a constitution refers simply to the principles and rules deduced or deducible from government as it was organised and as it operated in actual practice or, as Professor Charles McIlwain puts it in his classic, *Constitutionalism: Ancient and Modern* (1940), it refers to "the substantive principles to be deduced from a nation's actual institutions", procedures and processes of government. John Stuart Mill puts it quite clearly too: a constitution in its original sense is "an organic growth from the nature and life of a people; a product of their habits", of their national character and usages as reflected in the institutions, principles and procedures they have evolved for the management of their public affairs (*Representative Government* (1910 edition)). The notion of a constitution did not then exist as something apart and separate from government; it was co-eval and entirely integral with, not external or anterior to, government.

As something deduced or deducible from the organisation and working of a government in actual practice, a constitution was thus necessarily unwritten. The first attempt to reduce the organisation of government into writing was not called a constitution, but an **instrument of government**, i.e., the Instrument of Government drawn up for England by Oliver Cromwell in 1649.

A constitution as a deliberate creation in written form existing separately from government, something external and anterior to government, and from which government derives its existence, is entirely the invention of the American revolutionaries in the 18th century. As Professor Sir Kenneth Wheare explains in his book, *Modern Constitutions* (1966):

> Until the time of the American and French Revolutions, a selection or collection of fundamental principles was not usually called "the constitution" ... Since that time the practice of having a written document containing the principles of government organisation has become well-established and "constitution" has come to have this meaning.

But whilst a constitution in its modern sense as something separate from, and anterior to, government, has acquired other functions, *viz,* the guarantee of the freedom of the individual against the government and the declaration of the fundamental objectives of the nation, its primary function remains that of an act by which a state or government is constituted:

> the act of constituting (a state or government or both) as well as the law or rules of government that are constituted, be these embodied in written documents or, as in the case of the British Constitution, implied in institutions, customs and precedents. (Hannah Arendt, *On Revolution,* 1962).

Even in its modern sense as something external and anterior to government, "a unitary constitution for a federal system of government" remains a contradiction in ideas. A federal system, being an arrangement between separate, autonomous governments, implies a separate, autonomous constitution for each of the governments involved. A single constitution for all the governments involved, both federal and state, is a manifest contradiction. This is implicit in the definition of federalism by the Judicial Committee of the Privy Council in *Attorney-General v. Colonial Sugar Refining Co. Ltd.* (1914) A.C. 237 at p. 253. "The natural and literal interpretation of the word" (i.e., federal), said the Committee, "confines its application to cases in which these States, while agreeing to a measure of delegation, yet in the main continue to preserve their original constitutions". The constitutions of the governments of the federating states pre-date that of the federation, and continue to exist and operate with their original authority after the formation of the union – subject of course to modifications necessitated by the creation of the union. That is the constitutional form which modern federalism has taken in its birth-place, the United States. The constitutional form was followed when the states in Australia federated in 1900.

Apart from this "natural and literal" meaning, the Judicial Committee of the Privy Council acknowledges that federalism is also applied in another, if loose, sense, but even this loose application of the system is equally predicated upon the separateness and independence of the constitutions of the constituent governments. This occurs when, as in Canada, the federating states surrender their original constitutions and accept new ones – where, in the words of the Judicial Committee in the same case, "self-contained States agree to delegate their powers to a common government with a view of having entirely new constitutions even of the States themselves."

Historical Origins of the Unitary Character of the Constitution of the Nigerian Federal System

How did this contradiction become part of our federal system? The Federation of Nigeria differs in its origin from the older federations in the United States, Australia and Canada in that it was formed by a state hitherto under a unitary government, devolving part of its powers to three autonomous regional governments. Noting the uniqueness of this application of the federal concept, the drafting committee on the review of the Nigerian Constitution in 1951 observed:

> The federal governments of U.S.A., Canada and Australia have been built on the basis of separate states surrendering to a federal government some of their powers for the benefit of all. The reverse process on which we are engaged – that of the creation of a federal government by devolution – is a political experiment for which ... there is no precedent to guide us and we are very conscious of the dangers involved in such an experiment.

Based on the Committee's report, new regional governments were organised and powers devolved upon them by a common constitution with no differentiation of any kind. The same sections of the one, single constitution established the organs of both the federal and regional governments and defined their powers.

Independence in 1960 brought new constitutional forms. Separate constitutions were established for the federal and for each of the regional governments in separate schedules annexed to the Independence Order-in-Council. Though separate and independent of one another, the several constitutions derived from a common authority, namely the Independence Order made by the British Government. A common source of authority which is not that of the federal government is not inconsistent with the federal principle.

But the independence of the state governments (and consequently the federal principle) would be violated if their constitutions were established for them by the federal government. That was the issue that confronted the making of the Republican Constitution in 1963. Since the Imperial Constitution of 1960 had to be done away with on the transition to a republican status, and there being no intention to use any other body than the existing established legislatures for the adoption of a republican constitution, the only constitutional form consistent with the federal principle in the circumstances was for each government to enact its own constitution. There was however an initial legal hurdle arising from the fact that only the Federal Parliament had power to repeal the Imperial Constitution and the Act of the British Parliament, the Nigeria Independence Act 1960, which constituted Nigeria an independent state. In pursuance of its power in that respect, the Federal Parliament enacted the Constitution of the Federation Act 1963, which repealed and replaced the Nigeria Independence Act and the Order-in-Council in so far as they applied to the federation, and delegated a like authority to the regional legislatures, whereupon each region enacted its own Constitution Law repealing and replacing the Independence Act and the Order-in-Council in their application to it. (When the Mid-western Region was created in 1964, its Constitution was enacted by the Federal Parliament in pursuance of power conferred on it in the Constitution of the Federation, but that was after it had been approved by the people through a referendum conducted in the region and by the prescribed number of regions.)

The 1979 and 1999 Constitutions reverted to the 1951-54 form of organising the federal and state governments under one, single constitutional instrument. In the original draft of the Constitution prepared by the Constitution Drafting Committee, as under the 1951-54 form, agencies of the federal and state governments and their powers were dealt with in the same sections. As finally enacted, however, the Constitution segregates in separate parts of the same chapters, provisions relating to the federal and state governments, except that miscellaneous and transitional provisions common to both units of government are dealt with together in the same sections, as are the division of powers, fundamental objectives and directive principles, citizenship and fundamental rights.

It is pertinent to state in this connection that the 1979 Constitution, as well as the 1999 Constitution, with its unitary character, did not owe its origin as an act of the people, as a constitution is supposed to be, according to its famous definition by one of the 18th century American revolutionaries, Thomas Paine, in his *Rights of Man*: "a constitution", he says, "is not the act of a government, but of a people constituting a government." The 1979 and 1999 Constitutions were made by the Federal Military Government, a government of absolute power, by virtue of sovereignty seized by force or threat of it from the Nigerian people. In the result, the civilian governments, both federal and state, installed since 29 May, 1999 derive their existence and authority as a government from the military – a monstrous contradiction concealed behind the beguiling lie in the preamble to the 1979 and 1999 constitutions: "We the People of the Federal Republic of Nigeria ... **Do Hereby Make, Enact and Give to Ourselves** the following Constitution". Needless to reiterate, the people had no hand, not a direct hand any way, in the making or enacting of either of those constitutions.

Implications of a Single Constitution for the Autonomy of the State Governments

A single constitution for the federal system in Nigeria has quite serious implications for the autonomy of the state government, which is a cardinal requirement in a federal system truly so-called, viz –

Execution and Maintenance of the Single Constitution

The executive authority of the federal government, which is vested in the president, is defined to "extend to the execution and maintenance of **this constitution**"; likewise the executive authority of a state government is defined to "extend to the execution and maintenance of **this constitution**", (Section 5).

The question concerning the autonomy of the states which arises from the definition of the executive authority of both the federal and state governments to "extend to the execution and maintenance of **this constitution**" is this: does the definition mean that the president is thereby empowered to execute and maintain the provisions of the constitution relating to the state governments alone – for example, provisions establishing the organs of government, and prescribing their composition, functions, procedures, the appointment or tenure of their functionaries, and the relation of the organs *inter se*, and government property? Is the maintenance of the security of a state government, its instrumentalities and property under the constitution within the executive authority of the President? This question would not have arisen had each state government been constituted by its own separate constitution.

It should be stated right away that the question whether a state governor is authorised by the definition in Section 5 quoted above to execute and maintain the provisions of the constitution relating to the federal government alone does not arise. This is because a state government is expressly enjoined by the constitution not to exercise its executive authority in a way to impede or prejudice the exercise of the executive powers of the federal government, endanger any assets or investment of the federal government in the state, or endanger the continuance of federal government in Nigeria [S. 5(3)]. Any contravention of this prohibition may be checked by the use of force against the offending state government. As the US Supreme Court held in sustaining the use of force by the federal government to check or remove the obstruction of its authority by a state government:

> The entire strength of the nation may be used to enforce in any part of the land the full and free exercise of all national powers and the security of all rights entrusted by the constitution to its care. The strong arm of the national government may be put forth to brush away all obstructions... If the emergency arises, the army of the nation, and all its militia, are at the service of the nation to compel obedience to its laws. [*Re Debs* 158 U.S. 564(1894)].

If a state government is not merely impeding or interfering with the exercise in the state of the president's executive power, but is attempting to terminate it completely by armed insurrection or rebellion, then the President is bound to accept the challenge and try to suppress it, and, though a war cannot formally be declared against a region within a federal state, to engage the regional government concerned in open war if organised armed resistance is offered; in prosecuting such war he may blockade the region and capture as "enemy property" the property of any person, whether neutral or rebel, residing within the rebellious region. [*The Prize Cases* 2 Black (67 U.S.) 635 (1863)]. Insurrection or organised rebellion by a state government or group of state governments is unconstitutional because it is a unilateral attempt to oust the authority of the national government from part or parts of the country.

The power of the federal government to preserve, protect and defend the constitution can also be invoked against a state government violating the secularity or the religious neutrality of the Nigerian state as constitutionally ordained (s. 10), since the violation of the character of the state in its religious aspect has the potentiality of endangering the survival of the constitution and of the nation.

An act by a state government impeding the exercise of the executive authority of the federal government or endangering the continuance of federal government or the survival of the constitution may be checked not only by appropriate executive action by the President but also by appropriate legislation enacted by the National Assembly. Under the 1963 Constitution the power of the federal legislature to do this derived from a specific provision in the constitution, which authorised it to make laws for any state outside the legislative lists to an extent necessary to secure compliance with the provision (s. 71). The provision is omitted from the 1979 and 1999 Constitutions but even without it the National Assembly still has competence to act by virtue of its general power to make laws with respect to the maintenance and securing of public safety under Section 11, its implied power to preserve the constitution, and its defence power under item 17 of the exclusive legislative list.

As regards the president, clearly the provision in Section 5 could not have been intended to have a result so utterly subversive of the federal principle. It must be read as confining him to the execution and maintenance of the provisions of the constitution relating to the federal government and to the preservation of the safety of the people. This is probably part of what is intended by the opening words of Section 5 that the power is "subject to the provisions of this constitution".

There are, however, certain provisions of the constitution which, read in the context of the fact that the federal and state governments are constituted under a single constitution, seem apt to confer on the President authority to act when only the security of one state government, but not the security of any other state governments or of the people, is affected. For this purpose, it is necessary to consider separately (a) a period when no emergency situation exists, and (b) emergency situation.

(a) Period When No Emergency Situation Exists: The maintenance of the security of a state government during a period when no emergency situation exists is primarily a state matter falling squarely within the _

responsibility of the state governor. A situation endangering the security of the state government but without impinging on the safety of the people must be excepted from the provision of Section 11 making "the maintenance and securing of public safety and public order" concurrent to both the federal and state governments. In any case, the intention of that provision is to enable the federal government to step in to maintain and secure public safety and public order in a situation affecting more than one state, but not when a situation is confined entirely within the territory of a state, except as may be necessary to protect the security of the federal government, its agencies and property within that state.

It is therefore a contradiction of the federal principle for the constitution to establish only a National Security Council, and **none** at all for a state. Given that the state governments are constituted under one single constitution as the federal government, it is arguable whether a state government is not thereby precluded from establishing a security council for the state or appointing a state security adviser. Worse still, the state governors, who are supposed to be the chief security officers for their respective states, are not included by office in the membership of the National Security Council. The Council consists of the president as chairman; the vice-president as deputy chairman; the chief of defence staff; the ministers of the government of the federation charged with responsibility for internal affairs, foreign affairs and defence; the national security adviser; the inspector-general of police; and "such other persons as the president may in his discretion appoint." Its function is defined to be "to advise the president on matters relating to public security including matters relating to any organisation or agency established by law for ensuring the security of the federation."

The non-inclusion of the state governors in the membership of the National Security Council cannot of course be redressed by the president appointing them to the Council in exercise of his power to appoint such other persons as he likes. This is so because of the principle of the autonomy of each government in a federation, which forbids the federal and state governments from conferring functions or imposing duties on the functionaries of the other without the consent of its chief executive.

(b) Emergency Situation: An emergency situation confined entirely within the territory of a state and, *a fortiori*, a localised emergency situation affecting a local community in the state is also a state matter to be regulated by the state constitution and handled by the state government. Federal government involvement in such a situation is a contradiction of, and is therefore incompatible with, the autonomy of the state government, except again as the situation endangers or affects the security of the federal government, its agencies or property. Had the state governments not been constituted under one single constitution as the federal government, the involvement of the latter in such a clearly regional or local matter would scarcely have been possible unless, exceptionally, it is authorised by the federal constitution.

As it is well-known, the involvement of the federal government in such a situation gave rise to the greatest assault on federalism in Nigeria. A provision in the 1960 Constitution defined a period of emergency as simply any period during which the federation was at war or there was in force a resolution by Parliament declaring that a state of emergency existed or that democratic institutions in Nigeria were threatened with subversion (Section 70). Apart from war, an emergency was determined, not by the physical situation actually existing in the country as an objective fact, but simply by a resolution by Parliament declaring that an emergency existed, no matter that the situation might be perfectly peaceful. Parliament was thus able to declare an emergency in the Western Region merely on the strength of an affray among the members inside the chamber of the regional House of Assembly, although no disturbances or threat of them occurred anywhere else in the region – a clear abuse and perversion of constitutional power to further partisan political interests. A far worse perversion was to follow the declaration of a state of emergency in the region.

In pursuance of the power granted to it to legislate outside its normal sphere of competence for "the purpose of maintaining or securing peace, order and good government during any period of emergency," Parliament enacted the Emergency Powers Act, 1961, authorising the President-in-Council to make "such regulations as appear to him to be necessary or expedient for the purpose of maintaining or securing peace, order and good government in Nigeria or any part thereof." It is almost unprecedented in the established constitutional orders, even in time of war, for the legislature to delegate the full amplitude of its power to the executive. For it was the entirety of its emergency powers that Parliament passed on to the executive, in effect allowing itself to be supplanted by the executive for this purpose. A delegation of powers in these terms is impermissible partly because it destroys the already attenuated foundation of the separation of powers under the constitution. It also impaired that aspect of the rule of law which requires that executive acts be justified by law and that the executive should not be the body to confer the necessary legal authority upon itself. The principle is well-established by many judicial authorities.

Indeed the Emergency Powers Act, 1961 went even further in relegating the legislature. It also empowered the President-in-Council to amend, suspend, or modify a law enacted by any legislature in the country; furthermore any regulation made by him had:

> effect notwithstanding anything inconsistent therewith contained in any law; and any provision of a law which is inconsistent with any such regulation ... shall ... to the extent of such inconsistency have no effect so long as such regulation ... remains in force.

It is true that a regulation made under the Act became void if it was not approved by the resolution of both Houses of Parliament within four months, and that both Houses could at any time by resolution amend or revoke it. Yet so long as a regulation remained unrevoked, Parliament could not legislate inconsistently with it, except by first repealing or amending the Emergency Powers Act itself.

Even more destructive of constitutional government was the manner in which the unlimited powers thus delegated to the executive were used in Western Nigeria (the emergency area). Altogether twelve regulations were made by the President-in-Council under the Act. Of these the most far-reaching was the Emergency Powers (General) Regulations, 1962. Its provisions proceeded upon the view that the government of Western Nigeria could no longer be carried on by the representative political institutions established by the constitution of the region, a view that is clearly untenable, and appeared to have been motivated by a desire to oust the Action Group from its power base as part of a grand plan to liquidate it as a political force in the country. The regulation provided for the appointment in Western Nigeria of an administrator who was to administer the government of the Region. As the government of the region, the administrator was given full executive and legislative powers. He was empowered to legislate by means of orders for the peace, order and good government of Western Nigeria; and when so legislating, he could amend any law in force in the region or suspend its operation, whether it be an Act of Parliament, a law of the regional legislature or an ordinance. The regional governor, premier, ministers, president, speaker and members of the Regional Houses were forbidden to exercise their functions except to such extent and during such period (if any) as the administrator might direct. The administrator was responsible only to the federal prime minister for the exercise of his functions.

Was the suspension of the elected government of Western Nigeria and its replacement by a federal government appointed administrator warranted by the Constitution either in letter or in spirit? The most that could be said of the power given to Parliament to "make such laws for Nigeria or any part thereof with respect to matters not included in the Legislative lists as may appear to parliament to be **necessary or expedient** for the purpose of maintaining or securing peace, order and good government" during any period of emergency is that it brought within the sphere of concurrent powers matters ordinarily exclusive to the region. If that be the case, does the notion of concurrent powers in a federal set-up enable the unit of government with the overriding power to suspend the order completely? To admit that would be to turn concurrent power into exclusive power, and so abolish the distinction between them. Even the so-called doctrine of "covering the field" according to which the federal legislature can, by dealing completely and exhaustively with a particular matter, exclude the regional legislatures therefrom is limited to the specific subject-matter of a particular legislation. It does not enable the federal legislature to make a general legislative declaration excluding the regions completely from the concurrent field of power. Such a declaration would be manifestly subversive of the constitution, and, given the extension of the concurrent power to the whole sphere of regional exclusive competence during an emergency, would convert the system from a federal to a unitary one, thereby destroying the restraining role of federalism.

The doctrine of covering the field is of doubtful validity, anyway. Although under the Constitution of Nigeria a federal law on a concurrent matter prevailed over an inconsistent regional law, one could not invoke the doctrine of inconsistency unless there was actual legislation in being. Only then could a comparison be made to see if one conflicted with the other, or, whether the federal legislation covers the entire field of the subject-matter.

It is even doubtful whether the emergency power of Parliament extended to the whole sphere of regional exclusive competence. Surely, there is a difference, however difficult it may be to define, between a power to legislate to **maintain or secure** peace, order and good government, and a power to legislate generally for peace, order and good government. The former assumes the existence of peace, order and good government, which only needs to be maintained or secured. It is a supplemental power. In other words, Parliament could only lawfully have assumed a supplementary power in support of the government of Western Nigeria to maintain or secure peace, order and good government during the emergency. And assuming that Parliament had the power which it purported to exercise, suspension of the government of Western Nigeria could only be said to be **necessary or expedient** on the erroneous view that the government had been rendered inoperative.

It is simply inconceivable that the federal government in the United States, Canada or Australia could declare an emergency in a state of the federation merely on the strength of an affray inside the chamber of the state's legislative assembly among its members, and then proceed to suspend the elected state government and to replace it with its own appointed administrator. Nothing could be more subversive of the whole idea of federalism.

The crisis in Western Nigeria coupled with other crises caused by abuse or perversion of constitutional power eventually culminated in the overthrow of the Constitution in a military *coup d'etat* in January 1966. Except for a four-year period of civilian democratic rule from October 1979 to December 1983, the country has been ruled as a unitary state by the military from that date till 29 May, 1999.

Such were the outrage on the autonomy of the state governments and the disastrous consequences sequel to it – these must never be lost on us – which prompted the provision on emergency powers in the 1979 Constitution which are repeated in the 1999 Constitution. They mark a significant departure from those in the 1960 and 1963 Constitutions in three main respects.

First, the kind of situation that must actually exist as an objective fact to warrant the declaration of an emergency is explicitly set out in the Constitution, *viz*

(i)   war;

(ii) imminent danger of invasion or involvement in a state of war;

(iii) "actual breakdown of public order and public safety ... to such extent as to require extraordinary measures to restore peace and security";

(iv) "a clear and present danger of an actual breakdown of public order and public safety... requiring extraordinary measures to avert such danger";

(v)   "an occurrence or imminent danger or the occurrence of any disaster or natural calamity affecting the community or a section of the community"; or

(vi) "any public danger which clearly constitutes a threat to the existence of the Federation" [Section 305(3)].

The constitution is thus as clear and precise as can be expressed in words in spelling out the kind of situation which must exist as an objective fact to warrant the declaration of an emergency. No other constitution in the world rivals our own in the clarity and precision of its provisions upon this point. Every student of constitutional law should be familiar with the decisions of the courts, particularly decisions of the U.S. Supreme Court, expounding the meaning of the phrase "public order and public safety" and what amounts to its breakdown or to "clear and present danger" of such breakdown. It behoves the operators of the constitution – and they owe it to all of us – to be faithful always to these unambiguous and unequivocal provisions.

Secondly, while the power to declare an emergency is vested in the federal government – i.e., the president subject to the subsequent approval within a specified time by the National Assembly – the constitution takes due cognisance of the federal principle that an emergency situation confined entirely within the territory of a state is primarily and essentially a state matter falling squarely within the responsibility of the state government to maintain the constitution in its area of authority. Accordingly, it provides that when the situation specified in (iii), (iv) or (v) above is confined entirely within the territory of a state, the president is not to declare an emergency in that state unless and until he is requested to do so by the state governor, acting with "the sanction of a resolution supported by two-thirds majority of the House of Assembly" [Section 305(4)]. In clear, unequivocal terms designed to put the matter beyond doubt, it provides that the "president shall not issue a proclamation of a state of emergency in any case to which the provisions of subsection (4) of this section apply unless the governor of the State fails within a reasonable time to make a request to the president to issue such proclamation" [Section 305(5)].

Since the governor cannot request the declaration of an emergency in his state without the approving resolution of the State House of Assembly supported by a two-thirds majority, there can be no failure on his part to make such request unless and until the House has given approval by resolution. Only when a reasonable time has elapsed after the passing of the approving resolution can the question of failure to request a declaration of an emergency arise.

Thirdly, when an emergency is declared in a state in accordance with these provisions, the National Assembly is not to assume power to make laws on matters within exclusive state competence unless the state House of Assembly is "unable to perform its functions by reason of the situation prevailing in that State" [section 11(4)]. However, "a House of Assembly shall not be deemed to be unable to perform its functions so long as the House of Assembly can hold a meeting and transact business" [Section 11(5)]. And the extra legislative power thus given to the National Assembly during an emergency situation existing in a state only enables it to make such laws as may appear to it to be "necessary or expedient until such time as the House of Assembly is able to resume its functions." Finally, it is expressly declared that nothing in these provisions "shall be construed as conferring on the National Assembly power to remove the governor or the deputy governor of the state from office." The provision must be read as prohibiting suspension too.

These provisions seem eminently well-designed to reconcile with the autonomy of a state government in a federation, the power given to the federal government to declare an emergency in a state in a case where an emergency situation is confined entirely within the territory of that state.

The Respective Extent of the Judicial Powers of the Federal and State Governments

While the respective extent of federal and state legislative and executive powers are clearly spelt out in the Constitution (Sections 4 and 5), no

such clear delimitation of the respective extent of the judicial powers
of the federal and state governments is given. The provision in Section
6(6) that judicial power "shall extend .... to all inherent powers and
sanctions of a court of law", and "to all matters .... for the determination
of any question as to the civil rights and obligations" of a person is a
definition, not of the respective extent of the judicial powers of the
federal and state governments, but rather of what judicial power is — a
power for the determination of the civil rights and obligations of
persons in justiciable matters brought before the courts by such regular
proceedings as are recognised by law. The constitution thus leaves
undefined and uncertain the respective extent of the judicial powers
of the federal and state governments.

In both the United States of America and Australia, for example,
the judicial power of the federal government is explicitly defined to
extend, *inter alia*, to all justiciable matters arising under the constitution
and laws of the federation (Art. 3, Section 2 U.S. Constitution; Section
76 Constitution of Australia). Judicial power is power to adjudicate
all justiciable matters arising under the laws of a government and within
its geographical area. And laws for this purpose include the law of the
constitution of the government concerned.

The application in Nigeria of this general criterion of the extent
of judicial power is complicated by the fact that there are no separate
constitutions for the federal government and for each state
government, as had been the case before October 1, 1979, and as is the
case in the United States of America, Australia and most other
federations. Where each government in a federation is constituted
and organised under a separate constitution, there is no difficulty in
applying the general principle that its judicial power extends to the
adjudication of justiciable matters arising under its constitution and
laws. Where, however, both the federal and state governments are
organised under one, single constitution, some difficulty arises in
determining what comprises the law of the constitution of the
federation or the law of the constitution of a state for the purpose of
determining the extent of their respective judicial powers. Is the entire

single constitution part of the laws of each government including those of its provisions relating exclusively to the organisation, powers, rights and property of each government?

Does the fact that the federal and state governments are established and organised by one, single constitution have the effect that a government in a federation is thereby made amenable to the judicial power of another government regardless of the principle of the autonomy of each government? And can the courts of one government exercise jurisdiction in a matter arising under the provisions of the constitution relating to the organisation, powers, rights, property, etc., of another government?

According to Justice Nasir, then President of the Federal Court of Appeal, in *Federal Minister of Internal Affairs & Others v. Shugaba* (1982) 3 N.C.L.R. 915 —

> The president has no power or authority, save as may be clearly provided by the Constitution, to interfere with the powers or authority of a state governor. The governor also has no power or authority to interfere with the functions of the chief executive of the Federation. This same principle applies to the relationship of the National Assembly and a House of Assembly of a State in their respective powers of law making or other responsibility assigned to them by the Constitution. The same principle of non-interference applies to the relationship of the Judiciary of the Federation and the Judiciary of a state in the exercise and control of judicial powers and jurisdiction of the courts established for the federation and those for the State.

"Unless the Constitution specifically authorises a federal court", adds the learned president, "it cannot exercise the judicial power of a state and likewise a state court cannot exercise the judicial powers of the federation." These statements fall short of defining the respective extent of the judicial powers of the federal and state governments in the context of the one, single constitution.

Some insight into the issue is furnished by the provision in the 1999 Constitution to the effect that "the Federal High Court shall have and exercise jurisdiction to the exclusion of any other court in civil causes and matters" with respect, *inter alia*, to:

(i)   "the administration or the management and control of the federal government or any of its agencies";

(ii)   "subject to the provisions of this constitution, the operation and interpretation of this constitution in so far as it affects the federal government or any of its agencies";

(iii) "any action or proceeding for a declaration or injunction affecting the validity of any executive or administrative action or decision by the federal government or any of its agencies" [Section 251(1)].

It should follow, logically, that the jurisdiction of the courts of a state government in all such matters should exclude that of the federal courts insofar as such matters relate to the state government.

The question, otherwise known as the Doctrine of Mutual Non-interference, cannot be pursued further here due to limitations of space. It is one of the most intricate issues of federalism, made all the more so because of the unitary character of the Constitution of the Federal Republic of Nigeria. (The question is fully examined in my book titled *Federalism in Nigeria* (1983), pp. 3-17; 264-275).

Amendment of the Constitution

The amendment of the one, single constitution is put beyond the power of either the federal or state governments alone. For this, a two-thirds majority of the total prescribed membership of each House of the National Assembly (four-fifths for the amendment of the amending procedure itself, the procedure for the creation of states or the guarantee of fundamental rights) and the approval of the Houses of Assembly of not less than two-thirds of all the states is required (Section 9).

Conformable as it is with the federal principle that the amendment of the constitution is put beyond the power of either the federal or state governments alone, it is so only insofar as the amendment affects the constitution of the federal government. The question still remains whether the procedure fully satisfies the principle of the autonomy of each state government. Two-thirds majority of all the states (i.e., 36 states) is 24. What this means is that the organisation, powers, procedures, etc., of a state government opposed to an amendment can be changed against its wish. And there may be up to 12 state governments opposed to the amendment. Where each state government is established and organised by its own separate constitution, this will be clearly inconceivable, as only itself and/or the people of the state can change the state constitution. No affront to the autonomy of a state government in a federation can be worse than a change in its organisation, powers, procedures, etc., effected against its will. This compels the conclusion that there can be no true federal system in Nigeria until each of the constituent units in the federation has its own constitution. Only on the basis of such a constitution can the governments of the federating units be truly autonomous.

The restructuring of the federation into six regions should be an occasion for the regions to adopt their own constitutions, and to restore to the people their long-denied constituent power, the power to enact, by means of a referendum, a constitution suited to their peculiar character and circumstances. By democratising the constitution in this way, the contradiction of a democratic government under a non-democratic constitution would have been removed. The concept of a democratic constitution is further elucidated in Chapter 8 of Volume 5.

Power and Financial Relations of The Federal and State Governments

The federal system in Nigeria also contradicts the cardinal principle of true federalism which requires that the arrangement should not place such a preponderance of power and financial resources in the hands of either the national or regional governments as to make it so powerful that it is able to bend the will of the others to its own. The power and financial resources sharing arrangement should be so weighted as to maintain a fair balance between the national and regional governments. Federalism requires that the national and regional governments should stand towards each other in a relation of meaningful autonomy and equality resting upon a balanced division of powers and financial resources. Each must have powers and financial resources sufficient to support the structure of a functioning government able to stand on its own against the other. The sharing arrangement under Nigeria's federal system assigns to the federal government powers and resources overwhelmingly greater than those assigned to the states, thereby depriving the latter of any meaningful autonomy in relation to the federal government. The 36 states structure has added greatly to the weakening of the state governments, reducing them in status to poor relations of an over-powerful federal government. The matter is compounded by the continuing influence of a hang-over from our military past when the state governments were mere instruments of an all-mighty Federal Military Government.

The marked imbalance in the power and financial relations between the federal and state governments originated in the 1979 Constitution and the belief among its makers, since belied by experience, that a concentration of powers and financial resources in the federal government would bring about national unity and progress. The lesson from that experience shows that an over-strong national government increases the intensity of the competition for its control, with a consequent undermining of national unity and stability. It also increases the incidence of corruption and the perversion of power, with a consequent undermining of progress.

There are five main respects in which the 1979 and 1999 Constitutions have altered the power relations in the federation in favour of the federal government. First, 16 matters, hitherto concurrent to both the federal and regional governments under the 1960/63 Constitutions, are now made exclusive to the federal government *viz*: arms, ammunition and explosives; bankruptcy and insolvency; census; commercial and industrial monopolies, combines and trusts; drugs and poisons; fingerprints, identification and criminal records; labour (i.e., conditions of labour, industrial relations, trade unions and welfare of labour); prisons, professional occupations as may be designated by the National Assembly; quarantine; registration of business names; regulations of tourist industry; traffic on federal trunk roads; public holidays; regulation of political parties; and service and execution in a state of the civil and criminal processes, judgements, decrees, orders and other decisions of any court of law outside Nigeria or any court of law in Nigeria other than a court of law established by the legislature of a state. The complete exclusion of a state government from all of these areas is a significant change indeed, for it takes away completely the initiative which in the past, the regions undertook in some of these matters.

Secondly, not only is the scope of concurrent matters now severely restricted by the transfer of roughly 50 percent of them to the exclusive competence of the federal government, but also some of the matters still formally listed as such are actually dealt with in such a way as to make them exclusive to the federal government to a very large extent. For example, a state government's power over higher education is now restricted to merely making law for the "establishment of an institution for purposes of university, professional or technological education." Subject to this, the whole field of higher education – the regulation of admissions and standards, the question of free education at that level, etc., – is now exclusive to the federal government. While public safety and public order remain a concurrent matter (Section 111), the principal instrument for maintaining and securing them – "the police force and armed forces – are centralised in the federal government, without the concession made to the regional governments by the 1960/63 Constitutions to establish local police forces on a provincial basis.

Thirdly, the federal power over taxation of the income and profit of individuals is now, as in the case of company taxation, plenary, and not, as under the 1963 Constitution, limited to purposes specifically prescribed in the constitution such as the securing of uniform principles of taxation, etc. Even more important is the plenitude of its **exclusive** power over trade and commerce, which is not confined to trade and commerce with foreign countries and between the states as under the 1963 Constitution, but extends to trade and commerce **within** a state including the buying and selling of basic foodstuff, like garri, in the local market.

The federal power over trade and commerce is also significantly enhanced by the power given to the National Assembly;

(a)   to declare that any economic activity is to be managed or operated by the federal government to the exclusion of everybody else, including individuals;

(b)   to set up a body to review from time to time the ownership and control of business enterprises operating in Nigeria, and to administer any law for the regulation of the ownership and control of such enterprises.

It is not clear whether an activity outside the competence of the federal government can be so declared. It is not reasonable to suppose that by this provision the constitution intended that the National Assembly should have power to alter, by a mere resolution of its members, such a fundamental arrangement as the division of powers. An interpretation of this provision, in order to be consistent with the division of powers and with the procedure for the amendment of the constitution, must, therefore, limit its scope to activities within the competence of the federal government.

Fourthly, federal power is now extended to certain matters hitherto under exclusive regional competence. Minimum standard at the primary and secondary levels of education is now an exclusive matter for the federal government, so is the election of a state governor and the members of the State House of Assembly. Land title is now largely exclusive to the federal government, for not only is the Land Use Act 1978 entrenched in the constitution, but also its provisions are to "continue to have effect as federal enactments and as if they related to matters included in the Exclusive Legislative List set out in Part 1 of the Second Schedule to this constitution."

Local government too is no longer an exclusive state matter in its entirety. Aspects of it – registration of voters at local government elections, the procedure for such elections, local government finance and the creation of new local government areas – are subjected to regulation and control by the federal government; this is dealt with more fully in Chapter 6.

Fifthly, the federal government is granted yet another new source of power by the provision authorising the National Assembly to establish and regulate authorities to promote and enforce the observance throughout the country of fundamental objectives and directive principles enshrined in the constitution.

By these vast accretions, federal power now overwhelmingly predominates over state power. The federal government is also overwhelmingly predominant in the financial relations between it and the state governments. Without going into the complex details of the revenue sharing formula, as to which, see Chapter 5, the financial subordination of the state governments is clearly underlined by the mere fact that 95 percent of their revenue is derived from an account, the Federation Account, controlled and distributed by the federal government. The mechanism for the disbursement to the state governments of their share of the money due to them from the Account is not automatic or self-operating; they have to go physically to the federal government and hassle for it every month, and the process creates in them an understandable docility towards the federal government as pay-master.

In the result, the Nigerian federal system has become thoroughly unbalanced. The imbalance needs to be corrected by the restoration of the scheme of division under the 1960 and 1963 Constitutions.

Establishment of a Single Police Force and its Compatibility or otherwise with the Autonomy of a State Government Under True Federalism

Government can no more be divorced from the notion of a constitution than it can exist without an organised force to back up its authority. It is a contradiction in ideas to conceive of a government without a constitution or without an organised coercive force to enforce its authority, or to compel obedience to its commands. The organisation and control of the police force is yet another contradiction in Nigeria's federal system under its constitution.

The constitution establishes for the whole country a single police force – the Nigeria Police Force – and prohibits the establishment of any other police force in the federation [Section 214(1)].

In prohibiting the establishment of any other police force than the Nigeria Police Force, the 1979 and 1999 Constitutions differ from the 1963 Constitution which authorised local police forces to be established on a provincial basis [Section 105(7)]. This had made it possible for the northern and western regional governments under that constitution to retain and expand the local police forces established and maintained by some of their native authorities under the Native Authority Ordinance of 1943. For example, the Local Government Police Law, 1959 of the Western Region confirmed existing police forces in the region and authorised every local government council with the approval of the minister for local government to establish a police force. Local government councils in a province might form a joint committee for the purpose of the joint operation of a police force, and the minister might in the interest of efficiency require local councils in a province to form a joint committee, and in default might establish one himself. The office of a Superintendent-General of local government police forces was created, with power to supervise and discipline (by suspension, dismissal or otherwise) the members of the police forces and to give directions of a general character to a local government council or joint committee with respect to the training and employment of its police force. (The constitutional validity of the office of Superintendent-General of local government police forces was affirmed in *Olajire v. Superintendent-General of Local Government Services* (1961) ALL N.L.R. 826). Only in the Eastern Region was the power to establish local police forces not utilised. (It should be stated that the provision in the 1963 Constitution authorising the establishment of local police was abrogated by the military in 1966; the 1979 Constitution only followed that lead.)

The establishment of a single police force for the whole country raises two questions, *viz*, first, whether the Nigeria Police, as an institution, is a federal government agency or one common to the federal and state governments; and, second, the compatibility or otherwise of a single police force with the autonomy of each government under a federal system.

On the first question, the view of the Nigeria Police Force as a federal government agency is suggested by the listing of police as a matter within exclusive federal competence (item 45 exclusive legislative list). Regarded as a federal government agency, the consequence would follow that the state governments cannot confer functions or impose duties on it nor can the federal government authorise it to enforce state laws, unless authority for that is provided in the constitution. But this view of the matter can hardly be reconciled with the conception underlying the establishment of the Nigeria Police as a single police force for the maintenance of the authority and security of each of the federal and state governments as a government and for the enforcement of its laws.

It is in the light of this underlying conception that we must construe the provision in Section 214(2)(b) to the effect that "the members of the Nigeria Police Force shall have such powers and duties as may be conferred upon them by **law**" (emphasis supplied). The word 'law' seems to have been used advisedly, that is say, with due deliberateness, in contrast to the provision in Section 214(2)(a) which says that "the Nigeria Police Force shall be organised and administered in accordance with such provisions as may be prescribed by **an Act of the National Assembly**".

In the context of the two paragraphs of Section 214(2) and of the conception of underlying the establishment of a single police force for the whole country, the word 'law' is apt, and is intended, to include laws made by the National Assembly as well as those made by the state Houses of Assembly. This is not inconsistent with the listing of police as a matter within exclusive federal competence, since by Section 4(3) of the Constitution the exclusiveness of the power of the National Assembly to make laws with respect to any matter included in the exclusive legislative list is explicitly qualified by the phrase **"save as otherwise provided in this constitution"**, (emphasis supplied). It must therefore be concluded that the Nigeria Police Force, as a governmental institution, is an agency common to the federal and state governments, and that both can by law confer functions or impose duties on it, as is in fact the case – the Criminal Code (or the Penal Code in the northern states), which is largely a state law, is replete with provisions conferring functions or imposing duties on the police. Any other view would make nonsense of the idea of a single police as a coercive force for securing the authority and enforcing the laws of both the federal and state governments.

On the compatibility or otherwise of a single police force with the autonomy of each government under a federal system, it should be stated, to begin with, that a state and, *ipso facto*, a government exists or not according as it has the coercive force to compel obedience to its commands. In other words, a government implies a coercive force at the disposal of such government for maintaining its authority and enforcing its laws. A government not backed by such coercive force is a contradiction in ideas.

Yet it does not follow from this that there is an inherent incompatibility between a single police force and the autonomy of each government in a federal system. It all depends on how the control of the force is organised. A single police force has the advantage that it exposes the individual to less risk of oppression than one under the autonomous control of the state government. This consideration should override all others. What makes the arrangement under the 1979 and 1999 Constitutions objectionable is the fact that the control of the police is unduly centralised in the federal government. This undue centralisation manifests itself mainly in the power vested in the president to appoint and remove the inspector-general of police in whom the overall command of the police is vested.

We may note, in parenthesis, the bundle of contradictions in the provisions in the 1999 Constitution relating to the appointment of the inspector-general. Section 215(1) establishing the office provides that he "shall, subject to section 216(2) of this constitution, be appointed by the president on the advice of the Nigeria Police Council from among serving members of the Nigeria Police". Section 216(2) enjoins the president, before appointing the inspector-general or removing him from office, to "consult the Nigeria Police Council". The provision that the inspector-general "shall be appointed by the president **on the advice** of the Nigeria Police Council" imports a term of art implying an obligation on the part of the president to act only as advised by the council, whereas consultation implies an unfettered discretion to accept or not to accept advice given. The contradiction is made worse confounded by the Third Schedule which defines the functions of the Police Council as including "advising the President on the appointment of the inspector-general." The word `advising' in the context of the provision in the Third Schedule imports no obligation to act only as advised. These contradictions were not in the 1979 Constitution which simply provided that the inspector-general "shall be appointed by the president". It established no (or rather disestablished) Police Council, so no question of advice by, or consultation with, it arose.

The president's power to appoint and remove the inspector-general in his discretion under the 1979 and 1999 Constitutions is incompatible with the constitutional position of the police force as an agency common to both the federal and state governments, and designed to provide organised coercive support for the authority which each exercises as a government. It practically nullifies the value of vesting the command of the police in a non-partisan inspector-general, since he cannot afford to be too independent of the federal government in the exercise of his command, knowing that that might expose him to the sanction of removal.

It is incompatible with the autonomy of a state government under a federal system that the only organised coercive force on which it relies to maintain its authority and to enforce its law should be under the control of the federal government through the power to appoint and remove its head and commander. The autonomy of the state governments does certainly require that the appointment and removal of the inspector-general should either be a joint responsibility or be vested in a non-partisan body. That is necessary in order that the arrangement of a single police may be reconciled with it. It is for this reason that the 1963 Constitution vested the appointment and removal of the inspector-general in the Police Service Commission.

The undue centralisation of the control of the police force manifests itself in the second place in the fact that no machinery is provided for involving the state governments in its organisation and administration. The Police Council provided just such a platform under the 1963 Constitution. As earlier stated, its disappearance from the 1979 Constitution must be accounted a serious defect in the system, for the federal and state governments should be involved at least in the general supervision of the organisation and administration of a common agency, which is the mainstay of the power and authority of each. Happily, the Council is brought back by the 1999 **Constitution Section** 153).

Re-established by the 1999 Constitution, the Police Council comprising the president, as its chairman, the governor of each state, the Chairman of the Police Service Commission, and the inspector-general, is, in addition to advising the President on the appointment and removal of the inspector-general, responsible for:

(a)   "the organisation and administration of the Nigeria Police and all other matters relating thereto (not being matters relating to the use and operational control of the Force or the appointment, disciplinary control and dismissal of members of the Force); and

(b)   the general supervision of the Nigeria Police."

The appointment, removal and disciplinary control of members of the police force (other than the Inspector-General) are vested in an independent Police Service Commission.

Lastly, there is the failure of the constitution to provide, as did the 1963 constitution, that the state governor must be consulted by the Police Service Commission on the appointment and removal of a commissioner of police for his state. This has resulted in a considerable undermining of the authority of the governor *vis-a-vis* the state police commissioner, contrary to what the arrangement envisages, namely, that where public safety and public order is concerned, the state police commissioner should comply with all lawful directions of the governor, only insisting on reference to the president in cases of extreme gravity or sensitiveness. In a situation of danger to public safety and public order in a state, liberty on the part of the police commissioner to comply or not to comply with the governor's directions as he likes is incompatible with the autonomy of the state government, and is a recipe for trouble and eventual collapse of the system.

The danger inherent in the arrangement was manifested during the disturbances in Onitsha, Anambra State, in November, 2000 when the state police commissioner attacked the state governor in a press conference, accusing him of having encouraged or contributed to the situation. The contradiction in the arrangement highlighted by this incident is not removed by the reposting of the police commissioner concerned out of the state.

One final point, the vesting of the command of the police in a non-partisan, professional policeman, the inspector-general (assisted in a state by a commissioner of police) is subject to the power of the president to direct him with respect to the use of the police for maintaining and securing public order or public safety; the governor of a state has a like power to direct the state commissioner of police. The limits of the power are examined in Chapter 8.

CHAPTER 4

Fundamental Principles of Federalism and the Subversion of them and Other Aspects of the Constitution by a Federal Statute in Nigeria

The Subverting Federal Statute

The Corrupt Practices and Related Offences Act 2000 (hereinafter referred to as the Act) was enacted by the National Assembly in 2000. The execution or implementation of the powers and functions arising under the Act is vested in an agency, a body corporate with perpetual succession, called the Independent Corrupt Practices and Related Offences Commission (ICPC). The commission is a federal government agency not only because it is established by a federal law but also because its chairman and other members are appointed by the president upon confirmation by the Senate, and may be removed by him on an address by the Senate supported by two-thirds majority of its members (Section 3(6) and (8) of the Act). The appointment and removal power thus subjects the commission and its members to the authority of the president, and obliges them to carry out his wishes.

The Act also confers functions on other federal government authorities or functionaries. Section 5(2) provides that:

> if, in the course of any investigation or proceedings in court, in respect of the commission of an offence under this Act **by any person** there is disclosed **an offence under any other written law** not being an offence under this Act, irrespective of whether the offence was committed by the same person or any other person, the officer of the commission responsible for the investigation or proceedings, as the case may be, shall notify the director of public prosecutions or any other officer charged with responsibility for the prosecution of criminal cases, who may issue such directive as shall meet the justice of the case. (emphasis supplied).

Thus, the powers or functions of officers of the commission and of the Federal Director of Public Prosecutions are not limited to the investigation and prosecution of the offences of corruption, fraud or related offences under the Act but extend to all offences under any other written law committed by any person. In effect, therefore, the entire field of the investigation and prosecution of all criminal offences under any written law committed by any person is brought under the power of the ICPC, its officials and the Federal Director of Public Prosecutions, thereby resulting in the attenuation of the scheme of division of powers with respect to the matter under the Constitution.

Furthermore, under Section 61(1) of the Act, "every prosecution for an offence under this Act or **any other law prohibiting bribery, corruption and other related offences** shall be deemed to be done with the consent of the attorney-general" (emphasis supplied). By this provision the attorney-general of the Federation is given authority over prosecutions for bribery, corruption and related offences under any law, federal or state, in clear derogation of the authority of the attorney-general of a state under the constitution in respect of prosecutions for such offences under state law. And, as will be shown later, offences related to "bribery and corruption" may cover a wide range of offences under state law that have really nothing to do with corruption as such.

The reference in Section 61(1) to the attorney-general and to the

Director of Public Prosecutions in Section 5(2) of the Act must be read as a reference to the Attorney-General of the Federation and to the federal director of public prosecutions, since the federal government cannot, by its law, confer functions or impose duties on state government functionaries – so decided by the Supreme Court in *Attorney-General of Ogun State & Ors v. Attorney-General of the Federation & Ors* (1982) 3 NCLR 583. The 1979 and 1999 Constitutions contain no such provisions for the inter-delegation of functions as did the 1960 and 1963 Constitutions.

Principles Governing Constitutional Validity of Governmental Acts in a Federal System

The constitutional validity of a governmental act in a federal system is governed by two principles, *viz.* (1) the *ultra vires* doctrine, and (2) the doctrine of mutual non-interference.

The *ultra vires* doctrine is a trite principle of constitutional validity with undisputed acceptability and force, and may be stated simply by saying that a governmental act which is beyond or in excess of powers granted by the constitution is null and void. The only question arising in this case concerns the application of the doctrine, i.e., whether the Corrupt Practices and Related Offences Act 2000 is *intra vires* or *ultra vires* the National Assembly under Section 4 of the Constitution. This is considered below.

Nature, Basis and Effect of the Doctrine of Mutual Non-interference

The nature, basis and effect of the doctrine of mutual non-interference are entirely misconceived by the Supreme Court in its decision in *Attorney-General of Ondo State v. Attorney-General of the Federation & 35 Others* SC 2000/2001 where, in a lead judgment delivered by Uwais CJN and in which the other six participating justices concurred, the court said:

> It has been pointed out that the provisions of the Act impinge on the cardinal principles of federalism, namely, the requirement of

equality and autonomy of the state government and non-interference with the functions of state government. This is true, but as seen above, both the federal and state governments share the power to legislate in order to abolish corruption and abuse of office. If this is a breach of the principles of federalism, then, I am afraid, it is the constitution that makes provisions that have facilitated breach of the principles. As far as the aberration is supported by the provisions of the constitution, I think it cannot rightly be argued that an illegality has occurred by the failure of the constitution to adhere to the cardinal principles which **are at best ideals to follow or guidance for an ideal situation.** (Emphasis supplied, at p. 40).

Far from being "at best ideals to follow or guidance for an ideal situation", the doctrine is the basis, the foundation, of every true federal system, without which no such system can exist. It lies, not outside the constitution, but within it, operating by way of an implied prohibition against the **exercise** of a constitutional grant of power in a manner that, **in its practical effect,** impedes, frustrates, stultifies or otherwise unduly interferes with another government's management of its affairs or its continued meaningful existence as a government, e.g., the management of its finances, the appointment and control of its staff, the award of contracts for the provision of services and other projects, the exercise of other essential governmental functions, like that of law-making or its execution.

To quote a statement of the doctrine in B. O. Nwabueze, *Federalism in Nigeria* (1983) at p. 3:

> From the separate and autonomous existence of each government, and the plenary character of its powers within the sphere assigned to it by the constitution, flows the doctrine that the exercise of those powers is not to be impeded, obstructed or otherwise interfered with by the other government while acting within its own powers. The doctrine rests upon necessary implication from the establishment by the constitution of the federal and state governments as separate and autonomous governments, and the necessity for the maintenance of their capacity to continue to exercise their respective constitutional functions as such governments. It operates to invalidate an interfering act. The invalidity results from the act being inconsistent with the implied prohibition of the constitution against interference. From

the time when it was first explicitly announced in 1819, the doctrine
has become firmly established as a principle of federalism.

It was first announced in *McCullock v. Maryland* 4 Wheat 31 (1819).
The classic statement of it is in *D'Emden v. Pedder* (1904) 1 CLR 91,
at p. 111.

As has been rightly said, to construe a constitution without
necessary implications would defeat its intention (per *Dixon J.* in *West
v. Commissioner of Taxation* (1937) 56 C.L.R. 657 at p. 681; "what is
necessarily implied is as much part of the Constitution as that which
is expressed" per Sir Robert Garran, *Development of the Australian
Constitution* (1924) 40 LQR 202 at p. 215.

The doctrine rests on the pre-supposition that a governmental act
in a federal system is within powers granted by the constitution. Its
concern is rather with the practical effect which the exercise of the
power has on another government. If the practical effect is to impede,
frustrate, stultify or otherwise unduly interfere with another
government's management of its affairs or its continued meaningful
functioning as a government, then, the interfering act, though
unquestionably within the power granted by the constitution, is
unconstitutional and invalid.

Thus, as earlier stated, the constitutional validity of a governmental
act in a federal system raises two distinct issues: first, whether the act
is within powers granted by the constitution; if it is not, then, it is
unconstitutional and void as being *ultra vires*; second, whether the
exercise of the power is such as, in its practical effect, impedes
frustrates, stultifies or otherwise unduly interferes with another
government's management of its affairs. In the latter case, the act is
unconstitutional and void, not because it is *ultra vires*, but because the
frustration or stultification of, or interference with, another
government's management of its affairs would result in the federal
system itself being abolished in all but name.

As the High Court of Australia puts it in *R. v. Commonwealth
Court of Conciliation and Arbitration, Ex Parte Victoria* (1942) 66 CLR
488 the exercise by the federal government of its undoubted power

over labour so as to regulate or control the pay, hours and duties of all state public servants would have the practical effect of enabling it (the federal government) "to take complete control of all government administration within the country", thereby "abolishing in all but name, the federal system of government which it is the object of the constitution to establish". The preservation and maintenance of the federal system of government is something far more important, fundamental and therefore overriding than the grant to the federal government of a plenary power to legislate with respect to labour.

The doctrine is well-illustrated by another Australian case where a federal statute required banks not to conduct any banking business for a state or any authority of a state, including a local governing authority, except with the consent in writing of a federal minister, the aim being that the central bank should thereby become the sole banker to the state governments. The question that arose was whether the law was one with respect to a matter – banking – placed under the exclusive control of the federal legislature by the constitution or whether it was a law on how a state government should keep, manage or dispose of its money. If the latter, then, clearly the doctrine does not come into play, because the federal government has no power to make law with respect to the custody, management or disposition of its money by a state government. Had the law in question provided directly that state government money shall only be kept at the central bank and nowhere else or that the money, wherever kept, may only be withdrawn with the consent of the federal minister, then, that will be unquestionably unconstitutional and invalid, not because of the implied prohibition against interference (i.e. the doctrine under consideration), but simply because the federal government lacked power to enact it. The High Court of Australia (the highest court in the country) held that it was a law with respect to banking, but that it was nevertheless unconstitutional and invalid as being a law which interfered with the essential governmental function of the states, the power to keep, manage and dispose of their money (*Melbourne Corporation v. Commonwealth* (1947) 74 CLR 31, 82-83).

Similarly, the US Supreme Court has held that "a general non-discriminatory real estate tax .... or an income tax laid upon citizens and states alike could not be constitutionally applied to the state's capitol, its state house, its public school houses, public parks" in exercise of the federal government's plenary power over taxation – see *New York v. United States* (1946) 326 US 572. The point may be further illustrated by a hypothetical, if more striking, example. Suppose that a federal government, invested with plenary power over taxation, levies, by law, a tax of, say, ₦1 billion on every law made by a State House of Assembly and another ₦1 billion on every executive action taken under such law. Surely, the practical effect of the tax would be to cripple the state governments, to put them out of action or meaningful existence as governments, and thereby "destroy, in all but name, the federal system which it is the object of the constitution to establish".

See B. O. Nwabueze, *Federalism in Nigeria* (1983), pp. 3-17 for further discussion on the nature, basis and effect of the doctrine, and the numerous cases expounding and applying it.

The Principles of the Equality and Autonomy of the Constituent Governments in a Federal System as the Rationale for the Doctrine of Mutual Non-interference

The doctrine of mutual non-interference is predicated upon the principles of the equality and autonomy of the constituent governments in a federal system. Each government in a federal system has, by virtue of its independent existence, an equal status as a government with the others, and so entitled to an equal say, though not necessarily equal weight, in the common councils of the federal state. In the nature of things, the notion of equality between the national and regional governments can extend no further than this. The national government is necessarily bigger than a regional government in terms of the territorial area over which its powers are exercised. Its powers are exercised over the whole country while those of a regional government are confined to only a part of it. Secondly, while a fair balance should be maintained between the powers assigned to each, they cannot be so weighted as to be equal. Matters within their respective competence must necessarily differ in their relative importance, and equality is not determined by how numerous or few are the matters assigned to it. Nor can the financial resources available to each be made equal. Federalism accommodates a certain amount of inequality in powers and financial resources between the national and regional governments, so long as any preponderance in favour of one is not such as to reduce the other to virtual impotence. The conception of federalism as implying a dualism between two equal and competing sovereignties therefore gives a misleading picture.

The principle of autonomy in a federal system implies, further, that neither the central government nor the regional ones can confer functions or impose duties, obligations, restrictions and liabilities on the functionaries of the other. This particular implication of the principle was expressly enacted in the 1963 Constitution in the provision forbidding the President as well as the federal legislature from conferring functions or imposing duties on the governor or other functionaries of the state governments without the consent of the state governor, and *vice versa* (Sections 99 and 100). While these provisions are not repeated in the 1979 and 1999 Constitutions, the prohibition remains applicable as a necessary implication of the autonomy of the federal and state governments in relation to each other.

The application of the prohibition under the 1979 Constitution was affirmed by the Supreme Court in *Attorney General of Ogun State & Others v. Attorney-General of the Federation & Others* (1982) *ibid.* Speaking for a unanimous Court of seven Justices, Fatayi-Williams *CJN* said that:

> neither the President of the Federal Republic of Nigeria nor the National Assembly can unilaterally confer powers on a state functionary such as the governor or the Attorney-General of a State and thus bring him within the investigatory or scrutinising powers conferred upon the National Assembly by section 82 subsection (1) of the 1979 Constitution.

In more pointed language, Sir Udo Udoma *JSC*, concurring, said:

> Having regard to the autonomy of the state …., neither the National
> Assembly nor the president has the constitutional power to impose
> any new duty on the governor of the state. Such an imposition would
> normally meet with resentment and refusal to perform for the
> enforcement of which there is no constitutional sanction. For that
> reason it would have been unconstitutional for the president in the
> Adaptation Order (No. 5 of 1981) to have replaced the military
> administrator with the governor of the state.

Idigbe *JSC* spoke in the same vein in his own concurring judgment.

Whether the Act Impedes or Interferes with a State Government's Management of its Affairs

The Supreme court in the *Ondo State Case* is right when, in the passage
quoted above, it says that it "is true" that "the provisions of the Act
impinge on the cardinal principles of federalism, namely, the
requirement of equality and autonomy of the state government
and non-interference with the functions of state government", but
the judgment fails to consider the specific provisions of the Act
impinging on those principles and the nature of the interference.

To begin with, in punishing corruption, fraud and related offences
committed by public officers, the Act defines a public officer as:

> a person employed in any capacity in the public service of the
> federation, states or local government, public corporations or private
> company wholly or jointly floated by any government or its agency
> including the subsidiary of any such company whether located within
> or outside Nigeria and includes judicial officers serving in magistrates,
> area/customary courts or tribunals.

Public officers employed in the services of state or local
governments, and private persons too, are subjected to the power
vested in the ICPC to examine and prosecute persons alleged to have
committed corruption, fraud or related offences under the Act or
"under any other law" involving the money or other property of state
or local governments, as well of course as the money or other property

of the federal government. Thus, public functionaries in the service of a state government (other than the governor) are subjected by the Act to investigation, prosecution and punishment for corruption, fraud and related offences committed by them in the discharge of their official duties in relation to the money, property or affairs of the state government arising from the award of contracts, issuance of licences or permits, employment of staff or any other business or transaction – see Sections 8, 9, 10, 11 and 12 of the Act. The governor himself may be investigated for corruption, fraud or related offences involving the money or property of the state government by an independent counsel authorised in that behalf by a national functionary, the Chief Justice of Nigeria (Section 51(1) of the Act). The ICPC is:

> to examine the practices, systems and procedures of public bodies and where, in the opinion of the commission, such practices, systems or procedures aid or facilitate fraud or corruption **to direct and supervise** a review, to **instruct,** advise and assist any officer, agency or parastatal on ways by which fraud or corruption may be eliminated or minimised by such officer, agency or parastatal (Section 6(2); emphasis supplied).

Surely, the practical effect of all these provisions of the Act is that the management of nearly all aspects of the affairs of a state government is subject to control and interference by the commission, its officials and other authorities of the federal government. Little, if anything, is left of the autonomy of the state governments; the federal system would have ceased to exist in all but name, and would, for all practical purposes, have been converted to a unitary system.

The Act will be like the Sword of Damocles which the president can hold over the heads of the state governors to coerce them to fall in line with his wishes and schemes. The governors will have lost their independence as the heads of autonomous governments as the names of those opposed to his wishes and designs will be sent, one after another, to the commission to be investigated ostensibly for alleged corruption under Section 52(1) of the Act. This is the evil use to which the Act is susceptible, and for which it is being used.

The inequality flowing from a situation where the head of the federal government can submit to the Commission for investigation for alleged corruption, the name of the head of a state government, but the latter cannot do the same to him is too glaring and blatant to be compatible with true federalism. And a federal system which permits the removal, for corruption or for any other reason, of the head of a state government at the instance of the head of the federal government, or even *vice-versa*, is no true federal system at all. No interference could be worse than that. And it is no less an interference because the removal is for corruption, our abhorrence of corruption notwithstanding.

The autonomy of a state government is also clearly interfered with by the duty imposed on the chief judge of a state to "designate, by order under his hand, a court or judge or such number of courts or judges as he shall deem appropriate to hear and determine all cases of bribery, corruption, fraud or related offences arising under the Act or under any other law" – a court or judge so designated shall not, while the designating order subsists, hear any other cases (Section 61(3) of the Act). This provision is clearly unconstitutional, and void by the decision of the Supreme Court in *Attorney-General of Ogun State & Others v. Attorney-General of the Federation & Others* (1982) 3 NCLR 583.

Whether Section 15(5) of the 1999 Constitution and the Entire Chapter on Fundamental Objectives and Directive Principles of State Policy (Chapter Two) are a Grant of Power

The Act purports to have been enacted pursuant to Section 15(5) of the Constitution; it thus raises the question whether that subsection and the entire Chapter on Fundamental Objectives and Directive Principles of State Policy of which it is part is a grant of power.

(i) The Plenitude of Legislative Power Granted to the Federal and State Legislatures Under Section 4 of the 1999 Constitution.

The provision in Section 4 of the Constitution authorising the federal and state legislatures to make laws for "the peace, order and government of Nigeria or any part thereof" is a grant of sovereign law-making power in its entirety and plenitude. Every subject-matter with respect to which law can be made, including corruption and abuse of office, is embraced within the power. The phrase "peace, order and good government" does not, as the Judicial Committee of the Privy Council has held, delimit the purpose for which the power is granted, in the sense that a law must be for peace, order and good government in order to be valid; it is simply a legal formula for expressing the widest plenitude of legislative power exercisable by a sovereign legislature. Thus, under Section 4 of the constitution, the federal and state legislatures, each within the limits of its power under the division of powers between them, have all the power they need to legislate with respect to corruption and abuse of power; they do not need any more power to be conferred on them for the purpose by Section 15(5) of the Constitution.

(ii) Section 15(5) and the Other Provisions in Chapter Two of the Constitution Grant no Power but Only Impose a Duty Regarding the Purposes for which the Powers Granted by the Constitution are to be Employed.

Section 15(5) provides:

> The state shall abolish all corrupt practices and abuse of power.

With the greatest respect, the Supreme Court in the *Ondo State Case* (supra) erred in law and thereby distorted the whole scheme and design of the constitution when it held as follows:

> The **power** to legislate in order to prohibit corrupt practices and abuse of power is **concurrent** and can be exercised by the federal and state governments and, being a concurrent **power,** any law made on the matter by the federal government has overriding effect (emphasis supplied).

It also said in the passage of the lead judgment quoted earlier that:

> both the federal and state governments share the **power** to **legislate**
> in order to abolish corruption and abuse of office (emphasis supplied),
> i.e. power derived from Section 15(5) above.

But even if, in clear distortion of the scheme and structure of the
constitution, Section 15(5) is read as a grant of power to the federal
and state governments, then, the power so granted is not a **concurrent**
one, as the lead judgment erroneously says, but a **divided** power. Each
is to legislate on corruption within the limits of its powers under the
division of powers between the federal and state governments.

Two points may be made on Section 15(5). First, the provision
must draw its meaning and effect from the character of the
Fundamental Objectives and Directive Principles of State Policy in
Chapter 2 of the constitution of which it is part. The provisions of
that chapter are merely a **declaration** expressly made non-justiciable
by the Constitution itself (Section 6(6)), defining in the main the duties
of the state towards the individual; towards that end, they set out the
objectives and principles according to which powers conferred in other
parts of the Constitution are to be exercised, but they are not
themselves a grant of power. They grant no powers at all, but only
impose a non-justiciable duty on "all organs of government and all
authorities and persons exercising legislative, executive or judicial
powers, to conform to, observe and apply" the declared objectives
and principles (Section 13), one of which is the objective or directive
to use their power to abolish all corrupt practices and abuse of office.

The crucial distinction is between, on the one hand, a grant of
power, such as is contained in Sections 4, 5, 6, 11 and other enabling
provisions of the constitution, and, on the other hand, a declaration
of objectives and directive principles of state policy, imposing on the
organs and functionaries of the state a duty to use the **power** so granted
to accomplish desirable social goals for the benefit of the people. The
governments in Nigeria, federal and state combined, have the plenitude
of powers they need to govern to the fullest extent, but the problem
is to get them to use those powers to secure and promote the
welfare of the people. This is the problem at which the declaration in

Chapter 2 of the Constitution is directed.

By its nature, power implies no obligation to exercise it at all or to exercise it for a particular purpose or in a particular direction. The legislature is under no duty to exercise its power to make law on any matter nor is the executive obliged to execute the law when it is made. Thus, although government has the constitutional power to do so, it is not legally obliged to provide medical, educational and other social services and amenities for the welfare of the people. Similarly, the limitation on power arising from a constitutional guarantee of fundamental rights and freedoms imposes no duty on the state positively to do anything to promote the material well-being of the people, but only a negative duty not to violate them.

Until the second decade of the 20th century, constitution-makers had pre-occupied themselves largely with constitutional powers and limitations; the duty of the state to use its powers to secure and promote the welfare of the people was seldom ever their concern. In a society built upon *laissez-faire* and economic individualism, as most societies were before the 20th century, the securing to the individual of social and economic amenities is regarded as none of the state's business. But the economic and social consequences of the two World Wars proved to be a catalyst. First incorporated in the constitution of India (1948), Directive Principles of State Policy were adopted into the constitution of Nigeria (1979) from where it has spread in the 1990s to ten other African countries – Zambia 1991 Constitution, Ghana 1992, The Gambia 1996, Uganda 1995, Tanzania 1984 (as amended in 1992), Malawi 1992 (as revised in 1994 and 1995), Lesotho 1993, Sudan 1998, Sierra Leone 1991 and 1996, Eritrea 1997.

In the second place, the word "state" in Section 15(5) refers, not to the federal government alone, but to both it and the state governments, each within the limits of the powers assigned to it by the constitution (see the definition of "state" and "government" in Section 318 of the Constitution). In other words, the division of powers between the federal and state governments in the Constitution has to be read into Section 15(5), or, putting it differently, all the governments are "directed" to use their respective powers under the division of powers in the Constitution to abolish corruption and abuse of office.

To read Section 15(5) as directed to the federal government alone would be a manifest distortion of the unequivocal meaning and intention of Section 13 (quoted above) and of the purpose of the whole Chapter 2. Worse still, to read it as a grant of power to the federal government alone or as conferring concurrent power would be altogether subversive of the federal scheme of the constitution, since the power to abolish corruption and abuse of office, especially when taken together with the power to "enforce the observance" of the entire Chapter 2, embraces much the greater field of governmental power. The government under the constitution would have been transformed from a federal to a unitary system of government. At any rate, the preponderance of federal power would have been enlarged to a point utterly incompatible with the autonomy of the states.

With respect, happily, to the scheme of the constitution relating to the guarantee of fundamental rights, our courts have laid it down as not being the purpose or effect of the declaration of Fundamental Objectives and Directive Principles to curtail those rights. In the words of the Court of Appeal, relying on a decision of the Supreme Court of India and affirming the trial judge, "the Directive Principles of State Policy have to conform to and run subsidiary to the chapter on Fundamental Rights". (See *Archbishop Okogie & Others v. Attorney-General of Lagos State*, Suit No. FHC/L/74/80 delivered on 30.9.80; affirming *Agoro J* in Suit No. ID/17M/80 decided on 18.7.80; *Madras v. Champahan* (1951) SCR 252). It is submitted that the Fundamental Objectives and Directive Principles have also to conform to and run subsidiary to the autonomy of the state governments *vis-a-vis* the federal government and to the division of powers between them.

(iii) Non-justiciability of the Fundamental Objectives and Directive Principles in Chapter 2 and its Implications in Relation to the Question Whether the Chapter is a Grant of Power.

As earlier stated, the Fundamental Objectives and Directive Principles in Chapter 2 of the 1999 Constitution is expressly made non-justiciable by Section 6(6)(c) which provides as follows:

> The judicial powers vested in accordance with the foregoing provisions of this section .... shall not, except as otherwise provided in this constitution, extend to any issue or question as to whether any act or omission by any authority or person or as to whether any law or judicial decision is in conformity with the Fundamental Objectives and Directive Principles of State Policy set out in Chapter 11 of this Constitution.

The non-justiciability of the Fundamental Objectives and Directive Principles is predicated in part on the premise that they are not a grant of legislative power since, if they were, a large part of legislative power would be excluded from the jurisdiction of the courts contrary to Section 4(8) of the Constitution, which says:

> Save as otherwise provided by this constitution, the exercise of legislative powers by the National Assembly or by a House of Assembly shall be subject to the jurisdiction of courts of law ....

The saving phrase, "save as otherwise provided by this constitution", is directed, not to the provision in Section 6(6)(c) above, but rather mainly to that in Section 6(6)(d). It says:

> The judicial powers vested in accordance with the foregoing provisions of this section .... shall not, as from the date when this section comes into force, extend to any action or proceedings relating to any existing law made on or after 15th January, 1966 for determining any issue or question as to the competence of any authority or person to make any such law.

Needless to say, an existing law is deemed to be made by the National Assembly or a State House of Assembly according as its subject-matter is within the legislative competence of the one or the other (Section 315(1)).

The non-justiciability of the Fundamental Objectives and Directive Principles has another dimension, which is dealt with below.

Whether the Act is *Intra Vires* or *Ultra Vires* the National Assembly Under Section 4 of the 1999 Constitution

(i)   *The Extent of the Legislative Power of the Federal Government with Respect to the Creation and Punishment of Criminal Offences, with Particular Reference to the Offences of Corruption, Fraud and Related Offences.*

As the earlier paragraphs of this chapter would have made clear, the danger which the Act poses to the federal system and hence to unity and stability of Nigeria arises not so much from the Act being a usurpation of the powers of the state governments under the scheme of division of powers in the constitution as from its being a grave interference with the autonomy of the state governments, their co-equality with the federal government and with the doctrine of mutual non-interference upon which the entire federal system is built. But the Act is also incontestably beyond the power of the National Assembly under the federal scheme of division of powers in the Constitution (1999).

The creation and punishment of offences is undoubtedly a most complex aspect of the division of powers in our federal system. Under the constitution, it is **largely** a residual matter, since, except as noted below, it is not assigned to the federal government either in the body of the Constitution or in the legislative lists in the Second Schedule. The function belongs therefore exclusively to the state governments, subject again to the exceptions shortly to be noted. Thus, the Criminal Code (or the Penal Code in the northern states), which is a codification in 521 sections of ordinary offences applicable to the life of the ordinary citizens, is largely a state law.

These ordinary offences, as distinct from the technical offences referred to later, range from offences against religion and morality (insult to religion, disturbing religious worship, unnatural offences, indecent offences, defilement of under-age girls, prostitution, abortion, obscenity); offences against public health (exposing for sale things unfit as food or drinks, adulteration of food or drink intended for sale, dealing in diseased meat; etc); offences against the person (kidnapping, slave dealing, child stealing, assaults and violence to the person, grievous harm, wounding, homicide, suicide, infanticide, murder); offences against property (stealing, stealing with violence, extortion, burglary, house-breaking, obtaining property by false pretences, personation, cheating, corruption, fraud, receiving stolen property, forgery, arson, destruction of or damage to property, cruelty to animal); and a variety of miscellaneous offences involving acts injurious to the public (ordeal, witchcraft, juju, criminal charms, nuisances, gaming houses, misconduct relating to corpses).

The point to be specially noticed is that corruption, fraud and allied offences fall within this category of ordinary offences, and, being therefore a residual matter, the creation and punishment of them belong exclusively to the state governments, subject to the exceptions noted below.

Federal offences, i.e., criminal offences created by the federal government under the exceptions referred to earlier, fall into three categories, *viz*:

(a) Offences against the Nigerian state or the federal government, its agencies, functionaries or property. The offences in this category relevant to the issue under discussion are corruption, fraud and allied offences involving the property of the federal government or its agencies by whomsoever committed, whether its own functionaries or others. These are unquestionably within its power to punish. Thus, a conviction under a federal statute of certain persons conspiring to defraud the federal government of Australia of diverse and large sums of money by procuring the payment by it of excessive prices for the supply of goods for the use of the armed forces was affirmed by the High Court (R. *v. Kidman* (1915)).

(b) Offences against public safety and public order (other than offences against the Nigerian state or the federal government). The power of the National Assembly under Section 11 of the Constitution to make laws with respect to the maintenance and securing of public safety and public order is an important source of federal offences of the ordinary type, but it provides no authority whatsoever for the offences created by the Corrupt Practices and Related Offences Act.

(c)   Offences created with respect to matters on the exclusive and concurrent legislative lists. Sixty-six specific matters are enumerated on the Exclusive Legislative List. The 68th item on that list is stated as "any matter incidental or supplementary to any matter mentioned elsewhere in this list", and incidental and supplementary matters are defined in Part III of the Schedule to include the creation of offences. The question that arises is whether the creation and punishment of offences in relation to the 66 specific matters on the Exclusive Legislative List as well as the matters on the Concurrent List exist as an independent power or only as an incidental power.

In the view of the Judicial Committee of the Privy Council in a celebrated case (*Balewa v. Doherty* (1963)), "no offence can be created .... unless the creation .... is incidental or supplementary to some other matter." It held further, and rightly in this particular regard, that a matter does not become incidental to another matter merely by being closely connected with it; the latter matter must actually have been acted or legislated upon before something else, like the creation of offences, can be said to be incidental to it. In the words of the Committee:

> One cannot talk sensibly of an offence being incidental or supplementary to banks or banking, or to railways (Item 37) or to trunk roads (Item 39). But if there has been legislation about trunk roads, one can ask oneself whether the creation of the particular offence can properly be called an incidental or supplementary part of the legislation .... There must be actual legislation in being or a function of the federal government actually being discharged; only then can the connection between the two matters be examined to see whether it is sufficiently close.

By its nature as defined in the above quoted statement, an incidental power in relation to the creation of offence, implies therefore no more than a power to punish violations of or non-compliance with the law. Its express inclusion in the constitution imports no more than would have been implied without it, since, as Chief Justice Griffith said:

> the very notion of law, in the sense of a rule of conduct prescribed by a superior authority, connotes provisions as to the consequences which are to follow from its infraction. The imposition of such consequences, commonly spoken of as sanctions, which are generally in the form of penalties, is in the strictest sense of the term incidental to the execution of the power to make the law itself (R. *v. Kidman* (1915)).

In the same vein, Chief Justice John Marshall of the US Supreme Court has said:

> All admit that the government may, legitimately, punish any violation of its laws; and yet, this is not among the enumerated powers of Congress. *(McCollock v. Maryland* (1819)).

Such offences are known as technical offences; they concern only persons engaged in activities relating to the matter regulated by the law, such as arms and ammunition; aviation, including the carriage of passengers and goods by air; banks and banking; drugs and poisons, etc. Such technical offences are not included in the Criminal Code (or Penal Code).

The view of the Judicial Committee of the Privy Council that "no offence can be created" in relation to the specific matters in the Exclusive and Concurrent Legislative Lists "unless the creation .... is incidental or supplementary to" a matter on the lists seems unduly narrow. Many federal offences on these matters are created, not as penalties for violations of the provisions of a law on them, but separately and independently as a way of regulating such matters. The creation of these offences is explicable only on the view, as decided by the High Court of Australia, that a power to make law **with respect** to a given matter is wide enough to embrace the creation of offences in relation thereto as a separate and independent exercise (R. *v. Kidman* (1915)). The wider view of the matter is certainly preferable to that of the Judicial Committee of the Privy Council, as otherwise it would mean that the creation of the offences in the Criminal Code (or Penal Code) categorised as federal offences is unconstitutional, except for offences against the Nigerian state or the federal government as well as offences against public safety and public order generally and perhaps a few others.

The federal offences in the Criminal Code (or Penal Code) created on the wide view of the power to make laws "with respect to" given matters relate mostly to smuggling and other custom offences, infringement of copyright; counterfeiting the currency, revenue stamps or postage stamps; stopping mails, intercepting telegrams or postal matter, misdelivery or retarding delivery of postal matter, fraudulent evasion of postal laws, unlawful franking of letters, sending dangerous or obscene things by post, illegal setting up of post office, damaging post office, interference with telegraphs, intentionally endangering safety of persons travelling by railway, for example, placing things on the railway, obstructing or damaging railways or railway works; obstructing aircraft, trespass on aerodrome; fraudulent taking, concealment or disposal of mineral in or about a mine, injuring or obstructing the working of a mine; entering a ship or wharf without a ticket, obstructing the navigation or management of a ship.

The classification of offences under the Code into federal or state offences is not of course free from difficulty, as is attested by the divergent classifications made by the various commissioners who prepared the revised editions of the laws of some of the regions or states.

But the wider view of the power to make laws "with respect to" given matters has a significant implication in relation to the power of the federal government to punish corruption, fraud and allied offences. According to Mr. Justice Higgins of the High Court of Australia:

an Act making a conspiracy to defraud the Commonwealth a criminal offence may fairly be treated as an Act made 'with respect to' each and all of the subjects of legislation mentioned in the first thirty-eight placita of section 51; for a fraud on the Commonwealth affects its finances, and to cripple the finances tends to cripple, more or less, the exercise of all the legislative powers, and the execution of all the laws. (*R v. Kidman* (1915)).

This seems to be overstretching the power unduly. On this view, the federal government has power to punish corruption and fraud in relation not only to its property but also to all matters within its legislative competence. But that is the farthest extent of its power. Beyond this, the rest of the offences in the Corrupt Practices and Related Offences Act 2000 are unconstitutional, as being *ultra vires* the federal government.

(ii) *Extent of Power Conferred by Item 60(a) of the Exclusive Legislative List.*

Item 60(a) of the Exclusive Legislative List empowers the National Assembly to make laws with respect to:

> The establishment and regulation of authorities for the Federation or any part thereof to promote and enforce the Observance of the Fundamental Objectives and Directive Principles contained in this constitution.

Item 60(a) must also draw its meaning and effect from the character and purpose of the Fundamental Objectives and Directive Principles of State Policy. Construed in that light, it does not, nor is it intended to confer on the federal government power to create and punish offences outside its power to do so under other provisions of the constitution or power to derogate from the autonomy of the state governments. The words of the Item make this clear. They seem clear enough that the only power conferred on the federal government by Item 60(a) is power to establish and regulate authorities, but not power to prescribe the functions of any authorities so established, these being already prescribed and delimited by Item 60(a) itself, *viz.,* "to promote and enforce the observance of the Fundamental Objectives and Directive Principles". The term "establishment" or to establish raises no difficulty of interpretation. To regulate an authority within the meaning of Item 60(a) certainly does not, by any canon of interpretation, enable the National Assembly to confer upon the authority powers which the assembly itself does not otherwise possess. To regulate an authority within the meaning of Item 60(a) means simply to prescribe its membership, quorum, procedure, finances and such other matters, but not its powers and functions, which are already defined in Item 60(a) itself. Whatever else the word regulate may mean in the context, it does not enable the National Assembly to create offences outside the power in that behalf conferred upon it in other provisions of the constitution or to empower an authority to try, convict and punish persons for such offences, as is done by the Corrupt Practices and Related Offences Act 2000.

It needs also to be stressed that Item 60(a) speaks of "the establishment and regulation of authorities .... to enforce", not the Fundamental Objectives and Directive Principles as such, but rather their "observance". The duty of "observance" is laid by Section 13 only on "organs of government and .... authorities and persons exercising legislative, executive or judicial power", but not on other persons. It is clearly wrong to read Item 60(a) as if the word "observance" were not there, as if the authorities to be established were empowered to "enforce" the Fundamental Objectives and Directive Principles as such. A person not exercising legislative, executive and judicial powers, and on whom therefore no duty is laid to **"conform, observe and apply"** the Objectives and Directives cannot come within the power conferred by Item 60(a), whatever its true extent may be.

Even on the misconceived assumption that the Act is within the power of the federal government to enact by virtue of Item 60(a) still it would be unconstitutional and void as being an attempt to exercise the power in a manner calculated, in its practical effect, to impede, burden or interfere with the management of the affairs of the state governments – the doctrine of mutual non-inference noted above. This is so, because the offences created and made punishable by the Act encompass within their ambit not only money, property and other assets of the federal government but also those belonging to a state or local government, a statutory corporation or company owned wholly by it or jointly with others as well as to persons employed in any capacity in its services or in the services of any such corporation or company. The federal government would have been enabled to control, to a great extent, the administration of the affairs of the state governments thereby, in the words of the High Court of Australia quoted earlier, abolishing "in all but name, the federal system of government which it is the object of the constitution to establish".

(iii) Whether Power to "Abolish all Corrupt Practices and Abuse of Power", Assuming Item 60(a) to Confer Such Power, Embraces Power to Legislate with Respect to Fraud and Offences Related Thereto.

The issue raised here is whether power to legislate to "abolish all corrupt practices and abuse of power", assuming such a power to be conferred by Item 60(a), embraces power to legislate with respect to the entire wide field of fraud and offences related thereto. The question arises because the Act defines corruption to include "bribery, fraud and other related offences" (Section 2), and authorises investigation, prosecution, trial, conviction and punishment for fraud and related offences committed by any person under the Act or any other law.

Specifically, it punishes as a crime, certain acts committed by any person which are not corruption as such, e.g., the receipt of anything with knowledge that it has been obtained by means of fraud, stealing or other criminal offence (Sections 13 and 14); the destruction, alteration, mutilation or falsification, with intent to defraud or conceal a crime, of any book, document, valuable security, computer system, account, etc., or an entry therein or the making of any false entry therein, which belongs to his employer or which has been received by him on account of his employment (Section 15); the furnishing of a false statement or return by an officer charged with responsibility therefore in respect of money or property received by him or entrusted to his care (Section 16).

Corruption (or corrupt practices) and fraud are two distinct offences, differing in the constituent ingredients and the punishment prescribed for them by the law. The difference between them is recognised by the 1999 Constitution (see the Fifth Schedule), the Criminal (or Penal) Code, by the Act itself and other relevant penal statutes (e.g., the Corrupt Practices Decree 1975 – since repealed). The essential ingredient of corruption is the asking for or the receiving of property, money or other benefit or the promise or the giving of it as gratification for the performance of or forbearance to perform the functions of an office or position in abuse or perversion of such office or position. Its main constituent element is the exercise of or forbearance to exercise an office at a price, as in the buying and selling of merchandise; it is characterised by action or omission influenced or induced by the promise or receipt of gratification. It is this element that makes corruption pervert, venal or putrid.

Corruption does not, in its essence, entail deceit or trickery deliberately practised in order to gain some advantage dishonestly, which is the essential element in the definition of fraud. Corruption is an intentional act by a giver and taker; the giver, however grudging his participation may be, is not deceived or tricked by the taker; hence both the taker and giver are guilty of the offence. In the case of fraud, on the other hand, the person defrauded is an innocent victim of deceit or trickery dishonestly practised on him by the fraudster in order to gain some advantage.

Fraud takes a much wider variety of forms than corruption. Corruption is dealt with in Chapter 12 (Sections 98-111) of the Criminal Code, fraud in Chapters 38, 39, 40 and 41 (Sections 418-439 and 441) of the Code. And there are many offences which are or may be said to be related to fraud, but certainly not to corruption, e.g., forgery, personation, obtaining stolen goods knowing them to be so; even stealing (dealt with in Chapters 34, 35, 36 and 37, Sections 382-417 of the Criminal Code) shares with fraud a common element of dishonest acquisition of property from its innocent owner.

It is submitted that the term "corrupt practices and abuse of power" in Section 15(5) of the Constitution (1999) is used in the sense defined above, and does not embrace fraud and offences related thereto. Accordingly, Item 60(a) of the Exclusive Legislative List does not empower the National Assembly to legislate with respect to fraud and related offences; these remain, in spite of Item 60(a), matters within exclusive legislative competence of the States as residual matters — except of course as regard fraud in relation to the property of the federal government. In so far, therefore, as the Act defines corruption to include fraud and offences related thereto, and also authorises the investigation, prosecution, trial, conviction and punishment for them, it is unconstitutional and void. To hold otherwise would result in the federal government taking over a large part of the power with respect to the creation and punishment of criminal offences to the exclusion of the States to whom they belong under the division of powers. It would further distort the distribution of powers already heavily unbalanced in favour of the federal government, especially when this is taken together with the unlimited powers over criminal prosecution for all offences under any written law conferred on the Federal Director of Public Prosecutions by section 5(2) of the Act — referred to above.

(iv) Non-justiciability of a Law made Pursuant to Item 60(a) of the Exclusive Legislative List.

Section 6(6)(c) of the 1999 Constitution is also relevant in this connection and needs to be set out again. It says:

> The judicial powers vested in accordance with the foregoing provisions of this section .... shall not, except as otherwise provided in this constitution, extend to any issue or question as to whether any act or omission by any authority or person or as to whether any **law** or judicial decision is **in conformity** with the Fundamental

Objectives and Directive Principles of State Policy set out in Chapter 11 of this Constitution (emphasis supplied).

According to the definition in the *New Webster's Dictionary*, to conform is to bring into correspondence, to comply with requirements.

The question raised by the provision of Section 6(6)(c) above is whether the court has the jurisdiction or power to enquire into whether the Act is in conformity with, is authorised by, or is required for the enforcement of, the Fundamental Objectives and Directive Principles. It is submitted, with the greatest respect, that the court lacks the jurisdiction to embark upon such an enquiry, and that it erred in law when, in the lead judgment in the *Ondo State Case* (supra), it said on p. 35:

> The ICPC is by the provisions of Item 60(a) to promote and enforce the observance of the Fundamental Objectives and Directive Principles of State Policy as contained under Chapter 11 of the Constitution. The question is how can the ICPC enforce the observance? Is it to use force? Is it to legislate or what? The ICPC cannot do either of these because the use of force or coercion in enforcing the observance will require legislation. The ICPC has no power to legislate. Only the National Assembly can legislate.

What the Court is saying in effect is that the Act is in conformity with, is authorised by, or complies with the duty laid on the National Assembly to "abolish all corrupt practices and abuse of power." Surely, the Court is without jurisdiction to do that in view of Section 6(6)(c) of the Constitution.

(v)   *Whether Item 67 of the Exclusive Legislative List has any Bearing on the Power of the National Assembly to Enact the Act.*

The reliance placed by the Supreme Court in the *Ondo State case* (supra) on Item 67 of the Exclusive Legislative List seems, with the greatest respect, to be misplaced. Said the Court:

> Item 67 under the Exclusive Legislative List read together with the provisions of section 4 subsection (2) provide that the National Assembly is empowered to make law for the peace, order and good government of the Federation and any part thereof. It follows therefore, that the National Assembly has the power to legislate against corruption and abuse of office even as it applies to persons not in authority under public or government office.

Item 67 has nothing to do with the matter. It reads:

> Any **other matter** with respect to which the National Assembly has power to make laws in accordance with the provisions of this Constitution. (Emphasis supplied).

The Item only empowers the National Assembly to make law with respect to any matter other than those listed as Items 1 to 66 in the List on which exclusive power to make law is granted to the National Assembly in the body of the Constitution, e.g., the power conferred by the provisions of Sections 8, 9, 12, etc. There is no provision in the body of the constitution specifically granting to the National Assembly power to "legislate against corruption and abuse of office", unless it be Section 15(5). But if Section 15(5), assuming it to be a grant of power, is embraced in Item 67, then, the National Assembly's power to "legislate against corruption and abuse of power" will be exclusive, not concurrent. The reliance on Item 67 in the passage just quoted seems entirely misconceived.

Whether the Act is Unconstitutional for Uncertainty

The Act is unconstitutional and void for uncertainty. It defines corruption in Section 2 to include "bribery, fraud and other related offences". No one can say with certainty what offences are related to fraud. Are forgery and impersonation, for example, not related to fraud? The issue here concerns not only the competence of the

National Assembly to make law with respect to fraud but also the uncertainty as what offences are related to corruption.

Whether the Bad Provisions of the Act can be Severed

Nearly all the offences created by the Act affect the money, property or affairs of the state governments, and their functionaries are made liable to investigation, prosecution and punishment for corruption, fraud or related offences under most of the provisions committed by them in the discharge of their duties in relation to the money, property or affairs of the state governments. Persons not "exercising legislative, executive or judicial powers" are also made liable to investigation, prosecution and punishment for corruption, fraud or related offences under most of the provisions of the Act, notwithstanding that the power conferred by Item 60(a) of the Exclusive Legislative List by virtue of which the Act purports to have been enacted is not applicable to them. The good and bad provisions of the Act are thus so interwoven as to make it impracticable to severe one from the other.

CHAPTER 5

The Controversy over the Sharing of Money in the Federation Account among the Constituent Governments in Nigeria

The controversy over the sharing of money in the Federation Account (formerly the Distributable Pool Account) was probably the most vehement and clamorous in the relations between the federal government and the state governments in the Nigerian Federation. The federal government had brought an action in the original jurisdiction of the Supreme Court praying for "a declaration of the seaward boundary of a littoral State ... for the purpose of calculating the amount of revenue accruing to the Federation Account directly from any natural resources derived from that State pursuant to section 162(2) of the Constitution" of 1999.

The Judgment of the Supreme Court in the case, delivered on 5 April, 2002, is a devastating one for both the federal and state governments. It has perhaps settled nothing, has given satisfaction to neither side, has aggravated the controversy over the sharing of the money, and may intensify the agitation for resource control among the oil producing states. All these have put into serious questioning the wisdom of bringing the suit in the first place, and whether controversies of this kind which are of a highly explosive political nature, are really fit for resolution through the courts.

Conclusion in the Judgment Based on Boundaries

The question raised by the argument based on boundaries is correctly stated by the judgment as follows: "What is the boundary mark between Western, Mid-West and Eastern Regions (and, indeed, Nigeria for that matter) on the one hand and the sea, on the other?" That, indeed, is the crucial question. When the governing Orders-in-Council and Proclamation say that these Regions (or Nigeria) are "bounded" by the sea in the south or that their southern boundary is the sea, what is meant by the sea? Is it the coastline of the sea (or high-water mark), the low-water mark of the sea, or the outer limits of the part of the sea denominated as territorial waters, continental shelf or as exclusive economic zone?

After noting, quite pertinently, that: "the Orders-in-Council and Proclamation are silent on this", the judgment then goes on to conclude without first attempting to answer the crucial question posed:

> One thing, however is clear. If the boundary is with the sea, then, by logical reasoning, the sea cannot be part of the territory of any of the old regions. For this reason, therefore, I have no hesitation in rejecting the contention of the eight littoral Defendant States that their boundaries extend to the exclusive economic zone or the continental shelf of Nigeria. (At p.9 of the cyclostyled judgment delivered on behalf of the Court by Ogundare JSC.)

The above conclusion is certainly not supported by logic; far from that, it simply begs the question posed by the Court itself, which makes it contrary to logic.

It is only later in the judgment that the Court tried to answer the questions posed earlier, and it did that by locating the southern boundary of Nigeria (and *ipso facto* of the eight littoral states) at the low-water mark. In its words:

> the seaward extent of their land territory at common law is the low-water mark or the seaward limit of their internal waters .... The boundary-mark between a riparian owner, such as the littoral states are in this case, and the sea is the low-water mark pp. 10 & 12.

Thus, it conceded to the littoral states the foreshore, i.e., land between high and low-water marks at ordinary spring tides.

With respect to Cross River State which has a number of islands dotted on its internal waters and the sea, it held that "her southern boundary, in the circumstances, will be the seaward limit of her internal waters", p.13. And internal waters of all the littoral states include, in addition to the foreshore (as defined above), ports, anchorages, bays, gulfs and estuaries, any part of the sea separated by islands and all sea arms which are to the landward side of the base lines from which the territorial sea (or waters) is delimited, p.11.

The seabed and its subsoil up to the limits of the territorial waters is denied to the littoral states (and Nigeria too), p.17. The territorial waters of Nigeria is defined by the Territorial Waters Act (Cap 428, Laws of the Federation 1990) as including "every part of the open sea within thirty nautical miles of the coast of Nigeria (measured from low water mark) or of the seaward limits of inland waters". (Section 1 (1)). This represents a modification of international law, since, by the Geneva Convention on the Territorial Sea and the Contiguous Zone 1958, the territorial sea is a maximum of three miles, later extended to twelve nautical miles by the U.N Convention on the Law of the Sea 1982 which superceded the 1958 Geneva Convention.

Viewed from the standpoint of the term, "territorial waters" (or territorial sea), the denial of the littoral states' claim to it is difficult to support or justify. If the seabed and its subsoil to the limits of the territorial water is not part of the territory of the littoral states (or of Nigeria), what does the word "territorial" connote? It is obviously intended to convey a definite meaning. The explanation that "territorial waters" are "waters which wash the shores of the territory of the nation state, otherwise regarded as ending at the margin of the land" (per Barwick C.J of Australia) is unacceptable. The tides of the foreshore waters wash the shores of the territory of the state well enough, and those from 30 nautical miles away are unnecessary for the purpose.

It seems reasonable to say that territorial waters or sea connotes an area of the sea which international law allows a littoral state to appropriate as part of its territory. This conclusion has also a valid basis in law. In view of the provision in the UN Law of the Sea Convention 1982 (replacing the Geneva Convention on the Territorial Sea and the Contiguous Zone 1958), which defines the territorial sea as the part of the sea up to 12 nautical miles from the low-water mark (extended by Nigeria to 30 nautical miles), and the high seas as "all parts of the sea that are not included in the territorial sea or in the internal waters of a State", and considering the further provision that "the sovereignty of a State extends beyond its land territory and its internal waters to a belt of sea adjacent to its coast, described as the territorial sea", the territorial sea is not *territorium nullius* like the rest of the sea outside it. If it is so, the distinction drawn by international law between the two areas of the sea would have been rendered practically meaningless. The intention and purpose for the distinction is that the territorial sea is or should be part of the territory of the state to which it is contiguous (the littoral states in this Case), the contrary position under the common law notwithstanding. The legal basis and rationale for this conclusion is fully explained elsewhere in this chapter under the heading "The Concept of Sovereignty", which contains the crux of our position on the matter in controversy, and must therefore be closely studied.

In further support of the position here taken on this particular point, the situation may be supposed where the sea recedes some 3 – 30 nautical miles – a not too unlikely event (after all, Lake Chad is almost drying up). In that event, the boundary of the littoral states will indisputably be the new low-water mark, some 3–30 nautical miles into the space formerly occupied by the sea. What is the basis of the littoral states' right to this 3 – 30 nautical miles "retrieved" space which they did not have before the recession of the sea?

According to the Privy Council decision in *Attorney-General of Southern Nigeria v John Holt* (1915) A.C 599 and the English authorities on which it is based, where such recession resulted from alluvion or from a natural silting up of sand, gravel and the like or from other natural causes, and provided the recession is "so slow and gradual as to be in a practical sense imperceptible in its course and progress as it occurs" (per Lord Shaw), the retrieved land belongs to the riparian owners, and not to the state. This rule is founded upon security and general convenience; and its operation may bring either gain or loss to private riparian owners. If the sea, instead of receding, advances further into the land of the private riparian owners, that part of their land swallowed up by the sea together with the new high-water mark belongs to the State. The retrieved land, being the property of the private riparian owners, will indisputably form part of the territory (boundary) of the littoral states (or former regions). The question is : why should it belong to the littoral states to the exclusion of the inland states?

The strong language of the Privy Council in upholding the right of a private riparian owner to land resulting from recession of the sea is worthy of note. It said:

> To suppose that lands which, although of specific measurements in the title deeds, were *de facto* fronted and bounded by the sea were to be in the situation that their frontage to the sea was to disappear by the action of nature to the effect of setting up a strip of land .... between the receded foreshore and the actual measured boundary of the adjoining lands, which strip was to be the property of the Crown (i.e. the state), and was to have the effect of converting land so held into inland property would be followed by **grotesque and well-nigh impossible results,** and violate the doctrine which is founded upon the general security of landholders and upon the general advantage. at p. 612 (emphasis supplied).

As the Privy Council said, "beyond such rights as he possesses as one of the public," such as rights of navigation and fishing, a private riparian owner has also "special rights which are attached and add value" to his land (at p. 621); among them are the value conferred by frontage on the sea and the right to land resulting from the recession of the sea if and when such recession does occur.

If, as the Supreme Court held, the territorial sea, as defined above, does not belong to the littoral states, then, *a fortiori,* no part of the sea lying beyond it belongs to them. The latter conclusion is correct, of course. Although "no State may validly purport to subject any part of (the high seas) to its sovereignty" (art. 2, UN Convention on the Law of the Sea, replacing the Geneva Convention on the Territorial Sea and the Contiguous Zone 1958), international law accords to a coastal state the right of exploration and exploitation of mineral resources in the high seas up to a limit of 200 nautical miles from the low-water mark. (The high seas is defined as "all parts of the sea that are not included in the territorial sea or in the internal waters of a State" (art. 1, *ibid.*). The part of the 200 nautical miles lying beyond the territorial waters is known as the continental shelf, and forms a coastal state's exclusive economic zone.

Apart from the practical consideration that the sea may recede by, say, 3 – 30 nautical miles beyond the low-water mark, there is another practical consideration to be taken into account. Suppose the Federation of Nigeria breaks up or is dissolved. To whom will the oil in the territorial waters, continental shelf or the exclusive economic zone go? Will it be among the common property to be shared among all the states and, if so, in what proportions? I do not think that any right-thinking person will ever suggest anything so preposterous. I fear that the Judgment of the Supreme Court in this Case may well act as a spur, if not an incitement, to the peoples of the littoral states to break up the federation, so as to be able to take over what properly should be theirs by virtue of their location on the shores of the sea — the oil revenue, both on-shore and off-shore.

Even conceding that the territorial seas and the continental shelf or exclusive economic zone (as defined above) do not belong to the littoral states, considerations of ecological or environmental devastation caused by pollution, etc, clearly require or justify allocating to them a percentage of the revenue from mineral resources located there. In the words of the Okigbo Presidential Commission on Revenue Allocation Report (1980), Vol. 1, paragraph 351, "the production of minerals creates hazards to life and property in the areas concerned, and causes a general degradation of the environment and of the ecology of the producing areas," which creates for the state governments concerned "the additional responsibility for the increased cost of the welfare, and the rehabilitation (and in some cases resettlement) of the people and areas concerned". It is for these same reasons that, whilst in international law "the sea is *res nullius,* and is, therefore, available for the enjoyment of all nations of the world, land-locked nations inclusive," and no state may validly purport to subject any part of it to its sovereignty, international law nevertheless recognises, "that by the vulnerability of their proximity to the sea, maritime nations are entitled to some privileges not available to others to protect their security" p.14 of the Judgment. It recognises in, and accords to, them sovereignty over their territorial waters, and exclusive right of exploration and exploitation of natural resources over their continental shelf or exclusive economic zone.

If international law accords these special rights to coastal states because of the "vulnerability of their proximity to the sea", it smacks of meanness, insensitivity, injustice, unconscionableness and oppression for the Federal Government of Nigeria, as a beneficiary of the kind, indulgent concessions of international law, to deny to the country's littoral states a paltry 13 percent of revenue derived from mineral resources located in the territorial waters, continental shelf or exclusive economic zone contiguous to their territory. It might have been thought that their claim to such special compensatory allocation is so obvious and compelling as cannot be denied by any fair-minded person, least of all by a federal government whose right to the whole of the revenue in question arises by the generosity and concessions of international law. The whole thing seems so utterly unconscionable as to be unbelievable in a world where conscience, equity and fairness still have a place.

I discuss in subsequent sub-heads of this chapter, the legal basis of my conclusions that the decision of the Supreme Court is wrong, and is hardly "a just and equitable resolution of the dispute raised in this Case" at p.64 of the Judgment; and that the littoral states are entitled to a special compensatory allocation of revenue derived from oil or other natural resources located in the territorial sea and continental shelf or exclusive economic zone contiguous to their territory. But, first, what actually did the Case decide?

Outcome of the Case

The Judgment of the Supreme Court in this Case is a remarkable one – it runs to 64 pages. It is somewhat difficult to follow to know what exactly was decided. (A committee set up by the federal government is, I understand, still studying and analysing it to work out its implications.). As it will overburden the reader to detail all the points decided, only the more important or salient ones will be noted here.

The starting point in stating what exactly the Case decided is Section 313 of the 1999 Constitution, which provides as follows:

> Pending any Act of the National Assembly for the provision of a system of revenue allocation between the Federation and the States, among the States, between the States and local government councils and among the local government councils in the States, the system of revenue allocation in existence for the financial year beginning 1st January 1998 and ending on 31st December 1998 shall, **subject to the provisions of this constitution** and as from the date when this section comes into force, continue to apply. (emphasis supplied).

From this, the result must follow, as submitted on behalf of the federal government, that "until the authorities responsible are able to produce the formula envisaged under Section 162 of the 1999 Constitution the provisions enacted in the *Allocation of Revenue (Federation Account etc.) Act Cap 16* will continue to apply". Section

4A(6) of the Act aforementioned, inserted by Decree 106 of 1992 by way of an amendment, provides:

> An amount equivalent to 1 per cent of the Federation Account derived from mineral revenue shall be shared among the oil producing States based on the amount of mineral produced from each state and in the application of this provision, the dichotomy of on-shore and off-shore oil and mineral oil and non-mineral oil revenue is hereby abolished.

Applying its ruling that Cap. 16 is "only applicable in so far as it is not inconsistent with the provisions of the 1999 Constitution" and that the Act must give way in the event of an inconsistency, the Court held that, being inconsistent with the Constitution, (i) the 1 percent prescribed by the Act as against the not less than 13 per cent prescribed by the Constitution is void; (ii) the reference to "mineral revenue" in the Act is void as what is mentioned in Section 162(2) proviso of the Constitution is "natural resources"; (iii) the special allocation of 7.5 percent to the Federal Capital Territory, the development of the mineral producing areas, general ecological problems and stabilisation account is invalid – this point is taken up in the next sub-head of this chapter. From the tenor and thrust of the entire Judgment, and as reaffirmed in the Court's answer to the various counterclaims by some of the Defendants, where the Court held, in unambiguous terms, that the sea beyond the low-water mark is not part of the territory of the littoral states so as to entitle them, on the basis of derivation, to the revenue from the mineral oil located there, the abolition by the Act of the on-shore and off-shore dichotomy is void. In the result, therefore, the dichotomy remains applicable, and the littoral states are not entitled to the 13 percent of revenue from off-shore oil mineral on the basis of derivation. This, needless to say, is the central issue in the Case.

The Court also rejected the claim by the states for payment, on the basis of derivation, of 13 percent of revenue even from on-shore oil located in their land territory. The ground for the decision on this claim is that "there is no legal basis for the use of this figure". The reasoning behind this holding is stated as follows:

> In the absence of any legislation by the National Assembly pursuant to section 162(2) of the Constitution which fixes a figure that is not less than 13 per cent (but which may be more than that figure) in calculating the amount due to a State affected by the principle of derivation in the proviso to the subsection, it is for the President, as the prescribed authority, to modify Cap 16 (as amended) to bring it in conformity with the provisions of the Constitution, particularly section 162 thereof. Unless and until either is done, the 3rd Defendant cannot, as of legal right, lay claim to 13 per cent as a basis of working out the amount due it under the proviso to section 162(2). It is not in dispute that natural resources are located on his territory and that revenue accrued, and still accrues, to the Federation Account from such resources. **While it is not disputed that the 3rd Defendant is entitled to some share of that revenue,** it is the actual entitlement that is in dispute. And this can only be resolved by knowing the actual figure to be used in calculating the entitlement. (emphasis supplied).

The changes required are not such as the president can make by virtue of his power of adaptive legislation, which is restricted to changes of a verbal or textual nature; it does not extend to changes of substance in the law. The Court did not advert to the limits of the power in its pronouncements – as to these limits, (see my *Nigeria's Second Experiment in Constitutional Democracy* (1985), pp. 93–95).

It has been thought necessary to quote the relevant part of the Judgment in full to bring out how highly questionable the reasoning is. Since it is conceded that the 3rd Defendant (Akwa Ibom State) is "entitled to some share of that revenue" it has a constitutional right to be paid at least 13 per cent, pending the time the actual amount (which may be 13 per cent or more) is fixed by the National Assembly. Payment of the 13 per cent minimum cannot justifiably be withheld; the legal basis for it is Section 162(2) proviso of the Constitution. Upon a purposive interpretation, what the proviso says is that the share of a state based on derivation shall be 13 per cent or such higher figure as the National Assembly may determine, not that a state shal' be entitled to an amount to be determined by the National Assembly, not being less than 13 per cent. The former meaning seems to be the one indicated upon a close reading of the proviso. The wording is admittedly clumsy and lacking in clarity, but an interpretation is to be preferred which would not defeat the object intended and so result in avoidable deprivation against the states. The withholding of the payment is therefore unjustified, inequitable and oppressive.

Constitutionality or Otherwise of the Allocation Formula Embodied in Cap 16

Section 1 of the Allocation of Revenue (Federation Account etc) Cap 16 prescribes the following revenue sharing formula:

(i)   Federal Government   48.5 percent

(ii)   State Government   24.0 percent

(iii) Local Government   20.0 percent

(iv) Special Funds (allocated to Federal Capital Territory, Development of the Mineral Producing Areas, General Ecological problems, Derivation and Stabilisation Account) 7.5 percent

As earlier noted, the allocation of 7.5 percent under the heading "Special Funds" was declared void as being inconsistent with the constitution. This is because the only beneficiaries to the amount in the Federation Account are the federal government, the state governments and the local government (Section 162(3)).

Regrettably, the Judgment did not address the issue as to whether the nullification of the 7.5 percent allocation to Special Funds leaves still valid and operative the rest of the sharing formula prescribed by the Act. The Defendants (i.e., the 36 States) are entitled to have the entire amount in the Federation Account, not just 92.5 percent of it (i.e., 100 − 7.5), shared among the beneficiaries designated in Section 162(3). It is immaterial that only a small proportion or nothing of the 7.5 per cent Special Funds allocation may be allocated to them. The National Assembly may well take some more years to enact a new revenue sharing formula. Will the 7.5 per cent remain unallocated for so long as it takes the Assembly to enact a new formula? The unconstitutionality of the 7.5 per cent allocation to "Special Funds" has so distorted the entire revenue sharing formula under the Act as to render it unconstitutional and void. The bad is so intertwined with the rest as to make severance under the "blue pencil rule" inapplicable.

Some Misconceptions or Omissions Resulting in the Court Coming to a Wrong Decision

Three misconceptions or omissions that led the Court to come to a wrong decision are here noted, *viz* (i) whether the sea is a natural resource as claimed by Cross River State; (ii) the constitutionality or otherwise of extra-territorial legislation in Nigeria; and (iii) the concept of sovereignty.

(i) *Whether the Sea is a Natural Resource as Claimed by Cross River State*

Cross River State (9th Defendant) had counterclaimed that the sea is a natural resource, and that it is entitled to it by virtue of its contiguity to the State's on-shore land. The claim is of course more or less the same as the claim to the minerals under the bed of the sea. Earlier in the Judgment, the Court adopted the definition of "natural resources" in Black's *Law Dictionary,* which is as follows:

> Any material in its native state which when extracted has economic value. Timberland, oil and gas wells, ore deposits, and other products of nature that have economic value; the cost of natural resources is subject to depletion, often called "wasting assets". The term includes not only timber, gas, oil, coal, minerals, **lakes** and submerged lands, but also features which supply a human need .... (emphasis supplied).

The Court omitted to make a specific pronouncement on whether the sea is a natural resource. But, surely, if "lakes" is a natural resource, the sea should also qualify, at least up to the point where the territorial sea ends and the high seas begin. But, of course, the Court's decision upon the point would have been to say that, even if the sea is a natural resource, it does not belong to, or is not part of the territory of, Cross River State. As according to the Court, it does not belong to the federal government either, the oil mineral located under its bed belongs to neither. Whatever rights the federal government has and exercises over it are held by it and are to be exercised as "Trustee or Custodian of the State from where such natural resources are derived" – so Cross River State asserted at p. 47 of the Judgment. Regrettably again, the Court did not pronounce upon this claim. I reserve comments to subsequent portion of this chapter.

(ii)   *Constitutionality of Extra-Territorial Legislation in Nigeria*

The question raised here concerns the constitutional validity or otherwise of three statutes enacted to implement the 1958 Geneva Concentions on the subject (later replaced by the UN Law of the Sea Convention 1982), *viz*, the Territorial Waters Act Cap 428, the Exclusive Economic Zone Act Cap 116, and the Fisheries Act Cap 404. As the Court's decision turns so much on these Conventions and the implementing Acts, the constitutional invalidity of the Acts will affect a considerable part of the decision.

The question is whether the three Acts are extra-territorial laws, and, if so, whether extra-territorial laws are valid under the 1999 Constitution of Nigeria. The Territorial Waters Act defines Nigeria's territorial waters as including "every part of the open sea within thirty nautical miles of the coast of Nigeria (measured from low-water mark) or of the seaward limit of inland waters", and makes certain acts or omissions committed within the area a criminal offence. Cap 116 defines Nigeria's exclusive economic zone as "an area extending from the external limits of the territorial waters of Nigeria up to a distance of 200 nautical miles from the baselines from which the breadth of the territorial waters of Nigeria is measured". It vests in the federal government exclusive rights for the exploration and exploitation of natural resources located in the zone's seabed and subsoil. It also authorises the federal government to establish artificial islands, installations and structures in the zone, or to permit their establishment, operation and use by any other person; to prohibit ships from entering without its consent any part of the area. It makes certain acts or omissions committed within the zone a criminal offence. The Fisheries Act makes provisions for the regulation and control of fishing and the protection of fish in Nigeria's territorial waters and also makes certain acts and omissions in the area criminal offences.

As, according to the Court's decision, the southern limit of Nigeria's territory is the low-water mark, so that the territorial waters and exclusive economic zone are outside it, the three Acts are clearly extra-territorial laws. To the question it posed to itself as to "what gives validity" to these three Acts, the Court held, accepting the submission by counsel for the federal government, Chief Williams SAN, that "each of the enactments was validly enacted by the Federal Legislature pursuant to the power to make laws **for the Federal Republic of Nigeria** with respect to external affairs .... External affairs is on the exclusive legislative list" at p 14 of the Judgment (emphasis supplied). With the greatest respect, there is a misconception here which led the Court to a wrong decision on the constitutional validity of the three enactments.

External affairs, as an item on the Exclusive Legislative List (Item 26), is only a subject-matter of legislative power; its listing as an item on the Exclusive Legislative List does not determine the extent of the power to make laws with respect thereto. The extent of the power depends on Section 12 (2) of the Constitution, which says; "The National Assembly may make laws **for the Federation or any part thereof** with respect to matters not included in the Exclusive Legislative List for the purpose of implementing a treaty" (emphasis supplied, see also Section 4(2)).

The words "for the Federation" in the subsection makes it clear that the power it confers is only power to make laws applying to persons and things in Nigeria, not to persons and things outside its territory; it does not enable the National Assembly to make laws for foreign countries or foreign territories. Had the subsection said that "the National Assembly may make laws with respect to matters ......" omitting the words "for the Federation or any part thereof", as it might have done if those words were intended not to have any effect, then, the subsection would have conferred power to make extra-territorial laws for the purpose of implementing treaties. As the three Acts apply to persons and things outside the territory of Nigeria, the territorial sea and the exclusive economic zone not being part of it according to the Court's decision, the three Acts are not authorised by Section 12(2) of the Constitution, and are therefore unconstitutional and invalid. Given the constitutional invalidity of the three statutes, the international conventions relied on so heavily by the Court and which the Acts were enacted to implement do not apply as law in Nigeria, since, by Section 12(1) of the Constitution, "no treaty between the Federation and any other country shall have the force of law except to the extent to which any such treaty has been enacted into law by the National Assembly". It is therefore wrong for the Court to have relied on them, as it did.

No doubt, the statutes were enacted by the military government whose powers were unlimited by a supreme constitution, yet as laws in existence today within the meaning of Section 315 of the 1999 Constitution, their continuing validity depends upon their conformance with the provisions of that constitution.

(iii)   *The Concept of Sovereignty*

The misconception here is the most critical as lying at the root of the Court's wrong decision; for, it disabled the Court from appreciating the impact of changes in international law upon the common law. The misconception concerns the concept of sovereignty. When the UN Law of the Sea Convention 1982 (replacing the Geneva Convention on the Territorial Sea and the Contiguous Zone 1958) says that "the sovereignty of a State extends beyond its land territory and its internal waters to a belt of sea adjacent to its coast, described as the territorial sea", and that it also "extends to its bed and subsoil", what is meant by "sovereignty", and is not the intention and effect of the provision that the territorial sea, its bed and subsoil, should be appropriated and assimilated to the state to whose land territory they are contiguous? So much turns therefore on the meaning of the term "sovereignty" and of the provision in the Convention (quoted at p. 15 of the Judgment).

The misconception about the nature of sovereignty is manifested in various pronouncements upon the point by the Court, as, for example, that, while the low-water mark is the seaward limit of the country's territory, Nigeria, "in its sovereignty and by the custom of international law exercises **jurisdiction** beyond that limit" (at p.14); that "Nigeria as a sovereign State is a member of the international community"; that "the littoral Defendant States, not being sovereign, are not, either individually or collectively"; that, "in the exercise of its sovereignty, Nigeria from time to time enters into treaties – both bilateral and multilateral"; that "the notion of territorial waters whereby sovereignty is given to a maritime nation over a breadth of the sea adjacent to her coast, developed," (at p.14) (emphasis supplied).

Later in the Judgment, it again says: "the claim by the Plaintiff of sovereignty over the territorial sea of Nigeria and the Exclusive Economic Zone does not extend the land territory of Nigeria beyond what is provided for in sections 2 and 3 of the Constitution" (at p.17.) The Judgment finally sums up thus upon this point:

> the sum total of all I have been saying above is that none of the Territorial Waters Act and the Exclusive Economic Zone Act has extended the land territory of Nigeria beyond its constitutional limit, although the Acts give municipal effect to international treaties entered into by Nigeria by virtue of its membership as a sovereign State, of the Comity of Nations. These treaties confer sovereignty and other rights on Nigeria over certain area of the sea (the Atlantic/ Ocean) adjacent to her coastline (at pp. 18.)

These pronouncements betray a basic misconception that led the Court to a wrong decision upon the point in dispute.

To begin with, the sovereignty of Nigeria does not belong to the federal government alone, but is divided between it and the state governments; each is sovereign within the area of competence assigned to it by the constitution; in other words, the sovereign state of Nigeria is made up of the federal government and the state governments, with the former representing all of them in the country's relations to other countries and international organisations by virtue of external affairs having been assigned to it exclusively by the constitution under the division of powers between them. Power over external affairs is thus only part of Nigeria's sovereignty. In so far as the sea involves Nigeria's relations with other countries, it is an aspect of the country's external affairs and therefore within the exclusive jurisdiction of the federal government, but the exercise of that jurisdiction is subject to the supreme law of the constitution, just like the exercise of jurisdiction over any other matter assigned to the federal or the state governments under the constitution. With the greatest respect, it not only distorts the distribution of sovereignty in a federal system, but also gives a misleading picture of the matter to say in the rather sweeping language of the Court that the littoral defendant states are not sovereign.

But the really crucial question concerns the true nature of sovereignty. Sovereignty comprises two constituent elements, both of which must be present before it can arise or exist, *viz,* (a) ownership of territory, (albeit notional ownership), and (b) "power and jurisdiction". Sovereignty is therefore inseparable from ownership of territory or it will mean no more than "power and jurisdiction" which a state exercises in a foreign territory. Implying, by its nature, ownership of territory, sovereignty cannot meaningfully exist or be spoken of without such ownership; that will be a blatant contradiction in ideas.

"Power and jurisdiction" only, even to the fullest extent, acquired by one country in another country is not tantamount to sovereignty. Annexation of territory, following a conquest or following a treaty of cession, is the means by which the sovereignty of a country is acquired. Sovereignty connotes, therefore, *dominium* over territory as well as "power and jurisdiction" to its fullest extent. Hence the position of an imperial power in a colony and in a protectorate is expressed in terms of sovereignty in a colony and of only "power and jurisdiction" in a protectorate. The terms of a typical treaty of cession of sovereignty underline the cardinal significance of ownership of territory in the concept of sovereignty.

Ownership of territory implied by, or inherent in, the concept of sovereignty connotes **dominion**. Dominion, as Sir Ivor Jennings has said, conveys "to a lawyer bred in the tradition of Rome.... the idea of *dominium* or ownership, and etymologically that is the idea which it ought to convey". (see his *Constitutional Laws of the Commonwealth* (1957), p.9). Though the *dominium* implied by sovereignty connotes absolute ownership, the ownership is only notional; it does not carry with it beneficial ownership of land (except in conquered territories), but only power of administrative control of land by means of legislation, which may be exercised to take over beneficial ownership and generally to regulate the tenure of land.

As earlier stated, sovereignty, with the notional ownership of territory (dominion) which it implies, is what distinguishes a colony and a protectorate, the position of an imperial state being expressed in terms of sovereignty in a colony and of "power and jurisdiction" in a protectorate. "A protectorate", writes Sir Henry Jenkyns in his authoritative book, *British Rule and Jurisdiction Beyond the Seas* (1902), p.165, "is a country which is not within the British dominions" (i.e., territories). The difference is well portrayed in the statement of it by Lord Justice Kennedy in *R v. Earl of Crewe* (1910) 2 K.B 576 at p. 620, which has been quoted and requoted ever since:

> What the idea of a protectorate excludes and the idea of annexation on the other hand would include is that absolute ownership which was signified by the word dominium in Roman law, and which, though perhaps not quite satisfactorily, is sometimes described as territorial sovereignty. The protected country remains in regard to the protecting state a foreign country.

In international law this has the consequence of preserving treaty rights and privileges acquired or enjoyed by foreign powers before the establishment of the protectorate, but on annexation such rights and privileges automatically come to an end. Moreover, foreign nationals in a protectorate are not subject to the nationality laws of the protecting Power, as they will be in its dominion.

A further consequence of the lack of sovereignty by Britain in a British protectorate is that the inhabitants of a protectorate, unlike those of a colony, are not British subjects. Indeed not only are they not British subjects but they are also not British nationals at all, for in the contemplation of the English common law all non-British subjects, whether they be the nationals of foreign independent countries or the natives of a British protectorate, were aliens. The common law recognises no other class of British nationals outside British subjects. Not being British subjects, the inhabitants of a British protectorate do not, like those of a colony, owe any duty of allegiance to Britain "because allegiance exists only between the Sovereign and his subjects, properly so called".

Even when an imperial state's "power and jurisdiction" in a foreign country has become so full and plenary as to embrace the entire substance of political power, covering all matters connected with its peace, order and good government, as in the protectorate of Nigeria and the other African protectorates, denominated by the term **"colonial** protectorates", still, without sovereignty acquired through annexation of territory, the protectorate remains a foreign country in relation to the imperial state. The point is well-brought out by Lord Denning *in Nyali Limited v Attorney-General* (1956) 1 Q.B. 1 at p.15 (a Kenyan case):

> Although the jurisdiction of the Crown in the protectorate is in law a limited jurisdiction, nevertheless the limits may in fact be extended indefinitely so as to embrace almost the whole field of government. They may be extended so far that the Crown has jurisdiction in everything connected with the peace, order and good government of the area, leaving only the title and ceremonies of sovereignty remaining in the Sultan.

By the title of sovereignty, Denning means of course the title of ownership of territory.

In relation to Nigeria, Lagos, acquired by the cession of sovereignty through the annexation of its territory (see the terms of the treaty of

1861) was part of the dominions of Britain, while the rest of the country, acquired by the cession or the sheer arrogation of "power and jurisdiction", was a foreign territory under the protection of Britain, a protectorate. The difference in the constitutional status of the two areas of the country (amalgamated into one country in 1914 as the Colony and Protectorate of Nigeria), was maintained until October, 1960, even though Britain's "power and jurisdiction" in the Protectorate had since embraced the entire substance of political power covering everything connected with its peace, order and good government, exactly as in the Colony of Lagos; the absence of the title of sovereignty or dominion over territory in the protectorate accounted for the differentiation.

The position remained like this until October 1, 1960 when the necessity arose that the position of Britain (or its symbol, the Crown) in Lagos, expressed in terms of sovereignty or dominion over territory, and its position in the rest of the country, expressed in terms of only "power and jurisdiction" (i.e., the absence of dominion over territory), should be assimilated. Independence was to be granted to Nigeria as a single country, and it would have been monstrously absurd to have dealt with the sovereignty of its component parts separately. The only sensible course in the circumstances was therefore to assimilate the position of the Queen in the Protectorate to her position in the Colony; in other words, to enlarge her "power and jurisdiction" there into sovereignty. In a technical sense, this meant annexation of territory (dominion). This was in fact done by the Independence Act which provided that as from October 1, 1960, Nigeria shall form "part of Her Majesty's dominions" (Section 1(1)). See an insightful article in (1957) 1 J A L 99 – 112 where the writer, choosing to remain anonymous, exposed the British imperial technique in this matter. Martin Wight, in his *British Colonial Constitutions* (1952) has said that:

> no dependency (apart from territories formerly under A mandate, Iraq and Transjordan) has yet attained responsible government without having first been elevated into a colony (and its inhabitants promoted into British subjects) through annexation. When Southern

Rhodesia, still a protectorate, was granted responsible government in 1923, it was formally annexed as a preliminary (at p.33.)

The practice has changed since Wight wrote in 1952; the new practice was to delay annexation of territory until independence. See further on this subject my *Constitutional Law of the Nigerian Republic* (1964) pp. 14 – 26; 80 – 81; *A Constitutional History of Nigeria* (1982), pp. 1 – 19; 72 – 74.

Enough has been said above about the inseparability of ownership of territory, albeit notional ownership, from the concept of sovereignty to expose the blatant contradiction of saying in one breadth that the sovereignty of Nigeria "extends beyond its land territory and its internal waters to a belt of sea adjacent to its coast, described as the territorial sea" and to "its bed and subsoil" (at p.15 of the Judgment, quoting articles 1 and 2 of the Geneva Convention on the Territorial Sea and the Contiguous Zone 1958), and in another breadth that the territorial sea, its bed and subsoil, are not part of her territory. The contradiction manifests an utter misconception of the nature of sovereignty and its inseparability from ownership (notional) of territory (dominion); the one cannot exist without the other.

By way of emphasis, what the provision in the Convention (quoted above) does is to extend Nigeria's sovereignty in her land territory which gives her dominion over it, to her territorial sea; her sovereignty in the two areas is exactly of the same **nature,** and no differentiation is made by the provision between her sovereignty in the two areas; it is characterized by ownership of territory in the one as in the other – and of course by "power and jurisdiction", to the extent that "power and jurisdiction" can be exercised in or over the sea and its bed and subsoil.

The Supreme Court has relied for its decision on R *v Keyn* (1876) 2 Ex.D. 63 at p. 67, per Sir Phillimore, and other English decisions cited at p. 12 of the judgment, which held that "the county extends to low-water mark, **where the 'high seas' begin",** without taking into account the impact upon this common law rule of the new definition of the high seas as "all parts of the sea that are not included in the territorial sea", which is defined as "the part of the sea up to 12 nautical miles from the low-water mark" – extended by Nigerian law to 30 nautical miles (see the U.N Law of the Sea Convention on the Territorial Sea and the Contiguous Zone 1958, and Nigeria's Territorial Waters Act 1967 Cap 428).

The common law must adapt itself to the changing limits of the high seas as determined by agreement (treaty) among the countries of the world, a point acknowledged by the Privy Council in *Att-Gen of Southern Nigeria v John Holt (ibid)* when it referred to "the Crown (i.e., the state) as the owner of the sea and its bed within territorial limit" (at p. 611), which, varying according to changes in the definition of the high seas by international law, may be the low-water mark or the limits of the territorial sea.

It is sovereignty or dominion over territory that distinguishes Nigeria's position in her territorial waters (with its bed and subsoil) from her position in her continental shelf or exclusive economic zone. But for this, there would have been no need for demarcating the area of the sea thirty nautical miles from the coast of Nigeria from the area beyond that to the limit of 200 nautical miles from the low-water mark, called the continental shelf. If the whole area covering 200 nautical miles from the low-water mark is outside the territory of Nigeria, then, it should have been treated as just one composite stretch of sea (with its bed and subsoil) instead of being demarcated into two separate and distinct areas, denominated respectively as territorial sea and continental shelf. The reason for the demarcation is that, by international law, Nigeria has sovereignty or dominion over the territory (bed and subsoil) covered by the territorial sea but only a limited amount of "power and jurisdiction" over the continental shelf which is a foreign territory in relation to her. The Court seems to have allowed itself to be unduly shackled by the rules of the common law at the expense of the clear stipulation of international law, applicable in Nigeria, that the country's sovereignty, implying as it does, dominion over territory, extends to her territorial sea with its bed and subsoil.

Sovereignty does not have a different meaning under the relevant provision of the Geneva Convention on Territorial Sea and Contiguous Zone 1958 (now replaced by the U.N Convention on the Law of Sea 1982). Indisputably, therefore, the territorial sea (with its bed and subsoil) is part of the territory of Nigeria (and *ipso facto* the littoral states) by right of the sovereignty or dominion over it conferred on her by international law, as made applicable to Nigeria by the Territorial Waters Act.

This view of the matter derives additional support from Section 134(6) of the 1960 Constitution and Section 140(6) of the 1963 Constitution, each of which provides that "for the purposes of this section, the continental shelf of a Region shall be deemed to be part of that Region". The implication of applying this deeming provision to the continental shelf but not to the territorial sea, with its bed and subsoil, is that the latter is in reality part of the territory of a region, otherwise the deeming provision would have been applied to it as well. The point seems unanswerable.

What makes the Supreme Court's decision so palpably misconceived and wrong is not so much the holding that the territorial sea is not part of the territory of the eight littoral states as that it is not part of Nigeria's territory either. Perhaps its decision and pronouncements upon this latter point need, even at the risk of appearing tediously repetitive, to be set out here in order to put them in better context and to enable attention to be focused on them at one glance.

The Court has located "the southern boundary of Nigeria as the Atlantic Ocean, that is, the sea" (at p. 8 of the Judgment), and that of the eight littoral states as being "co-terminous with the southern boundary of Nigeria" (at p. 9). Re-affirming this, the Court again said that "Nigeria is a coastal or maritime Nation – its southern boundary is the Atlantic Ocean" (at p.14). It accepted the federal government's contention, as put forward by its counsel, Chief Williams SAN, that "the seaward limit of Nigeria is the low-water mark but Nigeria in its sovereignty and by the custom of the international community exercises jurisdiction beyond that limit" (at p.14). Accepting again the federal government's contention, it goes on to say:

> I have shown earlier in this judgment that the Imperial Power that created the country Nigeria put as her southern boundary the Sea – the Atlantic Ocean. I have also found that where the sea is a boundary, the boundary mark is the low-water mark. The low-water mark, therefore forms the boundary of the land territory of, not only the eight littoral States of Nigeria, but of Nigeria as well (at p. 14).

After considering the international conventions applicable to the matter, the Judgment then concludes as follows:

> The claim by the plaintiff of sovereignty over the territorial sea of Nigeria and the Exclusive Economic Zone does not extend the land territory of Nigeria beyond what is provided for in sections 2 and 3 of the Constitution ……. The sum total of all I have been saying above is that none of the Territorial Waters Act, Sea Fisheries Act and the Exclusive Economic Zone Act has extended the land territory of Nigeria beyond its constitutional limit, although the Acts give municipal effect to international treaties entered into by Nigeria by virtue of its membership, as a sovereign State, of the Comity of Nations. These treaties confer sovereignty and other rights on Nigeria over certain areas of the sea (the Atlantic Ocean) adjacent to her coastline (pp, 17-18).

The decision that the territorial sea lying off the coast of the eight littoral states is not part of Nigeria's territory is outrightly contradicted by decisions from other common law jurisdictions cited with approval by the Court (at p.12). It is enough to examine only the one among them with the most direct bearing on the Nigerian Case – *Re: Ownership of Offshore Mineral Rights* (1968) 65 DLR (2d) 353 where the Supreme Court of Canada held that

> the effect of that Act, coupled with the Geneva Convention of 1958, is that Canada is recognised in international law as having sovereignty over a territorial sea three nautical miles wide. **It is part of the territory of Canada** (at p. 375 emphasis supplied).

The Act referred to is the Territorial Sea and Fishing Zone Act 1964 (Canada).

The Supreme Court of Canada is certainly right that the territorial sea contiguous to one of the constituent provinces is part of the territory of Canada, so is the U. S. Supreme Court in awarding to the United States "ownership" of the territorial sea lying off the coast of one of the constituent states of the Union: see *United States vs State of California* 332 U.S. 19 — another of the cases cited with approval by the Nigerian Supreme Court.

Why, then, in the face of such decisions from other common law jurisdictions, accepted by the Nigerian Supreme Court, and which the learned Justice, Ogundare JSC who spoke for the Court, said he has "read" (at p. 12), did the Court decide that the low-water mark is the seaward boundary of Nigeria or that the territorial sea is not part of the territory of Nigeria? The reason lies in the dilemma created for the Court by the Constitution of Nigeria, which is different in this respect from those of the United States, Canada and Australia. Had the Court accepted that the territorial sea is part of Nigeria's territory, how is that to be reconciled with what the Court referred to as the "constitutional limit" of Nigeria's territory? The federal government and the Court would have had then to accept the contention of the eight littoral states that:

> Nigeria consists of the aggregate of the territories of all the 36 States of the Federation and the Federal Capital Territory and that, constitutionally, therefore, Nigeria cannot have any other territory outside this aggregate (at p. 13).

The contention is unanswerable, irrefutable. There is just no escape from it. Sections 2(2) and 3(1) of the Constitution provide that Nigeria shall consist of 36 named states and a Federal Capital Territory, not that it shall consist of 36 named states, a Federal Capital Territory and the territorial sea (with its bed and subsoil).

The territorial sea can only be part of the territory of Nigeria, as it undoubtedly is according to the international conventions, local statutes and decisions from other common law jurisdictions mentioned above, if it is part of the territory of the littoral states. It is the Nigerian Constitution that governs the matter, not that of some other country.

With the greatest respect, the Supreme Court should not have tried, as it did, to avoid the clear, inescapable effect of the international conventions, local statutes and decisions from other common law jurisdictions mentioned above taken together with Sections 2(2) and 3(1) of the Constitution of Nigeria. The territorial sea is and must be part of the territory of the eight littoral states for it to be part of Nigeria's territory, as it certainly is by international law and by the statute law of Nigeria.

The Beneficial Title to the Rights Vested in the Federal Government in the Territorial Sea (Assuming it not to be Part of Nigeria's Territory) and the Continental Shelf

Assuming for purposes of the discussions in this section that the territorial sea (with its bed and subsoil) is not part of Nigeria's territory – an erroneous position as shown in the last section – the question arises as to who is entitled to the benefits of the rights accorded to the country in the area by international law. The same question arises in respect of the continental shelf to which indisputably the country's sovereignty or dominion does not extend.

The contention of Cross River State (9th Defendant in the Suit), upon which the Court made no pronouncement, is that the rights are held and are to be exercised by the federal government as trustee or custodian for the littoral states by virtue, if not of their ownership, then, at least of the contiguity of the territorial sea (with its bed and subsoil) and the continental shelf to their land territory. There is certainly a point in the contention, though it is perhaps overstated. For, if it be correct, the littoral states will then be entitled to the entirety, not just 13 per cent, of the revenue from natural resources located in the territorial sea and the continental shelf. The littoral states are members of a comity of states in a federal union; the other members of the union are entitled to share in the benefits, but the littoral states have an undeniable right to a special compensatory allocation because of the hazards of ecological or environmental degradation by pollution resulting from their proximity to exploration and exploitation activities in the area. The rationale for this special compensatory allocation is stated more fully above.

Interpretation of Section 162(2) Proviso

For ease of reference and to help understanding of the discussion in this section, (which proceeds on the basis that the territorial sea is not part of the littoral states) the proviso to Section 162(2) of the 1999 Constitution needs to be set out in its exact terms. It reads:

> Provided that the principle of derivation shall be constantly reflected in any approved formula as being not less than thirteen per cent of the revenue accruing to the Federation Account directly from any natural resources.

There is an obvious imprecision, clumsiness and lack of specificity in the wording of the proviso. (The proviso would have connected more rationally and logically to the main provision in Section 162(2) had derivation been among the principles particularised there, instead of being introduced for the first time in the proviso, as it were, out of the blues.) Unlike the provision in the 1960 and 1963 Constitutions, which spoke specifically of revenue derived from **"mineral extracted from that Region"** (emphasis supplied), the proviso makes no explicit reference to the physical location of natural resources within the territory of a state. Had it done so, its meaning would have been put beyond dispute. Nor is the on-shore/off-shore dichotomy mentioned anywhere in the proviso. As it is, the proviso leaves it open for argument whether the "principle of derivation" applies only to revenue from natural resources located within the land territory of a state or whether it applies as well to revenue from natural resources located in the sea bed and its subsoil contiguous to the land territory of a state. In failing thus to make any reference whatsoever to the physical location of the natural resources to which the "principle of derivation" is to be applied, the proviso created a problem of interpretation. It may be that the omission was deliberate, and was based on a belief that the past history of revenue allocation in Nigeria has fixed a definite meaning upon the words "principle of derivation".

Apparently taking it for granted as something beyond dispute that "derivation" could only refer to revenue from natural resources located within the land territory of a state, the Judgment of the Supreme Court proceeded on the basis that the question for determination was the boundary of the littoral states, and that that would provide the answer to the matter in dispute. No attempt was therefore made to interpret Section 162(2) proviso from the standpoint of what it really means in the context. Had that been done, perhaps the Court might have come to a different decision. The Supreme Court therefore erred in treating the case as one for the determination of boundary, as prayed by the federal government, rather than one for the interpretation of Section 162(2) proviso of the Constitution which, properly and purposively construed, does not require the determination of boundary. It must be said, with the greatest respect, that the Judgment creates the impression in one's mind that, in some parts at any rate, it is an attempt to rationalise conclusions arrived at beforehand.

The decision reached by the Court may well have been suggested by the *prima facie* or literary meaning of the word "derivation" as defined in a dictionary, i.e., "a drawing or obtaining, **as from a source"** (emphasis supplied). But the etymology of the word is not conclusive. It is the meaning of derivation as a "principle", not as a mere isolated word, that needs to be ascertained as a matter of purposive interpretation. A principle is not defined by the etymology of words alone; practice over a period also supplies a relevant context to be taken into account, and may impress upon a word a meaning different from the *prima facie* or dictionary one. Such an approach is particularly necessary in the case of words used in a constitution whose interpretation, as the courts have constantly emphasised, calls for an approach informed by its character, not as a body of rules on paper, but as a living instrument for the government of a society comprising millions of people of divergent interests.

Thus, the interpretative question to which the proviso to Section

162(2) gives rise is whether the "principle of derivation", **as understood and applied in Nigeria over the long period from independence in 1960** gives to a littoral state a right to a compensatory share of revenue from oil located in the bed of the sea and subsoil contiguous to its land territory. Putting it differently, is the "principle of derivation", **viewed in its historical context,** to be applied to only one or both of the revenues from on-shore and off-shore oil, with the former (revenue from on-shore oil) predicated on "ownership" of land and the latter on contiguity? Speaking generally and before considering the historical evidence, there is no good, justifiable ground for discriminating between ownership of territory (dominion) and contiguity in the application of the principle of derivation. The considerations for a special compensatory allocation for the oil producing states are largely the same in both cases, namely, ecological or environmental degradation caused by pollution – see above. Except as a matter of pure legal sophistry, why, it may be asked, should it make a difference whether the entitlement of the littoral States to a special compensatory allocation of revenue from oil is because of their notional ownership of the territory where the oil is located or because of the contiguity of the oil location to their land territory? The whole on-shore/off-shore oil dichotomy is unreal and irrational, and is probably artificially invented to deprive the littoral states of what, in reason and equity, should be their due.

Now to the historical evidence. The history begins with the 1960 Constitution, Section 134(6) of which provides that "for the purposes of this section, the continental shelf of a Region shall be deemed to be part of that Region". (The implication of applying this deeming provision to the continental shelf but not to the territorial sea, with its bed and subsoil, is that the latter is in reality part of the territory of a Region, otherwise the deeming provision would have been applied to it as well.) This provision deeming the continental shelf to be part of the territory of a region was repeated in the 1963 Constitution (Section 140(6)), and remained in operation until the period after 1971. With the greatest respect, it is remarkable that, instead of treating the provision as a historical factor of great significance in the interpretation of the meaning of the "principle of derivation", as used in the proviso to Section 162(2), the Supreme Court indulged itself in a legal sophistry concerning the meaning of the word "deemed", saying "the subsection did not make the continental shelf part of the Region but only deemed it to be part of the Region solely for the purpose of the section" at p. 21.

The on-shore/off-shore oil dichotomy crept into the constitutional arrangements for revenue sharing during the period after 1971. Revenue sharing during that period alternated between the inclusion or exclusion of revenue from off-shore oil in allocations based on derivation until the 1979 Constitution, which made no provision for allocation based on derivation. It merely provided in Section 149(2) that "any amount standing to the credit of the Federation Account shall be distributed among the federal and state governments and the local government councils in each state, on such term and in such manner as may be prescribed by the National Assembly".

Pursuant to the power conferred upon it by Section 149(2) aforementioned, the National Assembly in 1982 enacted the Allocation of Revenue (Federation Account etc) Act Cap. 16, Laws of the Federation 1990, which, by the clear implication of its provisions, and by the omission of the deeming provision, reintroduced the on-shore/off-shore oil dichotomy. By its Section 2(2)(a), "a sum equivalent to 2 per cent of the revenue derived from **minerals extracted from the mineral producing areas of Nigeria** shall be paid directly to the mineral producing states in direct proportion to the value of minerals extracted from the area of each such State". (The Act is examined extensively in my *Federalism in Nigeria* (1983), pp. 192 – 215). And so matters remained until the Act was amended in 1992 by Decree 106 which, while providing for the allocation, on the basis of derivation, of "1 per cent of the revenue accruing to the Federation Account derived from minerals" (Section 1), goes on in section 4A(6) to state, in clear, unambiguous words, that "in the application of this provision, the dichotomy of on-shore and off-shore oil revenue is hereby abolished".

That remained the law until the 1999 Constitution came into force on May 29, 1999 or rather until the Supreme Court decision was handed down on 5 April 2002. Thus, for a period of more than 20 years from October, 1960 to April 5, 2002, including the 10 years up to and after the 1999 Constitution came into force, the revenue allocation to the oil-producing, littoral states on the basis of derivation included revenue derived from oil located in the territorial sea and continental shelf, with their bed and soil.

Interpreted in the context of this past history of revenue allocation in the country, and considering that the proviso to Section 162(2) of the 1999 Constitution does not say in explicit terms that the "principle of derivation" shall apply only to revenue from natural resources located in the land territory of a state, a purposive interpretation of the proviso should apply its derivation provision to revenue from both on-shore and off-shore oil. With great respect, the Supreme Court erred in failing to interpret the proviso in the manner here suggested and therefore came to a wrong decision; it failed to interpret it at all.

Compatibility or Otherwise with the Autonomy of the State Governments and with True Federalism of the Power Vested in the National Assembly to Prescribe a Revenue Sharing Formula

Although the point did not arise, and was therefore not addressed in the judgment of the Supreme Court in this Case, the compatibility or otherwise with the autonomy of the state governments and with true federalism, of the power vested in the National Assembly to prescribe a revenue sharing formula has a significant bearing upon the whole system of revenue sharing in Nigeria.

The essence of federalism is that both the general and regional governments possess, in respect of some matters, an authority which is both independent and exclusive of the other. There must be no subordination of the one to the other on matters within their respective exclusive spheres. But the independence required is not just independence with regard to power to regulate and execute such matters. It requires also independence with respect to the means or resources necessary for the effective performance of the functions of legislation and execution. A government invested with independent and exclusive legislative and executive powers over certain matters but with no independent financial resources for carrying them out has no real independence. Its lack of independent financial resources must necessarily subordinate it to the authority vested with control of those resources, which can be used to hamper or impede the performance of its legislative and executive functions, even to the point that its independence in those matters is altogether destroyed.

Financial independence is thus indispensable to real independence in legislative and executive matters. The principle must therefore be accepted that federalism requires that both the general and regional governments must each have under its own independent control the financial resources necessary for the performance of its exclusive functions – K.C. Wheare, *Federal Government (1953) p.97.* It is a principle that characterises the federal constitutions of the United States, Australia and Switzerland. It has been stated thus in the *Federalist*:

> It is as necessary that the state governments should be able to command the means of supplying their wants, as that the national government should possess the like faculty in respect of the wants of the Union. *Federalist No 31.*

Now, the effect of the power given to the National Assembly to prescribe the terms for sharing federally-collected revenue between the federal, state and local government is to place in the hands of an organ of the federal government the control of 90 per cent, of the total revenue sources of the states. By means of this power the National Assembly can reduce the state governments to the position of almost complete subordination to the federal government, by making the allocation on terms that will allow to the states only a very small share of the revenue – so small as not to have any meaningful bearing on their needs as determined by the functions assigned to them by the constitution. To take an extreme example, an allocation of, say 5 per cent, to the state and local governments, though it may be against the spirit of the provision, will be in accordance with its letters, and therefore a constitutionally valid exercise of the National Assembly's unqualified discretion to prescribe the proportion to go to the state governments.

It is not of course being suggested that there is any real likelihood of the National Assembly, in the exercise of its power, ever disregarding the needs and legitimate claims of the state and local governments in the way supposed in the example above. It is true that the National Assembly is an organ of the federal government, and that the relation of its members to the people in the various states is limited to matters within federal competence, which may thus dispose them to want to put their interest first in order to make sure that they and the federal executive have adequate funds for the discharge of their functions. On the other hand, since the members are removed from the actual disbursement of the funds of the federal government, they ought not really to have any personal involvement in the matter on the side of the federal government, such as to render them incapable of forming a detached and objective judgment on the matter. They ought therefore to be motivated rather by a desire to ensure that the allocation is properly guided by the probable cost of carrying out the functions assigned to each government, so far as this can be ascertained by an acceptable method of weighting them. Not being personally or institutionally involved in the disbursement of the funds of the federal government, therefore, the National Assembly members may be expected to approach the sharing from a national rather than a partisan standpoint.

Furthermore, it was envisaged that the exercise of the power by the National Assembly to prescribe the terms of allocation will be preceded in every case by wide consultations and report by a body of experts. The Constitution Drafting Committee (CDC) had in fact proposed a permanent fiscal review commission to be established by the constitution. The Constituent Assembly rejected this — not of course the idea of a permanent review commission but of one established directly by the constitution. A Revenue Mobilisation Allocation and Fiscal Commission (RMAFC) is now established by the 1999 Constitution with a representative from each state and with power, among other things, to "review, from time to time, the revenue allocation formulas and principles in operation to ensure conformity with changing realities". But the National Assembly, in the exercise of its power under Section 162(3) of the Constitution, is not limited or bound by a review carried out by the Commission.

As envisaged, the enactment by the National Assembly of a law prescribing the terms of allocation was in fact preceded by the appointment of a revenue allocation commission, which consulted widely throughout the country, by means of public sittings held in Lagos and in the then 19 state capitals, private consultations with interested individuals and groups, in particular the various governments in the federation, each of whom submitted a written memorandum embodying its views upon the matter. The terms of reference of the commission were, among other things, to examine the present formula for revenue allocation having regard to the need to ensure that each tier of government in the federation has adequate revenue to enable it discharge its functions as laid down in the constitution, and to recommend new proposals for revenue allocation between the federal, state and local governments. The report of the Commission showed a thorough and mature consideration of the problem from an objective and national standpoint. No assembly representative of the nation can fail to be guided by the recommendations of a commission conducted with such terms of reference and on lines such as those adopted in this case.

It is also not intended to suggest that prescribing the terms of allocation in the constitution, as the 1963 Constitution did, is necessarily to be preferred. While it guarantees to both the federal and state governments independence with respect to financial resources for carrying out their functions, it suffers from the serious disadvantage of being unalterable except by the rigid procedure for constitutional amendment, notwithstanding that some functions assigned to one tier of government may, in consequence of changing economic and social circumstances, have become more expensive than those assigned to the other. For this reason, revenue sharing should be seen as a problem to which, in the words of Sir Kenneth Wheare, "there is and can be no final solution," but only "adjustments and re-allocations in the light of changing conditions." (*Ibid,* p. 123). The adjustments required are perhaps best effected through the process of ordinary law-making rather than that of constitutional amendment. This is the consideration that induced both the CDC and the Constituent Assembly to entrust to the National Assembly the function of prescribing the terms of allocation.

The point being made here is not therefore that the power to prescribe the terms of allocation should not have been given to the National Assembly, but that it should not have been given to it without qualification designed to ensure that the terms to be prescribed would be rationally related to the functions to be performed by each tier of government under the division of powers as prescribed in the constitution. Thus, Section 162(3) of the 1999 Constitution should have read:

> any amount standing to the credit of the Federation Account shall be distributed among the federal and state governments, and the local government councils in each state, on such terms and in such manner as may be prescribed by the National Assembly, **based on (or having regard to) the relative cost of discharging the functions of each government and the other resources available to it under the constitution and after considering a report on the matter by an independent review panel (i.e. RMAFC).**

The words in bold are the kind of qualification needed to ensure that the state and local governments' share of federally collected revenue is not to be at the arbitrary whim of the National Assembly, but is to be determined by the Assembly according to some constitutionally laid down guideline which is also judicially enforceable. That is perhaps what the Aboyade Technical Committee on Revenue Allocation (1977) had in mind when, after stating the arguments against prescribing a formula in the constitution, it nevertheless concluded that "on balance we are convinced that it would be in the overall interest of the nation to provide a minimum basis for ascertained revenue to each constituent government, which is appropriately guaranteed by legislation against the vicissitudes of changing political administration at the Centre (*ibid* at p.77).

As regards sharing among the states *inter se*, and among the local government councils *inter se*, not only is the National Assembly an appropriate body for the purpose, but also its power is qualified by the principles set out in Section 162(2) of the Constitution.

CHAPTER 6

Local Government in a Federal and Presidential System

Proposal to Establish Local Government in the Nigerian Constitution as an Independent Tier of Government

From the inception of its work, the Constitution Drafting Committee (CDC) in Nigeria was faced with the novel demand that local government be separate from, and independent of, the state government. The demand seemed to have been encouraged or inspired by the new importance which the federal military government's reforms had given to local government. In a country which had been starved of political expression by ten years of military dictatorship, the popular participation in local government introduced by the reforms naturally excited great interest, and prompted the demand that the fruits of those reforms, described as the most important legacy of the military government, should be entrenched in the constitution.

The demand was well-intentioned. It was motivated by a desire to protect local government against the great political manipulations to which it had been subjected in the past. The aim, in the words of the sub-committee of the CDC, was to stop the state governments from "cavalierly and whimsically tinkering with local government organs." There had been too many cases of elected local government councils being capriciously dissolved and replaced by appointed agents of the state government, the so-called caretaker committees or management boards or sole administrators. There had also been neglect and denial of funds for carrying out the functions assigned to local government. In the result, local government had been reduced to mere tools in the hands of the state government to be used and manipulated as its whims dictated. Against this background, the local government reforms of the federal military government were seen as a great deliverance which should be consolidated and entrenched in the constitution.

But it is necessary to understand what is novel and objectionable about the demand. It was not just a demand that democratically elected local government councils and the functions appropriate to them should be given recognition in the constitution while at the same time maintaining their character as agencies of the state government. If that were what was being demanded, there would be nothing novel or strange about it. For, in this country we have become familiar with the device of having certain functions of government institutionalised in the constitution by vesting them in independent bodies. For example, under the 1979 Constitution, census and elections are, on account of their sensitiveness, vested in independent commissions established by the constitution, the aim being to insulate them from political influence and interference. But all that independence for this purpose really means is that the commissions are free from outside direction or control in the discharge of their functions.

Independence does not mean that the commissions exist as separate entities from the federal government. On the contrary, they are agencies of that government, and therefore integral parts of it, just like the other bodies or institutions – ministries, departments, etc – of which the federal government is composed. What is more, they are secondary agencies, ranking below the primary organs, i.e. the president, the National Assembly and the courts. Indeed they are subordinate agencies in that the appointment and removal of their members are controlled by the primary political organs – the president and the National Assembly.

The independence demanded for the local government councils goes beyond institutionalising local government functions in democratically elected councils which, while their existence is guaranteed in the constitution, would nevertheless exist and function as agencies of the state government. What was being demanded is to terminate the status of local government as an agency of the state government, and to establish it as a government existing separately from, and independently of, the state government. The division of governmental powers and revenue in the constitution would thus be transformed from a dual to a tripartite basis involving the federal and state and local governments on the same principle of equality between them. Under this proposal, a local government is to relate to the state government in exactly the same way as the latter relates to the federal government. Not only is its existence and democratic character to be guaranteed in the constitution, it is also to have reserved to it a sphere of functions from which the state government would be excluded. It is important to emphasise this point. The functions of local government, however they are defined, are not to be concurrent to the local government and the state government, they are to belong to the former to the complete exclusion of the state government.

The effect of a tripartite division of powers would be to bring a local government into direct relation with the federal government based, as already stated, on the principle of autonomy and equality between all three tiers of government. Local government would thereby cease to be a function of the state government, making it as unconstitutional for the state government to act on matters reserved exclusively to the local government as it would be for it to act on those reserved exclusively to the federal government. Herein lies the novelty and strangeness of the demand.

Consistently with this principle of equality, amendments to the draft Constitution prepared by the CDC were tabled in the Constituent Assembly, which sought to establish local government councils and the offices of chairman and deputy chairman of a local government council in the same sections that establish the federal and state assemblies and the offices of president, vice-president, governor and deputy governor. Thus, where the draft constitution had provided that "there shall be for the Republic, a president and a vice-president and for each state a governor and a deputy governor who shall each be elected to office in accordance with the provisions of this constitution," the proposed amendment sought to insert "and chairman and deputy chairman of each local government council" after deputy governor.

The mover of the amendment had boldly asserted that the chairman and deputy chairman of a local government council were the "structural equivalents" of the president, vice-president, governor and deputy governor, and must have "the same constitutional rights". Similarly, local government councils were said to be the structural equivalents of the National Assembly and the State Houses of Assembly. This brings out quite clearly the conceptual premise on which the amendments were based, i.e. that the local government is "the structural equivalent" of the federal and state governments. As was pointed out during the debates in the Constituent Assembly, the logic of the demand and the amendments based on it would make it necessary that the area of authority of a local government, its executive authority, the qualifications and disqualifications for elections, the method of elections, tenure of office of the chairman, his removal, etc., would all have to be provided in the constitution, just as in the case of the organs of the federal and state governments, with the result of course that they would become unalterable except by the rigid procedure for constitutional amendment - a procedure in which, in accordance with the requirements of federalism, the National Assembly, the State Houses of Assembly and the local government councils would have to be associated.

The involvement of the federal government in local government in the way implied in this demand would have the effect of abolishing the distinction between matters of local concern and those of national concern. The basis for the division of powers under federalism is that, within the framework of a general government charged with responsibility for matters of national concern, those of local concern should be managed by the state governments. Now, local government is an example **par excellence** of a matter of local concern. As such it is universally recognised as the exclusive responsibility of the state governments. Federal government involvement in local government is thus a contradiction of the very idea of federalism.

While accepting the general demand that the constitution should contain provisions on local government, the CDC had sought to minimise the departure from principle involved in this by putting those provisions in the form of a non-justiciable directive to the state governments on how to exercise their undoubted power over local government. By this device, a state government would constitutionally be under a duty to conform to, observe and apply the directive, but no court could enquire into the question whether or not any of its laws or acts is in conformity therewith. But to the advocates of an independent local government in the Constituent Assembly, this was unacceptable. The non-justiciability of the directive was considered incompatible with their view of local government as an independent tier of government. The provisions had therefore to be made justiciable in the constitution as finally adopted by the Constituent Assembly. Apart from this, the provisions are substantially the same as those in the CDC draft; none of the amendments in the Constituent Assembly mentioned above got incorporated in the end.

We shall now proceed to consider the exact nature of the arrangement embodied in the constitution as enacted.

Recognition of a State Government's Power over Local Government

The central principle of the provisions of the constitution on local government is the recognition of the state government's power over local government. This results from the fact that, under the division of powers, local government is not (except for certain aspects of it) mentioned either in the body of the constitution or in the legislative lists as being within federal competence; as a residual matter therefore it lies within the exclusive authority of the state governments (section 4(7) and section 5(2)). Thus the authority of a state government over local government derives from the fact that it is a residual matter, and not, as is commonly supposed, from the provision of the constitution requiring every state government to ensure the existence of democratically elected local government councils under a law which provides for their establishment, structure, composition, finance and functions (section 7(1)). That provision is not a grant of power; it is, instead, a limitation on power. It assumes that a state government has power over local government under some other provision of the constitution. Subject to exceptions to be mentioned later, the whole subject of local government is a residual matter, and as such within the exclusive competence of the state governments under sections 4(7) and 5(2) of the constitution.

However, the provision (section 7(1)) is an explicit recognition by the constitution that the power to establish local government, to define its structure, composition and functions belongs to the state governments. If local government is a function of the state government and only the state government has the constitutional power to establish local government and to define its structure and functions, it clearly and necessarily follows that local government is not an independent third tier of government, but only an agency or creation of the state government. No doubt, in common usage, it is often referred to as a third tier of government. There is nothing improper in the usage, so long as it is understood that a local government is only an agency of the state government. It is one of the agencies or bodies which, together with the primary organs - the governor, the House of Assembly and the courts - make up the state government. It is given a considerable measure of autonomy from the primary political organs of the state government, i.e. the governor and the House of Assembly, but it is not completely independent of them. For example, there are no constitutional fetters on the power of the State House of Assembly to prescribe the organisational structure of a local government in terms of the functionaries appropriate to it, e.g. chairman, deputy chairman, secretary, treasurer, supervisory councillors, etc., and to prescribe how many councillors should compose it and the division of a local government area into wards for this purpose as well as the terms and tenure of office and removal of office holders and other councillors. The point needs perhaps to be stressed that the things specified in section 7(1) - establishment, structures, composition, finances and functions - are only aspects but are not exhaustive of local government as a subject-matter of legislative power belonging to the state governments as a residual matter.

Restrictions on State Government's Power over Local Government

(i)   Guarantee of Local Government by Democratically Elected Local Government Councils

The constitution guarantees "the system of local government by democratically elected local government councils," and directs that "the government of every state shall ensure their existence under a Law which provides for the establishment, structure, composition, finance and functions of such councils," (section 7(1)). The purpose of this provision is to restrict the state government's power over local government by imposing a mandatory directive on how the power is to be exercised. With the restriction implied in the guarantee and mandatory directive, a state government cannot, as hitherto, conduct local government as it pleases; it is bound to conduct it through local government councils democratically elected under a law that provides for their establishment, structure, etc. the concern is to ensure that a state government will not abuse its power, by, for example, using its own appointed agents to conduct the business of local government. The effect of the provision is thus to take away from a state government the discretion normally implied in a power. Instead, it obliges a state government not only to enact the necessary legislation to provide for the establishment, structure, composition, functions and finances of local government councils, but, more importantly, to ensure the existence of democratically elected local government councils under such law.

Whether the duty thus cast upon a state government can be compelled raises an interesting question. But even if a state government cannot be compelled to establish democratically elected local government councils, it can be restrained from using its own appointed agents to conduct local government. Thus, where, pending such time as democratically elected local government councils could by established, management committees were established by law to conduct local government in Lagos State, and the state governor was authorised to appoint their members, the law was held to contravene section 7 of the constitution, and was accordingly declared void, (see *Adeniji-Adele & Others v. Governor of Lagos State & Others* (1982)). The suspension and subsequent dissolution by the governor of the elected local government councils, and the appointment in their places of management committees were also declared void as a violation of the guarantee of local government by democratically elected local government councils. An order of permanent injunction was issued against the state governor, his servants or agents restraining them from establishing committees of management and from appointing the members thereof.

(ii) Area of Authority of a Local Government

The extent of the power of a state government to prescribe the area of authority of a local government has been the subject of much dispute. Two provisions of the constitution failed to be considered. There is the directive in section 7(2) that "the person authorised by law to prescribe the area over which a local government council may exercise authority shall -

(a) define such area as clearly as practicable; and

(b) ensure, to the extent to which it may be reasonably justifiable, that in defining such area, regard is paid to
      i. the common interest of the community in the area,

      ii. traditional association of the community, and

      iii. administrative convenience."

This provision assumes the power of the State House of Assembly to prescribe the area of authority of a local government or to delegate the power to some functionary of the state government provided that the prescription conforms with the directive.

In a decision handed down on March 17, 1980, Justice Balogun of the High Court of Lagos State held unconstitutional and void the delegation to the state governor under the Local Government Law (1980) of power to delimit the areas of authority of local government councils in the state, on the ground that,

> this being a very important subject ... it was not within the contemplation of the makers of the constitution that the State Assembly will delegate to the governor the power to define the area of authority of a local government without the House of Assembly setting out the standards which an area of authority of a local government must conform with, (see *Balogun v. Attorney-General of Lagos State* (1980)).

While the absence of "standard of action" renders the delegation of legislative power unconstitutional, it seems clear on the authority of the American decisions on the point that the standards need not be set out in the statute itself if they can be gathered from the legislative programme of which the particular statute is part or from other relevant sources. The constitution being such a relevant source, the provisions in section 7(2) quoted above should be read into the Local Government Law. These provisions set out quite adequate standards to guide the creation of local government areas by the governor in pursuance of power delegated to him by the House of Assembly.

It is contended on the other hand that a state government has no power at all with respect to the extent of the area of a local government. The 1999 Constitution has radically altered the position on the matter. Whilst under the 1979 Constitution, the area of each state was defined by reference to named local areas, those named areas were not explicitly stated to be local government areas. Nowhere in the constitution were they referred to as local government areas. It just happened that they corresponded to the names of existing local government areas. But some of them. e.g. Abakaliki, Onitsha or Enugu in Anambra State, are also the names of existing towns. It follows that the areas named could be references either to existing local government areas, existing towns or simply local communities comprising a group of towns. They are perhaps better regarded simply as local communities. But whether they are regarded as local communities or as local government areas, the important point is that their designation in the constitution carried no implication as to the number of local government **councils** that may exist within each of them. The area of a state, as defined by reference to the named localities, would not have been increased or decreased by the establishment of two or more local government councils within each of the named areas.

Furthermore, the boundaries of each named area were not defined in the constitution so as to identify its territorial extent and thereby to preclude the transfer of any part of it to another area by a law made by the state legislature. So long as all the named areas remained in existence, the extent of the land area comprised in each of them had no constitutional significance; the constitution would not be amended or violated in any way by the transfer of any part of the territory of one area to another.

Under the 1999 Constitution, however, the areas named as forming the area of a state are explicitly designated as local government areas. Furthermore, it is provided that "there shall be seven hundred and sixty-eight local government areas in Nigeria as shown in the second column of Part 1 of the First Schedule to this constitution" (section 3(6)). This provision establishes no local governments for the local government areas so created. The distinction between the creation of local government areas and the establishment of local governments for the local government areas so created is one that needs to be appreciated.

Consequent upon the provision in section 3(6) above, a procedure is provided for the creation of new local government areas or the adjustment of the boundary of an existing local government area by a law of the State House of Assembly (section 8(3) and (4)). But for the creation of a new local government area under a state law to take effect, the National Assembly has to enact a law amending the provision of the constitution relating to the number of local government areas (section 8(5)). For this purpose, the House of Assembly concerned shall, after the creation of a new local government area, make adequate returns to each House of the National Assembly (section 8(6)). But suppose the National Assembly fails or refuses to enact the necessary law to amend the constitution for this purpose.

(iii) Local Government Elections

The power of a state government over local government elections is restricted in three respects. First, the regulation of registration of voters and of the procedure relating to local government elections is made concurrent to the State Houses of Assembly and the National Assembly, which means that in the event of conflict, the National Assembly's enactment prevails (Item E, concurrent legislative list). A question has arisen concerning the effect of this provision on the status of an existing state law, since at the commencement of the 1979 Constitution, local government elections and the registration of voters for purposes of such elections were regulated by the Local Government Edict 1976 and the Local Government Electoral Regulations 1976 made by each state government.

The provision of the 1979 as well as the 1999 Constitution regarding the status of an existing law is that such law is to be deemed to be an act of the National Assembly or a law of a State House of Assembly to the extent that it relates to a matter within the competence of the National Assembly or a State House of Assembly (section 274(1) 1979; s.315(1)1999). The High Court of Lagos State has construed this to mean that an existing law on a concurrent matter is thereby made an exclusively federal enactment, and is to be applied as such by the state courts; and that accordingly the Lagos State Local Government Electoral Regulations 1976 made by the state governor under section 20 of the Local Government Edict 1976 of the State became a federal law, *(Lawal v. Lagos State Electoral Commission* (1980)). While it is true that the electoral regulations became a federal law by virtue of the constitutional provision relating to existing laws, they do not thereby cease to be a state law. The effect of the constitutional provision (section 274(1)) is to make an existing law on a concurrent matter a federal as well as a state enactment. But, since its operation as a state law is suspended, it is as a federal enactment, rather than as a state enactment, that the state courts should apply it. The provision of the Local Government (Basic Constitutional and Transitional Provisions) Decree No. 36 of 1998 (repealed with effect from 29 May, 1999 by Decree 63 of that year) fixing the tenure of local government chairmen and councillors at 3 years must be deemed to be an exclusively state law, that (i.e. such tenure) being a residual matter.

But while a State House of Assembly may, concurrently with the National Assembly, legislate on the registration of voters, the compilation of a register of voters for all elections is vested exclusively in a federal agency, the Independent National Electoral Commission (INEC) (Section 78 and Schedule 3, Part 1, Paragraph 1). INEC is specifically empowered to ensure that the register of voters is prepared and maintained in such form as to facilitate its use for local government elections (Schedule 3, Part 1, Paragraph 1). A state electoral commission is also established in the constitution, but its role in this connection is merely to advise INEC on the compilation of the register in so far as it is applicable to local government elections in the state (Schedule 3, Part 11, Paragraph 4(b)).

While both the National Assembly and a State House of Assembly may legislate on the procedure for local government elections and on the registration of voters for that purpose, the elections are to be organised and conducted exclusively by the state government through the State Independent Electoral Commission which is specifically empowered to "organise, undertake and supervise all elections to local government councils within the state" (Schedule 3, Part 11, Paragraph 4(a)). But the holding of an election is conditioned by the existence of a register of voters prepared and maintained by INEC in a form designed to facilitate its use for the purpose of local government elections. A State Independent Electoral Commission cannot therefore organise, undertake and conduct local government elections if, for any reason, there is no register of voters prepared and maintained by INEC for the purpose. The point arose in a case in Lagos State in 1980.

The electoral commission for the state was organising local government elections to be held throughout the state on March 29, 1980. It had planned to use for the purpose of the register of voters compiled by FEDECO in 1977/78 for the presidential, gubernatorial and legislative elections in 1979. The register was based on constituencies for the legislative elections, which made it clearly unsuitable for use in local government elections based on wards. Besides, the law under which the register was prepared - the Electoral Act 1977 – explicitly excepted local government elections from its application.

The High Court held that the law relating to the registration of voters for purpose of local government elections in Lagos State is not the Electoral Act 1977, but the State's Electoral Regulations 1976, regulation 7 of which required registration of voters to be carried out for every local government election on dates to be prescribed by the state governor *(Lawal v. Lagos State Electoral Commission* (1980)). It follows that, unless and until a register has been prepared by FEDECO under regulation 7 above, the Lagos State Electoral Commission could not lawfully hold, organise, undertake and conduct local government elections in the state. The court accordingly made a declaratory order that the holding of local government elections by the State Electoral

Commission on the basis of the 1977/78 register of voters prepared under the Electoral Act 1977 would be null and void as being unconstitutional as well as contrary to public policy and repugnant to natural justice. It was contrary to public policy and natural justice because, even had the Electoral Act 1977 made the register applicable to local government elections, its use for the elections in 1980 after the lapse of nearly three years would have resulted in the disenfranchisement of a large number of people who qualified for registration in the interval.

By an order of perpetual injunction, the State Electoral Commission was restrained from holding, organising or conducting local government elections in the state unless and until a register of voters for the purposes of such elections is compiled by FEDECO or until a new register of voters for the purpose of election to the State House Assembly is prepared, and adapted to make it suitable for use in local government elections.

The third restriction on the power of a state government over local government elections relates to the franchise for such elections and the qualifications and disqualifications for candidates. The state government, to whom the power to legislate on the subject belongs exclusively as a residual matter, is not at liberty to make the franchise and the qualifications and disqualifications for candidates more restrictive than are prescribed by the constitution for election to the State House of Assembly. It is constitutionally directed to "ensure that every person who is entitled to vote or be voted for at an election to a House of Assembly shall have the right to vote or be voted for at an election to a local government council" (section 7(4)). Thus, the regulations made by a state governor in pursuance of the power given to him under section 20 of the Local Government Edict 1976 to prescribe the qualifications and disqualifications of electors and candidates are unconstitutional and void to the extent that the qualifications and disqualifications prescribed are different from, and inconsistent with, those prescribed in the constitution for voters and candidates in an election to the State House of Assembly.

There is a slight difficulty in the application of the directive in section 7(4) in that what the subsection on the face of it provides for is the entitlement to be registered as a voter at an election to a legislative house, but not the entitlement to vote. The provision must be read together with another one, which says that "every citizen of Nigeria, who has attained the age of 18 years residing in Nigeria at the time of the registration of voters for purposes of election to any legislative house shall be entitled to be registered as a voter for that election" (section 117(2)). Notwithstanding the way the provision is worded, the intention is clearly to confer the right to vote on every Nigerian citizen who has attained the age of 18 years or over, and is resident in Nigeria at the time. As the High Court of Lagos State has rightly held, registration as a voter is not an additional qualification for voting, but only a device for ensuring that those who vote at an election are legally qualified to do so; the aim is to reduce fraudulent voting (ibid). It follows that section 7(4) of the constitution does not provide that only persons registered as voters at an election to a State House of Assembly are entitled to vote at local government elections. What it does is to ensure that the franchise for a local government election shall be open to every Nigerian citizen qualified as a voter at an election to a State House of Assembly by virtue of having attained the age of 18 years or over and by virtue of being resident in the country at the time.

The residence qualification raises a further problem. Section 117(2) speaks of residence in Nigeria, but it has been suggested that the provision should be construed to refer to residence in the state (ibid) in order apparently to distinguish it from the residence in Nigeria prescribed for election to the National Assembly (section 77(2)). The intention seems to have been to make residence in Nigeria a uniform qualification for the franchise for all elections (including local government elections), though a person may only exercise it in the place in which he is actually registered. A state government cannot therefore make residence in the local government area a requirement for the right to vote at a local government election, but it can provide that a person qualified to vote at a local government election can only be registered in the place where he actually resides.

The qualifications for a candidate at an election to a State House of Assembly are that he must be a Nigerian citizen of the age of 30 years or above (section 106). A Nigerian citizen of the requisite age is nevertheless disqualified to stand as a candidate if —

(a)   he has voluntarily acquired the citizenship of another country or, except as may be permitted by the National Assembly, he has made declaration of allegiance to such a country;

(b)   he is adjudged to be a lunatic or otherwise declared to be of unsound mind under any law in force in any part of Nigeria;

(c)   he is under a sentence of death or imprisonment for more than six months for an offence involving dishonesty where such sentence is imposed by a court of law in Nigeria;

(d)   he has, within a period of less than ten years before the date of the election, been convicted and sentenced for an offence involving dishonesty or has been found guilty of a contravention of the code of conduct;

(e)   he has been adjudged or otherwise declared bankrupt under any law in force in Nigeria and has not been discharged; or

(f)   he is employed in the public service of the federation or of any state (section 107).

(iv) *Functions*

Not only does the constitution not create local governments but also it confers no functions directly on them. It merely provides that "the functions to be conferred by the law upon local government councils shall include those set out in the Fourth Schedule to this Constitution" (section 7(5)). No local government can therefore assume any of the enumerated functions by right of constitutional grant. They have to be first conferred on it by "Law," which is defined to mean a law enacted by a House of Assembly (section 318(1)). A state government is, however, under a constitutional duty to confer these functions on its local governments. Again, as earlier stated, it is a matter for argument whether a State House of Assembly can be compelled to make the necessary law.

The crucial question is whether a state government is not only obliged to assign these functions to its local governments but is also precluded thereafter from exercising them directly, or whether it can exercise them concurrently with the local governments. It need hardly be said that these functions are part of the power vested in a state government to make law on any matter not included in the exclusive legislative list, and to execute any law so made (sections 4(7) and 5(s)). A state government cannot confer these functions on its local governments if it does not itself possess them. The issue therefore is not as to a state government's right to these functions, rather it is whether the act of conferring them on the local governments operates to divest the state government of its own power over them.

The form in which the functions are provided for in the fourth schedule has an important bearing upon the question under consideration. It is necessary therefore to reproduce the schedule in full. The functions are enumerated in the constitution under two separate paragraphs as follows:-

1. The main functions of a local government council are as follows-

(a) The consideration and the making of recommendations to a state commission on economic development planning or any similar body on ·
    i. the economic development of the state, particularly in so far as the areas of authority of the council and of the state are affected, and

    ii. proposals made by the said commission or body;

(b) collection of rates, radio and television licences;

(c) establishment and maintenance of cemeteries, burial grounds and homes for the destitute or infirm;

(d) licensing of bicycles, trucks (other than mechanically propelled trucks), canoes, wheel barrows and carts;

(e) establishment, maintenance and regulation of markets, motor parks and public conveniences;

(f) construction and maintenance of roads, streets, drains and other public highways, parks, open spaces, or such public facilities as may be prescribed from time to time by the House of Assembly of a state;

(g) naming of roads and streets and numbering of houses;

(h) provision and maintenance of public conveniences and refuse disposal;

(i) registration of all births, deaths and marriages;

(j) assessment of privately owned houses or tenements for the purpose of levying such rates as may be prescribed by the House of Assembly of a state; and

(k) control and regulation of-
   i.   out-door advertising and hoardings,
   ii.   movement and keeping of pets of all descriptions,
   iii. shops and kiosks,
   iv.   restaurants and other places for sale of food to the public, and
   v.   laundries.

2. The functions of a local government council shall include participation of such council in the government of a state as respects the following matters, namely -

   (a) the provision and maintenance of primary education;

(b)   the development of agriculture and natural resources, other than the exploitation of minerals;

(c)   the provision of maintenance of health services; and

(d)   such other functions as may be conferred on a local government council by the House of Assembly of the State.

The separation of the functions are into two categories, and the language by which the enumeration in each paragraph is introduced seem to suggest that the functions enumerated in paragraph 1 are intended to be exclusive to local governments while those in paragraph 2 are concurrent. It cannot have been the intention that after assigning to local governments the functions in paragraph 1, the state government should continue to operate fully in those fields in competition with the local government and in derogation of its own grant. Clearly what is intended is that a state government is to exercise the functions only through its local governments.

It is necessary, however, to examine the functions closely in order to determine whether they embrace both legislation and execution, and whether, consequently, delegation will operate to exclude both the legislative and executive authority of the state government in respect of the functions. Except for items (e) and (k), paragraph 1 seems to proceed on the basis that the authority to regulate or prescribe remains with the State House of Assembly (or the National Assembly in the case of radio and television licences), and that local governments are to operate largely in the executive sphere of the functions enumerated. The context seems clearly to suggest that the words "maintenance" and "provision" are used in a physical, not a regulatory sense. Paragraph 1 must therefore be construed as not obliging a state government to confer upon its local governments authority to regulate these matters; the obligation cast on it is only to delegate to the local governments power to execute any regulations which it may make on them (except items (e) and (k)). It follows therefore that only the executive authority of the state government in respect of these matters is excluded by the delegation of them to the local governments. A state house may of course in its discretion additionally confer regulation-making power on local governments in respect of any of those matters.

In respect of matters mentioned in items (e) and (k), however, the function to be conferred on local governments must include power to make regulations. It does not appear that the power of the State House of Assembly to regulate those matter is thereby excluded. Some of the matters mentioned in the two items, e.g. markets, and shops, are so important as to make a uniform regulation of them by the State House of Assembly both necessary and desirable. The intention seems to be that these matters are to be regulated by the local governments within the framework of a central legislation enacted by the State House of Assembly. (Some of them may even be subject to the regulatory authority of the National Assembly.)

The functions enumerated in paragraph 2 remain fully the responsibility of the state government, but the local governments are to be involved in them in some way. The nature and extent of such involvement is entirely at the discretion of the state government. A proposal to include these functions among those to be conferred on local governments was rejected in the Constituent Assembly on the ground that they would be beyond the executive capacity of a local government to undertake. With the exception of item (d), their inclusion in the constitution in the form in which they now appear in paragraph 2 of the fourth schedule was never approved by the Constituent Assembly; they were put there by the Federal Military Government.

(v) Finances

Local governments have complete financial independence from the state government. They have three sources of revenue all of which are independent of the state government. First, the constitution gives them a direct share of federally collected revenue, though the amount of such share and the terms of apportioning it among the groups of local governments in the various states are left to the National

Assembly to prescribe (section 149(2)). The share due to the local governments in each state is paid, not directly to them, but through the state government. The payment is made to the state government as trustee to distribute it to its local governments in accordance with a formula to be prescribed by the State House of Assembly (section 162(3) and (5)). The state government is not entitled to keep any part of the money for its own use. Under the Allocation of Revenue (Federation Account, etc.) Act, 1982, the local governments' share of federally collected revenue was fixed at 10 percent.

Grant by the state government from its own resources is another source of revenue for local governments. The state government is under a constitutional duty to make the grant, which is to be a proportion of the state government's total revenue as may be prescribed by the National Assembly (section 162(7)). Again this was fixed at 10 percent by the 1982 Allocation of Revenue Act.

The act also established a committee charged with the function of ensuring that allocations made to local governments from both federal and state sources were promptly paid into the joint local government account and distributed to the local governments in accordance with a formula prescribed by the State House of Assembly. The state Accountant-General was to report such payments to the State House of Assembly and to each house of the National Assembly within ninety days of the end of each financial year, and his report must state whether the payments had been correctly made.

There is, thirdly, the local governments' independent revenue, which is derived from functions which the constitution directs to be assigned to them, *viz*, rates, radio and television licences; fees for the use of cemeteries, burial grounds, markets, motor parks, and public conveniences; licensing fee in respect of bicycles, trucks and canoes; registration fee in respect of births, deaths and marriages; fees for licensing shops, restaurants and other places for sale of food to the public (Schedule 4).

Application of the Presidential System at the Local Government Level

The application of the presidential system at the local government level is pre-determined by three factors. First, there is the logic of the fact that it is the system in use at the state and federal government levels. It seems to me necessary and logical that all three levels of government should be run and operated on the same principles and forms of governmental administration, if for no other reason than that of maintaining consistency and symmetry in the entire polity. But there is another reason besides. Local self-government is meant to provide a training ground for informed and effective participation by the citizen at the higher levels of the state and federal governments. It affords him, says Alexis de Tocqueville in his great classic, *Democracy in America* (1835), an opportunity to practise

> the art of government in the small sphere within his reach; he accustoms himself to those forms without which liberty can only advance by revolutions; he imbibes their spirit; he acquires a taste for order, comprehends the balance of powers, and collects clear practical notions on the nature of his duties and the extent of his rights.

But it makes no sense to train and educate the local citizen in a system different from that he is going to encounter at the state and federal levels. If he and the nation are to derive maximum benefit from the training and education afforded by local self-government, then, the system, the principles and the practices in use at that level should be the same as those in operation at the state and federal levels.

The second factor that predetermines the choice of the presidential system at the local government level is the fact that the chairman of the local government area is elected, not from a local constituency within it, but by the entire electorate of the area. This is consistent only with the presidential system, certainly not with the parliamentary system. He has a constituency which is not only different from that of a local government councillor, but also wider than that of all the counsellors put together. The implication is, in effect, to separate him from the local government council and its members, and to confer on him an authority and a mandate of office derived, not from the council, but directly from the electorate. If his position is to be merely that of chairman of the local government council, then, he ought, logically, to be chosen by the council, and be removable by it. But the fact that he is elected directly by the entire electorate of the local government area gives him an existence and authority separate from that of the council; it places him outside the council. It implies indeed headship of the local government area and its government.

The position of the Local Government Chairman as head and executive authority of the local government carries with it an implication which points logically to, if it does not predetermine, the presidential system as the system that should apply. Now, a functionary who is the executive authority of the government ought not at the same time to preside in the capacity of chairman over the legislative council of the government. Even the parliamentary system does not permit of so complete a fusion; the prime minister under the system, though a member and leader of the legislative assembly, is not its chairman, since, he were to be chairman, he would thereby have been established as more or less an absolute ruler.

Apart from these three predetermining factors, there are also other considerations which make it desirable that the presidential system should also be applied at the local government level. First, a requirement that the political executive functionaries, now designated as supervisors, must be elected members of the local government council would imply that they hold their office by virtue of membership of the council, and that they owe responsibility for the discharge of their duties to the council rather than to the chairman. Such a principle would undermine the authority of the chairman and the efficacy of the administration of the local government. It should not be left in doubt at all that it is to the chairman, and not to the council, that the supervisors owe responsibility for the performance of their duties. The responsibility for their appointment should be placed wholly and entirely in the chairman.

Secondly, an important merit of the presidential system is that it enables the net to be cast widely in the search for political executive functionaries, instead of restricting it to members of the legislature. In making such appointments, the president, governor or chairman is expected to look for the fittest persons who may not all be found among members of the legislature.

Having said all this, the question still remains whether, in view of the restricted scope of functions exercisable by local government and the fact that the functions are more in the realm of execution, the separation of legislative and executive powers makes enough sense at that level. What, in other words, is there to be separated? The fact that the functions of local government are mostly in the realm of execution is indeed a cogent enough reason for making their exercise the exclusive responsibility of the chairman, assisted by the supervisors. A council or a board, says John Stuart Mill, is "not a fit instrument for executive business." It is, he emphatically asserts,

> admitted in all countries in which the representative system is practically understood, that numerous representative bodies ought not to administer. The maxim is grounded not only on the most essential principles of good government, but on those of the successful conduct of business of any description. No body of men, unless organised and under command, is fit for action, in the proper sense. Even a select board, composed of few members, and these specially conversant with the business to be done, is always an inferior instrument to some one individual who could be found among them, and would be improved in character if that one person were made the chief, and all others reduced to subordinates. What can be done better by a body than by an individual is deliberation. When it is necessary or important to secure hearing and consideration to many conflicting opinions, a deliberative body is indispensable. Those bodies, therefore, are frequently useful, even for administrative business, but in general only as advisers; such business being, as a rule, better conducted under the responsibility of one.

It is therefore contrary to the principle of good government to vest executive responsibility in a local government council. It properly belongs to the chairman who, as the executive authority, should be separated from the council.

But then, it may be asked, does a local government's small range of legislative functions justify the maintenance of an elected council as a separate organ of government? Mill again provides us a cogent answer, one based on sound principle of good government. "There is", he writes, "hardly any kind of intellectual work which so much needs to be done, not only by experienced and exercised minds, but by minds trained to the task through long and laborious study, as the business of making laws." It demands specialisation, and the acquisition of expertise that comes from it. The necessity and importance of this specialisation and expertise are not negated because of the limited range of a local government's legislative functions. They still provide a training ground in the art of law-making, which can be used later to greater advantage at the state and federal levels.

The separation of the council as an organ distinct from the chairman and the supervisors would enable it, to quote Mill again, to "watch and control the government; to throw the light of publicity on its acts; to compel a full exposition and justification of all of them which any one considers questionable; to censure them if found condemnable."

The Local Government (Basic Constitutional and Transitional Provisions Amendment No. 3) Decree No. 23 of 1991, gave to a local government council the following functions, which ought to form part of its normal and regular functions, *viz*

(a) debating, approving and amending the annual budget of the local government, subject to the chairman's veto which may be set aside by two-thirds majority of the local government council;

(b) vetting and monitoring the implementation of projects and programmes in the annual budget of the local government;

(c) examining and debating monthly statements of income and expenditure rendered to it by the local government; and

(d) advising, consulting and liaising with the chairman of the local government

These, together with the function of passing legislative proposals into law in the form of bye-laws, limited though its scope is, seem clearly to justify the prevailing arrangement whereby a local government council is maintained as a separate organ chaired by someone other than the chairman. Needless to say, the State House of Assembly may, within the limits of its constitutional competence and within the limits of permissible delegation, assign to a local government council such additional functions as it may deem fit; a provision to that effect was indeed contained in Decree No. 23 of 1991, referred to above.

CHAPTER 7

Nature and Role of Legislation in Modern Government and the Struggle between Rival or Competing Interests for the Control of Legislative Power

Nature and Role of Legislation in Modern Government

"Legislation," writes the Nobel Laureate, Friedrich von Hayek, citing Julius Paulus, Roman jurist of the third century A.D., "has justly been described as among all inventions of man the one fraught with the gravest consequences, more far-reaching in its effects even than fire and gunpowder" (F.A. Hayek, *Law, Legislation and Liberty* (1982), p. 72). From its small beginnings in the ancient Greek city-states as isolated single instances, through its momentous development in Rome as a regular, systemic and leading instrument of rule, providing the superstructure of the famed *Pax Romana*, to its further vast expansion during the course of the centuries since then, legislation has become such familiar and common activity of government that we now tead to lose sight of its crucial role in government. The laws enacted by Rome provided not only an "imposing architecture of government," but also a sublime instrument for order, peace and regularity which served perhaps more than anything else to unify the provinces of the Empire (see Edward Gibbon, *The Decline and Fall of the Roman Empire, vol. 1*, p. 28; vol. iv, pp. 374-444). The peace and security established by Roman law and maintained by the Roman government within its borders and throughout its far-flung Empire has been acclaimed "the supreme achievement in the history of statesmanship" (Will Durant, *The Story of Civilisation, vol. iii*, p. 232).

Legislation has indeed a frightful potency as an instrument of control and coercion of the individual and society. The very language of legislation is that of command. Legislation is, for the most part, couched as commands directed to the individual as to how or how not to conduct himself and his activities. In particular, all criminal legislation is a command prohibiting some act or omission, or otherwise restricting the individual's freedom of action under penalty of death, imprisonment, fine, forfeiture or deprivation of other rights. But the coercion of criminal prohibition operates not only on those on whom the penalty has actually been exacted for violating it but on every one else who, being subject to the prohibition, is coerced, against their desire and will, to refrain from engaging in the prohibited act either because of the threat of legal punishment or because of their concern, as good, law-abiding citizens, not to incur it. Apart from the fact that the unimpeded exercise of individual freedom of choice is itself a value of great importance to human life, the frustration of human desires and will may involve the infliction of a special form of suffering. This, as Professor Hart has pointed out, is particularly so in the case of laws enforcing a sexual morality, which "may create misery of a quite special degree" arising from the individual being compelled to repress his sexual impulses in obedience to such laws.

Legislation is not only the most potent instrument of coercion, it is also the most far-reaching and crucial power in the government of society. It is the expression of the supreme power in the state, the distinctive mark of a country's sovereignty, and the index of its status as an independent state. Thus, the sovereign power in a state is identified in the organ that has the power to make laws by legislation.

The legislature is therefore the sovereign organ of state power. As the hallmark of a country's sovereignty, legislative power is a plenary power and as such has no inherent limits, that is to say, no limits flowing inherently and inexorably from its nature; it is subject only to such extrinsic limitations as may be imposed on it by the supreme law of a written constitution or by established convention.

Thus, a legislature, like the British Parliament, which is not subject to the supreme law of a written constitution by which it is created and its powers defined and *ipso facto* limited, can legally exercise the sovereignty of the nation reposed in it in any way and for whatever purposes it chooses; it can, in theory, at any rate, do anything it likes, except, of course, things that are physically impossible, like turning a man physically into a woman, or a woman into a man, but it can provide that a man shall be deemed - notionally, that is — to be a woman or *vice versa*. More to the point, it can, by means of legislation,

(i)   exercise executive power or authorise some other person or agency than the president to exercise it independently of his control;

(ii)   exercise judicial power or authorise the executive or some other agency than the judicature to exercise it;

(iii) abdicate its power either in whole or in part to the executive;

(iv)   confer rights or impose duties on the individual, and abrogate them, as it deems fit.

The form of words employed to express the plenitude of legislative power is that the legislative authority "shall have power to make laws for the peace, order and good government" of the country (Section 4, Constitution of Nigeria 1999). The phrase "peace, order and good government," as the Judicial Committee of the Privy Council has said, does not delimit the extent of the power or the purposes for which it is to be used, in the sense that a law must be for peace, order or good government in order to be valid. It is simply a legal formula for expressing the widest plenitude of legislative power exercisable by a sovereign legislature.

The emergence of deliberate **law-making** by legislation, with its sovereign and plenary character, **revolutionalised** government and transmuted it into what is known as a state strictly so-called. It is the change from the rule of custom to the rule of legislated law in written form, and from the settlement of disputes by private force or feud vengeance to the arbitrament of law that marked the emergence of the state in the strict sense. Hence state power (or political power) is defined by John Locke as "a **Right** of making laws ... and of employing the force of the Community, in the Execution of such laws, and in the defence of the Commonwealth from Foreign Injury." (John Locke, *Two Treatises of Civil Government* **(1690), new** student edition by Peter Laslett (1960), p. 268). And to John Austin, law, strictly and properly so called, is not custom, but obligatory rules of behaviour or action "commanded" by the sovereign (i.e., the state) in the form of legislation; "laws which are not commands of the sovereign," he maintains, "are laws improper, or improperly so-called." (John Austin, *Lectures on Jurisprudence*, 5th edition (1885) vol. 1, p. 79).

From the concept of legislated law as an indispensable index of statehood also emerged the concept of the state as a legal order. The latter concept is important for a true appreciation of the crucial role of legislation in the life and organisation of society. The intimidating, irresistible and awesome force behind the power of the state is not in the nature of a brute, savage and barbarous force, to be arbitrarily applied at the whims and caprices of those in control of the state from time to time. It is not, properly understood and applied, a kind of Leviathan. On the contrary, it is force bounded and moderated by law. Law is a necessary attribute as well as a necessary instrument of the state; law is made by the state but the state itself is grounded on law, i.e., law considered as a body of laws or in totality. The state is characterised by power and force. State power, the power to govern the affairs of men in society, is not just arbitrary power but rather one exercised in accordance with definite procedures and rules. And force, which is the central attribute of the state, and without which it cannot exist – "states exist or not according as they have the force to impose their commands" — is also not just brutish, unregulated force but rather "force displayed in a regular and uniform manner" in accordance with law that regulates, conditions and therefore qualifies it (see D'Entreaves, *The Notion of the State* (1967), p. 2). In more succinct language, the state denotes power and force exercised "in the name of the law;" it connotes a legal order, a body of laws that regulates, conditions and qualifies the exercise of power backed by force within a given community.

It follows that the state, as an organisation of power and force, can no more be defined apart from law. While law is created by the state, and is "an instrument more or less necessary for carrying out the state's activities and attaining its ends", the state, in its turn, is grounded upon law; it is the law that imparts to the state its character as an organisation whose "activities are systematised, co-ordinated, predictable, machine-like and impersonal" (see Poggi, *The Development of the Modern State*, p. 75). Law and the state are thus correlative entities neither of which can be properly conceived without the other. Each is conditioned by the other in the sense that the existence of each is a condition of the existence of the other. The state cannot exist apart from or without law any more than law can exist apart from or without the state. Accordingly, force or power and, *ipso facto*, a state not regulated and conditioned by law, that is to say, a lawless state, is a perversion, a complete distortion of the state concept. (The socialist state rests on a different conception of the relation between the state and law.)

The crucial importance of legislation as an indispensable instrument of government is further underlined by the fact that almost every activity of government requires the authority of some enabling law, whether it is the provision of social welfare, economic and industrial development, social or moral reform, land tenure, maintenance of peace and order, the security, safety and integrity of the state, etc. "It is largely by means of legislation that administrations ... react to the need for basic changes in the economic, social and political structure of the country." "The energy of legislatures", writes Sir Henry Maine, "is the prime characteristic of modern societies."

The necessity for legislation as the basis for governmental action stems partly from the principle that, under the modern constitutional state, the executive has no inherent power over the citizen; it has no power, by its own inherent authority, to do any act prejudicially affecting the right or interest of the individual without authorisation by some law, either the law of the constitution or an ordinary law. And since most executive acts of government operate on individuals in one way or another, legislation has thus a compelling paramountcy and decisiveness in government.

The intimidating volume of legislation poured out each year by the state shows the extent the population is subjected, in its affairs and activities, to regulation of various kinds by the state under sanctions of one form or another. We may get some idea of its sheer volume to note that, in the 13 years from 1966 to 1979, the Federal Government of Nigeria, enacted 627 laws, excluding the even more formidable volume of subsidiary legislation (rules and regulations) issued under them. Laws enacted by the state governments during the same period accounted also for quite a considerable number. The Nigerian Criminal Code, in some 521 sections, punishes as criminal offences a wide variety of acts or omissions by the ordinary citizens in the course of their lives. These are apart from the large number of technical offences created as sanctions or penalties for the violation of the provisions of particular legislation, e.g., the Companies and Allied Matters Act, the Banks and Financial Institutions Decree.

The importance of constituent power, the power to institute, by means of a written constitution, a frame of government for a community and to define its powers and its relations with the individual, needs no special emphasis. It is the ultimate mark of sovereignty, and from which the other elements of sovereignty are derived.

Legislation is thus a crucial factor that distinguishes government in Africa before and since the inception of colonialism. It is one of colonialism's greatest legacies to Africa. Government in pre-colonial

African society was essentially the rule of custom and the force behind the government was largely in the nature of brute, unregulated force. The rule of custom signifies a primitive society, one characterised by:

> a markedly static conception of social life, in consequence of which law, instead of being regarded as an instrument placed at man's disposal for betterment and change, appeared rather as a limit imposed by a mysterious and transcendent force on the expression of their preferences and the choices dictated by their needs. (see D'Entreaves, *The Notion of the State*).

It can be said with truth that no pre-colonial black African community, both acephalous and centralised ones, had advanced by organic evolution beyond the stage of the rule of custom into the stage of the rule of legislated law, which characterises the state, and provides the vehicle for the expression of its will and command, and for the discharge of the essential functions of government in society. Law, for all pre-colonial communities in black Africa, was not the command of the sovereign (i.e., the state), and its sanction was not organised force regularly applied by the sovereign as regulated and restrained by law. Law was simply customary or accepted modes of behaviour, and its sanction was partly spiritual or religious and partly brute unregulated force; it rested largely upon belief, passed from generation to generation, in some supernatural power to reward obedience to those rules or to punish violation of, and deviation from, them. Religion among Africans is concerned mainly with maintenance of rules of accepted behaviour, which alone makes the survival and expansion of the community possible. Religion in Africa, as Basil Davidson observes:

> is the selective codification, for its impact on everyday life, of a "two-way" network of moral pressure: of the workings of the principle of Good in its positive sense, on behalf of whatever supports or guards a specific social system; and of the workings of the same principle in a negative sense - the sense of Evil which promotes or provokes,

chiefly as one form or other of punishment or deterrent, whatever may go against the system (*The Black Man's Burden* (1992), p. 82).

Just as in medieval Europe the rule of custom sanctioned by religious beliefs had resulted in the decline of the state to the extent that it was considered non-existent, so also its exclusive rule in pre-colonial black Africa operating with the same spiritual sanction precluded the existence there of the state strictly so-called.

In the historical evolution of political societies, the rule of custom represents a phase that is incompatible with the notion of the state strictly so-called. There have been six eras in that evolution. These are:

(i)   the era of the theocratic state of society, as exemplified by the old Oriental Empires and the pre-colonial African societies, when human society was held together by religious belief or by social customs growing out of such belief;

(ii)   the Greek Age, characterised by great intellectual activity, democracy and civic freedom;

(iii)   the Roman Age, the great age of "empire, of conquests, of consolidation of nations, of law and government," of the development of the state into full maturity, characterised by legislation as the main instrument for carrying out the state's activities and attaining its ends;

(iv)   the Medieval Age, characterised by the ascendance of the Christian Church and Feudalism, the re-emergence of the rule of custom as against legislation, with the consequent decline of the state to the point it was considered non-existent;

(v)   the Modern Age, characterised by the absolutism of the state, with all the attributes essential to it; and

(vi)   the Democratic and Industrial Age, characterised by the constitutional state, which was ushered in by the American and French Revolutions and the Industrial Revolution.

We need to state for purposes of emphasis that the institution of a written constitution as a means of constituting a government was part of the legislated law brought to Africa by colonialism. From the inception of colonial rule (except in cases where the colonial territory was incorporated into the metropolitan state or was incorporated into the metropolitan state as part of a bigger imperial state), a government was instituted locally for the colony by a written instrument of government, the colonial constitution, made by the imperial government and which, as law, established the organs of the colonial state, conferred their powers and regulated the mode for exercising them.

But as a colonial legacy in Africa, legislation, together with the state of which it is an essential component, is nearly as baneful as it is beneficial. Both have been thoroughly perverted by post-colonial African rulers. Lee has aptly and pointedly described the perversion thus:

> The colonial state represented a body of laws, however illegitimate; the post-colonial state is a body of men which has captured the state apparatus, buttressed by the sanctions which had been expressed in the final stages of the nationalist struggle ... The state sometimes appears to be little more than a description which can be applied to those who succeeded to the public offices vacated by colonial administrators .... Circumstances encourage all those concerned in 'nation-building' to place a much greater emphasis on the state as an apparatus for government than on the state a system of law (J.M. Lee, *African Armies and Civil Order* (1969), pp. 9-11).

The perverted conception of the relation between the state and law is reflected in the fact that the state's force is sometimes regarded in terms of sheer brute force unregulated and uncontrolled by law, and the power as sheer arbitrary, lawless power, as when government, with thirty army personnel, all heavily armed, invaded and took forcible possession of the property of a person indebted to it, which happened to be in the occupation of a hospital, chased out and sacked the hospital staff, discharged all the patients, seized the hospital records, closed down the hospital and made structural alterations to the buildings, all in the belief, which was erroneous, that the hospital also belonged to the debtor personally *(Obeya Memorial Specialist Hospital v. The Attorney-General of the Federation* (1987)) or where government, claiming to be owner of property left behind by its real owner during a civil war, moved into it with some 150 armed soldiers, ejected the real owner's son who had been let into possession lawfully as tenant by the government's estate agents after payment of the agreed yearly rent, and while his suit was, to the knowledge of the government, pending in the court to determine the right of the government to eject him and its claim to be the owner. *(Governor of Lagos State v. Chief Odumegwu-Ojukwu* (1986)). There have also been instances of the perversion by African rulers of the notion of legislation as a system of general rules of prospective application to all persons alike – the state, rulers and the ruled. The instances are too numerous, making enumeration or discussion of them inappropriate or inexpedient here.

Role and Importance of a Democratic Procedure for Legislation

A democratic procedure for legislation has a role and an importance that call for special emphasis. It liberalises government, ensures regularity in its administration, and checks arbitrariness. Requiring laws to be made in accordance with pre-determined rules of procedure is perhaps the best guarantee of regularity. Regularity in the administration of government enables the individual to know in advance how he stands with the government, and when the latter is planning to interfere with the course of his life and activities.

In a constitutional government, legislative proposals are usually required to be presented in the form of a bill, with the precise wording of the provisions fully set out, and thereafter to be put through a ponderous process of long-drawn-out debates in the Assembly and its committees, during which the substance of the proposed law and the meaning and implication of its wording are examined in detail. The machinery of committees, hearing and long debates which characterises the legislative process of a democratic government may well be cumbersome, time-consuming and even inefficient, but it has an important virtue in minimising the incidence of arbitrary and ill-thought-out legislation. It serves to "prevent those inroads upon the law of the land which a despot ... might effect by ordinances and decrees ... or by sudden resolutions" (A.V. Dicey, *The Law of the Constitution*, 10th edition (1960), p. 407). It also helps to enhance the authority and fixity of a law enacted through that process.

The process of consultation with interested groups – trade unions, trade and professional associations and other interested sections of the community – which precedes the introduction of a bill in the legislative assembly is designed to serve the same purpose. In an ideal setting, even the seemingly simple function of drafting involves "interviews and correspondence with experts in various branches of the subject with which the measure deals. Notes will have to be written tracing the history of previous legislation or attempts at legislation, and explaining the reasons for and effect of the several proposals embodied in the draft bill, and stating the arguments which may be advanced for and against them, and these will soon grow into a formidable literature of commentaries".

All this is usually lacking in the process of legislation in a dictatorship, such as a military government. It is much too hurried and much too concerned with its aggrandising purpose to permit of consultations and lengthy discussions.

Legislation is too serious a business to be done in a haste. Providing the authority for most actions of government, legislation is the most fundamental, the most far-reaching and the most authoritarian of all governmental powers, and therefore the most prone to autocratic use. It thus requires to be exercised with due deliberation and after mature consideration of the matter in all its ramifications and implications, in order to "secure against the imperfection of decision-makers" and to "demonstrate to those who are disappointed ... our determination not to decide against them easily or casually. We should give time for thought, even though thought does not always take time" (L.R. Lucas, *On Justice* (1980), p. 95).

In this connection, the admonition of Lord Bryce is well worth noting, "In the field of legislation," he writes:

> the danger of doing too much is a serious danger, not only because the chances of error are manifold, but because the law ought to undergo as few bold and sudden changes as possible ... Even the certainty of law is apt to suffer if legislation becomes too easy, for the impatient autocrat may well be tempted, when some defect has been discovered, to change it forthwith, and then to find that the change has been too sweeping, so that steps must be taken backward, with the result of rendering doubtful or invalid transactions which have occurred in the meantime ... In reforming the law of a country the risk of going too slow is less serious than that of going too fast (see James Bryce, *Studies in History and Jurisprudence, vol. 2* (1901), pp. 317-318).

This is not, of course, a justification for inaction or for unwarranted tardiness, especially where bills of urgent national importance, like an annual appropriation bill, are concerned. Thus, the lapse of three months from the introduction of the 2000 Appropriation Bill in November 1999 to its passage by the National Assembly at the end of March 2000 has, quite justifiably, been called to question.

The Nigerian Constitution contains no provision stipulating the time in the year an appropriation bill should be introduced in the National Assembly or how long the Assembly may take to pass it. All it says is that the budget for the following financial year can be introduced "at any time" in the current financial year (Section 81(1)).

In this regard, the Nigerian Constitution differs from the Constitution of France 1958 and those of many Francophone African countries. The constitutions of a number of Francophone African countries (but not that of France itself) stipulate the time the annual finance bill must be introduced in the National Assembly, usually at the beginning of October preceding the financial year to which it relates. They also provide, as does the Constitution of France 1958 (Article 47), that it be passed by the Assembly within a prescribed time frame of varying length, usually between 60 and 85 days, failing which its provisions may be put into effect by ordinance issued by the government.

This latter provision reflects the dominating role of the government in the process of legislation in the French system, as will be explained later. The power given to the executive to put into effect by ordinance a finance bill in the circumstances specified in the provision above is foreign and anathema to English traditions and governmental principles bequeathed to Nigeria and other former British colonies.

It is well that President Obasanjo has indicated that in future the appropriation bill for the coming financial year will be introduced in October of the current year. On its part, the National Assembly should make it part of its standing rules to pass the budget within 60 days of its being laid before it by the president.

One last point, the provisions of the Constitution prescribing the mode, the manner and form, for the exercise of legislative power operates as a limitation on power, noncompliance with which renders its exercise null and void. As was held by the Judicial Committee of the Privy Council in a Sri Lankan case, *The Bribery Commissioner v. Ranasinghe* (1965), where a legislature is given power subject to certain manner and form, whether it be a simple or special majority of its members or the assent of the president, that power does not exist unless and until the manner and form is complied with. The supremacy of the constitution demands that the court should hold void any exercise of power which does not comply with the prescribed manner and form or which is otherwise not "in accordance with the constitution from which the power derives."

Struggle Between Rival or Competing Interests for the Control of Legislative Power

In view of the crucial role of legislation in government and its frightful potency as instrument of control and coercion of the individual and society, it should not surprise us that its control should be keenly contested, even to the point of feuding, among various interests in the country, setting them against each other – the people against the government, rival ethnic, religious or political groups and social classes against one another, the executive against the legislative assembly, the upper against the lower house in a bicameral legislative assembly, etc. Each of these interests, groups, institutions and bodies wants to control it or at least to have a significant share in its control, so as to be able to control or influence how the country is governed.

In the discussions which follow, nothing will be said about the relation between the legislative assembly and the executive with respect to the initiation of legislation or the management of proceedings on a bill in the assembly. These are subjects large and important enough to warrant treatment in a separation chapter of their own – see Chapter 8 below.

The People versus the Government

It used to be the conception that legislation was a function **only** of a political community, not of the people in their mass; in other words, that only a people organised as a political community could enact law through the machinery of the state. On this hypothesis, while the power of the people in their mass to constitute themselves into a political community is admitted, any such constituent act by which a constitution is established is purely a **political** act, giving the constitution only a political, as distinct from legal, existence. If it is intended that the constitution should also be a law, then it is for the resultant political creation, the state, to enact it as such through its regular procedure for law making.

The argument smacks of excessive formalism. If the state is a creation of the people by means of a constitution, and derives its power of legislation from them, it may be wondered why the people who constitute and grant the power cannot act directly, in a referendum or otherwise, to give the constitution the character and force of law. After all, the constitution, being the starting point of a country's legal order, its "lawness" should not depend upon its enactment through the law-making mechanism of the state, but rather upon its recognition as such by the people to be governed by it.

Happily, this conception has been, and is being, abandoned in an increasing majority of the countries of the world. From the time of the American Revolution in 1776-87, wrote Alexis de Tocqueville in his great classic, *Democracy in America* (1835), the:

> doctrine of the sovereignty of the people took possession of the state. Every class was enlisted in its cause; battles were fought and victories obtained for it; it became the law of laws. Sometimes, the laws are made by the people in a body, as at Athens .... The people reign in the American political world as the Deity does in the universe. They are the cause and the aim of all things; everything comes from them, and everything is absorbed in them.

As Palmer observed:

> European thinkers in all their discussion of a political or social contract, of government by consent and of the sovereignty of the people, had not clearly imagined the people as actually contriving a constitution and creating organs of government. They lacked the idea of the people as a constituent power.

Thus, the American Constitution of 1787, as law "ordained and established" by the people, is said to have broken with "the dominant tradition". Hardly anyone today disputes that the American Constitution "obtains its entire force and efficacy, not from the fact that it was ratified by a pre-existent political community or communities – for it was not - but from the fact that it was established by the people to be governed by it"– see Edward Corwin, *The Doctrine of Judicial Review* (1963), at p.100. The people as sovereign is not any more a mere matter of political theory. "We the People", the opening words of the U.S. Constitution, "does not", says David Mathews, "merely echo a revolutionary sentiment, it reflects a common practice."

The precedent of the American break with the dominant conception was adopted in France as a result of the revolution there in 1789. Ever since then the notion of the people as a constituent power and the legitimate authority to adopt a constitution through a constituent assembly specially elected for that specific purpose, followed by ratification in a referendum of the whole citizenry, has become firmly implanted in French governmental system. Thus, the

Constitution of the French Fourth Republic (1946) was first prepared in draft by a specially elected constituent assembly of 586 members, 64 of whom were representatives from Africa. The constitutional proposals as drafted by the constituent assembly were then submitted to a national referendum which rejected them on 5 May, 1945. Fresh proposals were adopted by a second constituent assembly elected on 2 June, 1946, and were later approved at a referendum on 13 October, 1946. Likewise, the Constitution of the Fifth Republic was submitted to, and approved at, a referendum held in metropolitan France and in all the overseas territories on 28 September 1958.

The French tradition in the matter has been transmitted to her former African colonies as part of their inheritance from French colonialism. With the exception of one or two, all of them have had their successive constitutions adopted through a constituent assembly or referendum or both.

The notion of the people as the rightful authority to adopt a constitution through a referendum or a constituent assembly specially elected by them for the purpose is also well rooted and accepted in Belgium, one of the European colonising powers in Africa. Its first and still surviving written Constitution of 1831 was adopted by a specially elected national congress of 200 delegates. The first amendment by which the suffrage was vastly expanded in September 1893 was likewise adopted by a constituent assembly elected for the purpose in April 1892. The monarchy being the central pillar of the constitution, the question whether or not Leopold III should be permitted to return to the country from exile after the Second World War to resume the throne from his brother regent was decided by a referendum in 1950 at which 57.68 per cent of the population voted in favour and 42.32 per cent against. (He was forced to abdicate soon afterwards because of widespread violent disturbances provoked by his return and the threat of civil war. He was succeeded by Baudouin.)

The course followed in the matter by the former Belgian territories in Africa had therefore been more or less predetermined by precedents in the former mother country. Thus, a new constitution for the Congo (Leopoldville) was adopted at a nationwide referendum between 25

June and 10 July, 1964. This was replaced by the 1967 Constitution likewise submitted to and approved at a national referendum from 4 – 24 June, 1967. The Constitution of Burundi's Second Republic was approved at a referendum on 15 November, 1981. Rwanda adopted a new constitution by referendum in December 1978, and a referendum on a national charter planned for 15 June, 1991 could not take place because of invasion by insurgent Rwandan forces in exile.

Outside former French, British and Belgian Africa, all the other African countries (with exceptions presently to be noted) have applied the process of a referendum in adopting their constitutions. Influenced no doubt by American precedent, Liberia's Constitution of 1847 was approved in convention on 26 July and later approved by the "people" in a referendum. Its 1984 Constitution was submitted to a constitutional assembly elected in conventions throughout Liberia from 12 May to 20 June, 1983, and was later approved in a referendum on 3 July, 1984. Ethiopia's Socialist Constitution was approved in a referendum in February 1987, so were those of Egypt (1964/80) and Somalia (1964 and 1979) while that of Libya (1951) was adopted by a national constituent assembly. (In proclaiming "the Socialist People's Libyan Arab Jamahiriya" in 1975, Gaddafi denounced plebiscites as "a fraud against democracy".)

The countries that became independent by armed revolt – Algeria, Angola, Guinea-Bissau, Mozambique, South Africa and Zimbabwe – belong in a different category (South Africa's 1983 Constitution was approved in an all-white referendum by 1,360,223 votes in favour and 691,557 against.) In none of them, however, except Algeria, was the independence constitution adopted through a referendum due, apparently, to the prevailing war condition.

Britain and most of her former colonies stand apart from this growing worldwide trend. Since she has never had a written constitution, Parliament acquired authority, firmly embedded in tradition, as the sovereign legislature and constituent power in Britain, precluding any question of the people as a constituent power and of a referendum as a means of exercising it. The tradition is again transmitted to her former colonies as part of their inheritance from British colonialism. This is the tradition and the conception underlying the provisions in the Constitution of Nigeria (1979 and 1999) vesting in the National Assembly and the State Houses of Assembly, the legislative power of the country, including constituent power, subject to the manner and form therein prescribed for its exercise (see Sections 4, 8, 9, 58, 59 and 100 of 1999 Constitution).

Remarkably, Ghana under Nkrumah was the first country in former British Africa where, in a radical break with the tradition inherited from British colonialism, the people were given legal recognition as a constituent power. Of the fifty-five articles of the 1960 Constitution, seventeen were made alterable only by the people in a referendum. In compliance with this procedure, the constitutional amendment by which the country was transformed into a one-party state in 1964 was submitted to a referendum and approved by 2,773,920 votes in favour and 2,452 against, out of a registered electorate of 2,988,598, thus giving a 99.9 percent majority in favour. This break with the inherited tradition has, since the 1990s, been followed in nine countries of former British Africa whose constitutions were adopted in a referendum (six countries) or through a constituent assembly specially elected for the purpose (three countries) –The Gambia, Ghana, Malawi, Seychelles, Sierra Leone, Sudan, Namibia, South Africa and Uganda. And in a referendum in February 2000, proposals for a new constitution for Zimbabwe were rejected by 697,754 votes against and 578,210 votes in favour. These encouraging beginnings may, hopefully, signal a new trend in former British Africa towards the growing universality of referendum as a means of adopting a constitution.

As the giant of Africa, Nigeria should be in the vanguard of this movement away from an outmoded tradition. A new constitution for the country, to be negotiated and agreed at a Conference of the ethnic nationalities, should be submitted to a referendum and approved by a simple majority of voters in not less than 60 per cent of the ethnic nationalities.

The concept of the people as lawmaker acting through a referendum has been carried further to approval of ordinary legislative proposals or other measures. From its origins in the United States and Switzerland, the submission for popular decision, of ordinary legislative or other measures proposed by government, is today a feature of modern democracy widely used throughout the world. Indeed, in some Swiss cantons, all legislative proposals originated by government, in particular constitutional amendments, are required to be submitted for popular approval or adoption whilst in other cantons as in the confederation itself and also in the American states submission is optional at the instance of the government or a prescribed number of citizens. Apart from the submission, whether compulsory or optional, of legislative proposals originated by government, there is also the method, known as the **initiative**, whereby a prescribed number of citizens can of themselves originate legislative proposals and have them submitted to the people for enactment into law, although the procedure is still restricted in its application to only a few countries, notably the Swiss Confederation as respects constitutional amendments as also many of the cantons and many American states as respects both constitutional amendments and ordinary legislation (see James Bryce, *Modern Democracies, vol.* 2 (1920), p. 460). The initiative is an example *par excellence* of a means whereby the people could obtain needed reforms in a constitutional manner, even against the will of the rulers. The constitutions of nearly all Francophone African countries recognise the referendum as a method of making ordinary law.

Both methods of direct legislation by the people are meant to supplement representative government, and to correct some of its shortcomings, including inadequacies on the part of representatives themselves. Representative government is afterall only resorted to as a substitute for direct democracy because of the impossibility, the inconvenience and expense in a large country of having every question touching upon its government decided by the people at large. But a substitute, a simulation, is scarcely ever quite the same as the real thing. When the people vote directly on ordinary legislative proposals or other measures whose significance cuts across all sectional boundaries, the influence of class, party and other group interests and sentiments is considerably reduced, whereas elections (even voting in the chambers of legislative assemblies) are dominated by ethnic or party interests and spirit, so that the real mind of the people does not receive as full an expression as might be desired. Voting at referenda on such matters is largely free of the dominating influence of partisan interests and spirit, depending of course on the question submitted.

Direct legislation by the people has the further advantage that it increases the opportunities for the people's political education, and it does so in a way unequalled by elections, because they oblige those who take part in them to try to understand the question submitted, and to reach a conclusion on it. The public discussion of the question in the media and at public meetings that precede the voting is a source of education for all, even for those who abstain from voting. And it permits a closer scrutiny of the merits and demerits of the questions or proposals submitted than would otherwise be possible.

Yet it has a limited use. The limits of its application are implied, firstly, in the reasons creating the necessity for representative government – the great inconvenience, expense and time involved in a frequent resort to the people in a large modern state; secondly, the fact that its ability to produce dispassionate decisions presupposes that only questions of great importance cutting across sectional interest should be submitted; thirdly, low turnout due to apathy or the absence of adequate publicity by means of organised campaigns unless when the political parties are sufficiently interested to call out their supporters; and fourthly, the fact that the questions submitted may be beyond the knowledge and competence of the mass of the people to understand and judge properly, and the danger that a desirable measure may be rejected out of ignorance on the part of the people. On the whole, however, referenda seem to have produced satisfactory results; witness, for example, the referendum in South Africa in March

1992 when the white electorate voted overwhelmingly in support of negotiations to end apartheid.

The Executive Versus the Legislative Assembly

Legislation through an assembly of men and women mandated in that behalf by popular consent, which is an important constitutive element of constitutionalism, took a revolution to get firmly established. Its history dates back again to antiquity. In Rome, following a revolt against absolute monarchy under which the city-state had been governed since its founding in 753 B.C., the system and law-making by the monarch were abolished and replaced with constitutional government under a republic (508 B.C.-27 B.C.). Law-making became a joint responsibility: the magistracy proposed, the senate deliberated and might approve or disapprove, and the measure was then submitted to the Assemblies, which might pass or reject it (but without debate). The significant point to emphasise is that a legislative measure initiated by the magistracy and approved by the senate did not become law unless and until passed by the Centurial Assembly or the Tribal Assembly, both of which were Assemblies of the whole people. We are told by Will Durant that by 200 B.C. the Tribal Assembly had become "the chief source of private law in Rome," (*The Story of Civilisation, vol. iii,* p. 27) but the Centurial Assembly also continued to function.

The incorporation of the people into the established processes of government, as the body with power to pass into law, measures initiated by the magistracy and approved by the senate, meant, as Charles McIlwain said, that the fundamental doctrine underlying the Roman state during this period was "constitutionalism, not absolutism" (see *Constitutionalism: Ancient and Modern* (1940), p. 59). Thus was introduced to the world the form of government limited **by law**, otherwise known as constitutionalism.

From 27 B.C. Rome reverted again to monarchy, first under a so-called principate (27 B.C.-192 A.D.), described by Edward Gibbon as "absolute monarchy disguised in the form of a commonwealth", and later under undisguised absolute monarchy (192 A.D.-1453). The description of the principate as absolute monarchy in disguise was because, except for the senate, the institutional restraints on the law-making power had disappeared leaving the prince/emperor as virtual absolute ruler. The Assemblies had ceased to function as law-making bodies, the people having become too large in number to meet for that purpose; they were not formally abolished, but were never again convened. Their role as the body to give force of law to legislative measures had passed partly to the senate whose *senatus consulta*, while not strictly law, had now acquired by convention the effect of law and were treated as such, but **mostly** to the prince/emperor who was recognised as having power, invested in him by the people (so it was rationalised), to make laws. And by 192 A.D. the senate itself had ceased to play any role in legislation, and was reduced to merely ceremonial functions. The praetorian edicts, which had formed a prominent part of the system of legislation in the republican period, had also ceased after the reign of Emperor Diocletian (284-303 A.D.) After the collapse of the Roman Empire in Western Europe in 455 A.D. and in Eastern Europe and Asia Minor in 1453, the absolute monarchy still continued to hold the stage there for several centuries more.

England was the first to rise against monarchy and to shorn it of its absolutism in the course of a series of revolutions there in the 17th century – the civil war which culminated in the establishment of the Commonwealth under the Instrument of Government of 1649, followed by the Restoration of Charles II in 1660 upon certain terms, and finally the Glorious Revolution of 1699 by which the crown was bestowed on William of Orange and his wife, Mary, after the flight to France of Mary's father, James II. Included in the terms of the offer was what was termed a Bill of Rights, which contained thirteen stipulations, among which were the abolition of the power of the monarch to make or suspend laws, to take executive actions not authorised or backed by law, and to act as supreme judge of acts committed against the government.

The stipulations, known as the Bill of Rights, established constitutional government as a definite principle of government in England, although limited in their terms and application to the executive, as it was also limited in Rome. The principle, thus firmly established in England, later moved across the seas and became also accepted in parts of Europe – France, Italy, Scandinavia, Poland and Hungary – and in North America. It has been rightly described as England's "pre-eminent contribution to the history of Western freedom".

Yet the assembly – parliament – which supplanted the monarch as the law-making authority was not a truly representative body in the sense of being mandated in that behalf by popular consent. Government freely elected by universal suffrage (as contra-distinguished from the direct democracy of the ancient city-states of Greece and Rome) did not begin to emerge until the 19th century. England was again the forerunner in that development, which took some 86 years to accomplish there through a process of piece-meal extensions of the franchise in 1832, 1867, 1885 and 1918. Universal adult suffrage was not attained in Europe and the United States until later in the 20th century.

In Africa since the advent of colonialism, the machinery of legislation also passed through various stages of development – from the colonial governor as sole legislature to the establishment of a legislative council composed of the governor and other designated colonial officials, to which were later added nominated unofficial members. The elective principle came in slow stages culminating towards the end of colonial rule in universal adult suffrage.

The victory of the assembly over the monarch in England for the right to make law by legislation does not establish the assembly, even after it has become a fully elected body, as the sole repository of the power to the exclusion of the monarch (i.e., the executive). For, whilst the power is not divided between them as two separate organs, each holding an allotted sphere of legislative competence independently of the other, the entity, called Parliament, in which the undivided legislative power is vested, is not the assembly alone, but rather the assembly and the monarch. In other words, the latter is as much a constituent part of Parliament as the assembly; their right or title to the legislative power is both joint and equal in the sense that the concurrence of both is indispensable in law-making. Neither the one nor the other alone can make law.

The indispensability of the monarch's concurrence to legislation in England is of course an attempt to reconcile monarchy with popular sovereignty. The monarch is the sovereign, and the cardinal essence of sovereignty in the legal sense is the power to make laws. Thus, while monarchy remains the formal framework of government, the monarch's title of sovereignty must need be given cognisance in the distribution of power to the representative organs of government. The device of making him a constituent part of the legislature seeks therefore to accommodate his title of sovereignty with the popular sovereignty of the people which the assembly represents.

The British expedient of making the executive a constituent part of Parliament was written into the constitutions of the countries in former British Africa all of which, with only two exceptions (Zambia and Botswana), acceded to independence with monarchy as the formal framework for government (the British monarch was the titular Sovereign and Head of State). It was retained even when these countries transformed into republics – many of them under a presidential form of government in place of the Westminster parliamentary system – but subject to some modification in the consequences attendant upon conflict between the president and the assembly. The basic position remained of course that no bill could become law without the president's assent. In Tanzania, Zambia, Malawi, Botswana and Gambia he had the choice of either assenting or dissolving the assembly, provided that the bill, after having been refused assent by the president, was passed again within six months by a two-thirds majority (or a simple majority in Malawi and Botswana); the president must then assent within twenty-one days unless before that he had exercised the option of dissolution. In Uganda (1967), he must assent to every bill passed by the assembly and presented to him. In Ghana (1960), however, a bill or part of a bill to which the president had withheld his assent was killed altogether.

The provision in the Kenyan Constitution seems to suggest that a bill could become law without the assent of the president. First, whereas the provision in the other constitutions was that the legislative power of Parliament was to be exercised by bills passed by the assembly and assented to by the president (Tanzania and Gambia even stressed that a bill shall not become law unless it was so passed and assented to), in Kenya it was to be exercised by bills passed by the National Assembly. Further, "upon a bill that has been passed by the National Assembly being presented to the president for assent, it shall become law and shall thereupon be published in the Kenya Gazette as a law." These provisions are somewhat curious in so far as they suggest that presentation alone and not actual assent was all that was required for a bill to become law; this is hardly consistent with an earlier provision making the president a constituent part of Parliament. During the debate on the Constitution Bill in 1964, the Minister of Justice and Constitutional Affairs, Mr Tom Mboya, explained that "the assent of the president will be a formality. We have decided not to retain or preserve the "royal veto" ... Only Parliament can pass laws and the president will have no power to veto any law passed by Parliament". This seems to suggest that presidential assent is legally necessary but must be given as a matter of course.

Following the American precedent in preference to the inherited British expedient of making the executive a constituent part of the legislature, the Nigerian Presidential Constitutions of 1979 and 1999 vest legislative power in the National Assembly alone (House of Assembly in the case of a state). Undoubtedly, the American precedent of vesting legislative power in Congress alone, i.e., the Senate and the House of Representatives, was greatly influenced by the framers' preoccupation with the doctrine of the separation of powers, but the principles of republicanism seem also to have been a conditioning factor.

It is true that the constitution also makes the signature of the president requisite to legislation. The rationale for this is that, legislation, being a solemn and authoritative act of state, would need to be authenticated by the state functionary who personifies the authority and majesty of the state. The president's signature is necessary to bestow the seal of authority of the state upon a law passed by the assembly. But the fact that his signature is necessary to the efficacy of a law does not by itself make him a co-beneficiary of the legislative power. His signature stands more or less on the same footing as the requirement that a company's corporate seal is essential to the validity of certain of its acts. The authority to do the act is something distinct from the act of appending a signature or affixing a seal.

That the significance of this is purely formal is illustrated by the fact that, whereas in British constitutional theory and practice the concurrence of the monarch to legislation cannot be dispensed with under any circumstances, under the American Constitution and under the Nigeria Constitution, a bill passed by the assembly can become law without the president's signature if he fails to sign it within a specified period of time of its being presented to him, and the assembly then re-passes it with a two-thirds majority. The power of the president to withhold his signature from a bill operates by way of a veto (a qualified veto) in the strict sense of the world, since it operates to block the effectuation of the decision of an otherwise competent authority. Had the constitution not required a bill to be signed by the president, passage of a bill through the National Assembly would have been enough to give it the force of law since the legislative power is vested in the assembly alone. It would be otherwise had the president been made a constituent part of the legislature. His consent, however it is to be expressed, would then have been integrally involved in the legislative power; so that the withholding of it would not strictly be a veto, since a veto implies that the power of decision-taking is elsewhere than in the person exercising the veto. A member of a body may be enabled to veto the decision of that body, but that is because the decision-taking power is for all practical purposes in the majority.

We may note the interesting question raised concerning the interpretation of the language of Section 58(4) of the Nigerian Constitution which says that "where a bill is presented to the president for assent, he shall within thirty days thereof signify that he assents or that he withholds assent." Presidential assent or the withholding of it is not meant by the constitution to be a mechanical exercise; it certainly permits the president to seek information or clarification from the assembly necessary for a decision whether to assent or to withhold it. But does it also enable him to return a bill to the assembly for reconsideration of either the whole or parts of it? Interpreted in the spirit of mutual co-operation and dialogue which should inform relations between the two arms of the government, a request for reconsideration seems to be within the legal ambit and intendment of Section 58(4).

The point is covered by explicit provision in the 1958 Constitution of France which is adopted into the constitutions of most of her former African colonies. It states, *inter alia*, that a request for reconsideration, made within a prescribed time limit, "may not be refused" (Article 10, France). The absence of such an explicit provision in the Nigerian Constitution should not preclude an interpretation of Section 58(4) based on the precedent in these other countries. Such an approach seems eminently sensible and desirable for harmonious relations between the two organs, especially where a finance bill is concerned, i.e., a legislation which appropriates money from the public funds or which authorises the payment, issue or withdrawal of money from such funds, or the imposition of or an increase in any tax, duty or fee or reduction, withdrawal or cancellation thereof.

The French precedent in the matter, which is bequeathed to all her former African colonies with the exception of Guinea (1958), Tunisia and Algeria (1963), is different from the British and American in a sense decidedly repugnant to constitutionalism. Acceptably, the executive is not made a constituent part of Parliament (defined in the 1958 Constitution of France as consisting of the National Assembly and the Senate), nor can the president refuse to "promulgate" into law a bill passed by the assembly. A bill passed by the assembly does not become law unless and until it is "promulgated" by the president but he is obliged to do so within a prescribed time – fifteen days in France – subject to his right within that time limit to return it to the assembly for reconsideration, which "may not be refused".

But then comes the objectionable aspect of the arrangement. Under the constitution, the subject matters of the legislative power are divided between the assembly and the executive, enumerated matters being vested in the assembly and the residue in the executive. The matters so enumerated are described as being "within the domain of law" or "within the legislative domain," while "matters other than these ... have an executive character", and are to be regulated by the executive by decrees. Also, the executive may, "in order to carry out its programme," "ask Parliament to authorise it to take, in the form of ordinances and for a limited period, measures that are, normally within the domain of law" (Article 38, France). It needs to be emphasised that this goes beyond delegated legislation as it is understood in the British and American systems.

"If it appears in the course of the legislative procedure that a bill or amendment is not within the domain of law or is contrary to a delegation of authority granted by virtue of Article 38, the government may declare it out of order" (Article 41, France). The point in dispute will then, upon a reference by the government or the president of a legislative house, go to the constitutional council for ruling.

Thus, under the system, the terms "law" and "legislation" have a restricted meaning as referring only to laws passed by the legislative assembly; they exclude regulations (decrees and ordinances) made by the executive. No readily intelligible meaning or sense is conveyed by the distinction drawn by these constitutions between legislative and regulatory powers (the Constitution of Chad 1962 has a part headed **"Legislative and Regulatory Power"**), the former being designated as the "domain of law," since executive decrees and ordinances made in the executive's "regulatory powers" have the same force as a primary source of law as "legislation" made by the assembly.

Both derive their force as law directly from the constitution, and neither is subsidiary or inferior to the other. Furthermore, the division in the constitution of the subject matters of the law-making power between the executive and the assembly leaves the nomenclature "legislature" without much meaning as a distinctive classificatory term differentiating the law-making organ of the state from the executive organ. Both organs, each within the area of law-making assigned to it by the constitution, constitute the "legislature" of the state.

But whether the term "legislature" still has any distinctive meaning in the context, there can be no doubt that an executive, invested directly by the constitution with a large, if not the greater, part of the law-making power of the state can become over-powerful, as has been borne out in France under de Gaulle and in many of the former French African countries.

The Upper versus the Lower House in a Bicameral Assembly

The relation of inferiority and subordination of the House of Lords (upper house) to the House of Commons with respect to law-making in Britain is a product of history arising from the fact that the latter is elected while the former is not. The House of Lords can hold up for a specified period of time but cannot veto a bill passed by the Commons. A veto power in an unelected House is an outrage on the democratic ideal.

Under the Nigerian Constitution, the two houses of the National Assembly, the Senate and the House of Representatives, equally as the two houses of Congress under the U.S. Constitution, are both popularly elected and have equal legislative power, so that neither can override the other in the event of disagreement between them over a bill. Because of this, a bill passed by one House but not by the other lapses completely; also, any amendment to a bill proposed by one House must be agreed by the other, or else it lapses.

A joint meeting of both Houses to resolve differences is not allowed by the Nigerian Constitution, except in the case of a money bill, as earlier defined. In the event of disagreement over a money bill, a joint finance committee, composed of equal number of members from both Houses, is convened to examine the bill with a view to resolving the differences, failing which the bill will be voted on at a joint meeting of the two Houses (Section 59). Should the president fail to assent to the bill within thirty days of its presentation to him or if he withholds his assent, then, it becomes law without his assent if it is re-passed at another joint meeting of the two Houses by two-thirds majority (Section 59(4)). The exception in respect of a money bill is predicated upon the imperative need for ensuring that the administration of government and its services is not to be paralysed by differences between the two Houses which prevent the enactment of an appropriation law.

Although the conception underlying the principle of equality is that the two Houses should be complementary, not competitive, parts of a single legislative assembly, and that conflicts over legislative or other proposals should be based on genuine differences of opinion rather than on institutional jealousy, yet, with each House jealously guarding its equality with the other, there is bound to be rivalry over the issue of primacy. Neither will like to concede primacy to the other. Hence struggle over primacy has proved to be the main factor in the rivalry between the two Houses of the National Assembly. The seniority (as distinct from primacy) of the Senate seems not to be disputed by the lower House. On this issue of primacy, the question has been raised whether a joint meeting to resolve differences over a money bill does not undermine the equality of the numerically smaller House (the Senate) with the larger one (the House of Representatives). It seems unnecessary to pursue the question here.

CHAPTER 8

Nature and Extent of Executive Power

Extent of Executive Power as Delimited by its Inherent Nature

The extent of executive power, one of the most contentious issues in government, is delimited by its inherent nature. Its limits are implicit in the very word "execute." The *Concise Oxford Dictionary* defines "execute" as to "carry (plan, command, law, judicial sentence, will) into effect." This, like every other definition of the word, suggests physical action of some sort, and would therefore exclude any function that does not involve such action, such as thought. It would be an abuse of language to say that thinking is execution or that a person is executing anything when he is thinking out a plan. Thought is of course a vital element in a process that may eventually produce a definite plan or policy which is to be executed. The thinking out of a plan or policy partakes of the same nature as the deciding of cases by the courts. The adjudicatory function cannot be said to involve execution. That arises when the court has given a decision and the decision is being carried into effect. The same is true of the function of administering a law, as distinct from its execution. Much of it is quasi-judicial or quasi-legislative, involving merely the taking of decisions which operate to determine individual cases or to lay down general regulations.

In the general practice of modern government, however, the thinking out of policy and the administering of laws are among the most vital functions of the executive. One cannot imagine an executive that is excluded altogether from the thinking out of policy and its formulation. The executive has the primary responsibility for government, and policy is squarely implicated in governing. So also the filling in of the details of complex, modern legislation and the determination of a variety of issues arising in its administration can only be undertaken by the executive. Neither the legislature nor the judiciary is really well suited for the task, because of their procedure and the limited time and personnel available to them. The Constitution of Nigeria (1999) recognises this practice by vesting in the president the function of determining policy (Section 148(s)).

However, the fact that, for reasons of convenience, governmental efficiency and the logic of the executive's responsibility to govern, it has become customary for the executive to assume these functions should not brand them with the character of executive power. While generally recognised practice has brought them under the umbrella of the executive, by nature they are still not executive; they fall therefore outside the ordinary meaning of executive power. A distinction is to be made between functions which are executive by their nature and those that do not partake of that nature but are merely treated as such by modern governmental practice. The latter is not part of the **executive power** strictly so-called. This distinction appears to have the support of the United States Supreme Court.

Like thought and adjudication, legislation is also not embraced in execution. Like judicial decision, legislation duly enacted calls into play the exercise of executive power, so that its making cannot at the same time be an inherent function of executive power. By the inherent nature of executive power, therefore, legislation falls outside its purview. This inherent limitation is reinforced by the provision in the Nigerian Constitution vesting legislative power exclusively in the

National Assembly. The inherent limitation relating to adjudication is also reinforced by the vesting of judicial power exclusively in the courts. The executive can make law only by virtue of power delegated to it in that behalf by the National Assembly within the limits dictated by the principle of the exclusiveness of the National Assembly's power over legislation. Hence legislation by the executive is called delegated or subordinate legislation. The extent of legislative power the assembly can delegate to the executive is severely limited by the separation of powers.

This is a feature that distinguishes our system of government from the French system (bequeathed to nearly all former French African colonies) in which the subject-matters of the legislative power are, by the constitution itself, divided between the legislative assembly and the executive, with the latter empowered to legislate by decrees or ordinances on all matters not specifically enumerated and assigned to the legislative assembly. In other words, under the system, enumerated subject-matters of the legislative power belong to the legislative assembly, and the residue to the executive to be regulated by decrees or ordinances.

But the limits set on executive power by its inherent nature still give rise to considerable disputation as to its exact extent. Three or rather two differing schools of thought have been adumbrated upon the matter – the Residual or Inherent Power Theory and the Specific Grant Theory. Depending on the provisions of a particular constitution, the difference between the two approaches may not be much. The adherents of the Residual or Inherent Power Theory maintain, in the words of Professor Alan Gledhill, that executive power "is not limited to execution of the laws and, provided it is not forbidden by law, action by government need not wait upon legislation expressly empowering government to do it."

The Inherent Power Theory of the extent of executive power has been given classic expression in the statement made on it by President Theodore Roosevelt in his famous "stewardship" doctrine. "The most important factor in getting the right spirit of my Administration", he wrote in his *Autobiography:*

> was my insistence upon the theory that the executive power was limited only by specific restrictions and prohibitions appearing in the constitution or imposed by the Congress under its constitutional powers. My view was that every executive officer, and above all every executive officer in high position, was a **steward of the people**, and not to content himself with the negative merit of keeping his talents undamaged in a napkin. I declined to adopt the view that what was imperatively necessary for the Nation could not be done by the president unless he could find some specific authorization to do it. My belief was that it was not only his right but his duty to do anything that the needs of the Nation demanded unless such action was forbidden by the Constitution or by the laws. Under this interpretation of executive power I did and caused to be done many things not previously done by the president and the heads of the Departments. I did not usurp power, but I did greatly broaden the use of executive power. In other words, I acted for the public welfare, I acted for the common well-being of all our people, whenever and in whatever manner was necessary, unless prevented by direct constitutional or legislative prohibition (emphasis supplied).

The Specific Grant Theory, on the other hand, maintains that executive power is simply power to execute the laws, to carry into effect the provisions of the laws, either by enforcement against persons contravening them or by doing work or taking some other action required thereunder. There must be in existence a law, including the law of the constitution, in execution of which the action of the executive is done. Whilst conceding that, in addition to the execution of the laws, executive power also embraces other specific grants contained in the Constitution, they maintain that the provision vesting executive power in the president is not itself a grant of power because it is not specific.

Extent of Executive Power as Defined in the Constitution

The Constitution of Nigeria attempts to answer the question as to the extent of executive power, not however with the degree of clarity and certainty that we would wish. It provides that,

> **subject to the provisions of this constitution,** the executive power
> of the Federation shall be vested in the president and ... shall extend
> to the execution and maintenance of this constitution, all laws made
> by the National Assembly and to **all matters** with respect to which
> the National Assembly has for the time being power to make laws
> (Section 5(1)) – emphasis supplied.

The three elements comprised in this provision need to be set out *seriatim, viz*

(a) execution and maintenance of the constitution;

(b) execution and maintenance of laws made by the National Assembly; and

(c) execution and maintenance of "all matters" within the legislative competence of the National Assembly but on which it has as yet made no law.

These elements mark an important point of difference from the U.S. Constitution, in that executive power is not there expressly stated to extend to (a) and (c) above (Article 2). "The vesting of the executive power in the president", said the country's Supreme Court, "was essentially a grant of the power to execute the laws" (*Myers v. United States* (1926)), but, although not expressly so stated, the laws, the President is to execute include the law of the constitution. As the Court held in a leading case in 1890 "the laws he (i.e., the president) is to see executed are manifestly those contained in the constitution, and those enacted by Congress" (*Cunningham v. Neagle*). Thus, it is (c) above that constitutes the real difference between the two constitutions in this respect.

Execution of Laws Made by the National Assembly

The execution of laws made by the National Assembly raises no problem. Laws validly made by the National Assembly within the limits of its power under the constitution are the predominant source of executive power, since there is hardly any law that does not call for one kind of executive action or the other. For example, the postal laws need to be executed by building post offices, printing stamps and generally by operating postal services; and the education laws by building schools, enforcing standards, conducting examinations, etc. For anything like an adequate picture of the extent of powers available to the executive in the administration of government one has therefore to consult the statute book.

Such executive action as is called for under the laws is the constitutional prerogative of the president by virtue of the vesting of the executive power in him and his more specific power to execute laws made by the National Assembly. The passing of a law requiring execution calls the power into existence without any specific authorisation to that effect in the law itself. Once the National Assembly enacts a law authorising, say, the provision of medical and health facilities, then, whether the law specifically vests him with the power to do so or not, the president can, by right of the power vested in him by the constitution, execute the law by building hospitals and organising medical and health facilities provided of course an appropriation has been made by the legislature. The National Assembly acts unconstitutionally if it vests the execution of the law in some person or agency who is independent of the president – subject, as noted below to the exception in the case of purely administrative or ministerial functions of a quasi-legislative or quasi-judicial nature.

Execution of the laws involves more than taking the specific actions required by particular statutes. The laws must be viewed not only individually but also as a mass forming a system. It is in this sense that one speaks of the duty to maintain law and order in society. As Chief Justice Vinson of the U.S. Supreme Court says:

> unlike an administrative commission confined to the enforcement of the statute under which it is created, or the head of a department when administering a particular statute, the president is a constitutional officer charged with taking care that a mass of legislation be executed (*Youngstown Sheet & Tube Co. v. Sawyer* (1951)).

There is, in this connection, another difference between the Nigerian and U.S. Constitutions, which deserves to be noted. The U.S. Constitution speaks of the execution of the "laws" (Article 2, Sec. 3) which, as earlier stated, includes the law of the constitution. "Laws" in this context is not limited to the law of the Constitution and those made by the Congress, but includes also international treaties which are incorporated into municipal law directly by Article 3 Section 8 of the Constitution, thereby making treaties part of the laws to be executed by the president. In contrast, Section 5(1)(b) of the Nigerian Constitution is explicit that the president is only empowered to execute the law of the constitution and those made by the National Assembly, but not treaties. This is reinforced by Section 12(1) which, adopting the position in English law, as do also the constitutions of other countries in former British Africa, provides that "no treaty between the Federation and any other country shall have the force of law except to the extent to which any such treaty has been enacted into law by the National Assembly".

There are many other countries of the world whose constitutions follow that of the U.S. in incorporating treaties directly as part of the municipal law, e.g., Bulgaria 1991 (Article 5(4)), Czechoslovakia 1991 (Article 2), France 1958 (Article 55), eleven countries in former French Africa, the Democratic Republic of Congo 1964 (Article 10) and Somalia 1960 (Article 6(1)).

Execution of the Constitution

The execution and maintenance of the constitution is not, however, free of uncertainty as to the actions it empowers the president to take. The uncertainty arises from the fact that what is to be executed and maintained is not just abstract concepts contained in a written document. The constitution in this connection is a living charter by which a government with a full amplitude of institutions, instrumentalities, powers and rights is created for the administration of public affairs. The government established by the constitution presupposes a community of people of differing individual interests but bound together by a common desire for the stability and security of the society as a nation.

Execution of government and its functions is covered for the most part by specific powers explicitly granted in the constitution, e.g., power to establish ministries, departments and offices; to appoint, control and remove ministers and other executive personnel and to assign functions to them; to determine and formulate policy; to maintain order; to suppress insurrection; to manage the finances of the government; to pardon offenders and commute sentences; to command the armed forces, etc. These, being specific grants, are known and regular powers, and therefore free of uncertainty.

The question has arisen whether the oath required of the president by the constitution to "preserve, protect and defend the constitution" imports specific and explicit grant of power to do so. Now, while an oath attaches criminal sanction in the event of its falsity, the question is whether it also operates as a grant of power. Neither the majority nor the minority of the U.S. Supreme Court in *Cunningham v. Neagle* (1890) dealt with the question directly. Edward S. Corwin has, however, pointed to "the obvious difficulty in claiming for the president powers that the constitution otherwise withholds from him, simply on the score of his obligation to protect and preserve it", and he concludes both on logical interpretation and upon available historical evidence that the oath is not an independent source of power.

The other question that has arisen on the effect of the oath is whether the obligation which it imposes upon the president to preserve and protect the constitution is a legally enforceable one. The president's oath may be compared with the Queen's coronation oath by which she swore "to conform to the people of England the laws and customs granted to them by the ancient Kings of England", and to "hold and keep the righteous customs" of the realm and to "defend and strengthen the same". Edward Corwin has again expressed the view that the "purpose, definitely, was to put the King's conscience in bonds to the law". In other words, violation of her or his oath of office by the Queen or president carries no criminal sanction. This interpretation is supported by a decision of the Ghana Supreme Court in 1961 in *Re Akoto* which, likening the declaration of fundamental principles, which the President of Ghana was required to make on assumption of office, to the Queen's coronation oath, held that "neither the oath nor the declaration can be said to have a statutory effect".

Apart from specific functions explicitly granted by the constitution, the execution of government also **implies** a host of other powers i.e., powers arising by implication: the execution of the business of government in all its ramifications; the protection of the instrumentalities established by the constitution for the purpose as well as government property; the preservation of the government and the nation by ensuring their stability, security and safety; direction and control of the departments of state, their activities and staff; pure administration; protection or preservation of the instrumentalities and functionaries of the government, including legislators and judicial officers; and co-ordination of the activities of government.

The U.S. case of *Cunningham v. Neagle* (1890) affords a good illustration of an implied constitutional grant of executive power. A Justice of the U.S. Supreme Court, while on circuit in California, was threatened with assault and murder by a person against whom he had given judgment. To protect him against the threatened attack, a marshal of the United States was, on the instruction of the U.S. Attorney-General, assigned to act as bodyguard to the justice. While the justice was at a railway station in the course of travelling from one circuit court to another, he was attacked by the author of the threats, whereupon the marshal shot and killed the attacker. The question before the Supreme Court was whether the attorney-general, on behalf of the president, had power to assign a marshal to act as bodyguard to a justice of the Supreme Court travelling on circuit, so as to constitute the killing of the attacker an act done in pursuance of a law of the U.S., which would entitle the marshal to be released on a writ of *habeas corpus* from the custody of the authorities of the State of California. There was no statute or any specific provision of the constitution enabling the president to protect judges, but it was argued that the action was justified by his power to execute the constitution, because the assignment of the marshal was made in discharge of an obligation fairly and properly inferable from that instrument, namely the preservation of the constitution against a person seeking to interfere with the discharge of his duty by a member of one of its agencies.

The argument was accepted by the majority of the court which held that the power to execute the laws extended to all the rights, duties and obligations growing out of the constitution and to all the protection implied by the nature of the government under the constitution. And the protection of the judges was essential to the existence of the government, since it would be a great reproach to the system of government of the United States if there was to be found within the domain of its powers no means of protecting the judges in the conscientious and faithful discharge of their duties from the malice and hatred of those upon whom their judgments might operate unfavourably.

A minority of two, while admitting that the president's executive power extended to the execution of the law of the constitution, held that the constitution established no law specifically requiring the protection of judges in their official capacity against murderous attacks. On the contrary, the Constitution vests in Congress the power "to make all laws which shall be necessary and proper for carrying into execution (its own powers) and all other powers vested by this Constitution in the government of the United States, or in any department or officer thereof" (Article 1, Section 8). Accordingly, in the absence of any enactment by Congress providing for protection as being necessary and proper for carrying the judicial power into execution, the president could not assign a marshal to act as a bodyguard to a judge and to follow him in his journey while in circuit. "The protection needed and to be given must proceed, not from the president, but primarily from Congress", and "the right claimed must be traced to legislation of Congress, else it cannot exist".

Execution of "all matters" within the Legislative Competence of the National Assembly

But is that all the powers the execution of government confers on the president? To what extent does it enable him to act on "all matters" within the legislative competence of the National Assembly but on which it has as yet made no law". In the absence of a law made by the National Assembly, what executive action can he take on any of the 66 specific matters on the federal exclusive legislative list?

Whilst the grant to the President of power to execute "all matters" within federal legislative competence is of an indefinite extent, i.e., it is not specific in the sense required by the Specific Grant Theory, it is nonetheless a grant of power explicitly made by the law of the constitution. It cannot have been the intention that the provision is to be a surplusage, adding nothing at all to the grants of power to execute the constitution and laws made by the National Assembly, especially as it appears together with them in the same sentence.

It can hardly be denied that the provision empowers the president, without any further authorisation by law made by the National Assembly, to manufacture or acquire arms, ammunition and explosives (Item 2, Exclusive Legislative List); to build airports (Item 3); to establish a bank under a general law on banking enacted by the Assembly (item 6); to borrow money for purposes of the government (Item 7); to construct and maintain roads (Item 11); to deport aliens (a citizen and an alien are defined in the Constitution) (Item 18); to establish diplomatic, consular and trade representation and generally to conduct external affairs (Items 20 and 26); to engage in fishing (Item 29); to insure government property (Item 33), etc. This is of course provided that the National Assembly has by law appropriated money for such projects. For, under Section 80 of the Constitution, all revenues or other monies raised by the government are public funds, from which no withdrawal can be made unless the withdrawal is authorised by an Act of the National Assembly and the manner of making such withdrawal is likewise authorised (Section 80(4)). And, provided also he does not thereby interfere with private rights. Subject to this, the power of the president to act on such matters before the National Assembly makes law on them, e.g., to borrow money, cannot be controlled by a resolution of the Assembly or of one only of the Houses, since the Assembly can take binding decisions by a mere resolution only in respect of matters specified in the constitution.

But it seems also clear that the power to take executive action on "all matters" within the legislative competence of the National Assembly does not enable the president to do so in respect of matters which, by their nature, do not admit of executive action in advance or in the absence of legislation regulating them, e.g., bankruptcy and insolvency (Item 5); banking i.e. the regulation of banks and banking (Item 6); commercial and industrial monopolies, combines and trusts (Item 10); control of capital issues (Item 12); copyrights (Item 13); currency, coinage and legal tender (Item 15); customs, excise and export duties (Items 16 and 25); evidence (Item 23); exchange control (Item 24); the creation of offences (Part III of the legislative list), etc. These matters, by their nature, require to be first regulated by law before executive action on them can take place.

On one point the two schools of thought on the extent of executive power are agreed, namely, that without authorisation by law, either the law of the constitution or one made by the legislative assembly, the president cannot, on his own inherent authority, i.e., authority flowing from his power to execute the government or to act on all matters within the legislative competence of the assembly, do anything that violates the rights or interests of the individual, or which interferes with his freedom of action. The Nigerian Constitution (1999) affirms this, but perhaps not in its entirety, by making executive power "subject to the provisions of this Constitution" (Section 5(1)); the provisions to which the power is made subject include, above all, provisions guaranteeing individual rights and freedoms. The constitutional guarantee of individual rights and freedoms can only be curtailed or interfered with by a constitutionally valid law, never by executive act not backed by a law validly enacted by the National Assembly. The limitations on executive as well as on legislative power in favour of the individual will be fully examined elsewhere.

Constitutional Restraints on the Powers of the President to Execute or Administer Government

It should be stated right away that limitations on executive power arising from the separation of powers (examined in Chapters 9-12 below) or from the legal protection of individual rights (Chapter 14 below) are not our concern here.

We are here confronted with one of the most significant respects in which the presidential system under the Nigerian Constitution differs from the American prototype. While the American Constitution clearly recognises the office of departmental head, as a collective body they (the departmental heads) have no existence whatever in the constitution. No obligation is cast upon the president to consult with them collectively as a cabinet with respect to the general programme or policy of the government. The reference to writing in the provision empowering the president to require the written opinion of a departmental head suggests that the constitution never contemplated a collective opinion or advice. However, collective consultation has developed informally in response to the demands and pressures of modern government faced, as it is, with ever-recurrent series of crises. The Cabinet in America as an institutionalised organ of government may be said indeed to have been the product of crisis. Before 1793 there was nothing that could be called a Cabinet. Although the first President, George Washington, occasionally called into collective consultation his departmental heads, of whom there were then only four (including the attorney-general), the meetings did not assume such frequency and regularity as to stamp them with an institutionalised character as an established machinery of the government. It was the diplomatic crisis of that year, arising out of the question whether or not America should adopt the position of neutrality in the war between England and France, that gave the Cabinet formal birth by impelling the president to meet his secretaries almost every day over the issue, the culmination being the meeting at which the decision was taken to proclaim American neutrality in the war.

But the point that deserves to be noticed about the Cabinet in America is that, after more than two centuries of existence as a definite institution of government, it has acquired no constitutional status by convention. There is no conventional obligation upon the President to consult it at regular intervals. How often he convenes the Cabinet is a matter entirely within the discretion of the President, and the practice has varied as between individual Presidents. Some hold meetings of the Cabinet fairly regularly; others, distrustful of meetings, consult their Cabinet at infrequent intervals, preferring informal consultations with various types of advisers. If there is no obligation to consult, much less is there a duty to accept the Cabinet's advice. Again individual presidents have differed as to the extent they defer to the advice of their Cabinet. Professor Sir Denis Brogan described the position accurately when he wrote: "There is in American theory and practice no question of *primus inter pares*. The famous story of Lincoln consulting his Cabinet and announcing, "Nos, 7; ayes, 1. The ayes have it" expresses perfectly the spirit of the American Constitution." The same president was reported to have said to his Cabinet on another occasion: "I have gathered you together to hear what I have written down. I do not wish your advice about the main matter – that I have determined for myself." And the matter in question was one indeed as momentous as the emancipation of slaves. Statements to similar effect are also credited to other presidents of similarly strong personality, like Andrew Jackson, Theodore Roosevelt, Woodrow Wilson and Franklin Roosevelt.

Without question the authoritarianism of Lincoln owed much to the failure of the constitution to provide for a Cabinet, and seemed to have vindicated those critics who at the time of the Constitution's adoption decried this omission as an open invitation to "despotism", "caprice, the intrigues of favourites and mistresses, etc." Individual consultation produces a different kind of effect from a collective one.

Modifications by the Nigerian Constitution of the American Presidential Executive

The American presidential executive, as described above, is modified in the following respects in Nigeria.

(a) The Subjection of the President to the Advice and Influence of Various Bodies Established by the Constitution

The most important modification in this respect is the establishment of a Cabinet in the Constitution and the obligation thus cast on the president to consult with it, the object being, by subjecting him to the advice and influence of a Cabinet, to prevent him from assuming dictatorial powers.

The constitution goes further than merely casting on the president an express or implied obligation to consult with the Cabinet. It requires him to hold regular meeting with the vice-president (or deputy governor) and all ministers (or commissioners) for the purposes of determining the general direction of domestic and foreign policies of the government, the coordination of the activities of the government, and also for the purpose of advising him generally in the discharge of his executive functions other than those functions with respect to which he is required to seek the advice or act on the recommendation of any other person or body. The word "regular" connotes constancy in time, and not as and when it suits the whim of the president or governor. In the context it does also imply a notion of frequency in time. A meeting once in every month, though it satisfies the idea of constancy in time, would not be in conformity with the spirit of the provision.

Although the determination of general policy and the coordination of government activities are not thereby divested from the president or governor, and made the collective responsibility of the Executive Council, the provision does have the effect of restricting the manner for exercising them. It requires him to exercise them, not alone in the solitude of his office or bedroom, but in council with the vice-president (or deputy governor) and ministers (or commissioners). The aim is to bring the collective views of the president (or governor), the vice-president and ministers (or commissioners) to bear upon such matters, but without depriving the president (or governor), as the sole repository of the power, of his authority to override the views of the rest of the council if and when he thinks fit. Having submitted a question on these matters to the deliberation of the council, the president (or governor) is within his constitutional right to refuse to accept the view of the rest of the council.

The provision does also oblige the president or governor to seek the advice of the Executive Council on the discharge of his executive functions generally. The implication of this is that, without an Executive Council, the political administration of the government by the president (or governor) alone is, to a large extent, unconstitutional. By making it mandatory for the president (or governor) to establish offices of ministers and, with the approval of the Senate (or House of Assembly), to appoint persons to such offices, and by casting upon him the obligation to hold regular meetings with the vice-president (or deputy governor) and ministers for the purpose of advising him on the exercise of his executive functions, the constitution does clearly manifest an intention that the president (or governor) is not to govern without the restraining and moderating influence of the collective advice of an executive council. Clearly, therefore, in a situation where the president (or governor) refuses or neglects to establish ministerial offices and to appoint persons to them or where, having appointed ministers, he refuses or neglects to hold regular meetings with them for the purpose of getting their advice on his executive actions, the administration of government by him in these circumstances would be a violation of both the spirit and letters of the constitution, no matter how benevolent or liberal his actions may be. "I am of the view", said the learned President of the Court of Appeal of Nigeria, "that if the governor ... refuses to hold these regular meetings, he constitutes himself as a dictator and this will be in my view not only contrary to the spirit of the constitution but is clearly a breach of the specific provisions of this section."

A unique situation not contemplated by the provision was created in Kaduna State during the first two years of the Second Republic (October 1979 to July 1981) by the refusal of the House of Assembly to approve four successive lists of commissioners submitted to it by the governor, leaving him to administer the government without the restraining influence of an Executive Council. The question to which the situation gave rise was whether the administration of government by the governor alone for nearly two years was, in the peculiar circumstances, unconstitutional. To this question, the Court of Appeal, in the passage quoted above, returned an affirmative answer.

The correctness of the decision may be questioned. The absence of commissioners was not due to a refusal or neglect on the part of the governor, but to the persistent rejection of his four successive lists of nominees by the House of Assembly in clear abuse of its power. The governor even sought, unsuccessfully, the court's intervention to compel the House to approve his nominations (*Governor, Kaduna State v. House of Assembly, Kaduna State* (1981)). It seems reasonable to say that the unjustified rejection by the House of all the persons nominated by the governor for appointment as commissioners created a grave exigency justifying the application of the doctrine of state necessity. In the stalemate created by the Assembly's refusal to approve commissioners for the governor, the necessity for government in the state was no less than at any other time. A complete abeyance of government would have resulted in chaos and the ruination of the society. In these peculiar circumstances, therefore, the governor was entitled to run the government without commissioners.

Be that as it may, the constitution does not contemplate or require that every executive action of the president (or governor) must be preceded by the advice of the executive council. That would involve the president (or governor) having meetings with the vice-president (or deputy governor) and ministers every day or even several times a day. What the provision seems to require is that the president (or governor) should have regular and frequent meetings with the vice-president (or deputy governor) and ministers in order to obtain their advice on general policy, coordination of government activities and other important executive functions.

Apart from the case of the Executive Council where consultation is made obligatory on the president or governor, there are other executive bodies established by the Nigerian Constitution and invested with the power to advise him on a variety of matters e.g., the National Defence Council on the defence of the sovereignty and territorial integrity of the Federation; the National Economic Council on economic affairs; the National Population Commission on population problems (that is, apart from its own independent functions with regard to census); the Council of State on the census, prerogative of mercy, award of national honours, matters relating to other executive bodies, and, when so requested, on the maintenance of public order and any other matters (again this is apart from the independent functions vested in it by the constitution); and the State Council of Chiefs on matters relating to customary law or cultural affairs, inter-communal relations and chieftaincy matters.

The intention of the constitution is to insulate these bodies from presidential control – there are altogether fifteen of them, including the five noted in the next section, i.e., Civil Service Commission, Police Service Commission, Police Council, Code of Conduct Bureau and the Code of Conduct Tribunal. To this end, the appointment of members (other than *ex-officio* members) is required to be confirmed by the Senate (except in the case of three of them - Council of State, National Defence Council and National Security Council), while their removal also requires a resolution of the Senate supported by two-thirds majority of its members praying removal for inability to discharge the functions of the office or for misconduct (Sections 153-157).

The difference between these bodies and the Executive Council is that the power vested in the former to advise the president or governor implies no obligation on his part to seek advice, so that failure by him to do so in no way affects the validity of decisions or actions taken by him, though the spirit of the provisions is that the president should seek their advice. But a "power" to advise does imply a right of initiative, a right to give advice without being asked. The power can be exercised independently of the wishes of the president; whether he requests it or not. These bodies can, from time to time, on their own initiative, meet to proffer advice to the president on matters on which they are respectively empowered to advise. They have, like any other body, an inherent power to determine, independently of the president's control, when and how frequently to meet to consider what advice to give. The president can of course request them to meet to advise him on particular questions, but it is not within his power to stop them agreeing on a schedule of meetings, whether it be monthly or quarterly. (The Council of State can advise on the maintenance of order only when requested.)

Consultation, when it does take place, whether as a constitutional requirement or at the discretion of the president must go beyond merely giving information or announcing a decision already taken. It implies that an opportunity must be given to the person or body consulted to express an opinion, to criticise any proposal brought forward by the president (or governor) and to offer advice; and that the opinion, criticism or advice so offered should genuinely be taken into consideration by the president (or governor) in arriving at a decision. Having done that, the president (or governor) is free to decide as seems best to him, whether in accordance with or contrary to the advice. No obligation is cast on him to accept it.

Consultation with a council as a condition for the exercise of the executive power vested in a single chief executive under the presidential system has obvious democratic virtue. First, as has truly been said, the interaction of many minds "is usually more illuminating than the intuition of one. In a meeting representing different departments and diverse points of view, there is a greater likelihood of hearing alternatives, of exposing errors, and of challenging assumptions." It is, we are told by John Stuart Mill, "a maxim of experience that in the multitude of counsellors there is wisdom; and that a man seldom judges right, even in his own concerns, still less in those of the public, when he makes habitual use of no knowledge but his own, or that of some single adviser." It is therefore necessary that, while the effectiveness of executive government requires that responsibility for it should be vested in a single individual, he "should, not only occasionally but habitually, listen to a variety of opinions, and inform his judgement by the discussions among a body of advisers." Perhaps even more important is what has been described as the "increased public confidence inspired by order and regularity and the increased *esprit de corps* of the participants". Modern government challenges the capacity of a single mind to deal with its many and complex problems. Crisis increases the intensity of the challenge, and modern government faces an ever-recurrent series of crises.

Second, collective consultation is likely to have a more restraining effect on the president than an individual one. It is less easy to ride roughshod over a determined opposition from a council than from an individual, and a president who does that faces a heavier responsibility in the event of failure or mistake; and where ministers are concerned he may also provoke the resignation of some and a consequent undermining of the unity of his administration as well as a possible loss of public support and confidence. There can be no doubt therefore that an obligation to consult a council does operate to restrain the president's exercise of his powers.

(b)　The Vesting in Independent Bodies Established by the Constitution and the Consequent Divesting from the President of Certain Functions Embraced in the Power to Execute the Government and the Laws

The Nigerian Constitution establishes certain independent functionaries or agencies charged with functions essential to the maintenance of democracy and liberty as well as to an impartial administration, which should, for that reason, be divested from the president to whom they belong as part of the executive power vested in him. Thus, while the executive power vested in the president embraces as a necessary incident the appointment, promotion, removal and disciplinary control of the staff in the ministries, departments and other executive agencies of government, these incidents of the power are largely divested from the president. With certain exceptions, the appointment, promotion, removal and disciplinary control of civil servants and members of the Nigeria Police are vested in independent bodies established by the constitution, the Civil Service Commission and the Police Service Commission respectively (Section 153 and Third Schedule). The only officers in the civil service and the police the president appoints and may remove are the secretary to the government, head of the civil service, ambassadors, high commissioners or other principal representatives of Nigeria abroad, permanent secretaries or heads of extra-ministerial departments, employees on his personal staff and the inspector-general of police, the latter on the advice of the Nigeria Police Council (Sections 171 and 215). Furthermore, the 1979 and 1999 Constitutions of Nigeria prescribed a code of conduct for public officers, including the president himself, and its implementation is vested in two independent bodies – the Code of Conduct Bureau and Code of Conduct Tribunal.

Two vital and sensitive functions, elections and census, which should normally form part of the power of the president to execute the constitution and the laws, are vested in independent executive bodies by the constitution – the National Electoral Commission and the National Population Commission. Also, the audit of accounts of government institutions is vested in an independent auditor-general. The control of the police is largely divested from the president. Its organisation and administration and all matters relating thereto (other than its use and operational control or the appointment, disciplinary control and dismissal of its members) as well as its general supervision are vested in the Nigeria Police Council composed of the president as chairman, all state governors, the chairman of the Police Service Commission and the inspector-general of police.

More important, the command of the police (i.e., its

operational use) is vested in the inspector-general to be appointed
from among its serving members (Section 215), and subject to the
overall authority of the inspector-general, in a commissioner of
police in respect of the contingent of the police stationed in a state,
though the president (or the governor in the case of the state police
commissioner) may give him lawful directions regarding the use of the
police for the purpose of maintaining and securing public security and
public order. It should be noted that the power of giving directions
vested in the president (or governor) does not extend to all police powers
but only to the use of the police for maintaining and securing public
security and public order; and that even as regards the use of the police
for maintaining public security and public order the power to give
directions does not cover all powers embraced in the inspector-general's
(or state police commissioners in respect of states) command power.
There are clearly aspects of the police power for the maintenance of
public order and security which lie outside the president's (or governor's)
power to give directions – for example, the power to decide the
individual policemen and the number to be deployed to a particular
public order assignment. The president is not part of the command
structure of the police force, as he is of the armed forces, and cannot
therefore command individual policemen or police units.

The divesting of the command of the police from the president
and the vesting of it in a professional inspector-general, save as regards
his power to give direction to the latter with respect to the maintenance
of public security and public order, constitutes a serious limitation,
since a considerable part of the president's power to execute the
government and the laws is covered in the function vested in the police
by the Police Act Cap. 359 Laws of the Federation 1990, *viz*, "the
prevention and detection of crime, the apprehension of offenders, the
preservation of law and order, the protection of life and property and
the due enforcement of all laws and regulations with which they are
directly charged". With the exception noted above, the police, under
the supreme command of the inspector-general, have a free hand in
the discharge of their wide-ranging functions, and cannot be directed

by, nor are they legally obliged to consult, the president, although any inspector-general, with enough political sense, is expected to keep him informed before taking action in a politically sensitive case, like the invasion of the Senate President's residence by a contingent of policemen in search of the mace said to have been removed from its proper place of custody in the Senate building.

The object of divesting the command of the police from the president is to ensure that the organised coercive force of the state represented by the police will not be abused for the oppression and victimisation of individuals for partisan political reasons. No doubt, the police themselves, like any other human organisation, are not free of ethnic, religious or other prejudices and influences.

There is one other police function, criminal prosecutions, in respect of which the police do not have a free hand, but here, unlike in the case of the maintenance of public security and public order, the control of the police in the exercise of this function is vested, not in the president, but in a professional functionary, the attorney-general, whose office, like that of the inspector-general of police, but unlike those of other ministers, is established directly by the constitution, which requires the holder to be a lawyer of at least ten years' post-call standing (Section 150). The office of the attorney-general is thus unique as being the only ministerial office established directly by the constitution and invested with constitutionally defined functions relating to the control of criminal prosecutions in the exercise of which he is specifically required "to have regard to the public interest, the interest of justice and the need to prevent abuse of legal process" (Section 174(3)). This requirement was an innovation introduced by the 1979 Constitution with the object of guarding against the abuse of the power, as happened on many occasions in the past.

Unlike the inspector-general of police, however, the independence envisaged for the attorney-general is attenuated by his being designated in the constitution as "a minister of the government" (Section 150(1)), the effect of which, it seems, is to subject him to political control in the exercise of his power over criminal prosecutions. During the First Republic

(October 1963 – January 1966), the attorney-general's position as a minister, with the obligation of collective responsibility for government decisions to which ministers were subject and with the control exercised over them by the head of government, deprived him of independence in the exercise of his power in respect of criminal prosecutions. In the inevitable conflict between the interest of justice and the political interests of the government, the latter were allowed to override. Prosecutions of political opponents upon trumped-up charges and the discontinuance of prosecutions instituted by the police against government party activists became quite a common phenomenon.

Against this background of abuse, the Constitution Drafting Committee (CDC), in its draft constitutional proposals in 1976, recommended that the attorney-general's power to take over or discontinue criminal prosecutions instituted by some other person or authority should be exercisable only with the leave of the court which, in deciding whether or not to grant leave, "shall have regard to the interest of justice, the public interest and the need to prevent abuse of legal process". As finally enacted, however, the constitution omitted the requirement to obtain leave of court, merely providing that "in the exercise of his powers under this section the attorney-general shall have regard to the public interest, the interests of justice and the need to prevent abuse of legal process." By thus bestowing constitutional force upon the principles of the common law which guided the exercise of the power, it was hoped to generate on the part of the attorney-general greater attachment to those principles.

The hope had unfortunately not materialised. The abuses of the past had reared their ugly heads again, and had attained such proportions that even the police, the agency handling most of the criminal prosecutions in the country, had to cry out loudly. Addressing a press conference in Benin on Tuesday, 13 July 1982, the Bendel State Commissioner of Police had protested vehemently against the intolerable frequency with which prosecutions instituted by his command, including prosecutions for murder, armed robbery, stealing, assault by party thugs, and even assault on the police were being withdrawn with "flimsy excuses" by the state attorney-general. The police commissioner had been compelled to employ the medium of a public protest through the press, because, as he said, his attempts to converse with the state attorney-general and his private complaints to the state chief judge and governor had yielded no result. Also on 5 April, 1983 at a ministerial briefing in Lagos, the minister of police affairs spoke about the "indiscriminate withdrawal of cases", saying that this had contributed immensely to the breakdown of law and order in the country, since it not only undermined the deterrent objective of the criminal law but might even operate as a positive encouragement to people with criminal tendencies to break the law.

In Kaduna State, the withdrawals were made even without an incumbent attorney-general to authorise them, none having been appointed since the inception of the presidential Constitution in October 1979. The absence of an incumbent attorney-general simply swept away the basis of the supposed safeguard – the expectation that the standing of the attorney-general as a leading lawyer of repute and the head of the Bar in the state would insulate him against pressure to use his power for political or personal reasons. Without an attorney-general duly appointed under the constitution and with the qualifications therein prescribed, the solicitor-general of Kaduna State and other officers of the Ministry of Justice simply assumed the power.

In one case, a prosecution for culpable homicide of a boy was withdrawn by the solicitor-general after committal on a preliminary investigation by a magistrate, who found a *prima facie* case to have been made out against the accused persons. But the solicitor-general thought the evidence at the preliminary investigation so contradictory as not to justify the prosecution being continued and accordingly withdrew it. The father of the dead boy, in a separate action in the High Court, then sought a declaration that only an attorney-general or a person duly appointed to act in the office could withdraw or authorise the withdrawal of a prosecution without leave of the court, and that in the absence of an incumbent attorney-general to authorise it, the withdrawal of the prosecution against the particular accused persons was unconstitutional and void (*Attorney-General, Kaduna State v. Hassan* (1983)).

The propriety of the exercise of the power by the solicitor-general and other law officers in the Ministry of Justice turns on the provision that the powers conferred by the constitution upon the attorney-general in respect of criminal prosecutions "may be exercised by him in person or through officers of his department" (Sections 160(2) and 191(2)). The interpretative question raised is whether the words "by him" govern both the exercise of the power by the attorney-general in person and its exercise "through officers of his department" – whether, that is, what is meant is that the power may be exercised by the attorney-general in person or by him through officers of his department. The contention of the solicitor-general was that the phrase "through officers of his department" confers upon the officers of the ministry an independent right to exercise the power, which does not depend upon delegation or authorisation by the attorney-general.

Affirming the decision of the trial judge, the Court of Appeal, by a majority of 3 to 1, rejected the interpretation contended for by the solicitor-general. Such a view of the provision would clearly do violence to its true meaning and intent. In the context of the provision the word "through" presupposes a person who is to act through others. It implies a delegated authority or agency, the officers of the department being merely agents through whom the attorney-general may act. Their acts done with his authority are presumptively his acts. In the contemplation of the law, the attorney-general is deemed always to be the person acting, whether the action is done by him in person or through officers of his department. As the learned president of the Court of Appeal, Justice Nasir, observed, "there is nothing in the constitution to vest the exercise of the constitutional powers of the attorney-general in any officer of his department without his authorisation".

The meaning intended is brought out clearly by the wording of the provision in Section 5, which says that the executive power vested in the president (or governor) may be "exercised by him either directly or through the vice-president and ministers of the Government of the Federation or officers in the public office of the Federation". It is exactly the same notion of delegated authority or agency that is intended to be conveyed by the provision authorising the attorney-general to exercise his power over criminal prosecutions through officers in this department.

The contention that officers of the attorney-general's department have an independent right to exercise it runs counter to the provision that no person that is not qualified as a legal practitioner with at least ten years' experience shall "hold or perform the functions of the office of attorney-general", in that, as Justice Wali pertinently observed, it will make it possible for officers without the prescribed qualification to exercise the power.

The interpretation contended for by the solicitor-general is also untenable for reasons of accountability. Being civil servants and removable only through a rigid procedure designed to guarantee them security of tenure, the officers of the attorney-general's department have no responsibility for their acts. The responsibility for acts done by civil servants falls upon the ministers and the president. They alone are accountable to the public for the acts of the civil servants. The exercise of the critical powers in respect of criminal prosecutions when there is no incumbent attorney-general would mean that the public has no responsible functionary to hold accountable for any abuses that may occur. It would also, as Justice Nasir said:

> lead to the ridiculous result of each and every officer of the department having power to terminate criminal prosecutions with or without the knowledge of the attorney-general in whatever case they so wish irrespective of the seriousness of the offence or the possible consequences of such termination and the courts will be powerless to intervene.

The Court of Appeal also rightly rejected the claim of right by the solicitor-general based on the necessity of maintaining orderly administration of the criminal law during any period when there is no incumbent attorney-general. "The issue of necessity", said the learned president, "does not arise as prosecution can still continue or be discontinued without reference to section 191. It is the method which is different."

Regrettably, the innovation of the 1979 Constitution has not proved effective in checking abuses, because all it does is to give constitutional force to the principles of the common law which are supposed to guide the exercise of the power by the attorney-general. It is not enough for the constitution to **direct** the attorney-general to have regard to the public interest, the interest of justice and the need to prevent abuse of legal process without making it **mandatory** for him to do so. The command to the attorney-general to have regard to these factors is merely **directory**, not **mandatory**.

Interestingly, the courts have entertained divergent opinions as to the effect of this provision. In a case where the Attorney-General of Benue State wrote to the court stating, in the bald form commonly used, that he no longer intended to prosecute the accused persons – or *nolle prosequi*, as it is called – Justice Idoko of the State High Court held that the provision has qualified the absolute discretion hitherto enjoyed by the attorney-general in the control of criminal prosecutions and that it requires him to state in his letter of discontinuance that he has in fact had regard to the public interest, interest of justice and the need to prevent abuse of legal process; and that, while he need not state the particular reasons of public interest on which his decision is based, the sufficiency or otherwise of such reasons being a matter entirely for him to judge, a *nolle prosequi* entered without an indication that these factors had been taken into account is improper and ineffective. In this view of the matter, significance of the innovation brought about by the provision is one of mere form, though the impression is created in some parts of the judgement that reasons must also be stated (*The State v. Akor & Others* (1981)).

The Court of Appeal, on the other hand, thinks that the provision has not altered the form of a *nolle prosequi* nor does it require the attorney-general to state reasons for his decision. "There is", said

Justice Adenekan Ademola speaking for the Appeal Court, "a presumption of law in his favour that the matters required to be taken into consideration have been so taken into consideration"; "it is", he continued, "for the people who allege contrarywise to say so and prove same". The latter part of the learned judge's statement implies that the provision does in fact qualify the attorney-general's hitherto absolute discretion. Expatiating upon this implication in a subsequent case, where it was alleged that the decision of the Lagos State Attorney-General to discontinue a prosecution instituted by a private person against his director of public prosecution and a police officer for conspiracy to bring a false criminal charge against the private prosecutor, could not have been based on consideration of public interest or the interest of justice, since he was thereby making himself a judge in his own cause, the Court of Appeal held that the effect of the provision under consideration is that the presumption in favour of the attorney-general can now be rebutted by evidence showing that he has not in fact had regard to these factors. If that can be successfully proved, then the courts can intervene with appropriate remedies. In this particular case, the complainant had neither proved that the withdrawal of the prosecution was motivated by ill-will nor that it was not in the public interest (*The State v. Ilori & Others* (1982)).

The Supreme Court has in turn reversed the Court of Appeal, holding that the provision is "merely a restatement of the common law", that the discretion of the attorney-general remains as absolute as before, and that it cannot be controlled by the courts, even if it can be proved that he had abused his power by prosecuting a person or discontinuing a prosecution for reasons other than those of the public interest or the interest of justice. To require regard to be had to the public interest, it was emphasised, does not mean that the decision finally arrived at must be justified by the public interest in an objective, judicially enforceable sense; what it means is that the public interest must be taken into account without being thereby elevated to a controlling principle for arriving at a decision. The court then concluded that, "except for public opinion, and the reaction of his appointor, he (the attorney-general) is still, in so far as the exercise of those powers are concerned, a law unto himself". With respect, it is not quite correct that the provision "has in no way altered the pre-1979 constitutional position of the attorney-general". Before 1979, the duty of the attorney-general to have regard to the public interest and the interest of justice existed merely under the common law, not under the constitution. Today, it has been given the force of the constitution, which is expected to bestow upon it greater sanctity and respect. It remains of course, as before a merely directory duty. That is, of course, the reason for its ineffectiveness as a safeguard against abuse.

The numerous abuses of the attorney-general's power over criminal prosecutions amply attest to the need to insulate the police and their functions from political control. Yet, regrettable as the abuses are, criminal prosecutions are a function the ultimate control of which should not perhaps be taken away completely from the government, since to prosecute or not to prosecute may in some cases be a major policy decision affecting the public order and public security and, consequently, the stability of the entire nation, as where, because of a person's great political standing, his prosecution and imprisonment for a certain offence might provoke his followers to violence, resulting in widespread public disorder. The case may even be one in which prosecution may have serious adverse repercussions on relations with a foreign country.

CHAPTER 9

Separation of Powers under the Constitution: Its Merits and Demerits

Relation of Separation of Powers to Constitutional Democracy

It is necessary for ease of reference to repeat here what was said on this issue in Chapter 1.

The question of whether separation of powers is a requirement of constitutional democracy is very much contested. Upon one view of the matter represented by Professor Charles McIlwain, a leading authority, all that constitutionalism requires is the legal restraint of a guarantee of civil liberties enforceable by an independent court and the restraint implied by the full responsibility of government to the whole mass of the governed. He emphatically rejects separation of powers as a requirement of constitutionalism. As he says:

> among all the modern fallacies that have obscured the true teachings of constitutional history few are worse than the extreme doctrine of the separation of powers and the indiscriminate use of the phrase 'checks and balances'[1].

Yet there is a school of thought that holds strongly that any

---

1 *Constitutionalism: Ancient and Modern* (1947), p. 414; see also his *Constitutionalism in a Changing World* (1940).

definition of constitutionalism that does not include the limitations
implied by the doctrine of the separation of powers is inadequate. It
is argued that only by separating the function of execution from that
of law-making, by insisting that every executive action must, insofar
as it affects an individual, have the authority of some law, and by
prescribing a different procedure for law-making, can the arbitrariness
of executive action be effectively checked. The idea of procedure has
an important controlling role. Where a procedure, separate from that
involved in execution, is laid down for law-making, and must be
complied with in order for the government to secure the necessary
authority for measures it contemplates taking, regularity in the conduct
of affairs is ensured. It is usual in most countries to subject proposals
for legislation to discussion and deliberation in a legislative assembly.
The separation of functions, between execution and legislation,
requiring separate procedures, is thus of the utmost importance, for
even if government is regarded as a single, indivisible structure, the
separation in procedure will necessarily operate as a limitation upon
the incidence of arbitrariness. The conduct of affairs in accordance
with predetermined rules is perhaps the best guarantee of regularity,
and restraint has little or no value in constitutionalising government
unless it is regularised. Regularity enables the individual to know in
advance how he stands with the government, and how far the latter
can go in interfering with the course of his life and activities.

   A separation in procedure carries with it, however, the idea of a
separate agency or structure. For although it may be theoretically
possible to prescribe different procedure for the two functions of
execution and legislation while at the same time vesting them in the
same agency, this hardly accords with common sense or experience.
A separation of the agencies to be entrusted with these functions would
seem, in the nature of things, to be inescapable if constitutionalism is
to be maintained. As Vile has put it:

> . . .we are not prepared to accept that government can become, on
> the ground of 'efficiency', or for any other reason, a single
> undifferentiated monolithic structure, nor can we assume that

government can be allowed to become simply an accidental agglomeration of purely pragmatic relationships. Some broad ideas about 'structure' must guide us in determining what is a 'desirable' organisation for government[2]

It may be concluded that constitutionalism requires for its efficiency a differentiation of governmental functions and a separation of the agencies which exercise them. For "the diffusion of authority among different centres of decision-making is the antithesis of totalitarianism or absolutism."[3] It must of course be admitted that, in the light of the practice and exigencies of modern government, governmental agencies are multi-functional; some over-lapping in the functions of the various agencies is inevitable. Thus the executive agencies do make rules. Yet this fact is only a qualification upon, and not a negation of, the basic idea about a division of functions and of agencies, since in its ordinary application, rule-making by the executive is subordinate to that of the legislature. This subordination accords with the concept of government as consisting of a "hierarchy of norms that will enable each of the decisions of an official to be tested against a higher rule"[4] This fact, as Vile pointed out, is further reinforced by the internal rules of behaviour by which, notwithstanding the considerable over-lapping of functions, agencies recognise that particular functions are the primary responsibility of a given organ, and so refrain from unwarranted encroachment upon each others' primary function.

In orthodox theory, separation is extended beyond functions and agencies to the personnel of the agencies. It is insisted that the same person or groups of persons should not be members of more than one agency. The most remarkable example of the application of this extreme separation is under the American Constitution, and the

---

2. M. J. C. Vile, *Constitutionalism and the Separation of Powers* (1967), p. 10.

3. Vile, *ibid*, p. 15.

4. Vile, *op. cit.*, p. 320.

American application of the doctrine finds justification perhaps in its federal and presidential systems of government. But, whatever may be the objections to this extreme separation, it is no argument for complete fusion of personnel. Even the parliamentary executive of the Westminster system is not a complete fusion. Though members of the executive are also members of the legislature, separation is maintained by the fact that such members form a very small proportion of the total membership of the legislature, and, more important, by the existence, in its British prototype, of an effective organised opposition whose role makes the legislature more than a mere reflection of the executive.

Not many of even the sternest critics of the doctrine of separation of powers deny its necessity as regards the judicial functions. For the rule of law as an element of constitutionalism depends more upon how and by what procedure it is interpreted and enforced. The limitations which the law imposes upon executive and legislative action cannot have much meaning or efficacy unless there is a separate procedure comprising a separate agency and personnel for an **authoritative** interpretation and enforcement of them. This separate procedure is provided by the ordinary courts of law. The unique virtue of the separate procedure and personnel of the courts is that, being unaffected by the self-interest and consequent bias of the legislature or executive in upholding their actions, it can be expected to apply in their interpretation of the constitution or a statute an impartiality of mind which inhibits any inclination to vary the law to suit the whim or personal interest of either the judge or a party to a dispute, thus ensuring "that stability and predictability of the rules which is the core of constitutionalism." Whilst admittedly judges may not be entirely devoid of self-interest in the subject-matter of a legislative act – for no human procedure is ever completely neutral – yet this impartiality serves at once as a safeguard against the possible danger of arbitrariness on the part of the judges in the discharge of their interpretative function, and is reinforced for this purpose by the doctrine of precedent and the tradition of judicial self-restraint.

Furthermore, the process by which the courts exercise their function affording as it does, ample opportunity for full argument by the parties or their lawyers on the interpretation of the law in the context of the facts before the courts, ensure that the court's decision would reflect the reasonable or acceptable view of the meaning of the law.

There is thus implicit in the doctrine of the separation of powers, the conception of constitutionalism as requiring that government be conducted through constitutionally established institutions and impersonal bureaucratic procedures and processes, that is to say, an institutionalised and bureaucratised government, with all the restraints on the behaviour of rulers, which it implies, as opposed to personal rule, i.e., a form of rule in which government is "largely contingent upon men, upon their interests and ambitions, their desires and aversions, their hopes and fears, and all the other predispositions that the political animal is capable of exhibiting and projecting upon political life."[5]

Constitutionalism is thus the antithesis of:

> . . . non-institutionalised government, where persons take precedence over rules, where the office holder is not effectively bound by his office and is able to change its authority and powers to suit his own personal or political needs. In such a system of personal rule..., the rules do not effectively regulate political behaviour, and we therefore cannot predict or anticipate conduct from a knowledge of the rules. To put this in old-fashioned, comparative government terms, the state is a government of men and not of laws.[6]

In point of historical fact, which not even Charles McIlwain disputes, separation of the powers of legislation and execution was well known in antiquity for over 500 years, though not in the extreme form instituted by the U.S. Constitution of 1787 – that was more than two millenia before the modern doctrine of the separation of powers was propounded by John Locke and Montesquieu in the 17th

---

5. Jackson and Roseberg, *Personal Rule in Black Africa* (1982), Preface, p. x.

6. Jackson and Roseberg, *ibid*, p. 10.

and 18th centuries respectively. It began in ancient Rome in 508 B.C. when, following a revolt against it, absolute monarchy was abolished and replaced with constitutional government under a republic (508 B.C.) in which executive power belonged to a senate and a magistracy; legislation, on the other hand, was a joint responsibility of the senate, the magistracy and two assemblies of the whole people (a Centurial Assembly and a Tribal Assembly): the magistracy proposed, the senate deliberated and might approve or disapprove, and the measure was then submitted to the assemblies, which might pass or reject it (but without debate). The significant point to emphasise is that a legislative measure initiated by the magistracy and approved by the senate did not become law unless and until passed by the Centurial Assembly or the Tribal Assembly. We are told that by 200 B.C. the Tribal Assembly had become "the chief source of private law in Rome."[7]

The incorporation of the people into the established processes of government, as the body with power to pass into law, measures initiated by the magistracy and approved by the senate, meant, as Charles McIlwain said, that the fundamental doctrine underlying the Roman state during the period was "constitutionalism, not absolutism."[8] Thus was introduced to the world the form of government limited by law, otherwise known as constitutionalism.

Merits and Demerits of Separation of Powers

The system of separated powers, with the friction between legislature and the executive necessarily attendant upon it, is a deliberate and calculated choice instituted by the Nigerian Constitution because of its cardinal virtue in protecting the people against governmental autocracy. "The doctrine of the separation of power," said Justice Brandeis of the U.S. Supreme Court in a dictum quoted and requoted by successive justices of the same court:

---

7   Will Durant, *The Story of Civilisation vol. III,* p. 27.

8   C. H. McIlwain, *Constitutionalism: Ancient and Modern* (1947), p. 59.

was adopted by the Convention of 1787, not to promote efficiency but to preclude the exercise of arbitrary power. The purpose was, not to avoid friction, but, by means of the inevitable friction incident to the distribution of the governmental powers among three departments, to save the people from autocracy.

The notion of partnership between the two political organs, desirable though it is, must therefore seek, not to abolish the friction and thereby destroy the cardinal benefit of the system as a protective mechanism against autocracy, but to prevent the inevitable friction from degenerating into a showdown that may cripple the entire machinery of government. How does the system protect the people against governmental autocracy? By its nature, the executive function is inherently prone to arbitrary use, but its propensity to arbitrariness would be greatly accentuated where the function of law-making also reposes in the same hands. For it is not just that the repository of the combined power can pass oppressive laws and then execute them oppressively; he can also oppress individuals by executive acts not authorised by law and then proceed to legalise his action by retrospective legislation. Government in such a situation is not conducted according to predetermined rules; it is a government not of laws but of will, a government according to the whims and caprices of the ruler. By separating execution from the law-making function, by insisting that every executive action must, in so far at any rate as it prejudicially affects an individual, have the authority of some law, and by instituting a different agency and procedure for law-making, the arbitrariness and autocracy of executive action may be effectively checked. Separation of powers and procedures serves therefore to limit the executive's capacity and scope for arbitrary and oppressive action against the people, by reason of the fact that most executive acts violating or interfering with private rights or interests require to be authorised by law made by the legislature.

Separation also imposes a similar restraint upon oppression by the legislative assembly since, assuming that an oppressive law made by the assembly is not unconstitutional for one reason or another, e.g., as violating constitutionally guaranteed rights, the legislature cannot itself execute or enforce it. The execution of law usually involves the exercise by the executive of a discretion whether or not to do so, and he may refuse to execute or enforce a law that he considers oppressive.

Moreover, the fact that the legislature has no control over the execution of its laws and cannot therefore prevent them from being enforced against its members may deter it from passing oppressive laws knowing that the executive may enforce such oppressive laws equally against the legislators themselves as against other citizens. Separation thus contributes in maintaining the equality of all before the law by ensuring that lawmakers, through not enforcing the laws against themselves, would not become a special group distinct from the rest of the community, a group that cannot be reached or touched by the law.

Also, the device whereby both the legislature and the executive are enabled to check each other in the exercise of their legitimate functions reinforces the safeguards against oppression provided by the separation of powers. A proposed law considered oppressive by the executive may be vetoed by him, and the legislature may not be able to muster the special majority needed to override the veto. The legislature, by reason of its large numbers which brings them closer to the people, is said to be especially prone to "enterprising ambition" and to a temptation to take liberties with the people's rights, which need therefore to be checked by a power in the executive to veto its laws. "Ambition", argued James Madison in *The Federalist*, "must be made to counteract ambition." An ambitious legislature must be checked and frustrated by an ambitious executive, and *vice versa*, in order that the liberty of the individual might be adequately protected.

Partial veto of this kind must be distinguished from an absolute veto, i.e., one that cannot be overriden by the legislative assembly, such as that in the 1960 Constitution of Ghana. The latter is more than a mere "check and balance", because it gives to the president a right in the exercise of the legislative power equal to that of the legislative assembly. Its effect is to negate the separation of powers so far as concerns the exercise of the legislative power.

Senate confirmation of persons nominated by the president for appointment to designated offices is designed also to safeguard the public interest, and to ensure, in particular, that appointments to such offices are not used to serve purely personal, partisan or sectional interests. "Such a check", James Madison has said, "enables the Senate (representing the legislative organ) to prevent the filling of offices with bad or incompetent men or with those against whom there is tenable objection" – quoted in *Myers v. United States* (1926). Again the nature of the Senate's approval as a mere check should be emphasised. The two vital functions of nomination and the actual making of an appointment belong exclusively to the president. The U.S. Supreme Court has laid it down emphatically in the landmark case of *Marbury v. Madison* (1803) that "the nomination ... is the sole act of the president" equally as the making of the appointment, "though it can only be performed by and with the advice and consent of the senate." "The advice of the Senate," said the Court in a later case (*Myers v. United States* (1926)) "does not make an appointment." Once the nomination has been confirmed by the Senate, and the appointment has been made by the president, then, provided the Senate was properly constituted when it gave the confirmation, the appointment is complete, and cannot be affected by a subsequent withdrawal or reversal of its confirmation by the Senate. Chief Justice John Marshall puts the point clearly when he said in *Marbury v. Madison* that after the process of appointment is completed by the formal act of appointment, "the time for deliberation has then passed. He has decided. His judgment, on the advice and consent of the Senate concurring with his nomination, has been made, and the officer is appointed."

The Senate has no power whatever in relation to a completed appointment. Its power relates only to nomination, and is completely exhausted once an appointment is made by the president on the strength of the confirmation. An appointee acquires a vested right in the office by virtue of his appointment. He cannot be divested of that right by the Senate, particularly considering that he might have been induced to resign from an appointment which he was holding at the time. If the Senate could withdraw or reverse a confirmation validly given and if the appointment could thereby be affected, the effect would be to enable the Senate to revoke an appointment made by the president, which it has no power to do under the constitution.

For, if it be supposed that the Senate's consent were also requisite to removal, or to revocation of all appointment already made, this would have imposed upon the president a limitation going beyond a mere check. "A veto by the Senate ... upon removal," said the U.S. Supreme Court, "is a much greater limitation upon the executive branch and a much more serious blending of the legislative with the executive than a rejection of a proposed appointment." If a proposed appointment is vetoed by the Senate, this would not frustrate completely the president's discretion in respect of the appointment nor greatly embarrass the work of his administration. He can nominate another person of his choice, and he has a wide field from which to exercise his choice. A veto on removal, on the other hand, will, whenever it is exercised, frustrate completely the president's discretion, thus making the Senate the final judge in the matter and so putting it above the president. And by overriding him in favour of a subordinate, such a veto will greatly undermine not only his authority with his assistants but also the principle of dependence and responsibility upon which the unity of the whole administration rests. For it would impose upon the president subordinates whom he cannot discipline through the ultimate sanction of removal, although there may no longer be any confidence between him and them.

In contrast to the fusion of the members of the executive and legislature under the British parliamentary system, their separation under the American presidential system implies a certain degree of opposition between the legislature and the executive, each eager to assert and guard its independence. The entire legislative assembly is thus in a sense in opposition to the executive. In asserting and guarding its independence, the legislative assembly is helped by its freedom from the dominating presence of the prime minister and his ministers.

Admittedly, separation is fraught with some danger arising from the fact that there are separate popular elections for the president and for members of the legislature and that their constituencies are different, which carries with it the possibility that the majority of the members may belong to a different political party from the president. A legislative majority is not a necessary condition of the presidential system as it is of the parliamentary. Indeed, a majority in the legislature controlled by a party different from the president's party is by no means an infrequent phenomenon under the former system. And, the rejection by the legislature of an important legislative proposal initiated by the president in no way affects his tenure.

An opposition majority in the legislature, when it does occur, affords the greatest opportunity for the effective control of the government by the legislature. It creates a situation which is almost the reverse of that under the parliamentary system. The business of the legislature is controlled by the leaders of the opposition majority almost as completely and effectively as it is controlled by the executive under the parliamentary system. Its members dominate the speeches and use them to subject executive proposals to severe scrutiny and criticism. Every executive measure including indeed its financial proposals, faces the risk of the sanction of rejection. It is as if the government of the country is transferred from the executive branch to the legislative assembly. No executive government, faced with an opposition majority in the legislature, can afford to bring before it arbitrary or otherwise objectionable proposals, knowing that they would almost certainly be thrown out, to its own discredit. The potency of legislation as an instrument for the coercion of the individual makes such a system of check and restraint necessary.

But this fact, beneficial though it is, also contains the seed of danger. An opposition majority in the legislative assembly tends to accentuate the risk of a confrontational or capricious assertion of the assembly's independence. As the experience of the United States shows, separation coupled with an opposition majority tends to produce mutual antipathy and antagonism between the president and congress, resulting in a lack of "cohesion and rational completeness" in policy. For although, in response to the exigencies and complexities of modern government, the president is now allowed a preponderant role in the initiation of legislation, Congress still considers itself the authority over policy. And an excessive consciousness of its authority under the influence of an opposition majority often leads it into too minute questioning, through its numerous committees, of policy programmes initiated by the president, so that by the time it has finished with them, the programmes are reduced to a patchwork of disorganised policy. The result is that the governmental process is rendered incapable of co-ordinated leadership. A well-organised system, it is argued, ought to have a centre of gravity, serving as "the stomach and the brain, into which all is taken, digested, and assimilated, and by which the action of the whole is regulated by a common intelligence." "Among all the modern fallacies that have obscured the true teachings of constitutional history," writes Professor Charles McIlwain in criticising the resulting enfeeblement of government, "few are worse than the extreme doctrine of the separation of powers and the indiscriminate use of the phrase 'checks and balances'", adding that "the limiting of government is not the weakening of it." He maintains that the framers, "in their fear of the government's doing harm," have "incapacitated it from doing much good."

Yet, in spite of this danger, an opposition majority in the legislature is healthy for a country experimenting with constitutional democracy. It would provide a most effective safeguard against the tendency of presidential rule towards autocracy. The danger of a capricious use of its power by an opposition majority in the assembly is admittedly a serious one, but the opposition of power by power may produce a *modus vivendi* that would enable the government of the country to be carried on effectively without the arbitrariness and autocracy of presidential power. A working partnership between the two organs will help to produce the needed *modus vivendi*.

To the extent that the National Assembly in Nigeria under the current democratic dispensation is acting like one controlled by a party in opposition to the president's party, it is doing a fine job, provided it is able to resist the temptation to carry opposition to the point of capricious confrontation in defence of its independence. Independence of the organs is a principle instituted by the constitution, not for the sake of self-aggrandisement, but as a bulwark for the people against autocracy.

The way the separation of powers serves to protect the people against the oppressive use of legislative power by the legislative assembly calls for further remarks, partly by way of elaboration. Where a bill passed by the Assembly is considered unconstitutional or oppressive by the president, four lines of action are open to him under the system, *viz*,

(i) he may withhold his assent to the bill – the provision in the 1960 Constitution of Ghana empowering the president to assent to the whole or part only of a bill (Article 24(1)) seems convenient and desirable and worthy of consideration for adoption in a future review of the Nigerian Constitution;

(ii) if the Assembly then re-passes it with two-thirds majority, he may refuse to execute or implement the law;

(iii) where unconstitutionality is the reason for his veto, he may disregard the law by acting contrary to it;

(iv) he may challenge the law in the courts on the ground of unconstitutionality.

Like the power to make law vested in the National Assembly, the power to execute the laws vested in the president by the constitution imports, as earlier stated, a discretion whether or not to exercise it. Just as the Assembly is not bound and cannot be compelled to make law on any matter within federal legislative competence, say, the construction and maintenance of roads, posts, telegraphs and telephones, trade and commerce, electric power, industrial, commercial and agricultural development, so also is the president not bound or compellable to execute a law when made, unless the law itself, by express words or by necessary implication, imposes a duty on him to do so. He can therefore refuse to execute a law which he considers unconstitutional. As Udo Udoma JSC said in *Att-Gen of Ogun State & Others v. Att-Gen. of the Federation & Others* (1982), "the governor is bound only to enforce laws constitutionally made by the State House of Assembly," but not unconstitutional laws.

The president is also not bound to accept or acquiesce in an unconstitutional encroachment on his executive power or other unconstitutional legislation by the National Assembly. He can act contrary to an unconstitutional legislation, as in the many instances of the removal of public officers by the president in the United States without the approval of Senate or without complying with other conditions for removal required by a law considered by the president as an unconstitutional interference with his executive power. The most remarkable instance was the removal of his secretary of state by President Johnson in 1868 without the consent of Senate as required by the Tenure of Office Act 1867. The removal was upheld, and the Act declared unconstitutional and void by the U.S. Supreme Court. The court also upheld the president's removal of a first-class postmaster in 1926 in disregard of an Act of 1876 which required Senate approval for it, declaring the Act to be unconstitutional and void. (It is noteworthy that the bill for the Act was vetoed by President Johnson but was re-passed over his veto.)

When the president disregards a law which he considers unconstitutional, or acts contrary to it, he acts conformably with his **power** to "maintain" the Constitution (Section 5(1)(b)) and with the **duty** imposed on him by the oath of office which the Constitution prescribes for him and requires him to take before assumption of office (Section 140(1)). The oath enjoins him, among other things, to "preserve, protect and defend the constitution" and to discharge his "duties to the best of his ability, faithfully and in accordance with the Constitution" (7th Schedule.) A duty is thus cast on him to protect and defend the constitution against violation by any person or body, the National Assembly included. The constitution is superior to and overrides any inconsistent law made by the National Assembly (Section 1); accordingly the president's duty to protect and defend the constitution and to act in accordance with it overrides his duty, also enjoined on him by his oath of office, to discharge his duties in accordance with the law. The president, as chief executive, and the National Assembly, being co-equal organs, each independent of the other, have equal rights to interpret the constitution, so that the interpretation of the National Assembly, embodied in its law, does not and cannot override a contrary interpretation by the president. By the separation of powers under the constitution, the power to determine, authoritatively and with finality, the correct interpretation of the constitution on a disputed issue is assigned to the courts.

Furthermore, the checkmating of each political organ by the other derives legitimacy from the popular basis of their respective mandates of office. Since both are directly elected by popular votes in separate elections, they are alike representatives of the people, and it is a "fundamental misconception," as the U.S. Supreme Court has described it, to portray the president as unrepresentative or an enemy of the people, and the legislative assembly as the custodian and protector of their interests against presidential encroachment. In the emphatic words of the U.S. Supreme Court in *Myers v. United States* (1926) "the president is a representative of the people just as the members of the Senate and of the House are, and it may be said that the president elected by all the people is rather more representative of them all than are the members of either body of the legislature whose constituencies are local and not countrywide." McConnell puts it perhaps more pungently thus:

> The president represents the nation as a whole, while the Congress represents it as a collection of states and congressional districts ... It would be comforting to assume that the many different positions that congressmen and senators take add up together to a position as national and as public-spirited as the president's ... The men of Capitol Hill represent different publics, different from each other's and from the president's. Their constituencies are vastly different,

some consisting largely of farmers, some of large cities, some of working class districts, some of states where mining is overwhelmingly important, and so on; but the president's constituency consists of all the people. Because the smaller constituencies emphasize particular interests, the aggregate representation offered by Congress does not equal that of the presidency.[9]

The question of acquiescence, mentioned in passing earlier, has arisen in concrete form as to whether the president's assent to a bill which he considers unconstitutional amounts to acquiescence and waiver of his right to challenge the law in court on the ground of unconstitutionality. The question was raised obliquely before the U.S. Supreme Court in the postmaster's case *(Myers v. United States* (1926)), but without the Court pronouncing upon it. But there is a Nigerian case in which the Governor of Kaduna State, through his solicitor-general, challenged the Kaduna State Appropriation Law 1980 which he had earlier assented to, just so as to avoid the consequence of the state being without an annual Appropriation Law *(Maigida (Solicitor-General & Permanent Secretary, Ministry of Justice, Kaduna State) v. House of Assembly, Kaduna State & Another* (1981)).

The right of the president to challenge a law in court on the ground of unconstitutionality is not his personal right but the public right of the people which cannot be waived by acquiescence on his part. There is a division of judicial opinion on whether even a private person can, by acquiescence, as by taking a benefit under a statute, waive his right to challenge it on the ground of unconstitutionality. In the view of the U.S. Supreme Court, "there is no sanctity in such a claim of constitutional right as prevents its being waived as any other claim of right may be" *(Wall v. Parrot Silver & Copper Co.* (1917)). On the other hand, the Supreme Court of India has, gratifyingly, rejected the doctrine of waiver of a constitutional right, on the ground that it has no "relevancy in construing the fundamental rights conferred by Part III of our

---

9   *The Modern Presidency* (1967), p. 35.

Constitution ... These fundamental rights have not been put there in the constitution merely for individual benefit ... They have been put there as a matter of policy, and the doctrine of waiver can have no application to provisions of law which have been enacted as a matter of constitutional policy" (*Pesikata v. State of Bombay* (1955)). This view of the matter applies with greater force in the case of the challenges of an unconstitutional law by the president in exercise of a public right; the right to do so, not being his personal right, cannot be waived by him as a legally binding act.

CHAPTER 10

Limits of the Separation of Powers

Initiation of Legislation

The Constitution of Nigeria (1999) vests federal legislative power in the National Assembly (Section 4), thereby separating it from executive power, which it vests in the president (Section 5). The question raised is whether this implies that legislative power, **in all its aspects**, in particular its initiation, belongs to the National Assembly to the total exclusion of the executive, i.e., the president. It needs to be pointed out that the issue here raised is not just a matter of the manner and form for the exercise of the power, which requires, among other things, legislative proposal to be in the form of a bill which will then be presented to the National Assembly, and must be passed by both Houses and assented to by the president before it can become law binding on the community.

The initiation of legislation is a vital part of the legislative power going beyond mere manner and form for the exercise of the power. (The initiation of legislation is to be distinguished from the function of introducing or presenting it in legislative assembly, which latter is a mere manner and form, and is governed by the standing orders).

The vesting of legislative power in the National Assembly is not conclusive as to whether the initiation of legislation belongs exclusively to it. The determination of policy is, by the express provision of the constitution, vested in the president acting not alone but at a meeting with the vice-president and ministers (Section 148(2)) — a provision, be it noted, absent in the Constitution of the United States. But policy — its determination and formulation — and legislation are like siamese twins. There is hardly any legislation that does not embody policy of one kind or another. It follows from this that the initiation of legislation is concurrent to both the National Assembly and the president, since, if it were to be exclusive to the legislative assembly, the president would, for all practical purposes, have been deprived of the power to determine and formulate policy. Neither can exclude the other from the legislative initiative. Indeed, by vesting in the president, acting at a meeting with the vice-president and ministers, the determination of policy in respect of all matters within the legislative competence of the National Assembly, the constitution manifests a clear intention that the president is to be the main organ for the initiation of legislation.

This conclusion, based, as it is, upon inference from the right vested in the president to determine policy, is perhaps not altogether beyond disputation, as it would have been had the constitution provided, as do the Constitution of France 1958 and those of many of the francophone African countries modelled on it, that "the premier (or the government in the African constitutions) and members of Parliament alike shall have the right to initiate legislation" (Article 39 France). This provision is complemented by others that dispel any doubt that the executive is the principal organ for the initiation of legislation under the French system. The American Constitution is also more specific on the point than the Nigerian; it empowers "the president from time to time to recommend to (the Congress) such measures as he shall judge necessary and expedient."

Even had the constitution been completely silent on the matter, the realities of modern government make it impracticable to regard the legislative initiative as belonging exclusively to the legislative assembly as an integral part of the legislative power. In a recent report, the Study of Parliament Group in Britain has sought to dispel the popular misconception on this point. "Legislation today," the Group affirms, "is pre-eminently a function of government. It is largely by means of legislation that administrations implement party programmes, react to the need for basic changes in the economic, social and political structure of the country, and bring the law into conformity with current standards of what is acceptable or tolerable. That being so, it is misleading to regard the legislative process as something in principle separable from government, still less to see it as beginning and ending in parliament."

This statement underlines the change that has taken place in the character and content of modern legislation. In the days before the emergence of the positive welfare state, the matters that needed to be regulated by legislation were few and simple — domestic relations, land, criminal offences, etc. These were easily within the initiative of individual legislators. The concern of the government was mainly with foreign relations, the maintenance of law and order, and execution generally. Modern government has an infinitely wider concern, involving active intervention in the life of society with a view to improving its quality. This, as has just been observed, require legislation, and legislation with high policy content. But policy is essentially an executive function. It is implicit in the right to govern, a fact which the constitution recognises in the provision vesting the responsibility for policy in the president acting in council with his vice-president and ministers.

There is another reason why the initiation of high policy legislation must be a function of the executive. Much of it is of an extremely complex and technical nature, with wide-ranging ramifications, which at once put it beyond the capacity of an individual legislator to manage or even to comprehend. The dimension of the issues with which it deals may be beyond his vision; they may be issues arising in the administration of the departments or other institutions of state and about which only someone inside the government can have knowledge and experience; such are questions of fiscal policy, social reform, economic development and even pure administration. Their complexity and technical nature require special expertise. Thus we find that because of this, the introduction of such legislation in the legislative assembly is usually preceded by a long and protracted period of gestation during which it is put through an elaborate process of consultation and discussion among various interested groups — the government party, the sponsoring department, the cabinet and its committees, and other interested sections of the community, such as trade unions, trade associations, etc. When at last the policy aspects have been thrashed out, then comes the drafting stage. Even this may be a complex and complicated matter.

These, then, are some of the factors which have necessitated that the legislative initiative should be largely in the hands of the executive, rather than of the legislative assembly. In Britain, the reality of the matter has been recognised since at least the middle of the eighteenth century. Most bills in Britain, estimated at 85 per cent, are government bills. In most of Africa executive monopoly of the legislative initiative is complete, to an extent that most legislators simply take it for granted that the initiation of legislation is the exclusive prerogative of the government, and that they themselves have no role in the matter at all.

In the United States, however, Congress regards itself as the main organ for the initiation of legislation by reason of the separation of powers in the constitution. Congress (or rather, its leaders) exercise the final discretion as to which bills should be introduced. It is these leaders who determine and control the business of Congress; no government ministers are in Congress anyway. Naturally these legislative leaders are quite jealous of their own and their colleagues' right of initiative. Indeed, until the later part of the 19th century, congressional control over the initiation of legislation was total and exclusive; there was then nothing like bills initiated by the executive and sent to Congress. And there exist in Congress facilities to assist members in the preparation and drafting of bills; of which the committee system, with the legislative expertise which it has developed, is perhaps the most helpful.

Yet even in the United States, Congress is gradually yielding legislative leadership to the executive, because of the latter's superior resources and capacity for action. From the time of President Theodore Roosevelt down to that of President Franklin Roosevelt, presidential leadership in the process of legislation, particularly in its initiation, has become established by practice as a principle of the working of the Constitution, so much so that today bills initiated by the executive account for a substantial proportion, estimated at about half, of all bills introduced in Congress. As President Franklin Roosevelt himself put it in his annual address to Congress towards the end of his first year in office in 1933, "the letter of the Constitution wisely declared a separation, but the impulse of common purpose declares a union." In the same vein, if somewhat exaggerated, a writer in *The New Republic* had said that "the traditional separation of powers has broken down for the simple reason that it results only in confounding them." This development has been aided by the budgetary reform of 1921, which entrusted to the president the responsibility for the preparation of an annual budget to be presented to Congress, thereby enabling him to "work out a general and integrated plan of government programmes and operations, which hitherto had been lacking." The present position is summed up thus by McConnell:

> The relationship between the president and Congress is considerably different from that formally drawn in the great scheme of the constitution. The separation of powers between these two branches has not indeed been removed; a vast gap separates the two. Nevertheless, the increasing complexities of modern political life have required an increasing role for the president, and the presidency has become increasingly institutionalised. Correlatively, the legislative branch has become less and less capable of mastering the daily flow of events of which policy is so largely composed; it is compelled to leave much to the executive branch. If present trends were to be projected into the future, we could envision a government system

in which the president with the whole executive branch under his effective control governs, and Congress checks and criticises. Already, this picture accords with what happens in some areas of policy, military and foreign affairs for example.

Constitutional Limitations on the Powers of the National Assembly with Respect to the Initiation of Financial Legislation

The right to initiate financial legislation is covered by specific provision in the Constitution of Nigeria, though it is not couched in terms as unequivocally exclusionary or prohibitory as the provision in the Constitution of France 1958 and the constitutions of most francophone African countries modelled on it, which says: "Bills and amendments introduced by members of Parliament shall not be in order when their adoption will have as a consequence either a diminution of public revenues or the creation of increase of public expenditures" (Article 40 France).

Though not couched in such unequivocally exclusionary or prohibitory terms, the provision in the Nigerian Constitution is clear and specific enough. It provides that the president shall cause to be prepared and laid before the National Assembly annual estimates of revenues and expenditure (i.e., a budget), and that the heads of expenditures contained in the estimates so prepared by him (other than expenditure charged upon the Consolidated Revenue Fund directly by the constitution which includes the salaries and allowances of certain designated public officers) "shall be included" in a bill, to be known as an appropriation bill, providing for the issue from the Consolidated Revenue Fund of the sums necessary to meet the expenditure and the appropriation of those sums for the purpose specified therein (Section 81(1) and (2)). If, in respect of any financial year, it is found that the amount appropriated by the appropriation act for any purpose is insufficient, or that a need has arisen for expenditure for a purpose for which no amount has been appropriated by the act, a supplementary estimate (again to be prepared by the president) showing the sums required shall be laid before the legislative assembly and the heads of any such expenditure "shall be included" in a supplementary appropriation bill. It seems clear from the fact that an appropriation bill or supplementary bill is to contain only the heads of expenditure in the estimates prepared and laid before the assembly by the president that its initiation is the prerogative of the president to the exclusion of the National Assembly.

There is very good reason for lodging exclusively in the president the right to initiate financial legislation. Orderly government requires that only those who administer the government, and therefore have an intimate connection with it, should propose national expenditure, and how the money needed for it can be raised; there would certainly be financial chaos if every member were to be free to propose expenditure, since members would then be competing among themselves to secure as much of the public funds as possible for the constituencies or interests which they represent. Desirable as it may be that only the executive should propose expenditure, its effect is undoubtedly to increase the dominance of the executive over policy. For finance and policy are intricately interwoven. Finance is the lever that links all activities of government, from which it follows that the organ controlling it is also given an overview of the entire functions of government, including policy.

Not only can the National Assembly not initiate financial legislation, it also cannot increase the **total** amount of the budget beyond what is proposed in the president's appropriation bill. It can reduce but not increase. This is because an increase in the total amount partakes of the nature of initiation. The excess amount over and above the total figure in the appropriation bill must be regarded as having been initiated by the Assembly, not by the president, and is therefore unconstitutional. And it is undesirable that such an increase should be permitted when the Assembly is not in a position to source the money to cover it.

Besides the denial of the right of initiative, the power of the National Assembly with respect to financial legislation is limited in other ways, as the amendments, declared unconstitutional by the court, made by the Kaduna State House of Assembly to the State's

Appropriation Bill in 1980 illustrates. The amendments consisted in the deletion of some heads of expenditure, including indeed the entire vote for one particular ministry, the Ministry of Social Development. Not only did the Assembly by these amendments purport, through the deletion of their votes, to abolish the executive departments affected, but it also purported to transfer some executive agencies from one department to another through the transfer of the votes meant for them. Also new expenditure subheads totalling ₦34.6 million, which were not included in the Appropriation Bill as submitted by the governor, were introduced into it by the Assembly. (The governor felt obliged to sign the Appropriation Bill with these amendments just so that the state would not be without an Appropriation Law.)

The establishment of office of minister is a prerogative explicitly vested in the president (or governor) by the Constitution (Section 147(1)); this is unlike in the U.S. where the establishment of offices is vested in Congress (Art. 2, Sec. 2). Although the Assembly may reduce, even to a nominal amount, the votes proposed by the governor for running them, their outright abolition by the Assembly through the total deletion of their votes is a usurpation of the governor's power to establish and disestablish ministries and executive departments. The purported transfer by the Assembly of executive agencies from one department to another by the device of the transfer of their votes is equally a usurpation of the governor's executive powers. Affirming this view of the matter, the Kaduna State High Court has held that "since it is the governor who can rightly establish ministries, the (House of Assembly) cannot transfer ... duties and responsibilities to any ministry either directly or indirectly or impliedly."

The Kaduna State High Court also held that the deletions and transfers of expenditure heads and subheads and the introduction of new ones are a usurpation of the governor's powers under the provisions of the constitution noted above and are therefore unconstitutional. The decision thus clearly establishes quite severe limitations on the power of the Assembly in respect of an appropriation bill. It may refuse to pass it (no money can be withdrawn from the public fund of the government except by the authority of a law enacted by the Assembly in conformity with the provisions of the Constitution — Section 80). Or it may pass it with amendments, but the amendments it can make are limited to decreases in the expenditure heads and appropriations proposed by the governor; in any event, the total amount of the appropriation proposed by the governor must not be exceeded. Deletions and transfers of expenditure heads and subheads and the introduction of new ones seem clearly not to be contemplated by the provision. As Justice Aroyewun of the State High Court has said, "what should be the heads of expenditure and the estimates for those heads are the exclusive preserve of the governor ... There is nowhere in the whole of S. 113 where directly or impliedly the House of Assembly has power to transfer funds from one head to another."

The conclusions above can be supported on the grounds both of rational interpretation, the historical origins of the provision and governmental practice in the past. Whilst the word "include" indicates a statement, e.g., an enumeration, that is not meant to be all-inclusive or exhaustive, unless the context suggests otherwise, "shall be included" in the context of Section 81 of the 1999 Constitution means that the heads of expenditure contained in the estimates shall be **embodied** in a bill, to be known as an Appropriation Bill. There is a clear difference between "shall be included" and "shall include".

This view of the matter is affirmed by the Finance (Control and Management) Act, cap. 144 Laws of the Federation 1990, which is the law governing the matter and is therefore binding on the National Assembly, unless and until repealed by it. Section 13 provides:

> (1) In accordance with the provisions of the constitution, the minister shall cause to be prepared in each financial year estimates of the revenues and expenditure of the Federation for the next following financial year, which shall be presented to the president for approval and when so approved by him shall be laid before the House of Representatives at a meeting commencing before the 1st day of January of the financial year to which they relate.

(2) **The proposals for all** expenditure to be made out of the Consolidated **Revenue** Fund contained in **such** estimates ... shall be submitted to the vote of the House at that meeting **by means of an Appropriation Bill,** which shall **contain estimates** under appropriate Heads for the several services required. — emphasis supplied.

This puts it beyond question that an appropriation bill shall contain only proposals for expenditure contained in the estimates prepared and laid before the Assembly by the president.

The history of the provision in the Constitution (quoted earlier) has a relevant bearing on its meaning. It is reproduced from the 1979, 1963 and 1960 Constitutions (Sections 75, 130 and 124 respectively) and the pre-independence constitutions since the introduction of responsible government in the country. The wording is identical in every respect in all the constitutions, except that the "president" in the 1999 and 1979 Constitutions replaces the "minister of the government of the Federation responsible for finance" in the earlier constitutions. Now, the same provision cannot mean different things in the various constitutions.

The constitutions prior to the 1979 and 1999 ones instituted a parliamentary system on the British model, so it is to the British Constitution, the original source from which the provision is derived, that we must go for its meaning. The principle of the British parliamentary system which the provision in the Nigerian Constitution seeks to enact is stated as follows in the authoritative book, *Constitutional and Administrative Law* (9th edn 1977) by Wade and Phillips:

A charge may not be considered by the Commons unless it is proposed or recommended by the Crown. The financial initiative of the Crown is expressed in a Standing Order of the Commons which in part dates from 1713: "This House will receive no petition for any sum relating to public revenue or proceed upon any motion for a grant or charge upon the public revenue unless recommended from the Crown" ... The estimates were considered by the House sitting in the Committee of Supply, which had **formal** authority to **reduce but not to increase a departmental vote** ... The estimates

are embodied in the annual Appropriation Act, which authorises
the issues from the Consolidated Fund of the money required for
maintaining the supply services for the year at pp. 188-189 (emphasis
supplied).

The authors said at p. 271: "While the annual cycle ensured that
Parliament should regularly approve the government's financial
proposals, the government retained a firm control over the House;
thus by a Standing Order of the House dating from 1713, the House
could not consider new charges on public revenue or new taxes except
on the recommendation of the Crown signified by a minister. This
emphasised that the government of the day bore the primary
responsibility for all taxation and expenditure." The renowned English
constitutional lawyer, Professor Stanley de Smith, in his *Constitutional
and Administrative Law* (3rd edn 1977) at page 278 puts it succinctly
thus: "No member can move a motion to increase an estimate or to
spend money on another object." Such, then, is the principle of the
British parliamentary system which Section 81 of the Nigerian
Constitution seeks to blend with the American presidential system.

In his highly regarded and influential book, *The English
Constitution* (2nd edn. 1872), Sir Walter Bagehot explains the rationale
behind the principle thus:

> The ministry is (so to speak) the breadwinner of the political family,
> and has to meet the cost of philanthropy and glory, just as the head
> of a family has to pay for the charities of his wife and the toilette of
> his daughters. In truth, when a Cabinet is made the sole executive, it
> follows it must have the sole financial charge, for all action costs
> money, all policy depends on money, and it is in adjusting the relative
> goodness of action and policies that the executive is employed. — at
> p. 155 — emphasis supplied.

Earlier at page 154 the author stated the principle thus: "On
common subjects any member can propose anything, but not on
money."

In governmental practice in parliamentary times in Nigeria, before
1979, the appropriation bill was sent together with the estimates to

the House of Representatives. The bill merely indicated the heads of expenditure without describing or explaining them in detail. The details were supplied by the estimates. The two were therefore complementary documents. Hence the provision in Section 81 of the 1999 Constitution that the heads of expenditure contained in the estimates shall be included, i.e., embodied, in an appropriation bill. That was how the system was operated in practice in the past, and there never was any question of an expenditure head or subhead being increased by the legislative house, or of a new head being added.

The American Constitution and budgetary process provide no reliable guide on the matter, because that constitution has no provision like that in Section 81 of the Nigerian Constitution. It has no provision at all specifically empowering the president to initiate financial or other legislation. The only provision with some bearing on the point is that authorising him to "recommend to their (i.e., Congress's) consideration such measures as he shall judge necessary and expedient" (Article 2, Sec. 3). Section 81 is a deliberate modification superimposed by the Nigerian Constitution on the American presidential system, a superimposition drawn from the British parliamentary system. (The American presidential system is modified in several other respects in the Nigerian Constitution, two such modifications, already mentioned above, being the provision specifically empowering the president to determine policy and to establish offices of ministers.) It is, as earlier stated, a blending of the two systems. The blending in this and several other respects is a characteristic feature of all the other presidential constitutions in the countries of former British Africa.

The initiation of legislation for the raising or expenditure of public revenue in the United States belongs, by express stipulations in the Constitution, to Congress, to whom alone is granted the power to "originate bills" for raising revenue (Article 1, Sec. 7) as well as the power to "lay and **collect** Taxes, Duties, Imposts and Excises, to **pay the Debts** and provide for the common Defence and general welfare of the United States" (Article 1, Sec. 8) – emphasis supplied. Under the constitution, Congress has full control of the finances of the country, including the initiative in regard to the raising and expenditure of money. What function the president exercises in the budget process and in the initiation of financial legislation is conferred on him, not by the constitution, but by an act of Congress who can, by another legislation, curtail, modify or withdraw the function, as it deems fit. The financial relations between the president and Congress in the United States are thus altogether different from those enshrined in Section 81 of the Nigerian Constitution, and can have no relevance to its interpretation. It is a false analogy to compare two things which are so completely unlike each other as the U.S. and Nigerian Constitutions are in this respect.

It should be pointed out that the annual appropriation law is not the only means available to the National Assembly for the control of public funds. Not only are all revenues or other monies raised or received by the government required to be paid into one or the other of the statutorily created public funds from which no withdrawal can be made except on the authority of an Act of the National Assembly (Section 80), but also the "manner" of making the withdrawal must likewise be prescribed by the Assembly (Section 80(4)). The manner is so prescribed by the Finance (Control and Management) Act Cap. 144 Laws of the Federation 1990, which provides that withdrawals shall be by warrant signed by the minister of finance or by the president.

Constitutional Mechanisms Enabling the President to Influence or Lead the Process of Legislation in the Legislative Assembly

Legislation, being the supreme directing instrument of rule in a modern society, we should expect the executive, whatever the form of government, to be deeply interested in how the process of legislation in the legislative assembly is managed in order to ensure the passage through the assembly of legislation required to implement its programme and electoral promises, and that private members' bills embarrassing, inimical or otherwise objectionable to it do not get passed. Its interest in this regard is often in conflict with that of the assembly and, depending on the system, such conflict of interests may give rise to confrontation between them, degenerating sometimes to a feud.

Conscious of this, the British parliamentary system and the French system are avowedly designed to avoid such conflict and confrontation, whilst the American presidential system more or less entrenches it, thereby thrusting upon the executive the problem and the responsibility of conducting its relations with the assembly so as not to allow the inevitable conflict, with the confrontation not infrequently attendant on it, from jeopardising the passage of its legislative programme. Accordingly, the executive under the system is judged as much by its performance in managing the executive branch and in shaping public opinion as by its performance as legislative manager — what Edward Corwin refers to as "the dual role of the president as catalyst of public opinion and as legislative leader" (*The President: Office and Powers* (1957), p. 264).

Underlying the strained relation between the executive and the legislature in Nigeria since the inception of the democratic dispensation on 29 May, 1999, therefore, is the natural ambition on the part of the executive under any form of government to control the process of legislation in the legislative assembly, and the inevitable conflict of interests, with the not infrequent confrontation attendant upon it, which this ambition generates under the American presidential system, compounded, as it no doubt is, by President Obasanjo's military mentality, which is a hangover from his military past as military commander and, later, head of the military government. The strained relation is thus by no means an unusual phenomenon under the system nor is it made any more unusual because the president and the majority of the members of the National Assembly belong to the same party. For, we are told by Edward Corwin, writing about the presidency in the United States, that "some of the bitterest feuding between the two branches has often occurred when both were of the same party" (*op. cit*, p. 298). But the proportions the confrontation has assumed in Nigeria do reflect inadequacy in President Obasanjo's skills as legislative manager and party leader as well as shortcomings in the constitutional structure of the relationship between the two organs.

The presidential system, as instituted by the U.S. Constitution, has little of the devices of the British and French systems which enable the executive to direct and control the process of legislation in the legislative assembly. Such devices as it provides are relatively few and inadequate in themselves alone to enable the executive to manage or lead, not to say dominate or control, the process of legislation in Congress. These devices consist in the provisions making the vice-president of the country president of the Senate (Art. 1 Sec. 3); requiring (not merely authorising) the president from time to time to give Congress information of the state of the union, and to recommend for its consideration such measures as he shall judge necessary and expedient (Art 11 Sec. 3); empowering the president to veto a bill passed by Congress subject to his veto being overridden by Congress re-passing the bill by two-thirds majority when it then becomes law without his signature (Art. 1 Sec. 7); empowering him to convene either or both Houses on "extraordinary occasions", or, in case of disagreement between them as to time of adjournment, to adjourn them to such time as he shall think proper (Art. 11 Sec. 3).

These devices serve as a link between the executive and Congress, and enable the former to exercise a measure of control, however comparatively little, over the process of legislation in Congress. The presidency of the Senate by the vice-president of the country is certainly an important link between the two organs. The person presiding over a legislative assembly is in a position to influence the conduct of its proceedings through his power to interpret standing rules of the assembly, to rule on the relevance of a member's contribution and on other points of order, to ensure orderliness of debates and generally to enforce order and discipline. Information to Congress consists partly in the annual state of the union message but more in the special messages which may be as frequent as the president deems necessary. We are told by Edward Corwin that nearly 30 were sent by President Franklin Roosevelt to the 73rd Congress, about 15 to the 74th and about 70 to the 75th Congress, and that "some of these communications merely drew attention in general terms to the need for legislation on a particular subject; others contain specific recommendation as to the content of the needed legislation; a few were accompanied by draft bills" (*ibid*, at p. 274). Then there are the personal appearances by the president before Congress to present an address. President Woodrow Wilson, for example, addressed Congress in special session twice in less than three months seeking its support and co-operation and urging legislative action.

The veto power has been quite an effective presidential check on Congress. From 1792, when it was first used by the first President, George Washington, to 1930, we are again told by Edward Corwin, there had been 750 vetoes, of which only 49 were overridden, which indicates the effectiveness of the power in nine cases out of ten (*ibid*, at p. 282). Whilst the president's power to adjourn Congress to such time as he may think proper had never been used up till 1957, the power to convene it on "extraordinary occasions" has been used so often that "extraordinary occasions" has come to mean simply "extra" or "special" sessions.

Extra-constitutional means used by American Presidents, notably Eisenhower, to exert influence on congressmen have also played a considerable part in the relations of the two organs; these consist in the main of regularly scheduled weekly conferences with congressional leaders, to which committee chairmen with an interest in the subjects the president wishes discussed, are invited; interviews by the president with recalcitrant members; lobbying by the president's men in the lobbys of Congress; etc. (See Corwin, *op. cit*, pp. 271-302).

The presidential system as applied in the Constitution of Nigeria (1979 and 1999) features none of the above devices except the veto power. It casts on the president no duty to give information to the National Assembly on the state of the Federation; it only empowers him in his discretion to "attend any joint meeting of the National Assembly or any meeting of either House ... either to deliver an address on national affairs, including fiscal measures or to make such statement on the policy of the government as he considers to be of national importance" (Section 67(1)). A minister may be invited, and is then obliged, to attend either House to explain the conduct of his ministry (Section 67(2)). The president can only convene the first session of the National Assembly after its election and immediately after he himself is sworn-in (Section 64(3)). The National Assembly cannot be dissolved before the expiration of its normal life of four years on which date it stands automatically dissolved but a proclamation by the president is needed to formalise it (Section 64). It is thus a serious shortcoming in the system that the only link provided by the Constitution between the two organs is the president's power, exercisable as and when he likes, to attend and address the National Assembly on national affairs, no duty is cast on him to do so, as in the United States. Without such links it should not surprise us that relations between them have been marked by so much face-off. Nor have the extra-constitutional means mentioned above been adequately utilised.

Although the inevitable friction between the executive and the legislature attendant upon the separation of their powers has tended in Nigeria to degenerate into a destabilising confrontation because of the inadequate constitutional links between the two organs and because the art of managing his relations with the National Assembly has not been sufficiently developed by the president, yet the liberty of the people is better safeguarded under this type of constitutional government than under a system, like the British, or even the French, in which control of the legislative process in the legislative assembly is vested in the executive by the constitution, especially in the fledgling democracies in Africa lacking the tradition and culture of liberty. The relation between the two organs under the French Constitution (1958), which is bequeathed to most of its former African colonies, fails to strike an acceptable balance between the independence of the legislative assembly and its control by the executive.

Acceptably, the president under the French system is not made a constituent part of parliament and must promulgate into law, bills passed by parliament. Nor are the premier and other ministers required to be members of the assembly. Indeed, not only are they not required to be members of parliament as a qualification for appointment, but they cannot be such members while in office as ministers, the ministerial office being explicitly declared by the constitution to be "incompatible with the exercise of any parliamentary office" (Art. 23). The exclusion of ministers from membership of the legislative assembly is applied in all the countries of former French Africa except in the few cases where a minister may, but need not, be a member — Benin (1964), Togo (1963) and Gabon (1961). However, ministers have a right of access to the assembly, and also a right to be heard, assisted by such commissioners of government as they might wish to bring with them (Art. 31). The ministers' right of access to Parliament and to be heard at its meetings facilitates executive control.

Bills on matters within the legislative domain may be introduced in Parliament either by the government (when they are called government bills) or by a member of Parliament (parliamentary bills), but it is natural that, because of the nature of the matters enumerated as being within the domain of law, most bills will be government bills. Government bills and government-approved parliamentary bills are accorded priority on the agenda of parliament as may be fixed by the government (Art. 48), which means that parliamentary agenda is determined largely by the government.

Parliament could of course refuse to pass a government bill or propose amendments to it, but its discretion to do so is subject to the government's control. Every bill (including parliamentary bills) must be examined in one of the permanent parliamentary committees but, if the government so requests, then, it must be referred to a special committee for special study (Art. 43). The committee system thus provides a vital instrument for the control of the legislative process by the government.

Amendments to bills are subject to more rigorous government control. To begin with, "no amendment shall be in order without the government's consent" (Art. 45); this applies equally to parliamentary as to government bills. The consideration of any amendment to a bill which has not previously been examined in committees may be opposed by the government (Art. 44). The premier is given the option of calling a meeting of a joint committee composed of an equal number of members from both Houses (the National Assembly and the Senate) to try to resolve disagreements between them over a bill (Art. 45). In the event that the joint committee fails to agree on a common text, the government may ask the National Assembly to rule definitively on the matter (Art. 45).

A bill, after it has been passed by Parliament, is transmitted to the government, and must then be promulgated by the president within 15 days, subject, however, to his right, within the 15 days time limit, to return it to parliament for re-consideration, which may not be refused (Art. 10).

When a finance bill is introduced by the government in the National Assembly, the Assembly must reach a decision on it within forty days, failing which, the government shall refer it to the Senate, which must rule within fifteen days; and if the bill is not passed by both houses within seventy days, the government may put it into effect by ordinance (Art. 47).

On the proposal of the government, a government bill dealing with the organisation of public authorities or which is intended to authorise the ratification of a treaty affecting the functioning of existing institutions may (provided the treaty is not contrary to the constitution) be referred to referendum by the president, who shall promulgate it into law if approved by the referendum (Art. 11). This thus constitutes an exception to the stipulation that "all laws shall be passed by Parliament" (Art. 34) – i.e., on matters specified in the Constitution as within the domain of Parliament.

Recognising the importance of information in enabling the executive's perspective on policy to be properly appreciated so as to avoid or minimise the incidence of misunderstanding, and in generally fostering a healthy relationship, the constitution establishes a channel of communication from the president to the Assembly by means of messages (Art. 18).

Finally, Parliament shall, at the request of the premier, convene in extraordinary session on a fixed agenda, and may, again on the premier's request, sit in secret session (Arts 29 and 33). Subject to this, Parliament shall convene as of right in two ordinary sessions a year, one of which shall commence on the second Thursday after its election; in addition, it shall convene as of right during a period of emergency (Arts 12 and 28). The Lower House of Parliament (but not the Senate) may be dissolved any time by the president, after consultation with the premier and the presidents of the two Houses, provided that no dissolution shall take place during the year following its election (Art. 12), nor during a period of emergency (Art. 16). (The provisions regarding dissolution differ in the Constitutions of some of the African countries concerned, notably Congo (Brazzaville) 1963, Mali 1961, Central African Republic 1959 and Gabon 1961).

CHAPTER 11

Consequences Flowing from the Separation of Powers

Separation of powers under a written constitution normally operates as a limitation on power, and so renders unconstitutional and void any violation of the limitation by an organ of government, as by the usurpation of another organ's power. The consequences flowing from the separation of powers in the constitution need to be elaborated by reference to concrete cases.

The Unconstitutionality of the Usurpation of, or Encroachment on, Executive Power by the Legislature

Save as it may be authorised in that behalf by the constitution, an encroachment upon executive power by the legislature, as by exercising it directly, by authorising some other person or agency than the president to exercise it independently of his control or by controlling the exercise of it by the president, is unconstitutional and void. Without attempting to define the nature and extent of executive power or what functions properly pertain to it as being of an executive nature, it would suffice for present purposes to illustrate this limitation by reference to acts indisputably executive in character.

The power to execute the government of a country, including the execution of its laws, carries with it, as an essential incident, power to appoint, direct and control executive personnel of various grades. For, it is not to be supposed that the president is to execute the government alone, unaided by subordinates appointed by him and who are subject to his control and direction. The power to remove such subordinates is equally an essential incident of the executive power as the power to appoint them in the first instance, removal being an instrument of control of last resort, since otherwise the president might be saddled, to the prejudice of his administration, with subordinates whom he could not remove, notwithstanding that they are disloyal, incompetent or otherwise unfit. The power to appoint, direct, control and remove subordinate executive assistants is thus cardinal to executive power, and pertains exclusively to it, subject, however, to any restrictions contained in the constitution. "To turn a man out of office," said Oliver Ellsworth, later Chief Justice of the United States, "is an exercise neither of legislative nor of judicial power." It partakes peculiarly of the nature of executive power. Similarly, "designating the man to fill an office," James Madison has said, "is of an executive nature." The statements of both Oliver Ellsworth and James Madison were quoted with approval by the Court in *Myers v. United States* (1926).

The attempt by the Congress of the United States to control the exercise by the president of power to remove subordinate executive personnel appointed by him, as part of the executive power vested in him by the Constitution (Article 2 Section 1), became a major constitutional issue before the country's Supreme Court in the celebrated case of *Myers v. United States* (1926). By an Act of Congress of 1876, the consent of Senate was made requisite for the removal by the president of postmasters of the first, second and third grades: Myers, a first-class postmaster, was removed from his office by the president without the consent of the Senate, and he sued for arrears of salary on the ground that, the consent of the Senate not having been obtained as required by the Act, his removal was wrongful. Whilst the power of appointment is expressly made subject to confirmation of the president's nomination by Congress, the removal power is not. The requirement of Senate consent for removal was accordingly declared unconstitutional and void.

As regards the appointment power too, the U.S. Supreme Court stated emphatically that the qualification in favour of the legislature, i.e., the requirement of Senate approval, should not be extended outside the cases in respect of which the approval of the Senate is explicitly required by the constitution, as by requiring Senate approval in respect of other appointments or by super-adding the approval of the House of Representatives. The appointments or nominations for appointment for which the approval of the Senate is required by the Constitution of Nigeria (1999) are those of ministers (Section 147(2)), auditor-general (section 86(1)), the chairmen and members of certain bodies established by the Constitution other than ex officio members (Sections 153(1) and 154(2), ambassadors, high commissioners or other principal representatives of Nigeria abroad (Section 171(4)).

We must now turn to other categories of functions indisputably executive in nature. Such is the doing or execution of physical acts, e.g., construction works, provision of infrastructural facilities or welfare services, other activities involving physical action, like the conduct of military operations, the minting of coins, the printing of currency notes and stamps, and the award of contracts for such. Interference with such functions by the Assembly is unconstitutional and void. The decision of the Kaduna State High Court in a case in 1981 (*Governor, Kaduna State v. The House of Assembly, Kaduna State*) affirms the unconstitutionality of legislative encroachment on a function in this category — the award of contracts for works to be done or services to be provided.

Also embraced indisputably within the domain of executive power is pure administration, i.e., purely administrative work within the executive departments not involving physical action in the sense mentioned above. This, too, cannot be controlled by the legislature, subject to what is said below about purely administrative or ministerial functions of a quasi-legislative or quasi-judicial nature entrusted to an agency created by statute.

Executive power embraces not only activities involving physical action or pure administration, but also the making of instruments as a means of carrying the provisions of a law into execution. Legislative power is meant for use in prescribing rules of general and uniform application to persons and things, whereas the application of those rules to individual cases, whether by means of executive instruments or judicial decrees, is inappropriate to its true nature. Furthermore, by the explicit stipulation of the constitution, legislative power is exercisable only by means of bills (Section 58(1)). Accordingly, in the case mentioned above, the Kaduna State High Court also held unconstitutional and void, a law by which the State House of Assembly transferred to itself powers of the governor exercisable by executive instruments or orders under the State's Local Government Law, *viz.,* power to create individual, named local governments with designated capitals, to constitute an emirate or traditional council for an emirate or traditional area and to prescribe for it the device of its seal, the composition of its governing council, its area of authority with detailed demarcation of boundaries; power to order an inquiry into the affairs of a local government council, and following upon such inquiry, to dissolve the council and either appoint a committee of management or order an election.

One more illustrative example of a function distinctly executive in nature may be mentioned. The organising and planning of celebrations to mark the anniversary of an event of great national importance pertains peculiarly to executive power; there is nothing legislative or judicial about it. It belongs therefore exclusively in the domain of the executive. Comity needed for fostering a harmonious relationship between the two political organs may well demand that the executive consult and involve the legislature in planning and organising such celebrations, but the demands of comity must not be confused with or be elevated to a constitutional requirement.

There are, however, exceptions which must be noted. One such exception relates to the appointment, direction, control and removal of staff employed in agencies created by statute and invested with functions of a non-executive nature, that is, purely administrative or ministerial functions of a quasi-legislative or quasi-judicial nature. The exception became firmly established by the decision of the U.S. Supreme Court in *Humphrey v. United States* (1935). The Federal Trade Commission Act 1914, created a commission charged with responsibility for the prevention of unfair methods of competition in commerce. The Commission is empowered to prefer and try charges of unfair competition, to issue a "cease and desist" order against any person, partnership or corporation found guilty after due hearing of using unfair method of competition. If the order is disobeyed, the Commission may apply to the appropriate circuit court of appeals for its enforcement, subject to the right of the person against whom the order is made to apply to the circuit court of appeals for a review of the order. The Commission also has wide powers of investigation in respect of certain matters; when it investigates any matter it must report to Congress with recommendations. Its members are appointed for a fixed term of years by the president by and with the advice and consent of the Senate, and may be removed by him for inefficiency, neglect of duty or malfeasance in office. Humphrey, a member of the Commission, was removed by the president before the expiration of his normal term, not for any of the causes specified in the Act, but because he and the president entertained divergent views with respect to matters of policy. Humphrey then sued for arrears of salary for wrongful dismissal. For the president it was argued that the provision of the Act prescribing the grounds upon which a member of the Commission may be removed was unconstitutional as being an interference with the president's executive power.

In its opinion on the case, the Supreme Court defined the status of the Commission to be that of an agency, created by statute to carry out the policy, not of individual presidents but of the law; accordingly it is to be independent of executive authority and direction, whether it be that of the president or any regular executive department. Its functions, the court held, are purely administrative, and do not involve the exercise of "executive power". "In administering the provision of the statute in respect of "unfair methods of competition" — that is to say filling in and administering the details embodied by the general standard — the Commission acts in part quasi-legislatively and in part quasi-judicially. In making investigations and reports thereon for the information of Congress under Section 6, in aid of the legislative power it acts as a legislative agency. Under Section 7, which authorises the Commission to act as a master in chancery under rules prescribed by the court, it acts as an agency of the judiciary. To the extent that it exercises any executive function — as distinguished from executive power in the constitutional sense — it does so in the discharge and effectuation of its quasi-legislative powers."

Unlike a member of the Commission, a postmaster involved in the Myers case "is an executive officer restricted in the performance of executive functions. He is charged with no duty at all related to either the legislative or judicial power." The Commission is in its character like the Interstate Commerce Commission, and must be governed by the same principle as is laid down in *Illinois C.R. Co. v. Interstate Commerce Commission* (1906) and *Standard Oil Co. v. United States* (1930). It is also analogous in character to the legislative court of claims (*Williams v. United States* (1932)).

Since, they are not comprehended in the president's executive power, the functions of the Federal Trade Commission and the tenure of its members are unquestionably within the power of Congress to prescribe. "The authority of Congress," the Supreme Court declared, "in creating quasi-legislative or quasi-judicial agencies, to require them to act in discharge of their duties independently of executive control, cannot well be doubted; and that authority includes, as an appropriate incident, power to fix the period during which they shall continue, and to forbid their removal except for cause in the meantime." The court explained its earlier decision in *Myers v. United States* as being confined to "executive officers" such as postmasters, i.e., officers whose functions form part of the executive power vested by the Constitution in the president. It concluded: "whether the power of the president to remove an officer shall prevail over the authority of Congress to condition the power by fixing a definite term and precluding a removal except for cause will depend upon the character of the office."

Whilst the correctness of the decision in the *Humphrey* case is not questioned, its implications have caused concern, if not alarm, in some quarters in the United States. The Committee on Administrative Management in the country has thus been prompted to comment in 1937:

> The multiplication of these agencies cannot fail to obstruct the effective overall management of the Executive Branch almost in geometric ratio to their number. At the present rate we shall have 40 to 50 of them within a decade. Every bit of executive and administrative authority which they enjoy means a relative weakening of the president, in whom, according to the constitution, "the executive power shall be vested". As they grow in number his stature is bound to diminish. He will no longer be in reality **the Executive**, but only one of many executives, threading his way around obstacles which he has no power to overcome. (emphasis supplied)

The disagreement between the President of Nigeria and the National Assembly over the bill for the creation of the Niger Delta Development Commission must be viewed in the light of the exception established by the decision in the *Humphrey* case (The bill was passed into law over the president's veto by two-thirds majority in the House of Representatives and by a unanimous vote in the Senate in the first week of June, 2000). What is the character of the Commission? Are its functions non-executive in nature; are they purely administrative or ministerial functions of a quasi-legislative or quasi-judicial nature, like those of the U.S. Federal Trade Commission, so as to bring it within the above exception, as regards the appointment and control of its staff and the control of its finances?

The functions of the Commission are not at all, like those of the U.S. Federal Trade Commission, quasi-legislative or quasi-judicial. The Commission is a body established, not by the constitution, but by statute and charged with the development of the Niger Delta in the area of transportation (including the building of roads and jetties), health, education, industrialisation, agriculture and fisheries, housing and urban development, water supply, electricity, telecommunications, pollution prevention and ecological preservation, and other functions incidental or necessary to the implementation of promotion of such development. Being thus executive in nature, its functions are embraced in the president's power to execute the government, and to appoint, as a necessary incident thereof, all assistants and personnel needed for the purpose without restrictions or control by the National Assembly by requiring Senate approval for the appointment of the Commission's members, such appointments not being among those for which Senate approval is required by the constitution.

In contrast, the Commission established by the Corrupt Practices and Related Offences Act 2000 is not an executive body. Its functions are partly administrative (e.g., advising on ways to eliminate or minimise corruption and fraud, and review of practices, systems and procedures that aid or facilitate corruption or fraud); partly promotional (educating the public about the evil of corruption and fostering public support in combating it), but mostly quasi-judicial (investigation and prosecution of cases of corruption, fraud or related offences). The National Assembly is therefore within its constitutional powers in requiring the approval of the Senate for the appointment by the president of members of the Commission.

In the light also of the exception relating to the appointment, control and removal of staff employed in agencies created by statute and invested with purely administrative or ministerial functions of a quasi-legislative or quasi-judicial nature, the conclusion must follow more compellingly that the appointment, control and removal of the staff of the legislature and judicature are not embraced within the president's executive power. The question became a major bone of contention in 1980 between President Shehu Shagari and the National Assembly during the Second Republic in Nigeria. The National Assembly had at the time some 2,500 staff of different categories (excluding the legislators themselves), who performed various functions and services: managerial, budgeting and planning, legislative drafting, accounting, audit, library and research, protocol and public relations, security, investigation, publications, printing, maintenance, transportation, procurement of stores, catering, medical and so forth. Such functions and services are not, in their nature, strictly legislative, but the question is whether the fact of their being connected with the work of the legislature brings them within the domain of legislative power.

It cannot be disputed that the functions performed by the staff of the legislature and the judicature are incidental to the effective discharge of the law-making and adjudicatory functions. The latter can only be performed in a suitable environment: there must be facilities for typing and clerical services for the drafting and printing of legislative proposals and motions, for the printing of the report of proceedings, for catering and medical services for members, and for the enforcement and maintenance of order and security in the chambers of the Assembly. Stationery and other stores must be procured. Members and the staff must be paid their salaries and other entitlements. And there must be receptionists and messengers to distribute papers and mails and to run errands generally. All this must be accepted as being necessarily incidental to the effective discharge of the law-making and adjudicatory functions. The separateness and independence accorded the legislature and judicature and their strictly law-making and adjudicatory functions ought logically to extend to all other functions reasonably incidental thereto.

The president had claimed, however, that the executive power vested in him extended to the appointment of staff of the legislature. On this ground, he vetoed the National Assembly Service Commission Bill, 1980, which vested the appointment of National Assembly staff in a commission consisting of designated functionaries of the National Assembly, arguing that it was a usurpation to take the power away from him and vest it in a commission so composed. The bill, he further argued, raised a point of policy as to whether the Federal Civil Service Commission should, by an act of the National Assembly, be designated as the commission to appoint National Assembly staff or whether an entirely new body should be set up for the purpose. He maintained that the National Assembly Service Commission, if it were to be created at all, should, like the Judicial Service Commission, be confined to the appointment and removal of "only such professional posts as are related to the National Assembly functions," while the other posts should continue to be part of the general pool of officers for which the Federal Civil Service Commission is responsible.

The argument is clearly misconceived. First, the power vested in the president to execute the constitution and the laws is expressly made "subject to the provisions of this Constitution" (S. 5(1)). The separation of powers is such a provision, and a fundamental one at that. It follows therefore that the power of the president to execute the Constitution and the laws is limited by the separation of powers. Apart from the general limitation implied in the separation of powers, it is, as concerns the legislature, specifically limited by the provision empowering the National Assembly to establish staff complements for itself and to prescribe the method of appointment of such staff (S. 51 but see also S. 310). Since no qualifications are put on the legislature's power to prescribe the method of appointment of its staff, appointment by a commission composed of persons not appointed by the president, and who are entirely independent of him, is unquestionably authorised by the provision, and is therefore within the discretion of the legislature to prescribe. Furthermore, being a particularised power, the power to prescribe the method of appointment of the legislature's staff must be taken as an exception to the general power vested in the president to execute the Constitution and the laws.

Second, the constitutional function of the Civil Service Commission relates only to the civil service, which, as regards the federal civil service, is defined to mean "service of the Federation in a civil capacity as staff of the office of the president, the vice-president, a ministry or department of the government of the Federation, assigned with responsibility for any business of the government of the Federation" (s. 318). It seems clear that only staff in the executive branch of the government are included in this definition. The specification of "staff of the office of the president, vice-president" and the juxtaposition of the word "department" with "ministry" suggest that "department" refers to department within the executive branch. Its meaning is further delimited by the phrase "assigned with the responsibility for any business of the government of the Federation," which is used in the same sense as under the provision empowering the president to "assign to the vice-president or any minister of the government of the Federation responsibility for any business of the government of the Federation, including the administration of any department of government" (S. 14(1)).

Thus the constitution makes a clear differentiation between the staff of the executive departments which it designates as the civil service, and staff of the legislature and the judicature. The latter are not part of the civil service, and accordingly not subject to the power of the Civil Service Commission under the constitution. The Civil Service Commission can exercise power over the staff of the legislature only if it is authorised in that behalf by law made by the legislature within the permissible limits of delegation, but the legislature can grant it no such power in respect of the staff of the judicature; it cannot delegate someone else's power.

Senator Akpata had a point when he said that there is no "meaningful separation of powers" and "no independence for the National Assembly" where the receptionist, the messenger and driver serving its members are appointed and may be removed by the president. A man, he said, is not master in his own house if his domestic staff are under the control of another person exercised through the power to appoint, remove and discipline them, for then their first loyalty and obedience would be to that other person. If that is in fact the constitutional position, then, he maintained, "something is wrong with the constitution." A constitution that proclaims the separateness and independence of the legislative and executive organs while at the same time making the one dependent upon the other for the staff it needs to be able to discharge its functions is indeed a blatant piece of self-contradiction. As earlier stated, no such contradiction exists under the constitution, so the constitutional position is in complete accord with the logic of the Senator's argument.

In the event, the National Assembly Service Commission Bill was re-passed, and assented to by the president, with all the original provisions disputed by the President. The Commission was duly established as the authority to appoint, promote, remove and discipline all categories of staff of the National Assembly as listed in a schedule to the Act. However, the appointment and removal of the members of the commission were conceded to the president, subject to the confirmation of the National Assembly as regards appointment, and to an address by it praying removal for inability or misconduct. In the exercise of its functions, the commission was not subject to the control or direction of any other authority or person. (A House of Assembly Service Commission was similarly established in the states).

Lacking the capacity to stand on its right and force its acceptance, the judicature had continued to suffer the degradation of having to depend upon the Civil Service Commission for the staff it needed for the effective discharge of its functions. Its demand for autonomy to recruit its own staff had been met with the argument that under the 1979 Constitution the power of the Judicial Service Commission related only to the appointment, removal and disciplinary control of judges, chief registrars and deputy chief registrars (3rd Schedule). This, it was said, suggests that the constitution did not intend that the judicature should appoint its own staff. The argument is again misconceived. A grant of power to do something does not imply a prohibition against doing anything else; it does not affect or limit the capacity of the grantee of the power to do other things if so authorised by law. It would be perfectly constitutional and lawful for the Judicial Service Commission to be authorised by law to appoint the staff of the judicature. Happily, power to do so is now granted to it directly by the 1999 Constitution (Third Schedule).

Independence of the legislature and the judicature must also imply a power to control and manage their own funds: to pay salaries to their members and staff, to purchase stores and other requirements and to provide the facilities they need for their work. The battle for its financial autonomy in such matters has been won by the legislature during the Second Republic, but the judicature was still held in subjection by the executive in the disbursement of its recurrent budget, including indeed the payment of the salaries of judges, which is an expenditure charged on the Consolidated Revenue Fund directly by the constitution itself. The control had unfortunately been exercised to the prejudice of the judiciary, as evidenced by the irregular payment of judges' salaries, which in some states had sometimes been allowed to be in arrears for two months. Judges had sometimes also had to use their own money to run and maintain their official cars. It is intolerable that the judicature should, in the language of a *Daily Sketch* editorial, be reduced to the position of a "poor relation" of the executive, who has to go "cap in hand" to the senior partner for the money to buy typewriters and stationery with which to type judgment. The separateness of the judicature and the conception of the three organs as co-equal partners become a farce in these circumstances. The judicature does have the right under the constitution to be self-accounting in the disbursement of its budget, a right now, happily again, affirmed and enshrined in the 1999 Constitution (Section 81(3)).

But does the independence of the legislature and judicature to control and manage their own funds also give them the right to execute works for the construction of residential quarters for their members and staff, the provision of infrastructural facilities like roads and street lights in an area dedicated exclusively as residential quarters for their members, and the award of contracts for such works? As concerns the judicature, although its capital expenditure is not, like the recurrent expenditure, charged on the Consolidated Revenue Fund by the Constitution, and is not therefore required to be paid directly to the National Judicial Council for disbursement to the heads of the courts under Section 81(3), the Council is empowered to "collect, control and disburse all moneys, **capital and recurrent**, for the judiciary" (Third Schedule — emphasis supplied).

Whilst no such explicit provision is made for the legislature, the logic of the matter demands that its independence in the disbursement of its capital budget should be no less than is now accorded the judicature.

But there are stronger grounds than logic to support this view of the matter. The decisive consideration is whether the disbursement of its capital budget by the National Assembly may properly be regarded as an incident of the exercise of the legislative power vested exclusively in it by the Constitution (Section 4) and to be exercised by it independently and free of control by the president. Will the disbursement of the Assembly's capital budget by the president not enable him to exert, even if indirectly only, control and influence over the exercise of its legislative function, will it not make the Assembly amenable to such control and influence in order to get him favourably disposed to execute its capital projects? The words of the U.S. Supreme Court in *Humphrey v. United States* (1935) suggest, if they do not compel, an affirmative answer:

> The fundamental necessity of maintaining each of the three general departments of government entirely free from the control or coercive influence, direct or indirect, of either of the others, has often been stressed and is hardly open to serious question. So much is implied in the very fact of the separation of the powers of these departments by the constitution, and in the rule which recognises their essential co-equality. The sound application of a principle that makes one master in his own house precludes him from imposing his control in the house of another who is master there ... The independence of each department requires that its proceedings 'shall be free from the **remotest influence**, direct or indirect, of either of the other two powers' (emphasis supplied).

If follows that, since the separateness of legislative power and the independent exercise of it by the National Assembly "free from the remotest influence, direct or indirect" by the president is a cardinal principle of the constitution, it is a provision to which the president's power to execute the laws is made subject by Section 5(1); in other words, the power is subject to the provision in Section 4, **read with all its incidents**. After all, the president's power to appoint and remove the staff of the executive agencies of the government is derived as an incident from his power to execute the government and the laws. ("Incidental matters" is listed as Item 68 in the exclusive legislative list. The subject of incidental powers is a complex one — see the relevant chapter in my *Federalism in Nigeria* (1983).

To put the limits of the president's power to execute the government in a fuller perspective, it needs to be pointed out that there are other provisions of the Constitution the limiting effect of which are brought into play by the words "subject to the provisions of this Constitution" in Section 5(1) .— the guarantee of individual rights and freedoms (which can only be curtailed or interfered with by constitutionally valid law enacted by the National Assembly but never by executive action unbacked by such law); the provisions (Third Schedule) vesting in the Federal Civil Service Commission or the Police Service Commission, as the case may be, the appointment, dismissal and disciplinary control of civil servants and policemen (with some exceptions), and in the Nigeria Police Council, the organisation and administration of the Nigeria Police and all other matters relating thereto; the provision vesting the use and operational control of the police in an inspector-general of police free from direction by the president, except as regards the maintenance and securing of public safety and public order (Section 215), etc.

The tendency to construe the extent of the president's executive power without due regard to the qualifying words "subject to the provisions of the constitution" is one that should be guarded against.

The Unconstitutionality of the Usurpation of, or Interference with, Judicial Power by the Legislature

It is a usurpation of judicial power for the legislature under the Nigerian Constitution to exercise same directly by legislation, or to authorise the executive or some other agency than the judicature to do so. But the problem is to determine when legislation amounts to an exercise of judicial power; on this, there is a conflict of judicial opinion. Upon one view of the matter, represented by the decision of the Supreme Court of Nigeria (*Lakanmi v. Attorney-General (West)* (1970)), a statute which confiscates or forfeits the property of named individuals found guilty of corruption by a tribunal of enquiry is a legislative exercise of judicial power and therefore void as a usurpation of judicial power. Also the United States Supreme Court, by a majority decision, held invalid an Act of Congress which permanently debarred from government employment certain named American citizens believed to have been engaged in subversive activities against the United States, on the ground that the Act inflicted punishment on the named individuals without the safeguards of a trial, and was therefore in the nature of a Bill of Attainder prohibited by the constitution, *United States v. Lovett* (1945). (The decision was not based on the view of the Act as an exercise of judicial power, though this was clearly implied). This view of the matter has also the support of Sir William Blackstone who wrote: "Therefore a particular act of the legislature to confiscate the good of Titus, or to attaint him of high treason, does not enter into the idea of municipal law ... it is rather a sentence than a law." Though this passage from Blackstone has been quoted with approval by the Judicial Committee of the Privy Council in 1966 (*Liyange v. R.*), in another case in 1967 *(Kariapper v. Wijesinha)* the committee declined to express an opinion as to the circumstances in which a confiscating act may constitute a legislative exercise of judicial power, saying that in the sphere of constitutional law it is unwise to go beyond what is necessary for the determination of the case in hand.

But this view of the matter is open to objection as being too wide in that its effect is that every *ad hominem* law that takes away the right of a named individual or otherwise prejudicially affects his interest is, on this view, a legislative exercise of judicial power. The essential attribute of a legislative exercise of judicial power is that **judgment** adverse to a named individual is passed by means of legislation without the due process of trial. Hence it is called **legislative judgment**. Not every act or decision has the distinctive quality of a judgment. However, it is well settled on high judicial authority that judicial power is not necessarily involved because an act or decision affects the legal rights of an individual or is made binding on him. But conviction and punishment for a criminal offence necessarily involve judicial power because they determine authoritatively and conclusively the legal standing of a person as a member of society and incarcerates him by the infliction of physical pain, the deprivation of personal liberty or by death.

In the light of the points above, the other school of thought holds, and rightly in our view, that two elements must be present for a legislative act to constitute an exercise of judicial power, *vis* (i) it must make a declaration of guilt against a named person in respect of an offence alleged to have been committed by him; and (ii) it must impose punishment on him therefor. By such an act the legislature pronounces upon "the guilt of the party, without any of the forms or safeguards of trial, it determines the sufficiency of the proofs produced, whether conformable to the rules of evidence or otherwise; and it fixes the degree of punishment in accordance with its own notions of the enormity of the offence" (*Cummings v. State of Missouri* (1866)). Without these two elements, a legislative act is not an exercise of judicial power, notwithstanding that it may be directed against a named individual. In other words, the legislation must pass **judgment** on the person concerned in order to be an exercise of judicial power. The most obvious example is a Bill of Attainder or a Bill of Pains and Penalties; both are legislative acts which condemn a person for a specified offence and impose punishment on him therefor, the punishment being in the former case death and in the latter any punishment less than death.

The view of the matter was endorsed by the Judicial Committee of the Privy Council in a Ceylonese appeal, which arose out of a law enacted by the Ceylonese legislature in 1965 *(Kariapper v. Wijesinha)*. The law imposed certain disabilities on named persons who had been found guilty of bribery by a commission of inquiry. It vacated their seat in Parliament or the local authority of a person so named and also disqualified him from being a voter or a candidate for Parliament or a local authority for seven years. The Judicial Committee held the Act to be, not an exercise of judicial power, but a legitimate exercise of legislative power. The grounds for this decision were that the two elements mentioned above were absent from the Act. First, it contained no declaration of guilt of bribery or of any other offence. Parliament did not by the Act make any finding of guilt against the persons named therein; that finding had been made by a commission of inquiry independently of the Act.

> The question of the guilt or innocence of the persons named in the schedule does not arise for the purpose of the Act, and the Act has no bearing on the determination of such a question should it ever arise in any circumstances. Secondly, the disabilities imposed by the Act are not, in all the circumstances, punishment.

They were intended, not really to punish, but to discipline and to "keep public life clean for the public good." In the view of the Board there is a difference between a disciplinary penalty and a punishment for an offence.

As the Judicial Committee observed in another case:

> A lack of generality in criminal legislation need not, of itself, involve the judicial function, and their Lordships are not prepared to hold that every enactment in this field which can be described as *ad hominem* and *ex post facto* must inevitably usurp or infringe the judicial power (*Liyanage v. R*).

Usurpation of judicial power by means of legislation that authorises the executive or some other agency than the judicature to exercise it is illustrated by a Swaziland case (*Ngwenya v. deputy prime minister* (1973)). On 25 May, 1972, one Ngwenya, who earlier that month had been elected to Parliament, was deported from the country as a prohibited immigrant on an order made by the deputy prime minister under the Immigration Act, 1964. He challenged his deportation on the ground that, being a Swazi citizen, he was not liable to deportation, since the Act under which the order was made expressly excepted from the power a person who "belongs to Swaziland." The High Court held the plaintiff to be a Swazi citizen, and so declared his deportation invalid. From this decision the government appealed. While the appeal was pending, the government in November, 1972 amended the

Immigration Act. The amendment established a special tribunal to decide, upon a reference by the Chief Immigration Officer, or the Permanent Secretary of the office of the Deputy Prime Minister, questions as to whether "a person belongs to Swaziland" in terms of the principal Act. The jurisdiction thus vested in the special tribunal was declared to be exclusive, and to be exercisable "notwithstanding any judgment, decision or order previously made by any authority, tribunal or court." There was however a right of appeal to the prime minister, whose decision was to be final. It was expressly provided that a decision of the special tribunal or of the prime minister would not be subject to appeal to any court, and would be deemed to supersede and nullify any previous decision or order given in the matter by any court or tribunal.

Despite the High Court's declaration of Ngwenya as a Swazi citizen, the question whether he belonged to Swaziland was nevertheless referred to the special tribunal by the Chief Immigration Officer. Ngwenya challenged the validity of this reference on the ground that the enabling Act was invalid or, alternatively, did not apply to him assuming it to be valid. He alleged that the Act infringed jurisdiction expressly vested in the High Court by the Constitution, namely jurisdiction for the enforcement of guaranteed rights, and for the determination of the validity of elections. Among the rights protected by the constitution was the right of a citizen not to be expelled from, or denied entry into, the country. This right being dependent upon citizenship, its enforcement presupposed that the Court should also have jurisdiction to determine the question of citizenship itself. Among the qualifications for election was the requirement that the person must be qualified for registration as a voter, which in turn required the person to be a citizen.

The Court of Appeal for Swaziland held, reversing the trial judge, that the exclusive and final jurisdiction conferred on the special tribunal and the prime minister ousted completely the jurisdiction of the High Court to determine questions of citizenship as a qualification for election to the National Assembly; accordingly it declared the Act *ultra vires* the constitution and void. The decision of the Appeal Court was handed down on 27 March, and on 12 April, following upon it, the King of Swaziland, on a petition by Parliament, abrogated the separate existence of judicial power in the country.

The constitutional position is stated in clear, unequivocal terms by Chief Justice Griffiths of Australia. "It is impossible under the constitution," he said, "to confer such functions upon anybody other than a court, nor can the difficulty be avoided by designating a body, which is not in its essential character a court, by that name, or by calling the functions by another name. In short, any attempt to vest any part of the judicial power ... in anybody other than a court is entirely ineffective": — *Waterside Workers Fedn of Australia v. J. W. Alexander Ltd* (1918).

Legislative interference with judicial power not involving its exercise directly by legislation or by the executive or other agency authorised in that behalf by legislation is illustrated by a legislation enacted by the Ceylonese Legislature in 1967. The facts giving rise to the legislation were that certain individuals, alleged to have been involved in an abortive *coup d'etat* to overthrow the government, were indicted for this. After their arrest, and while in detention awaiting trial, the legislature enacted a law which altered retrospectively the mode of trial, the offences, the admissibility of evidence and sentences, not for the generality of the population but specifically for the purpose of the trial of the individuals implicated in the *coup*, its operation being limited to the duration of the trial. Instead of trial by jury as the pre-existing law required, the Act empowered the minister of justice to direct trial by three judges without a jury. Whereas no minimum but only maximum penalty of twenty years' imprisonment was previously prescribed for the offences in question, the Act imposed a minimum penalty of ten years' imprisonment and the confiscation of property. It also created a new offence *ex post facto* to meet the circumstances of the abortive *coup*. It made admissible certain statements which had hitherto been inadmissible, for instance confessions made to or in the custody of a police officer, or statements made to a police officer in the course of an investigation. It was no longer for the prosecution to prove that a confession was voluntary, but for the accused to prove that it was not. The statement of an accused person against his co-defendants was made admissible. No appeal was to be allowed.

Read in the light of a government statement issued after the discovery of the plot, a statement which assured the people that the government "will do its duty by them," and that "a deterrent punishment of a severe character must be imposed" on the conspirators, these changes were held by the Judicial Committee of the Privy Council to be an interference with the functions of the judiciary, "a grave and deliberate incursion into the judicial sphere." The Act, the Committee observed, was "a special direction to the judiciary as to the trial" of particular and identifiable accused persons; its "pith and substance ... was a legislative plan *ex post facto* to secure the conviction and enhance the punishment of those particular individuals ... Quite bluntly, (its) aim was to ensure that the judges in dealing with these particular persons on these particular charges were deprived of their normal discretion as respects appropriate sentences. They were compelled to sentence each offender on conviction to not less than ten years' imprisonment, and compelled to order confiscation of his possessions, even though his part in the conspiracy might have been trivial ... If such acts as these were valid the judicial power could be wholly absorbed by the legislature and taken out of the hands of the judges."

Accordingly, the Act, together with the convictions based upon it, were declared *ultra vires* and void.

There was another form of legislative interference involved in this case. The Act empowered the minister of justice not only to direct trial before three judges without a jury but also to nominate the judges himself. The nomination was duly made. On a preliminary objection that the nomination and the authority on which it was made were *ultra vires* the Constitution, the three judges held that "the power of nomination is one which has hitherto been invariably exercised by the Judicature as being part of the exercise of the judicial power of the State, and cannot be reposed in anyone outside the Judicature"; its vesting in the minister of justice was therefore an interference and void. The Act was later amended to divest the minister of justice of his power, and to nullify his previous nomination; the Chief Justice was now empowered to make the nomination.

The legislative interference with judicial power in the Ceylonese case pales in enormity when compared with that by the legislature in Ghana under Nkrumah. It was a case of the use of legislation to secure the conviction and punishment by the court of persons accused of an attempt to assassinate President Nkrumah in August, 1962 at Kulungugu as he was returning from a state visit to Upper Volta.

The Criminal Procedure Code had been amended in 1961 to create a special Criminal Division of the High Court for the trial of offences against the state, offences against the person, and such other offences as the president might specify by legislative instrument. The court was to be constituted, with a bench of one judge and two other members, by the Chief Justice in accordance with a request made to him by the president. Trial was by a summary procedure and the decision of the court, to be arrived at by a majority, was final. By legislative instrument made by the president the trial procedure was changed so as to deprive the presiding judge of the power to rule that there was no case to answer; he must call upon the accused person' for his defence, whether or not a *prima facie* case was made out against him. The intention was of course to facilitate the conviction of persons charged with these offences. It did not however guarantee conviction, and failed indeed to secure it in respect of those charged with involvement in the abortive assassination attempt. Their acquittal, which led to the dismissal of all three judges involved in the trial, including Chief Justice Sir Arku Korsah, provoked a second amendment, which authorised the president, if it appeared to him that it was in the interest of the state so to do, to declare by an executive instrument the decision of the court to be of no effect, the instrument to be deemed a *nolle prosequi* entered in terms of Section 54 of the

Criminal Procedure Code by the attorney-general before the decision in the case was given. The operation of the Amendment was backdated to 22 November, 1961, the date of the first Amendment. The acquittal of the accused persons having been nullified by the president in pursuance of this power, a third Amendment was brought in which reconstituted the special division. It was now to consist of the Chief Justice or one other judge, sitting with a jury of twelve whose verdict was to be by a majority. The re-constituted court then re-tried and convicted the accused persons (they had been kept in prison all the time under the Preventive Detention Act), and sentenced them to death, later commuted by the president to a prison term. It is remarkable that the constitutionality of the legislation was not challenged in the court having regard to the fact that judicial power was expressly vested in the courts by the 1960 Constitution of Ghana.

The Unconstitutionality of the Abdication of Legislative Power to the Executive

The issue here does not call in question the constitutionality of delegation within certain limits, of legislative power to the executive which is recognised as necessary and expedient under the system of separation of powers as under that of fused powers. Delegation of legislative power is necessary and expedient because it assures the use of the power to the fullest extent not realisable were the legislative assembly alone, with its democratic procedure of protracted debates in plenary session and in its various committees, left to make all the laws needed for the regulation of the social and economic life of the modern state in all its details and varied ramifications. It is simply impracticable for it to attempt to do so. Given the complex conditions of modern social and economic life, involving masses and masses of details, it seems hardly practicable that the legislative assembly should attempt to do more than lay down general policies and prescribe standards, leaving it to the executive, as the organ equipped for the purpose, to apply, by subordinate rules and regulations, the policies and standards embodied in its statutes to the varied circumstances and facts of social and economic life. Such is the extensive use made of delegated legislation by statutory instruments, regulations, rules and public notices that it forms the greater proportion of the law in many countries, notably Britain and (before 1966) Nigeria.

Apart from its acknowledged necessity, the delegation, within certain limits, of legislative power to the executive has undoubted advantages – greater knowledge of what will work; increased speed enabling the need for urgency to be met; more flexibility; greater suitability in cases of great technicality or cases requiring a course of continuous supervision; need for local variation, etc.

Yet, the necessity and desirability of delegation must not be allowed to obscure the limitations on the authority to delegate necessarily implied by the separation of the legislative and executive organs and their functions. Whilst delegation, within certain limits, is permitted by the system, abdication is manifestly inconsistent with it, and is therefore not permitted. Congress, said the U.S. Supreme Court, "is not permitted to abdicate or to transfer to others the essential legislative functions with which it is thus vested" by the Constitution. Abdication, it affirms, is "unknown to our law and is utterly inconsistent with the constitutional prerogatives and duties of the legislature." (*Schechter Poultry Corp v. United States*).

What, then, is the difference between delegation and abdication of legislative powers? Delegation, as earlier stated, occurs where the legislature enacts a law which lays down policies and standards with respect to a particular subject-matter, leaving the detailed application of the laid-down policies and standards to be regulated by subordinate rules made by the executive; on the other hand, abdication implies the transfer to the executive of the power of general law-making or power to legislate on an area covering an undefined variety of matters, e.g., the regulation of the whole field of industrial activity. The transfer of the power of general law-making does not have to be permanent and irrevocable to be an abdication.

Abdication of the former type, i.e., the transfer of the power of general law-making, is exemplified by the Emergency Powers Act enacted by the Nigerian Parliament in 1961. (The Act is not now extant on the statute book). The Act empowered the Governor-General in Council to make "such regulations as appear to him necessary or expedient for the purpose of maintaining and securing peace, order and good government in Nigeria or any part thereof." Furthermore, the Governor-General in Council may amend, suspend or modify a law on any subject whatever enacted by any legislature in the country; also any regulation made by him had "effect notwithstanding any thing inconsistent therewith contained in any law; any provision of a law which is inconsistent with any such regulation ... shall ... to the extent of such inconsistency have no effect so long as such regulation ... remains in force." This amounts clearly to abdication or the transfer of the power of general law-making, since the term "peace, order and good government of Nigeria" covers the whole field of the legislative power possessed by the Parliament itself under the constitution.

It is true that the transfer was for the purpose of dealing with an emergency situation. Yet, under the system of separation of powers, abdication remains unpermitted and unconstitutional during a period of emergency as during normal times. Emergency increases the need for delegation, but it does not remove the limitation on the power to delegate. It gives to the legislature no greater power to delegate than it ordinarily possesses. Rejecting the argument that it does, the U.S. Supreme Court has said that "extraordinary conditions may call for extraordinary remedies, but they do not create or enlarge constitutional power" *(Schechter Poultry Corp v. United States)*. In the words of Justice Douglas of the same court in a case *(Youngstown Sheet and Tube Co. v. Sawyer* (1951) arising out of a declared emergency:

> There can be no doubt that the emergency which caused the president to seize these steel plants was one that bore heavily on the country. But the emergency did not create power; it merely marked an occasion when power should be exercised. And the fact that it was necessary that measures be taken to keep steel in production does not mean that the president, rather than the Congress, had the constitutional authority to act. (...) The president can act more quickly than the Congress. The president with the armed services at his disposal can move with force as

well as with speed. (...) Legislative power, by contrast, is slower to exercise. There must be delay while the ponderous machinery of committees, hearings, and debates is put into motion. That takes time; and while the Congress slowly moves into action, the emergency may take its toll in wages, consumer goods, war production, the standard of living of the people, and perhaps even lives. Legislative action may indeed often be cumbersome, time-consuming, and apparently inefficient. But ... 'the doctrine of the separation of powers was adopted by the Convention of 1787, not to promote efficiency but to preclude the exercise of arbitrary power. The purpose was, not to avoid friction, but, by means of the inevitable friction incident to the distribution of the governmental powers among three departments, to save the people from autocracy' — quoting Justice Brandeis in *Myers v. United States* (1926).

In the light of this, it is questionable whether the Supreme Court of Nigeria in *Williams v. Majekodunmi* (1962) was right in rejecting an application for a declaration that the Act was inconsistent with the Constitution (1960) under which it was enacted and therefore invalid as tantamounting to an abdication or the transfer of the power of general law-making by Parliament to the executive. The decision is remarkable for its lack of insight into the issue raised, namely the difference between delegation, which is, in general, permitted, and abdication. The judgment contains no more insight on the issue than the bland statement by Justice Bairamian, delivering the unanimous decision of the Court constituted by four justices. "Everyone", he said:

> who assisted in the framing of the Constitution, and in particular the legal advisers who attended the Conference, were all aware of this method of legislation, and that there was no intention to require that every bit of legislation made after Independence had to be made by the Legislature itself, whether Federal or Regional, or else it would be of no effect. There is, of course, no abdication; for the Legislature still has control under section 5 of the Emergency Powers Act, 1961; to subsidiary legislation *per se* there can be no objection ... Suppose, for example, that the emergency is that the Federation is at war; it would be desirable to conserve petrol for military operations and undesirable to expend it on frequent meetings of Parliament — which would make it wise to have regulations made by the Governor-General in Council; and as action should be swift, it would be desirable to enable, say, the administrator of some remote parts of Nigeria, to do what may be necessary in his area forthwith.

This clearly misses the point; the issue is not as to the validity, propriety or desirability of delegated legislation *per se*, which is not disputed, but whether the transfer of the power of general law-making in the guise of "delegation" is constitutionally permitted, even during an emergency which, as stated by the U.S. Supreme Court in the passages quoted above, does not abolish the limitation on the power to delegate. And, as earlier stated, the transfer does not have to be permanent and irrevocable to be an abdication. The Court also failed to consider the degree of the separation of legislative and executive powers under the 1960 Constitution and whether it was such as forbade the abdication of legislative power to the executive, i.e., whether the governor-general being a constituent part of Parliament made a difference. We need not go into that here.

Abdication in the form of the transfer, not of the power of general law-making, but of power to legislate on an area covering an undefined variety of matters, is exemplified by the authority given by statute to the President of the United States to make codes of "fair competition" for any industry or trade in the country where such code will tend to effectuate the policy of the statute. The authority given to the president was thus not confined to any single, defined enterprise, but embraced the entire field of industry and trade. Not only was it not confined to one particular industrial or commercial enterprise, there was also no limitation as to the kind of activity, conduct or relations to be regulated. Its scope is indicated by the fact that the code made for the live poultry industry dealt with such things as working hours, age of employment, wages, collective bargaining, trade practices constituting unfair methods of competition, and machinery for the protection of consumers, competitors, employees and others. Neither in the statement of policy nor in any other part of it did the statute provide a definition of "fair competition" which would serve as a measure for. delimiting the scope of a code. Far from limiting the meaning, fair competition was given an extended meaning in the statute so as to embrace whatever might be considered wise or beneficent for the welfare of any industry or trade. This comes quite close indeed to a power of general law-making. Holding the delegation unconstitutional and void in a unanimous decision, the U.S. Supreme Court observed that a code of fair competition, given the absence of limitation as to subject-matter and the absence of any statutory measure of fair competition, 'becomes as wide as the field of industrial regulation. If that conception shall prevail, anything that Congress may do within the limits of the commerce clause for the betterment of business may be done by the president ... by calling it a code. This is delegation running riot. No such plenitude of power is susceptible of transfer.' (*Schechter Poultry Corp v. United States*).

Limits of Delegation Truly So-called

Cases of abdication apart, delegation truly so-called is' not without limits, although the limits are uncertain. Two decisions of the U.S. Supreme Court may be contrasted to illustrate the uncertainty. In one (*Panama Refining Co. v. Ryan (1935)*), a statutory grant of power to the president to prohibit the transportation in interstate and foreign commerce of petroleum and petroleum products produced in excess of the amount permitted by state law was held an unconstitutional delegation, on the ground that, though it related to a single, defined subject-matter, namely the transportation in interstate and foreign commerce of excess production of petroleum and petroleum products, the statute had left the president free to impose prohibition or not as he liked without laying down any intelligible standard or principle to control the exercise of the discretion. It declared no policy on prohibition, whether it considered transportation of excess production as injurious to the national interest or as involving unfair competition, and it laid down no conditions or circumstances in which prohibition might be imposed.

In contrast, the delegation of power to fix maximum prices of commodities as a temporary wartime measure was upheld, because it was limited by the statutory requirement that such prices must be generally fair and equitable, and be based so far as practicable on prices prevailing in a stated base period and on such other relevant factors as general increases or decreases in costs of production, distribution and transportation, and general increases or decreases in profit earned by sellers of the commodity during the period subsequent to a prescribed date; the statute also prescribed that the power was to be exercised only when prices had risen or threaten to rise to an extent or in a manner inconsistent with the purposes of the statute, which were declared to be the prevention of inflation and its enumerated consequences. These, the court held, were adequate standards to control the delegated discretion as regards both the occasion for its exercise and as to the particular prices to be fixed. It is noteworthy that one of the justices considered the delegation unconstitutional as not setting any really meaningful limits as to whether, and, if so, when, the price of any commodity shall be regulated; in his view the delegation amounted to the grant of a commission "to take any action with respect to prices which he believes will preserve what he deems a sound economy during the emergency" *Yakus v. United States* (1944).

The power delegated to the President of Nigeria by the Public Holidays Act, Cap 378, Laws of the Federation 1990 to appoint by public notice "a special day to be kept as a public holiday" "in addition to the days" specified as public holidays in a schedule to the Act is certainly within the permitted limits of delegated legislation. The Public Holidays Act, as a law in existence on May 29, 1999, is continued in force by Section 315(1) of the 1999 Constitution, and, being a law on a matter in the Exclusive Legislative List (item 51), is deemed to have been enacted by the National Assembly (Section 315(1)(a)) in exercise of the legislative power vested in it by Section 4(1). It is thus the National Assembly which, by the Public Holidays Act (Section 2(1)), delegated to the president power to make subsidiary legislation "by public notice: appointing a special day to be kept as a public holiday". The public notice issued by the president appointing May 29 as a public holiday is part of the laws of this country, just like any other subsidiary legislation by the executive in the form of statutory instruments, regulations, rules and public notices, which are as voluminous if not more so than, statutes enacted by the legislative assembly.

The test of permissible delegation laid down in the American decisions admittedly lacks precision. A commentator has thus pointedly remarked that "the question still remains, however, 'what is a standard?' How much of a standard has been set up ... that rates be 'just and reasonable' ... and that ... rules be consistent with the public interest?" And in many cases where delegation is upheld, it is questionable whether what is accepted as a "standard" imports any really intelligible principle or yardstick. The impression is thus created that the application by the courts of the doctrine of limited delegation is often arbitrary. Yet the imprecision of the test does not negate the principle of limitation. The reason for a limitation is clear. For unless the enabling statute lays down a standard to guide the exercise of the delegated power, then the concept of limited government which underlies the separation of powers may be subverted, especially where this results in vital decisions of policy being given force of law binding on the country without being put through the process of discussion prescribed in the constitution for law-making, with the object that legislation should have as wide a basis in popular consent as possible.

It is important that delegated legislation should not only be strictly confined within its proper limits but also be strictly controlled by the legislature through such means as the affirmative procedure whereby subsidiary legislation may be required to be laid in draft before the legislative houses and is not to come into operation until they have resolved affirmatively that it should do so; or the procedure of requiring in the enabling Act that copies of a subsidiary legislation shall be laid before the legislative houses which may resolve to annul it. Then there is the procedure whereby a select committee scrutinises statutory instruments either in draft or after they have been made, and draws the attention of the House to any objectionable provision such as a provision making the legislation unchallengeable in the courts or giving it retrospective effect where the parent statute confers no express authority to that effect.

Unconstitutionality of Executive Usurpation of Legislative or Judicial Power

Lacking the sovereign and plenary character of legislative power, executive power has little, if any, scope of being used to trench on the legislative or judicial domains, except as an act of brazen perversion of the constitution, which would be manifestly null and void.

By governmental practice that has become customary in many countries in the former British empire, the executive is usually empowered by the constitution to make adaptations in existing laws necessary to bring them into conformity with a new order established following a change from one system of government to another under a new constitution, such as occurred in Nigeria in October 1960, October 1963, October 1979 and May 1999. In line with this customary practice, all Nigerian constitutions from 1960 have always given the executive the power to make the necessary adaptations in existing laws. The practice is predicated upon expediency because of the intricate nature of the task.

Section 274(2) of the 1979 Constitution, following the wording in the earlier Constitution of 1963, empowered the president (or the governor of a state), by order, "to make such **changes** in the **text** of any existing law as he considers necessary or expedient to bring that law into conformity with the provisions of the Constitution" (emphasis supplied). The reference to **textual changes** indicates the nature and scope of the power, as being limited to clerical or verbal changes, like changing names, titles and designations, substituting appropriate functionaries and so on. This is exemplified by an order made by the Governor of Kaduna State under the provision in Section 274(2), whereby the title Chief Justice in any existing law of the state was changed to Chief Judge, Military Governor, Executive Council or Governor-in-Council to Governor, minister to commissioner, native authority to local government council, North-Central State to Kaduna State, and Edict to Law. (See KDS L.N. No. 15 of 1980)

The provision (S. 274(2)) was not intended to authorise changes of substance or policy in the law. Deletion or repeal otherwise than for the purpose of effecting such clerical or verbal changes was thus outside its pale. To make changes in the text of a law — that is, in its wording — presupposes that the law continues in force with all its substantive provisions. If the law or any of its substantive provisions is abrogated, the text will not be there to be adapted to bring it into conformity with the constitution.

It is necessary to distinguish the power of adaptation vested in the president or governor under the provision of Section 274(2) and the provision under Subsection 1 of the same section. Section 274(1) provided that "an existing law shall have effect with such **modifications** as may be necessary to bring it into conformity with the provisions of this constitution", and "modification" was defined in Section 274(4) as including "addition, alteration, omission or repeal." Since the word "modification" did not appear in Section 274(2), its definition in Section 274(4) was for purpose of Section 274(1) only. It is not permissible to apply in the interpretation of a provision the definition of a word not used in it. The provision in Section 274(1) together with the definition of "modification" in Section 274(4) is directed, not to the president or governor, but to the courts as to how to interpret existing laws. Only a court can, in the exercise of its interpretative jurisdiction, say that an existing law has been impliedly repealed by the constitution. The power of the president or governor under Section 274(2) did not enable him to **modify** an existing law by repeal or by the addition or omission of **anything of substance.**

Now, it needs hardly be said that the making of alterations, deletions and additions in existing laws or their repeal for the purpose of bringing them into conformity with the constitution embraces a considerable part of the legislative power vested in the National Assembly and the State Houses of Assembly. The extent of legislative power which this will put in the hands of the president and the State governors must be viewed in the light of the fact that the military government which preceded the 1979 Constitution (and the 1999 Constitution as well) was an absolute, autocratic one, and had enacted many laws which may not be in conformity with the democratic standards of the 1979 Constitution. Suppose, then, the president or governor took the view that any of these laws was not in conformity with the constitution, did the power vested in him by Section 274(2) enable him to repeal it either in whole or in part? To admit that he could was to subvert one of the central planks — the separation of powers — upon which the whole constitutional edifice was built. A president or governor endowed with such wide legislative powers was not the type contemplated by the constitution — one who, in the words of Chief Justice Fatayi-Williams, "can only exercise executive powers." Such certainly is not the meaning nor the intention of the adaptive power.

It was thus a usurpation of the legislative power vested in the State House of Assembly for the Governor of Kaduna State, shortly after the transition from military rule to civilian democratic government in October 1979, to have used his power of adaptive legislation under Section 274(2) of the 1979 Constitution, to make changes of substance in the existing laws of the state. Purporting to act under Section 274(2), he issued the Local Government Edict (Modifications) Order, 1979 repealing the provisions of the Local Government Edict (now adapted to read Law) relating to emirate or traditional councils, nominated councillors and traditional presidents of local government councils. The effect was that these bodies and offices were thereby abolished. Also repealed by the Modification Order were the provisions in the Local Government Edict empowering the governor to approve the election of chairmen of local government councils and to determine their terms and conditions of service. These repeals and abolitions which, as they clearly went beyond the power of adaptive legislation, were a usurpation of legislative power, provoked a massive counter-usurpation of the governor's executive power by the State House of Assembly, thus intensifying the crisis that had held the State in its stranglehold since the transition.

The 1999 Constitution has altered the wording in its corresponding Section 315(2) which empowers the president (or the governor of a state) to make by order "such **modification** in the text of any existing law as (he) considers necessary or expedient to bring that law into conformity with the provisions of this constitution" (emphasis supplied). The change in wording from 'changes' in Section 274(2) of the 1979 Constitution to "modifications" has serious consequences. It imports into the provision in Section 315(2) the definition of "modification" in Section 315(4)(c), thereby enabling the president (or governor) to make changes of substance in all laws existing on May 29 1999 by "addition, alteration, omission or repeal" as he considers necessary or expedient to bring them into conformity with the provisions of the Constitution. It vests him with the power of substantive legislation derived, not from delegation by the National Assembly, but directly from the constitution.

In effect, therefore, the change of just one word, from "changes" to "modifications," has, perhaps without intending it, encroached on the exclusiveness of the National Assembly's power to "make laws for the peace, order and good government of the Federation" (Section 4(2)), an exclusiveness which the separation of powers contemplates and affirmatively requires. This is particularly the case because, although Section 315 appears in a Part of the Constitution headed "Transitional Provisions," no date is fixed on which the power is to cease to be exercisable. On the contrary, it is, by the express terms of Section 315(2), exercisable "at any time;" it is thus a continuing power covering the entire body of existing laws. It was limited to six months by the 1960 Constitution and three years by the 1963 Constitution.

The president will be acting like a true constitutionalist and in the true spirit of the separation of powers underlying our Constitution if he restricts his power of adaptive legislation under Section 315(2) to purely verbal or textual changes in existing laws.

CHAPTER 12

Efficacy of Separation of Powers and Other Constitutional Limitations on Power: The Question of Enforcement and Remedies

Enforcement Machinery

The efficacy of separation of powers as a constitutional device for limiting government depends on how the limitation on power arising from it are policed or enforced. It seems generally agreed that some means of enforcement is necessary to its efficacy; what is disputed is whether the enforcement machinery should be the ordinary courts of law or some other kind of machinery.

It may be thought that the issue is concluded where, as is usually the case, the constitution has the character of a law, and the limitations it imposes on government, the character of legal limitations, which will inexorably indicate the courts as the proper medium for their enforcement, a court being "the place where law is to be sought." For, as Charles Black remarked, "where but in a court would the

---

1. Charles Black, *The People and the Court* (1966), p. 118.

people look for the skilled reading and application of law?"[1] "The institution of judicial review," he further observed, "is the practical embodiment of **binding legal limitations** on the power of immediately elected government." No less categorical upon the point are the words of Alexander Hamilton. "Constitutional limitations," he maintains, "can be preserved in practice no other way than through the medium of the courts of justice ... Without this, all the reservations of particular rights or privileges would amount to nothing."[2] Whatever might be said against it (see below),[3] enforcement of constitutional limitations by the ordinary courts of law is, as was said by Chief Justice John Marshall in *Marbury v. Madison* (1803), "the greatest improvement on political institutions."

Indeed, true constitutional democracy can hardly exist unless the courts have the power to enforce the law of the constitution against the legislature and the executive, to ensure that their actions conform with it and that the rule of law is maintained as a principle governing the administration of the state. An independent judiciary, it has been truly said, is, by the nature of its function, "the citizens' last line of defence in a free society, that is, the line separating constitutionalism from totalitarianism." How effectively the courts perform this vital role is of course another matter.

But the French and others following in their footsteps are unpersuaded by the compelling logic of the argument about the inexorability of the courts as the enforcement authority. Their rejection of judicial review was probably borne out of national pride and prestige: if the British Parliament is not subject to judicial review, the French Parliament should not be on any lesser pedestal, but they forget that the supreme authority of the British Parliament is a product of the historical fact that Britain does not have, and never has had, a written constitution.

---

2. *The Federalist*, no. 78; 328; quoted with approval by the U.S. Supreme Court in *United States v. Lovett*, 328 U.S. 303, 314.

3. See also B. O. Nwabueze, *Judicialism* (1977), pp. 230-236; *Ideas and Facts in Constitution-Making* (1993), pp. 17-19.

In place of the ordinary courts as the reviewing body, the French Constitution (1958), whose precedent in this regard is followed with or without modification by the constitutions of eight African countries mentioned below, reposes in a Constitutional Council the determination of disputes between the two political organs on whether a subject-matter of the law-making power lies within the domain of the one or the other as well as the determination of questions concerning the constitutionality of organic or ordinary laws passed by Parliament and the standing rules of the legislative houses (Art. 62). By this provision, therefore, judicial review of legislative acts of parliament as well as decrees and ordinances made by the executive is totally precluded. It follows that the ordinary courts in France are confined to the administration of justice in disputes or matters arising under the ordinary law, and are excluded from those in which questions of constitutionality are involved, unless and until a decision on such question has been handed down by the Constitutional Council, thereby making the decision part of the law to be applied by the ordinary courts.

The total preclusion of the review of the constitutionality of legislative acts has serious constitutional implications. In the view of Dicey, commenting on the same provision in the Constitution of the French Third Republic (1875):

> The restrictions placed on the action of the legislature are not in reality laws, since they are not rules which in the last resort will be enforced by the courts. Their true character is that of maxims of political morality, which derive whatever strength they possess from being formally inscribed in the constitution, and from the resulting support of public opinion.[4]

That is, as far as legislative acts are concerned. They apply to purely executive acts with coercive legal force.

The correctness of this view of the matter depends on the character of the constitutional council and of its decisions. Certainly, the Council

---

4. A. V. Dicey, *The Law of the Constitution*, 3rd ed., p. 157.

is not a court of law nor does it partake of the character of a court. This is so for two main reasons. It consists of members appointed for a fixed, non-renewable term of nine years — three by the President of the Republic, three by the President of the National Assembly and three by the President of the Senate — in addition to all former Presidents of the Republic as life members (Art. 56).

In the second place, its functions are not judicial, because its decision on a question of constitutionality of a legislative measure can be rendered only before the measure, whether an organic law, an ordinary law or standing rules of the legislative houses, is actually promulgated into law or before it is put into effect, and then only on a reference to the Council by the President, the Premier, the President of the National Assembly, President of the Senate, sixty deputies or sixty senators, but not by a private person who is a party in a dispute (Art. 61). Now, a ruling given even by an ordinary court on a legislative measure before its promulgation into law or before it comes into operation and before a dispute has arisen on its application or threatened application to identifiable persons is not a judicial decision.[5] because the issue on which it is given is not a justiciable one;[6] it is only an advisory opinion.[7]

It is true that, unlike an advisory opinion strictly so-called, the French Constitutional Council's rulings are expressly made "binding upon the governing authorities and all administrative and judicial authorities," and that a legislative measure declared unconstitutional by the Council may not be promulgated or put into effect (Art. 62). No doubt too, preventive adjudication by means of an advisory opinion has certain cardinal advantages.[8] Yet, whilst an actual legislation passed by the legislature but not yet put into effect is an attempt by it to deal

---

5. *Hayburn's Case* 2 Dall 409 (1792); *United States v. Ferreira* 13 How. 40 (1851); *United States v. Evans* 213 U.S. 297, pp. 300-1 (1909).

6. *Att-Gen for Ontario v. Att-Gen for the Dominion* [1896] A.C. 348 (P.C.).

7. On the difference between judicial decision and an advisory opinion, see further Nwabueze, *Judicialism* (1977), pp. 84-97)

8. As to which, see Nwabueze, *loc. cit.*

with concrete situations of real life, it nevertheless does not have all the "impact of actuality and the intensity of immediacy"[9] created by the operation of a legislation on the rights or interests of identifiable persons. The meaning of words in which legislation is expressed can only be adequately and correctly ascertained in the light of the particular facts of a particular dispute involving the rights of particular persons. It is impossible, said the Judicial Committee of the Privy Council, to attempt before hand to imagine "all possible cases and facts which might occur to qualify, cut down, and override the operation of particular words" used in a statute.[10] Thus, whatever the advantages of preventive adjudication by means of advisory opinion, it cannot be a substitute for judicial review.

Happily for constitutionalism, the other countries of Europe, Italy, Germany, Australia, Turkey, Romania (1991) and Bulgaria (1991), which have adopted the device of a special review machinery, do not share France's total rejection of judicial review of statutes in any form. The special constitutional court established in the constitutions of all six of them is a court strictly so-called, both because it is so styled in the constitution and because its functions are judicial in nature. Whilst its jurisdiction varies in extent between the six countries, it includes in each case the review of the constitutionality of legislation on certain specified grounds. It is widest in Germany and Bulgaria, embracing (in Bulgaria) the interpretation of the constitution, adjudication of the constitutionality of laws and other acts of the National Assembly and the acts of the president, competence suits between the National Assembly, the president and the council of ministers, and between the bodies of local self-government and the central government, the compatibility between the constitution and the international instruments concluded by the country prior to their ratification, and the compatibility of domestic laws with the universally recognised

---

9.   Felix Frankfurter, "A Note on Advisory Opinion," Harv. L. Rev. 37 (1923), pp. 1002-7; see also his "Advisory Opinions" in *Encyclopaedia of Social Sciences*, p. 475.

10.   *Att-Gen of Ontario v. Hamilton Street* Ry [1903] A.C. 524 at p. 529.

norms of international law and the international instruments binding on the country, the constitutionality of political parties, the legality of the election of the president, vice-president and members of the National Assembly and the impeachment of the president or the vice-president.[11]

Significantly, however, the adjudication of violations of constitutionally guaranteed rights is not, except in Germany, among the matters within the jurisdiction of the constitutional court. Equally significant is the fact that in Bulgaria and Turkey, but certainly not in Germany and Austria, and probably not in the other two countries too, the jurisdiction of the court cannot be invoked by a private person; in Bulgaria it can only be invoked by the president, the council of ministers, the Supreme Court of Cassation, the Supreme Administrative Court, the Chief Prosecutor or at least one-fifth of all members of the National Assembly.[12] A constitutional court without power to enforce constitutionally guaranteed rights and whose jurisdiction cannot be invoked by private persons to enforce the other limitations on powers affords but little protection for individual liberty or for constitutional democracy.

In Italy, Bulgaria and Turkey, the effect of the constitutional court's decision is to nullify a law or Act adjudged to be unconstitutional.[13] The relevant constitutional provisions merely state in Romania that the decision of the court is "binding," which in the context may be taken to mean that it operates to nullify any law or Act adjudged unconstitutional,[14] and in Germany, that a federal law "shall specify in what case its decisions shall have the force of law"[15] which also seems to imply that in cases so specified a law or Act declared

---

11. Art. 149, Bulgaria; Art. 93, Germany; Art. 134, Italy; Art. 144, Romania; Arts 137-148, Austria; Arts 146-153, Turkey (1982).

12. Art. 150 (1), Bulgaria.

13. Art. 136, Italy; Art. 151(2), Bulgaria; Art. 153, Turkey.

14. Art. 145(2), Romania.

15. Art. 94(2), Germany.

unconstitutional is thereby nullified. The binding force of the constitutional court's decision in Romania applies only where a law duly promulgated or put into effect is declared unconstitutional. But the court is also given power to pronounce on the constitutionality of laws before their promulgation at the request of the president, one of the presidents of the two legislative chambers, the Supreme Court of Justice, at least 50 deputies or at least 25 senators, and to pronounce on the constitutionality of regulations of Parliament at the request of one of the presidents of the two legislative chambers, a parliamentary group, at least 50 deputies or at least 25 senators.[16] In these two cases, the ruling of the court is overridden if the law or regulation is, on a re-examination, adopted in the same form by a majority of at least two-thirds of the members of each of the legislative chambers.[17] As earlier stated, the use of preventive adjudication to supplement judicial review of statutes enhances the efficacy of constitutionalism.

It is important to note that the ordinary courts in these countries, unlike in France, are not completely excluded from matters within the jurisdiction of the constitutional court. They can interpret the constitution when it is applicable in cases before them, but in Germany, Turkey, Bulgaria and Romania they must stay the proceedings and obtain the decision of the constitutional court where an applicable law is considered to be at variance with the constitution;[18] in other words, they are competent to apply the constitution only when no conflict or discrepancy is found between it and an applicable law. The Italian Constitution has explicit provision on the point, but the position seems to be that, while an ordinary court can pronounce a law unconstitutional, its decision does not nullify the law, as does that of the constitutional court; it operates merely as a refusal to apply the law.

---

16. Art. 144(a) and (b).

17. Art. 145(1).

18. Art. 100(1), Germany; Art. 152, Turkey; Art. 150(2), Bulgaria; Art. 144(c), Romania.

There can be no doubt, we may venture to say in conclusion, that the new device instituted in these countries of Europe for the enforcement of constitutional limitations upon power by a special constitutional court affords less effective safeguards for liberty than their enforcement by the ordinary courts.

Enforcement by the Courts of Law and Democracy

It seems appropriate at this juncture to examine the arguments upon which the French might have based their rejection of the enforcement of constitutional limitations by a court and its replacement by a Constitutional Council constituted in the manner indicated above (apart from a desire, born out of national prestige, to put the French Parliament on the same pedestal as the British Parliament). It has been argued that a court of law, being an unelected body and a "counter-majoritarian force," it is undemocratic that it should be enabled to frustrate the will of an elected legislature (or an elected executive) on a policy measure which may have been passed by the votes of an overwhelming majority of its members or even by a unanimous vote.[19]

This clearly misrepresents the meaning and processes of democratic government. Democracy is not restricted to rule by an elected majority. The ideal and processes implied in the concept are more complex and subtle than that. Essentially, it connotes self-government, that is to say, government conducted by the people collectively and as individuals. The "self" there refers not only to the people as a free and independent community but also to the attribute of personal participation by the several individuals comprising the community. Democracy is thus a form of government in which the highest premium is placed on the participation of the individual in government. The primary meaning of democracy, Professor Arthur Lewis has said, is that all those affected by a decision should participate in making it.[20]

---

19. Alexander Bickel, *The Least Dangerous Branch* (1962), pp. 16 and 17.

20. Arthur Lewis, *Politics in West Africa* (1965), p. 75.

Majority rule is thus only one element in the processes of democratic government, dictated as it is by the inexpediency of unanimity in decision-making. It is the most practical expedient for reaching decisions in a society of men with differing interests and prejudices. But the majority referred to here is not a majority of the people. It is a majority of the legislature or of a plural executive, to whom the people, by a majority, have delegated their power of self-government, the delegation being necessitated by the inexpediency of collective decision by the entire population of a large, complex community comprising millions of people spread over a wide territory. The act of delegation, which is effected through the mechanism of a constitution, adopted by means of a referendum, is complemented by election at reasonably frequent intervals, whereby the people, again by a majority, choose those to represent and act for them in the legislative and executive organs of government. The democratic theory of self-government by the people is assured, however approximately, by these two processes of delegation and election.

But the ideal of individual participation has also to be assured in some form for the system of government to be fully democratic. Since they are determined by a majority, the processes of delegation and periodic elections do not effectively assure individual participation. It is in this connection that the terms of the delegation through the mechanism of a constitution acquires vital importance in a democracy. Democracy presupposes that the delegation is not to be unencumbered, but should rather be subject to terms designed to safeguard the position of the individual, and to enable him to intervene where the safeguards are being transgressed. If the size and complexity of modern society make it inexpedient for every individual to participate personally in decisions which affect him, then his liberty as an individual needs to be protected against those elected to the governing bodies. This is the function of a constitutional guarantee of individual rights, otherwise known as a Bill of Rights, and the separation of powers. Such a guarantee or Bill of Rights and the device of separation of powers becomes a necessary element of constitutional democracy. A government of the people by the people is not fully democratic and constitutional unless the instrument constituting it also protects the liberty of the individual by the two devices of a guarantee of basic rights and the separation of powers.

Yet the safeguard of a constitutional Bill of Rights and the separation of powers would be rendered practically nugatory if an individual who alleges violation of them by the legislature or executive is not able to appeal to a body independent of these organs, whether the ordinary courts or some other kind of tribunal. Review of governmental acts by an independent body at the instance of an aggrieved individual in the interest of maintaining the efficacy of the constitutional limitations is thus also an essential and important mechanism of democratic government. Being at the instance of an aggrieved individual, the democratic virtue of such a review is that it assures the individual's personal participation in government through his personal intervention to protect the terms of the delegation against infringement or abuse by the wielders of power, thus imparting greater reality to the concept of self-government.

The review of governmental acts, through the agency of an independent tribunal and in accordance with the limitations set out in the basic instrument of government, is the people's own device for the control of the power they have entrusted to their elected representatives. Judicial review, writes Professor Charles Black, "is the people's institutionalized means of self-control,"[21] the "self-restraint of democracy."[22] Being a practical incident of the terms and conditions upon which the majority in the legislature and executive holds its powers, the review of governmental acts in terms of the constitutional limitations upon government is indeed a constituent element of majority rule; to regard it as antithetical thereto is to misconceive the true basis of majority rule.

The counter-majoritarian argument asserts, however, that the concept of the "people" in relation to the limitations imposed on

---

21. Charles Black, *op. cit.*, p. 107.

22. *ibid*, p. 115.

government by the constitution is a "myth," an "abstraction," and one that obscures "the reality that when the Supreme Court declares unconstitutional a legislative act or the action of an elected executive, it thwarts the will of the representatives of the **actual people of the here and now**; it exercises control, not on behalf of the prevailing majority, but against it."[23] This is a fallacy. The concept of the people, with its imperfections and limitations, has as much reality in relation to the two processes of delegation and periodic elections. Once adopted, a constitution binds not only the generation of the people who adopted it but also posterity, though the latter have a right to refuse to be ruled by their ancestors long deceased. They can exercise this right to change the constitution in its entirety or to amend only such parts of it as do not meet with their approval. It is their birthright, but non-exercise of it indicates approval of or at least acquiescence in, what the people of the past have bequeathed to them. A constitution, though made 200 years before, has a continuing basis in current popular consent and approval. The suggestion that the U.S. Constitution has no democratic basis, that it is an imposition from a past age, is one from which most Americans would recoil.

It is further asserted that, "although democracy does not mean reconsideration of decisions once made, it does mean that a representative majority has the power to accomplish a reversal."[24] If by this is meant that a representative majority has the power to reverse the limitations imposed upon it by the constitution, then this is the exact antithesis of a constitutional democracy. "By definition," writes an eminent authority, Professor Carl Friedrich, "a constitutional democracy is one which does not grant all power to the majority."[25] It is rule by the majority according to predetermined rules. A representative majority that is not bound or limited by rules beyond

---

23. Bickel, *op. cit.,* pp. 16-17; (emphasis supplied).

24. Bickel, *op. cit.,* p. 17.

25. Carl J. Friedrich, *Constitutional Government and Democracy* (1950), p. 123.

its power to reverse is not a democratic body, but an autocratic and arbitrary one.

Granted that review of governmental acts by the court is a people's institution, it is said to be nonetheless undemocratic unless the personnel of the court are responsible to the people. Power, especially critical political power, is unsupportable without responsibility, which is attained only through the process of election. Three observations may be made upon this argument. First, the equation of responsibility with accountability through the process of election is much too narrow. While elections at reasonably frequent intervals are indispensable to democracy because they enable the people to give practical expression to their changing outlook and wishes on government, the concept of responsibility is wider than that. Responsibility demands not only the accountability of the government to the people through the electoral and other communication processes, but also that governmental actions should respond to the needs of the people as revealed in public opinion, which should therefore be among the factors informing policy.

So conceived, judges are unquestionably responsible, because they are responsive to the needs of the people, not so much to their immediate material needs, but to their need for principle in government, for those enduring values which are the ultimate end of government, and which serve to give lasting meaning and purpose to the life of the people. The legislature and executive, preoccupied as they are, with the expedient resolution of pressing problems, have failed all too often to take account of society's fundamental moral values in framing their measures. Insulated from the clash of interests and the pressures for expedient accommodation, the courts are well placed to distil principle out of society's fundamental presuppositions, establishing them as active principles of the constitutional system according to which the propriety (i.e., constitutionality) of actions of the legislature and executive are to be judged. In this way the court serves the ends of constitutional democracy.

Judicial decisions are also responsive to the attitude of the public towards questions of the day. The changing positions adopted by the U.S. Supreme Court on race relations have reflected the attitudes prevalent in the society; the spirit of equality prevailing in the immediate aftermath of the Civil War led to decisions unfavourable to segregation;[26] the swing in public attitude back to racial segregation produced the decision establishing the separate-but-equal formula[27] while the desegregation decisions of the 1950s may be accounted, in part at least, as the Court's response to the mood for unseparated equality dominant in the nation at the time.[28] Further, although considerations of what is good or desirable for society are primarily a matter for the political organs, the courts should not be unconcerned with them. Policy in its widest sense should be among the factors informing judicial decision.

Secondly, as Dean Eugene Rostow says, "the task of democracy is not to have the people vote directly on every issue, but to assure their ultimate responsibility for the acts of their representatives, elected or appointed."[29] This ultimate responsibility or control is assured by the right of the people, or the legislature in most African countries, to reverse the judges' interpretation of the constitution through a constitutional amendment, as has happened not infrequently. Professor McWhinney has even asserted, citing the experience in the U.S. and South Africa in 1937 and 1956 respectively, that in a conflict that becomes an election issue the Court will always pipe down if the government obtains a renewed mandate in the election.[30] This seems to take too cynical a view of the Court's checking function in practice. Was it really, as Charles Black "conjectured," the "crushing decisiveness of the 1936 election and the high public emotion swirling around the

---

26. *Railroad Company v. Brown*, 17 Wall 445 (1873).

27. *Plessy v. Ferguson*, 163 U.S. 537 (1996).

28. *Brown v. Board of Education*, 347 U.S. 483 (1954).

29. Eugene Rostow, *The Sovereign Prerogative: The Supreme Court and the Quest for Law* (1962), p. 153.

30. McWhinney, *Judicial Review in the English-Speaking World* (1965), p. 196.

Packing Plan"[31] that brought about the change in the Court's earlier position over the New Deal in the U.S.? While, as Charles Black also admits, "the decisive factor in producing the change will perhaps never be known,"[32] it seems nearer the truth to say that the change was largely the result of a genuine and honest conviction on the part of the two of the justices that their earlier position was wrong, and that there was sufficient warrant in the constitution for many of the New Deal measures.   Nor can it be said with certainty that in eventually affirming the Senate Act, 1955, and the South Africa Act Amendment Act, 1956, the South African Supreme Court merely bowed to the renewed mandate given to the government in the 1953 election at which the conflict with the Court was the dominant issue.

Thirdly, in democratic practice, election is not an invariable requirement regardless of its suitability or desirability for particular decision-making processes. "Every democracy divides issues of policy into several categories, to be settled by different means."[33] as appropriate.   It is just not appropriate or desirable that judges should be elected or removed by election. The office of a judge requires special qualifications and ability, which cannot adequately be judged by the electorate, whose judgment must inevitably be swayed by other considerations. Moreover, the process of election, characterised as it is by party or group interests and by political campaigning, is likely to impair the image of a judge as an impartial and independent guardian of the limitations imposed upon the majority for the protection of the individual.   These considerations make elections wholly inappropriate for the selection or removal of judges.   The case could not be put more strongly than in the words of John Stuart Mill. If, he says:

> a judge could be removed from office by a popular vote, whoever was desirous of supplanting him would make capital for that purpose out of

---

31.   Charles Black, *op. cit.*, p. 60.

32.   *ibid*, p. 60.

33.   Rostow, *op. cit.*, p. 173.

all his judicial decisions; would carry all of them, as far as he found practicable, by irregular appeal before a public opinion wholly incompetent, for want of not having heard the case, or from having heard it without either the precautions or the impartiality belonging to a judicial hearing; would play upon popular passion and prejudice where they existed, and take pains to arouse them where they did not. And in this, if the case were interesting, he would infallibly be successful, unless the judge or his friends descended into the arena, and made equally powerful appeals on the other side. Judges would end by feeling that they risked their office upon every decision they gave in a case susceptible of general interest, and that it was less essential for them to consider what decision was just than what would be most applauded by the public, or would least admit of insidious misrepresentation.[34]

Contrary to what Thayer says,[35] the checking function of judicial review exercises a sobering influence on government by inducing in it a humane and tolerant attitude towards power. It has certainly not made government careless of the need for fair dealing and common honesty. Rather it has introduced into governmental processes standards of judicial behaviour, such as those of openness, good faith, fairness, reasonableness and the more specific requirements of natural justice. Constitutionalism, it has been truly said, "is the application of judicial methods to basic problems of government; administrative justice, extending this application, attempts to extend the judicial methods to the wider sphere of activities which government is handling today."[36] And it has sharpened, not deadened, the people's "sense of moral responsibility," witness the court's desegregation decision in the U.S. which have awakened many Americans to their moral responsibility towards the underprivileged negroes in their midst. It has also enhanced, not dwarfed, the people's political capacity, witness the lively interest in government which recent Supreme Court decisions have generated among Americans, an interest which cannot

---

34. J. S. Mill, *Representative Governments;* reprinted in *Utilitarianism, Liberty and Representative Government* (Everyone's Library edn.) pp. 369-370.

35. James Thayer, *John Marshall* (1901), pp. 103-4; 106-7.

36. Bickel *op. cit.*, particularly chap. 4.

but increase their capacity to influence government, thus ensuring that "legislative and executive policy would be formed out of free debate, democratic suffrage, untrammelled political effort, and full enquiry."[37]

The argument about the checking function of judicial review being a counter-majoritarian force dissolves completely where the government is a minority one as in apartheid South Africa and Ian Smith's Rhodesia. The existence of such a government underlines most conspicuously the great importance of the checking function as the disenfranchised individual's only avenue for effective intervention or participation in government. The constitutional crisis in South Africa in 1952 provides a good illustration of this.

The Union of South Africa came into existence in 1909 by the union of four separate colonies under the South Africa Act of that year, which was enacted by the British Parliament. The Act, which became the Constitution of the Union, made membership of the bicameral legislature exclusive to Europeans. By the laws in force in the constituent colonies at the time of the union, the franchise was exclusive to Europeans in two of them, Transvaal and the Orange Free State (originally Boer republics), and in the other two, Natal and the Cape of Good Hope (originally British colonies) while not avowedly limited to Europeans, the franchise was qualified mainly by literacy and property/income requirements, which operated in Natal to exclude virtually all non-whites. However, in the Cape of Good Hope, where the requirements were less restrictive, a small but significant number of natives and "Coloured" persons had by 1909 been able to qualify as voters and had been registered in the Common Roll of voters. When the Union was established in 1909, the Union Act recognised existing franchise rights in the Cape by prohibiting any disqualification based on race or colour. Further, no registered voter in any province should be removed from the register by reason

---

37. Carl Friedrich, *op. cit.,* p. 117.

of any disqualification based on race or colour. These provisions were made unalterable by the Union Parliament except by a two-thirds majority of the total membership of both Houses sitting together. The Constitution had no Bill of Rights nor (apart from the entrenchment of the English and Dutch languages as the official languages) were there any other limitations on the government whose law-making powers were thus plenary and unlimited, except as just indicated. The government established by the Constitution is thus undemocratic both because of the denial of the vote to the overwhelming majority of the population and because of the absence of a constitutional Bill of Rights. (The total population of the country at the time consisted of 9,000,000 native Africans, 1,000,000 Coloureds, 300,000 Indians, and 2,275,000 whites. In 1935 there were 10,628 native voters on the Cape Common Roll). There was thus a very restricted scope for the Court's checking function as far as parliamentary legislation was concerned. Yet, restricted as it was, it proved supremely important in the face of the government's attempt to deprive the non-whites in the Cape of the existing franchise rights otherwise than as provided in the Constitution.

The story of this attempt began in 1936. In that year Parliament, using the prescribed procedure, passed an Act, the Representation of Natives Act, removing all natives (but not Coloureds) in the Cape from the Common Roll of voters, establishing instead a separate Cape native voters' roll, with a right to elect three representatives (Europeans) to the lower House. The Act was immediately challenged by one Ndlwana, a native registered voter, on the ground that the requirement of a two-thirds majority of both Houses sitting together had by implication been repealed by the Statute of Westminster, 1931, of the United Kingdom, and that accordingly Parliament could only function bicamerally.[38] For the government, it was contended that by the Statute of Westminster the South African Parliament acquired

---

38. *Ndlwana v. Hofmeyr* (1937) A.D. 229.

a sovereignty that was both unlimited and supreme, and in all respects equal to that of the British Parliament, so that the Court was not competent to question a duly promulgated and enrolled Act. The Appellate Division of the South African Supreme Court not only accepted the government's contention, saying emphatically that "it is obviously senseless to speak of an Act of a sovereign law-making body as *ultra vires*,[39] It went further to hold that a sovereign legislature is not subject to procedural limitations but could adopt any procedure it thought fit, from which it followed that the requirement of a two-thirds majority at a joint sitting was "at the mercy of parliament like everything else."

The government next moved against the Cape Coloured voters. By the Separate Representation of Voters Act, 1951, they were removed from the Cape Common Roll, and placed on a special roll, with a right, together with other Coloured voters in the country (about 50,000 in all) to elect four special representatives to the Lower House. Unlike the Representation of Natives Act, however, the 1951 Act was passed by a simple majority of each House sitting separately, the reason being that the government did not then have a two-thirds majority of the total combined membership of both Houses. Upon challenge by a "Coloured" voter, the Appellate Division held the Act void as being *ultra vires* the constitution.[40] Overruling its earlier decision in 1937, it held that the Statute of Westminster, 1931, had not impliedly repealed the stipulation about a two-thirds majority at a joint sitting, which remained binding on Parliament. To hold otherwise, it said, would be to enable Parliament "to deprive by a bare majority in each House sitting separately individuals of rights which were solemnly safeguarded in the Constitution of the country. This is a potent reason why this court, on being satisfied that its previous decision was wrong, should not hesitate in declaring the error of that decision."[41]

---

39.   *ibid*, p. 237.

40.   *Harris v. Minister of the Interior* (1952) (2) S.A. 428.

41.   *ibid, p. 472.*

The government retaliated by enacting another Act, the High Court of Parliament Act, 1952, which was passed by a bare majority in each House sitting separately. The Act constituted Parliament a court of law, composed of all members of both Houses under the chairmanship of a member appointed by the governor-general, with power to review any judgment of the Appellate Division, whether given before or after the commencement of the Act whereby the Appellate Division invalidated any enactment of Parliament or in any way denied it legal effect. It was made mandatory for a minister to bring any such judgment to the High Court of Parliament for review, but no one else could invoke the "Court's" jurisdiction. An application would first be heard by a judicial committee consisting of ten members of the "Court". The report of the committee would then be considered and voted on by the full "Court" which might by a bare majority resolution confirm, vary or set aside any judgment under review. The decision of the "Court" was declared final and binding.

On an application by the successful party in the earlier case, the Appellate Division, affirming the trial court, held that, as the Act, judged by its substance rather than its form, would enable Parliament under a different name to achieve the alteration, otherwise than in the prescribed manner, of the franchise rights guaranteed and entrenched in the constitution, it was unconstitutional and void;[42] further, that "invalidity in law as determined by Courts of Law"[43] is the sanction implied in the provision of the constitution that no law altering or abolishing the guaranteed franchise "shall be valid" unless passed by a two-thirds majority at a joint sitting.[44] The High Court of Parliament was not such a court as was envisaged by this provision, in as much as:

(i)　only a minister, but not the parties to the proceeding in the Appellate Division, could invoke its jurisdiction;

---

42. *Minister of the Interior v. Harris* (1952)(4) S.A.

43. *ibid at p. 779.*

44. S. 152.

(ii) the minister might so invoke its jurisdiction although the parties themselves might not wish to carry the matter any further;

(iii) its members, unlike real judges, had to pronounce upon the validity of legislation passed by them in another capacity, an invidious position completely foreign to the rules of natural justice on which the administration of justice in the country was founded.

Since the High Court of Parliament was not a court of law within the meaning of the entrenched provisions of the constitution, the Act creating it was void as an unconstitutional attempt to deprive the Court of its constitutionally entrenched power to adjudicate questions concerning the validity of Acts of Parliament. Even assuming the High Court of Parliament to be a court, the Act was still void as an attempt to contest the issue of constitutionality, a right which was also entrenched. This effect followed from the fact that the High Court of Parliament was not accessible to an individual, but only to a minister. For once the "Court" had ruled that Parliament had power to alter the entrenched provisions bicamerally, its decision would be conclusive both on the other courts in the country and on the individual, and would not be open to re-consideration even by the "Court" itself.

It was argued that, because Parliament had undoubted power to alter bicamerally the judiciary provisions of the constitution, by, for example, creating a court or courts superior to the Appellate Division, it could also competently have abolished by bicameral legislation the jurisdiction of the courts to adjudicate questions of the constitutionality of Acts of Parliament, provided that the requirement of a two-thirds majority at a joint sitting was not itself tampered with. Rejecting this argument, Chief Justice Centlivres observed:

> This is a startling proposition ... As I understand ... (the) argument the substantive right would, in the event of such an Act having been passed, remain intact but there would be no adjective or procedural law whereby it could be enforced; in other words the individual concerned whose

right was guaranteed by the constitution would be left in the position of possessing a right which would be of no value whatsoever. To call the rights entrenched in the constitution constitutional guarantees and at the same time to deny to the holders of those rights any remedy in law would be to reduce the safeguards enshrined in section 152 to nothing. There can to my mind be no doubt that the authors of the constitution intended that those rights should be enforceable by the Courts of Law. They could never have intended to confer a right without a remedy. The remedy is, indeed, part and parcel of the right. *Ubi jus, ubi remedium.*[45]

Remedies

The constitutions made by Britain for her former colonies at independence have introduced a significant innovation as regards remedies for the redress of violations of constitutional limitations. After proclaiming themselves the supreme law of the land, these constitutions affirmatively declare null and void, any law that is inconsistent with their provisions – see, e.g., section 1 of the Constitution of Nigeria (1999). Thus, nullity of a law inconsistent with the constitution follows from an express declaration to that effect by the constitution itself, and does not rest upon mere implication from the supremacy of the constitution, as in the Untied States.

The significance of the express declaration of nullity made by the constitution against any law inconsistent with its provisions is that, once a court rules that a law is inconsistent, its nullity follows inexorably from the declaration made in the constitution, and the court is under a duty, and has no discretion but to echo and enforce it. A declaration, as a remedy for the enforcement of constitutional limitations on government, is thus anchored and entrenched in the constitution. The discretion which the court possesses and exercises in ordinary cases to grant or refuse a declaration is completely taken away in cases of violations of constitutional limitations; its discretion in the latter case is limited to deciding whether a law is inconsistent with the constitution or not.

---

45. *ibid.* pp. 780-1.

The point is underscored with great clarity in Nwabueze, *Judicialism in Commonwealth Africa* (1977), at pages 109-110:

> From the constitutional declaration of invalidity arises an obligation on the part of the court to echo it and apply it in all cases of justiciable violation properly brought before it, notwithstanding anything to the contrary in the general law of remedies relating to declaratory judgment. If, to use an extreme example, a statute forbids the courts to make declarations of invalidity against governmental measures, this would conflict with the constitutional declaration, and the court would be obliged, under the syllogism of *Marbury v. Madison,* to apply the constitution and disregard the statute.

> It cannot be for nothing that the constitution, having imposed limitations and prohibitions on government, couples it with a declaration of invalidity against governmental acts transgressing those limitations and prohibitions. The constitutional declaration of invalidity must have some significance. It is intended to, and, it is submitted, does confer upon any person adversely affected by an unconstitutional governmental act, a right to apply to the courts to administer and enforce the constitutional declaration... Upon such an application, the court is obliged to pronounce upon the question of constitutionality. The constitutional declaration is thus also a direction to the court to apply and enforce it upon the application of a person adversely affected by an unconstitutional governmental act.

The view that a court has discretion to decline to grant a declaration in respect of a law found by it to be inconsistent or not in "consonance" with the constitution is manifestly subversive of the express declaration of invalidity made by the constitution itself against such law. As Chief Justice John Marshall said in *Cohen v. Virginia* 19 US 264 at 404 (1821): "We have no more right to decline the exercise of jurisdiction which is given, than to usurp that which is not given. The one or the other would be treason to the constitution."

The court cannot decline to exercise jurisdiction to grant a declaration of invalidity against a law found by it to be inconsistent with the constitution on the ground that the matter involved is "prickly", "hypersensitive" or because "it is impolitic or inexpedient" to do so, or because to do so "may lead to a widespread disruption of national life". Whatever risks of disruption of national life may be

attendant upon the nullification of a law found to be inconsistent
with the constitution, "we must decide it if it be brought before us" –
per John Marshall CJ in *Cohen v. Virginia,* ibid.

Being the only remedy constitutionally ordained in express terms
in the constitution (apart from the reliefs constitutionally ordained
for violations of guaranteed rights shortly to be noted) the declaratory
judgment is thus unlike other remedies – damages, injunction,
prohibition, *mandamus, certiorari;* these latter are not constitutionally
ordained, and may be limited or even taken away by law. The
declaratory judgment has indeed a very wide scope which should not,
in cases raising a question of invalidity on the ground of inconsistency
with the constitution, be whittled down by importing into its exercise
the discretion which the court exercises in granting or refusing it in
ordinary, non-constitutional litigation. Its wide scope coupled with
its amicable character and its avoidance of the language of compulsion
and command of the coercive remedies, which is calculated not to
excite government antagonism, the simplicity and cheapness of the
procedure, and above all its effectiveness has made the declaratory
judgment the "most ubiquitous (and) perhaps the most generally useful
of the remedies" against public authorities.

In regard to remedies for violations of the constitution, there is
another respect in which the constitutions made by Britain for her
former colonies at independence mark a significant innovation from
the American, namely, remedies for violations of guaranteed rights.
Unlike the American Constitution under which the jurisdiction of
the court to enforce guaranteed rights depends on implication, these
constitutions expressly provide that the "court shall have original
jurisdiction to *hear and determine* any application" made to it by a
person alleging that rights guaranteed by the constitution have been
violated in relation to him, and "may make such orders, issue such
writs and give such directions as it may consider appropriate for the
purpose of enforcing or securing the enforcement" of the rights in
question. The court must "determine", and has no discretion to decline
to "determine", whether, upon such application, a guaranteed right

has been violated, and to declare the offending law) or other governmental act) uncor.stitutional and void. To decline, in its discretion, to exercise the jurisdiction conferred on the court by this provision would, to quote Chief Justice John Marshall's words again, be treason to the constitution.

Indisputably, consistency with the provisions of the constitution as a criterion for the validity of a law applies to and governs both the substantive provisions of the law as well as the manner or procedure by which it is enacted. It follows therefore that a law is a nullity when the manner or procedure by which it is enacted is not in consonance with that prescribed by the constitution equally as when its substantive provisions are inconsistent with the constitution. The point is settled beyond dispute by a series of decisions by the highest courts in various jurisdictions.

In an appeal from Ceylon, *The Bribery Commission v. Ranasingbe* [1965] AC 172, the Judicial Committee of the Privy Council has held that under a written constitution which prescribes a procedure for law-making, the courts are not only entitled to go outside the official copy of a statute in order to enquire into the question of procedure, but have a duty, not a discretion, to declare it invalid if in fact it was passed without due form. For, where a legislature is given power subject to certain manner and form, whether it be a simple or special majority, or some other procedural requirement as that in Section 58(5) of the Nigerian Constitution, that power does not exist unless and until the manner and form is complied with. The supremacy of the constitution (as proclaimed in Section 1(1) of the Nigerian Constitution) demands that the court should hold void any exercise of power done otherwise than in the manner and form prescribed by the constitution or which is otherwise not "in accordance with the constitution from which the power derives".[46] As it further held, the proposition is not acceptable that "a legislature, once established, has some inherent power derived from the mere fact of its establishment to make valid law by the

---

46.   *Liyange v. R.* [1967] 1 A.C. 259.

resolution of a bare majority which its own constituent instrument has said shall not be a valid law unless made by a different type of majority or by a different legislative process... The minority are entitled under the Constitution of Ceylon to have no amendment of it which is not passed by a two-thirds majority".[47] The decisions of the Appellate Division of the South African High Court on the point have already been noted above.

---

47.   *The Bribery-Commissioner v. Ranasingbe*, ibid, at pp. 198 & 200.

CHAPTER 13

Fostering Partnership between the Legislature and Executive for Sustainable Democracy: A Constitutionalist Perspective

A harmonious partnership between the legislature and the executive is an imperative necessity for sustainable democracy. But it is not attained by merely wishing or talking about it. Four requirements for fostering such a relationship are here identified, *viz:*

(i)   keeping within the limits of power and within the constitution generally;

(ii)   a disposition not to abuse power while keeping within its limits;

(iii) restraining the arrogance and intolerance of state power;

(iv)   consultations and dialogue.

But before embarking on a discussion, one preliminary issue with crucial bearing on our subject needs to be first examined, namely, the constitutional primacy between the president, the legislature and the executive.

The Constitutional Primacy between the President, the Legislature and the Executive

Legislative power, not executive power, is the distinctive mark of a country's sovereignty, the index of its status as a state, and the source of much, if not the preponderant portion, of the power exercised by the executive in the administration of government. The sovereign power in a state is thus Identified in the organ that has the power to make laws by legislation, to issue "commands" in the form of legislation binding on the community. The legislature is therefore the sovereign organ of state power. The order in which the two organs are dealt with in the Nigerian Constitution (1999), which was also the order in the 1979 Constitution, the legislature in Chapter V (Sections 47-129) and the executive in Chapter VI (Sections 130-229), is a constitutional recognition of the primacy of the legislature over the executive.

The constitutional primacy of the legislature over the executive is not contradicted by the fact that the head of the legislature is not the first citizen. The chief executive is not the first citizen either. The president is. The Office of President, created by Section 130(1) of the Nigerian Constitution, is distinct from that of chief executive. The president is designated "the head of state, the chief executive of the Federation and the Commander-in-Chief of the Armed Forces of the Federation" (Section 130(2)). The president is the first citizen, not by virtue of being the chief executive, but by virtue of being the Head of State. The concept of Head of State has great significance transcending that of chief executive. The Head of State symbolises, he incarnates, i.e., he embodies in his person, the artificial entity, the state.

Oppenheim expresses the notion aptly thus:

> As a State is an abstraction from the fact that a multitude of individuals live in a country under a sovereign government, every State must have a Head as its highest organ which represents it within and without its borders in the totality of its relations.

The conception underlying the office is perhaps best stated in a provision in the Constitution of France 1958, which is adopted in the Constitutions of nearly all her former African colonies. The president is conceived as the "guarantor" of the regular functioning of the governing authorities ... the continuity of the State, ... of national independence and territorial integrity" (Article 5, France).

The undoubted primacy of the president, as head of state, over the legislature and the executive suggests, if it does not affirmatively require, that the office should be dealt with in a separate chapter of its own before the legislature and the executive, and not be lumped with the executive in one chapter after (or even before) the legislature. Remarkably, the three organs, the president (or governor-general), the legislature and the executive in that order, were segregated in separate chapters in the 1960 and 1963 Constitutions of Nigeria. They are also segregated in separate titles but in a different order in the Constitution of France 1958 and in the constitutions of nearly all her former African colonies. Whilst the president is dealt with in a separate title in the Constitution of Italy 1947, the order followed is the legislature, the president and the government. The segregation of the president in a separate chapter or title of its own is the more common arrangement followed in the constitutions of the countries of the world. Nigeria should revert to the arrangement in its 1960 and 1963 Constitutions. It is difficult to understand why the 1979 and 1999 Constitutions abandoned that eminently sensible and rational arrangement, and lumped the president with the executive in one chapter after the legislature.

Certainly, lumping the president, as head of state, in one chapter with the executive either before or after the legislature tends to confound the proper relationship that should exist between the three organs. To regard the president as just the chief executive and commander-in-chief and nothing more cannot but degrade and lower him in public estimation, depriving the office of much of the dignity, esteem and respect that should belong to it. As the speaker of the Zambian National Assembly once remarked in a stern rebuke to opposition members "a head of state is a head of state for everybody," no matter that he and they may be in different political camps. The president embodies, or at least represents, the state, which comprises the legislature, the executive and the people. A harmonious partnership can hardly be fostered between the three organs unless the primacy of the president, as Head of State, is constantly kept in mind, and due respect given to him as one who embodies in his person the majesty of the sovereign people.

Herein lies the rationale for the immunity from suit, arrest or imprisonment and from court process requiring or compelling his appearance which the Nigerian Constitution grants him while he is in office (Section 308(1)). The special protection afforded by the immunity is for the office, not for its individual holder as such. It is the majesty and dignity of the nation as symbolised by its head that is at stake. To drag an incumbent president to court and expose him to the process of examination and cross-examination cannot but degrade the office. The affront to the nation involved in this could be more easily perceived if it is imagined that a foreigner temporarily resident in the country were to take its president to court for, say, a breach of contract, and attempt to discredit him in cross-examination as a liar and a disreputable person. It should make no difference that the complainant is a national. The interest of the nation is the preservation of the integrity of its highest office should outweigh the inconvenience to the individual of the temporary postponement of his suit against the president. Where, however, the president holds office for life, there may be a real injustice, for the individual would have been deprived permanently of his suit. Even so the principle underlying the protection still demands that it should be maintained, though the situation does illustrate the undesirability of a life presidency. It needs to be emphasised, though this is already implied, that the immunity is limited to the period of incumbency only. It is thus only a procedural immunity. It in no way removes the president's liability, which becomes enforceable again in the ordinary mode of proceeding at the end of his term of office, without any limitation as to time for the period covered by his incumbency.

The protection does not immune the president against police investigation and interrogation. Furthermore, "appearance" not compelled by the process of a "court" is not covered by the immunity. Court in the context of Section 308(1)(c) is used in the same sense as in Section 6, and does not include a tribunal which is not a court in the constitutional sense. But there is a certain ambiguity about the coverage of the provision in Section 308(1)(a) to the effect that "no civil or criminal proceedings shall be instituted or continued against" an incumbent president. The ambiguity arises from the absence of an explicit reference to civil or criminal proceedings before **a court**, although it might be said that a court is suggested by the word "instituted."

We have become familiar in Nigeria with a host of tribunals which, though not courts in the constitutional sense, were entrusted with the trial of a variety of criminal cases under a procedure patterned more or less on that of a court, including representation by counsel, presentation of the case for the prosecution and for the accused, the ascertainment of facts by means of evidence given on oath or affirmation, the examination and cross-examination of witnesses, a finding by the tribunal based on the evidence and the law, etc. Even the procedure of an ordinary tribunal of inquiry into an alleged criminal offence, say, official corruption, is also closely assimilated to that of a court. Proceedings before such tribunals are certainly criminal proceedings, and the setting up of the tribunal and the arraigning of a person before it may without impropriety be described as the instituting of criminal proceedings within the meaning of Section 308(1)(a) of the Constitution.

Be that as it may, proceedings of a criminal nature against an incumbent president before any kind of tribunal, whether a court strictly so-called or not, affront the dignity of the office. As the embodiment of the state, which is the complainant in criminal proceedings, an incumbent president should not be proceeded against for a criminal offence, corruption or any other offence, before any tribunal. It simply ridicules the whole idea of protecting the office to say that a president, immuned against criminal proceedings before a court, can be proceeded against for a criminal act before a tribunal which is like a court in almost everything but name. The suggestion comes close to a quibble, a play on words, and a jettisoning of the substance and spirit of the immunity. The redress against an incumbent president for official corruption or any other criminal act is to have him removed upon an impeachment, whereupon he becomes amenable to civil and criminal proceedings and. other coercive processes, just like any other private citizen.

Analogy with the United States is unavailing in this matter, because the U.S. Constitution confers on the president no immunity corresponding to that in Section 308(1) of our Constitution. "Under our system of government," said Chief Justice Bartley in granting a *mandamus* against a state governor, "no officer is placed above the restraining authority, which is truly said to be universal in its behest, all paying it homage, the least as feeling its care, and the greatest as not being exempt from its power." These observations, it is argued, should apply with equal, if not greater, force to the President of the United States. The argument was indeed accepted by Chief Justice John Marshall when he sustained an application for a *subpoena duces tecum* against President Jefferson. Rejecting the president's contention that he could not be drawn from the discharge of his duties at the seat of government and made to attend the court sitting at Richmond, the Chief Justice drew a distinction between the President and the King of England. and held that all officers in the United States were subordinate to the law and must obey its mandate.

In any case, we must not close our eyes to social reality. The Nigerian society is different from the American society, and has not reached anything like the same level of equality in social relations that characterises American society, which is itself a product of the level of economic development. In the balanced words of Lord Bryce describing the social relations of an American President to the people:

The social relations of an American President to his people are eminently refreshing. There is great respect for the office, and a corresponding respect for the man as the holder of the office, if he has done nothing to degrade it. There is no servility, no fictitious self-abasement on the part of the citizens, but a simple and hearty deference to one who represents the majesty of the nation ... He is followed about and feted, and in every way treated as the first man in the company; but the spirit of equality which rules the country has sunk too deep into every American nature for him to be expected to be addressed with bated and whispering reverence.[1]

Having said all what is said above, it must be admitted that the distinction between the president as head of state and the president as chief executive is difficult to respect in practice. Ideally, a head of state should be above politics in order that his embodiment of the state and its majesty should attract maximum respect. But an apolitical head of state is possible, if at all, only if he is a titular head. Such a head can be above partisan politics because he exercises no political function and belongs to no political party. An executive head of state is in a different position. The exercise of executive powers necessarily invites criticism. One should not accept the office and refuse its price. That would be like eating one's cake and having it. Moreover, an executive president is not just the chief functionary of the government; he is the government itself. And to ban criticism of him is unduly to inhibit criticism of government. Where an executive president is a partisan leading a political party in a two- or multi-party system, then, he attracts even more criticism, since the system necessarily implies political competition. The president should not be a partisan in politics and at the same time refuse to accept its price. Verbal attacks, sometimes of a very derogatory kind, are inseparable from political competition. Within reason it is legitimate for politicians to try to discredit each other as part of the effort to enhance one's standing and undermine that of opponents. The leader of the opposition in Kenya, Mr. Ngala, put the point aptly when he said that, as a political head,

---

1.   James Bryco, *The American Commonwealth*, ed. Hacker, Vol. 1 (1959), pp. 25-26.

the president is "a person who throws mud at other fellow-politicians and mud can be thrown at him and he can have political fights with other leaders." This should not, however, be turned into a licence for vulgar insult against the head of state, though the danger in prohibiting vulgar insult which is not an offence by the ordinary law of libel or sedition lies in the difficulty of drawing the line between it and permissible criticism.

Affirmative Requirements for a Harmonious Partnership

Keeping Within the Limits of Power and the Constitution Generally

There can be no harmonious partnership between the legislature and the executive unless each keeps within the limits of its power and within the constitution generally. Usurpation of the other's power invites a resistance, leading to a fight. President Obasanjo said, quite rightly, in his Democracy Day Broadcast to the Nation, that he has no intention of conceding his powers to the legislature. No one would expect the legislature to concede its powers to the executive either. With each determined not to concede any of its functions to the other, a showdown (not mere friction) can only be avoided by each keeping strictly within the limits of its power.

Experience shows that usurpation of power is a big source of acrimony and instability in the relations between the two political organs, and we do not need to travel outside Nigeria for an incident to illustrate the point. The events in Kaduna State during the first two years of the Second Republic (October 1979 to July 1981) were an experience not to be forgotten. The State Governor, Alhaji Balarabe Musa, purporting to act under his power of adaptive legislation under Section 274(2) of the 1979 Constitution, but clearly exceeding it, made certain substantive and fundamental changes in the existing law of Kaduna State. By a Modification Order, he repealed the provisions in the State's Local Government Edict (after suitably adapting it to read "Law") relating to the emirate or traditional councils, nominated councillors and traditional presidents of local government councils with the effect of abolishing those institutions and offices in accordance with his radical egalitarian ideas. Also repealed were the provisions in the said Edict (Law) empowering the governor to approve the election of chairmen of local government councils and to determine their terms and conditions of service. These repeals and abolitions were clearly a usurpation of the power of the State's House of Assembly in whom the power of substantive legislation was exclusively vested by the Constitution.

Provoked to retaliate, the House of Assembly countered by a massive usurpation of the governor's executive functions – it first repealed the governor's usurping Modification Order. But whereas the usurpation by the governor was the result of an honest misinterpretation of the extent of his own powers under Section 274(2) of the Constitution, the usurpations by the Assembly were deliberate and intended as a retaliation. These acts of usurpation were contained in various statutes, three of which purported to divest the governor of all his functions in respect of local government. These functions, indisputably executive or administrative in nature, were either abolished or transferred to the Assembly or to other independent agencies (such as the State Electoral Commission, the Local Government Service Board, the local government councils or the High Court). The net result was to leave the governor without any functions at all in respect of local government, thus virtually severing the link between the executive government of the state and the local government councils. More drastic perhaps was the take-over by the Assembly of the award of all tenders where the amount involved exceeded ₦100,000. The power of the governor under the existing law to authorise, by special warrant, the issue of money from the public funds to meet urgent and unforeseen expenditure which could not without serious injury to the public interest, be postponed until appropriation was made by law, was abolished, the intention being to hamstring the governor's administration of the government. In an action by the governor, most of these transfers, take-overs and abolitions of the governor's functions were declared void by the State High Court as an unconstitutional usurpation or encroachment

(*Governor, Kaduna State v. The House of Assembly, Kaduna State* (1981)).

The two political organs had embarked on a course of confrontation that stalemated government work and created so much instability in Kaduna State.

Keeping within the limits of power and within the constitution generally required also, observance of the forms for the exercise of power. The powers of the National Assembly are exercisable, for the most part, in the form of legislation, and only in a few specified cases by means of a mere resolution of the Assembly or of one only of its Houses. The two forms differ both in their effect and in the process required for them. A mere resolution is not law, but in the specified cases in which a decision by a mere resolution is authorised by the constitution, it has a binding legal effect of which the courts and the community must take cognisance. Outside the specified cases shortly to be mentioned, whilst the Assembly or any one of its Houses is not expressly prohibited to pass any resolution it likes, such resolution, like the House of Representatives' resolution directing the president to stop negotiations for an IMF loan, binds no one, neither the executive nor private persons.

Because it is not law as such, a mere resolution involves no such elaborate process as characterises legislation – careful study based on facts, consultation with various interests, formal presentation in the form of a bill, prolonged debate on the merits and demerits of the matter and clause-by-clause examination in committee. All it needs is a substantive motion by a member, seconded by another. Indeed a motion involving no exercise of constitutional power need have no factual basis at all apart from the

> strong feeling that something needs to be done about a given issue. And
> in taking a position on a motion, facts are far less important than
> eloquence. Bills, on the other hand, quite often mean a lot of drudgery,
> of poring over statistics, of hard work and patience.

Even the formality of a substantive motion proposed by one member and seconded by another may be dispensed with where all that is required is just the approval of the Assembly or one of its Houses. And while legislation normally requires the president's assent, a resolution does not.

The following are the matters that may be decided or sanctioned by the National Assembly by resolution: presidential declaration of war with another country (approving resolution at a joint session required: S. 5(4)(a)), proposal for the creation of a new state (two-thirds majority: S. 8(1)(d)), proposal for boundary adjustment (S. 8(2)(b)(I)), declaration of economic activities to be managed and operated exclusively by the federal government (S. 16(4)), removal of the President of the Senate or Speaker of the House of Representatives (resolution of the appropriate house: S. 50(2)(c)), extension of the life of the National Assembly or of the president's tenure of office beyond four years because of a war involving the territory of Nigeria and which in the president's opinion makes it impossible to hold elections (Ss. 6(2) and 135(3)), directing investigation in aid of legislation or for the purpose of exposing corruption, inefficiency or waste in the execution or administration of its laws or in the disbursement or administration of funds appropriated by the Assembly (S. 88), ordering investigation into allegation of gross misconduct by the president or vice-president (two-thirds of all members: S. 143(3) and (4)), acceptance or rejection of a report by an investigating committee finding the president or vice-president guilty of gross misconduct (two-thirds of all members: S. 143(9)), prescribing the number of special advisers and their remuneration and allowances (S. 151(2)), approval of a proclamation of a state of emergency made by the president (two-thirds of all members: S. 305(6)), and extension of such a proclamation beyond six months (two-thirds of all members).

It is provided that where in the legislative lists scheduled to the Constitution (Sch. 2) "the National Assembly is required to designate any matter or thing or to make any declaration, it may do so either by an Act of the National Assembly or by a resolution passed by both Houses of the National Assembly." The Assembly's power in this respect relates to the declaration of any roads as federal trunk roads; designation of any internal waterway (other than the River Niger and its affluents) as an international or inter-state waterway; declaring of ports as federal ports; designation of occupations as professional occupations and of parks as national parks; declaration of ancient and historical monuments and records and archeological sites and remains as of national significance or importance; designation of any agricultural produce as an export commodity; designation of goods or commodities as essential goods or commodities for purposes of price control; declaration of sources of water as sources affecting more than one state; designation of antiquities and monuments as national antiquities or monuments; and designation of any professional education as within federal legislative competence.

The matters that require the sanction or approval of the National Assembly or of the Senate alone but without the formality of a resolution following on a substantive motion are the deployment of any members of the armed forces on combat duty outside Nigeria (Senate alone: S. 5(4)(b)); proposal for the (state) boundary adjustment (S. 8(2)(b)); alteration of senatorial districts or federal constituencies by the electoral commission following upon a change in the number of states in the federation or upon a census pursuant to an Act of the National Assembly (S. 74); appointment of a vice-president in the event of vacancy (S. 146(3); revocation of a proclamation of emergency (S. 305(6)(d)); appointment and removal of specified public functionaries.

It will have been noticed that the functions enumerated above lie mostly in the executive domain. The intention is, by involving the National Assembly in the executive field, to enable it to exercise a check and moderation on the actions of the executive. They enable the Assembly, for example, to ensure that the appointment and removal of important public functionaries are not abused for purely personal, sectional or partisan motives, that the country should not needlessly be dragged to war on the whims of a reckless president, that the deprivations and repressions of a state of emergency are not inflicted on the people by the president unless justified by the exigencies actually existing in the country, that the country's affairs and its resources are not mismanaged through corruption, inefficiency or waste, and that in the last resort the nation is rid of a president who flagrantly violates the constitution or grossly misconducts himself in other ways.

Among the functions listed above the exercise of which may be assumed by either House of the National Assembly simply passing an enabling resolution is investigation, either by the House or through a committee, into any matter or thing within federal legislative competence or into the conduct of affairs of any person, authority (including the House itself), ministry or government department charged with responsibility for (i) executing or administering laws enacted by the National Assembly or (ii) disbursing or administering moneys appropriated by the Assembly (Section 88(1)). As clearly stated in Section 88(2), investigation under the provision is **"only** for the purpose of enabling" (emphasis supplied) the House to: "(a) make laws with respect to any matter within its legislative competence and correct any defects in existing laws; and (b) expose corruption, inefficiency or waste in the execution or administration of laws within its legislative competence and in the disbursement or administration of funds appropriated by it."

No doubt, the words in which the purposes of the investigatory power are set out are very wide indeed. Yet they fall short of giving to the legislative houses, as they are now arrogating to themselves, power of general oversight of the activities of the executive in the administration of government. For such a power would be subversive of the separation of powers, which overrides the investigatory power of the legislative houses by reason of the fact that it (the investigatory power) is expressly made "subject to the provisions of this constitution," including the provisions relating to the separation of powers. The arrogation by the legislative houses of the power of general oversight of the activities of the executive is naturally resisted by the latter, and is thus a potent source of perilous confrontation between the two organs. In the apt metaphor used in the Report of the Panel on the Relationship between the Executive and the Legislature set up by the ruling Peoples Democratic Party (PDP), Section 88 does not "authorise the National Assembly to go into a fishing expedition in executive waters."

As further illustrations of the limits of the power, it does not also authorise the legislative houses to conduct an investigation into a publication which has no bearing whatsoever on the purposes for which the power is given, or to interfere with guaranteed fundamental rights (these being among the provisions of the Constitution to which the power is made subject). Thus, it was *ultra vires* the section and unconstitutional for the Senate in the Second Republic to have passed a resolution inviting the editor of the *Daily Times of Nigeria* to appear before it to substantiate a story in an issue of the newspaper which alleged that senators spent their time playing cards in the House and hunting for contracts in government offices (*Momoh v. Senate of the National Assembly* (1981)), or for the House of Representatives to have invited the editor of the *Sunday Punch* newspaper to appear before its committee investigating a story in an issue of the newspaper alleging fraud against its members, and to bring along all documents and facts relating to the allegation. (*Adikwu & Others v. Federal House of Representatives & Others* (1982)). The invitation in the latter case was nullified on the ground that, while the investigation was for an authorised purpose – i.e., fraud in the disbursement of federal government funds – it was a violation of the freedom of speech and press guaranteed by the constitution.

Another illustrative case which bears out the need for a proper appreciation of the limits of the power, and to keep within them in order to avoid needless confrontation with the executive was that in which a State House of Assembly passed a resolution appointing a committee of its members to investigate the general administration of a limited liability company owned partly by the state government (*Okitipupa Oil Palm Company Ltd v. Jegede & Others* (1982)). As part owners, the executive organ of the state was involved in the general administration of the company. The interesting question raised in the case is whether a limited liability company in which government has substantial shareholding is a person or authority charged with responsibility for disbursing or administering government funds within the meaning of the provision under consideration. Clearly, shareholding in a limited liability company is governed by contract. The money so invested represents the purchase price for an interest in the company thus acquired. It belongs to the company. The investment is purely a commercial venture, and the company cannot in any reasonable sense of the term be regarded as a person or authority charged with responsibility for disbursing or administering government funds.

But refraining from usurpation of or encroachment on each other's domain presupposes that both the legislature and the executive have adequate understanding of the limits of their respective powers and the method for exercising them or are anxious to acquire it. Such understanding can only be acquired by reading widely upon the subject and through practical experience in the art of democratic self-government over many years. The legislature and the executive in the current democratic dispensation in Nigeria inaugurated since May 29, 1999 clearly lack the understanding. The situation is understandable after nearly 30 years of political void inflicted on the country by an oligarchic military autocracy during which the Nigerian people were denied the opportunity to practise, and to learn by trial and error, the art of democratic self-government, to acquire the habits and spirit required for its success and sustenance.

The democratic experiment begun since May 29, 1999 is therefore properly regarded as a learning process. However, a learning process, if it is to offer a promise of change for the better, presupposes on the part of all concerned a sincere acknowledgement of lack of the necessary knowledge, an eager disposition and preparedness to acquire it by seeking counsel from informed sources of knowledge (books and other expert opinions), a capacity to imbibe the necessary knowledge from those sources, and a willingness to admit error and accept corrections. Without this, ignorance, rather than give away to knowledge, will only wax stronger and be asserted with greater boldness.

Viewed in the light of these considerations, the one year of the democratic experiment (May 29 1999 to May 29 2000) can be rightly described as a learning process only if any enduring lessons have been learnt from the numerous mistakes that have been made. But we seem only to be making more and more mistakes every day, and never learning from them. Learning is also precluded where a point of view, so palpably mistaken, is clung to so tenaciously and unrepentantly as the correct view on a disputed point – as in the argument about the illegality of President Obasanjo's declaration of May 29 as a public holiday (its legality is clearly incontestable). In the result, what is supposed to be a learning process is deprived of its value as a time for self-correction and self-improvement. So much time has been spent on fruitless bickering. With nothing much really learnt, the process is more one of unrewarding bickering than of learning. And we are all the losers for it.

There is considerable doubt whether the capacity to imbibe the necessary knowledge from informed sources of knowledge (books and other expert opinions) exists among many of our rulers. The feeling of satisfaction engendered by the provision in Sections 65(2)(a) and 131(d) of the 1999 Constitution prescribing a minimum educational qualification of "School Certificate level or its equivalent" for members of the National Assembly and the president (absent in the 1979 Constitution) is doused by the definition of school certificate or its equivalent in Section 318(1) – also absent in the 1979 Constitution – as meaning:

> (a) Secondary School Certificate or its equivalent, or Grade II Teacher's Certificate, the City and Guilds Certificate, or (b) education up to Secondary School Certificate level; or (c) Primary Six School Leaving Certificate or its equivalent and
>
> – (i) service in the public or private sector in the Federation in any capacity acceptable to the Independent National Electoral Commission for a minimum of ten years, and
>
>   (ii) attendance at courses and training in such institutions as may be acceptable to the Independent National Electoral

Commission for periods totalling up to a minimum of one year, and

(iii) the ability to read, write, and understand and communicate in the English language to the satisfaction of the Independent National Electoral Commission; and

(iv) any other qualification acceptable by the Independent National Electoral Commission.

In these days of widespread "expo", certificate faking and general degeneration in the standards of education in our schools and colleges, primary six school leaving certificate is really next door to illiteracy. What little literacy is acquired from the educational system at the primary school level is soon lost owing to the lack of a reading culture that pervades our society, caused to a considerable extent by the enthronement of wealth as the determinant of social standing and the consequent inordinate pursuit of it and of other mundane, non-intellectual pursuits. No one with this kind of thoroughly inadequate educational background can be expected to read, with understanding, the Constitution of Nigeria, laden, and it is, with difficult and perplexing concepts, or the books on constitutional law, political science and sociology where the knowledge of these concepts can be found. And knowing that he cannot understand them, he would have no inclination or disposition to buy the books or to read them.

The desire to accommodate educationally backward areas, which no doubt is the reason underlying the provision, is no justification for prescribing such low level of education for a National Assembly charged with responsibility to make laws for the peace, order and good government of Nigeria or any part thereof. The prescribed level of education may be alright for membership of the House of Assembly of the states in the educationally backward areas, but certainly not for the membership of the National Assembly for the whole country, which is the mirror through which the country is seen and judged in the world outside. The uniformity is part of the problem of having one constitution for both the national and state governments.

A Disposition not to Abuse Power while Keeping Within its Limits

More than anything else perhaps, the abuse of power by the executive or the legislature, while keeping within its limits, for reasons of the aggrandisement of personal, partisan, ethnic or religious interests, is the greatest obstacle to fostering a harmonious partnership between them. The history of the relations between the two organs under the system of separated powers both in the United States and Nigeria attests to this.

The impeachment of President Johnson of the United States in 1868 – the first and only impeachment of an American President until the recent impeachment move one hundred years later of President Clinton in 1998 – was a disreputable abuse of power for purely partisan motive. The ostensible ground of the impeachment was that the president had violated the Tenure of Office Act, 1867, by removing his secretary of state without the consent of the Senate as was required by the Act. (The Bill for the Act was passed into law over President Johnson's veto). His conduct was certainly not treasonable or otherwise criminal – these are the grounds for impeachment provided in the U.S. Constitution – but at worst only an improper exercise of a power which, under the constitution, belonged to him. Even its impropriety depended upon the constitutionality of the Act of Congress itself, and in the view of the president and his advisers the Act was a manifest contravention of the constitution. It was upon this view of the Act that he acted in removing the secretary of state without the consent of the Senate, a view which half a century later the Supreme Court affirmed when it declared the Act unconstitutional and void (*Myers v. United States* (1926)). In view of the Court's decision one may perhaps reflect what a great injury would have been done to the president and the entire American governmental system had the impeachment succeeded (it failed by only one vote).

The real reason for the impeachment was that, being a southerner, Johnson, hitherto Vice-President until the assassination of President Abraham Lincoln at the end of the civil war, had stood out against the several Acts of Congress designed to reconstruct – the

Reconstruction Acts – the southern states lately engaged in rebellion against the United States (he vetoed all of them). Being thus a by-product of the civil war – an event which had embittered and estranged relations to a degree no other event had done in the whole history of the United States – the impeachment was clearly an abuse of power.

The confrontation, noted above, between the governor and the House of Assembly in Kaduna State, which featured the usurpation of each other's power, was climaxed by the Assembly's refusal to approve the nomination of commissioners submitted by the governor for confirmation in accordance with constitutional requirement, by the resultant situation of the governor having to administer the government of the state without commissioners for nearly two years and, finally, by the impeachment and removal of the governor.

While the legislative assembly had, under the constitution, unfettered power to approve or to refuse to approve the governor's nominations for appointment as commissioners, yet, like all discretionary powers, such refusal must be in good faith. It must also not be arbitrary. It is an abuse of power to reject a candidate out of personal prejudice or for purely political considerations or for other reasons not rationally or reasonably connected with his suitability for the post. The question then is whether the rejection by the Kaduna State House of Assembly of all the persons in the four successive lists submitted to it by the governor could have been in good faith and entirely free from arbitrariness. The reasons given by the Assembly for its action must therefore be examined to see whether they were valid, rational and reasonable or whether they were based on personal prejudice or on considerations which had no rational or reasonable bearing upon the suitability of the nominees. An arbitrary or ill-motivated rejection is not of course invalid. This is because abuse of constitutional power, such as the power of the Assembly to reject a nomination for appointment as commissioner, does not attract the sanction of invalidity as does abuse of statutory powers. Nevertheless, an arbitrary or ill-motivated exercise by the Assembly of its power of rejection is not any the less an abuse of power because it is not amenable to the sanction of invalidity.

The first list of nominees was rejected on 17 October 1979. There were 13 names on it. Each nominee was considered on the basis of information submitted on him by the governor, and rejected for one reason or another, which had to do with either his constitutional qualifications, place of origin, education, age, character, public-spiritedness, political affiliation, health and so on. The general ground for most of the rejections, which affected as many as 9 nominees, was that the nominees had not, as at that time, resigned the appointments which they were holding in the public service. Under the Constitution, a person cannot be **appointed** a commissioner if he is not qualified for election to the House of Assembly. Among the grounds of disqualification for such election is employment in the public service. Literally interpreted, what the provision requires is that a person must not be the holder of an appointment in the public service at the time of his **appointment** as a commissioner. A person employed in the public service is not **disqualified from being nominated** for such appointment and submitted to the Assembly for confirmation, but if approved by the House he cannot be appointed unless and until he resigns his existing employment in the public service.

The literal meaning of the provision also accords with common sense, justice and the practice in some other states of the federation. A person should not be made to give up the security of a job which he presently holds in the public service when he is not sure that his nomination will be confirmed by the House. It is only reasonable and fair that his resignation should await the confirmation of the House. Nor is the public interest prejudiced by his resignation being delayed until after he has been confirmed. To the Kaduna State House of Assembly, however, common sense, justice and the practice in other states were irrelevant to what it erroneously believed to be the correct interpretation of the constitutional provision – namely, that resignation must precede nomination and confirmation.

The constitution was given another twisted interpretation when the Assembly rejected a nominee because he belonged to a local government area from which two commissioners had been appointed at different times during the military regime. Two commissioners in the past were considered more than a fair share for any local government area. Accordingly, the nomination of a candidate from the same area was thought to fly directly in the face of the provision requiring appointment of commissioners to reflect the diversity of the peoples comprised within the area of a state and the need to promote a sense of belonging among them (see. 14(4) & 173(2)). Clearly, the provision does not require that the distribution of ministerial appointments among the local government areas in the state should take into account appointments previously made by the military government. The rejection on this ground is thus also based upon an erroneous and unjustified application of constitutional requirement.

The House is undoubtedly right in insisting on a reasonable level of education for appointment as commissioner. (No qualification was prescribed in the 1979 Constitution). A grade III teachers' certificate holder was thus rejected on the ground that he was insufficiently educated to be able to deliver the goods. However, the rejection of a graduate on the ground that he was not the best qualified man in his local government area seems altogether irrational and unreasonable. A retired lieutenant-colonel was rejected because there were two retired major-generals, a retired inspector-general of police and a retired secretary to the military government in the same town. How then came a retired colonel in a town that could boast of thousands of capable people? – a member queried. From the point of view of educational qualification, the list was not a bad one, 7 out of the 13 nominees being graduates.

A graduate nominee aged 35 years was rejected because he was not "old enough to be a commissioner." Two 28-year-old nominees, both graduates, could therefore fare no better. A 53-year-old nominee was considered all right as far as age was concerned. This is ridiculous if the intention is to suggest that 53 is the right age for appointment as commissioner.

All 13 nominees, without exception, came off badly on the score of character. Such was the indiscriminate condemnation of all the nominees that a non-NPN member of the House was prompted to ask whether the governor was expected to have only angels as his commissioners, to which several NPN members replied in union: "Let him bring the angels." The allegations against the character of the nominees were very wide-ranging indeed, such as being pompous, arrogant, selfish, inaccessible, unsociable, irresponsible, untrustworthy, dishonest, a drunkard, a drug addict, a malingerer, associating with rogues and people of dubious character or not being generally the right type of person for the post of commissioner. One nominee was accused of embezzling fares paid by pilgrims, another of criminal conversion and a third of having been found in illegal possession of examination papers. Yet a fourth was said to be mentally ill.

This raises a serious question concerning the propriety of members using personal information of this type, much of which may be nothing more than sheer fabrication or rumours. There is also the danger of accusations based on personal prejudice, such as the condemnation of a journalist candidate for writing against an association to which a member belonged. The speaker had ruled that members were entitled to evaluate a nominee from their personal experience and opinion of him. This is no doubt correct, but a nominee should not be condemned for irresponsibility, dishonesty and such like without being given a hearing in his own defence and without evidence to substantiate the allegation. The report of the debates creates a distinct impression in the reader's mind that the members were using the opportunity of the confirmation exercise to vent their personal jealousies and grievances. In any case, arrogance, selfishness and unsociability are hardly justifiable grounds for rejecting a nominee for appointment as a commissioner if he is otherwise capable and of good character.

Incompetence, lack of leadership capability and of public-spiritedness and non-payment of tax were also among the grounds for rejection. These are certainly matters which the House is entitled to take into consideration. Although payment of tax is no longer required as a qualification for election to the House as it was at the time of the election in 1979, the House was perfectly justified, in the **exercise of its discretion**, to refuse to approve the nomination of a person found not to have lived up to his basic civic responsibility to pay tax.

The rejection of two nominees for having campaigned on behalf of a political party – the governor's party, no doubt – during the 1979 election seems clearly arbitrary, since a nominee for appointment as a commissioner is not supposed to be a non-partisan. The House felt greatly affronted by the inclusion in the list of a non-indigene of the state, who was then the solicitor-general of the state and was intended to be made attorney-general upon confirmation. "This is an insult," declared one member, while another urged that the name be not mentioned again!

As was said by one member, it is impossible to believe that out of 13 nominees none was considered suitable for appointment. The wholesale rejection certainly suggests an ulterior motive. It seems that behind all of the publicly stated reasons for the rejections was a motive of political retaliation against the governor for saying that he would not work with the NPN. This political motivation was betrayed in the statement by one member that the governor should not expect them to approve his nominees when he had vowed at his inauguration not to work with the NPN, a resolve which he had demonstrated in practical terms by the non-inclusion of NPN members in the list. If the governor could not tolerate NPN commissioners in his cabinet, then he shall have none at all.

On October 23, 1979 the list of the 13 rejected nominees was re-submitted to the House for reconsideration. The governor had requested that a small committee should be formed to interview the nominees. The request for reconsideration was spurned by the House, on the ground that it was ridiculous, and an insult on the intelligence of the members, to ask them to reverse the earlier decision, and thereby make a fool of themselves. Nor would the House take directive from the governor on how to do its work. Its earlier decision was therefore final and irrevocable, and the re-submitted list should simply be thrown into the waste-paper basket. The House was unmoved by an appeal that it should be considerate because the absence of commissioners was paralysing work in the ministries. "It is not the public," said Dahiru Maigana, "that is suffering, it is the governor." And so the list was thrown out for the second time.

The House was emphatic that it would consider only an entirely fresh list of new nominees. A fresh list, with completely different names which included three NPN members of the Assembly, was accordingly submitted, but was again rejected in its entirety by the House. A fourth list of new nominees was submitted to the House on 22 August, 1980, and referred to a special *ad hoc* committee of 11 members for screening. On the recommendations of the committee, all the 14 nominees on the list were rejected by the House on 29, August 1980: 12 on the ground that, being public servants, they had not resigned their existing public appointments before their nomination; and 2, who were not holding any public service appointments, for non-submission of three years' tax clearance certificates. An additional reason for rejecting 1 of the 2 latter nominees was that there was no information as to whether it had been three months since his resignation from the public service. The House would not accept written undertakings signed by those nominees holding public appointments, whereby they undertook to resign on the confirmation of their nominations. On this occasion a division was held, which showed 46 members in favour of rejection, and 21 against, with 3 abstentions.

After the fourth list was rejected in its entirety on 29 August, 1980, the governor brought an action in the Kaduna State High Court for an order of *mandamus* to compel the House to confirm the 14 nominees on the list, arguing that the power of the House to reject a person nominated for appointment was limited to disqualifications prescribed for election to the House, that there was a duty on the House to confirm a nominee who was not affected by the prescribed disqualifications, and that rejection for reasons not connected with such disqualifications amounted to a refusal to perform a public duty. The arguments are of course completely misconceived, and were rightly rejected by the court. The House, as earlier stated, is certainly not limited to the disqualifications prescribed in the constitution for election to the House. Confirmation implies not a duty but a power which, being discretionary by definition, is not amenable to *mandamus*, it being a settled principle that *mandamus* does not lie to compel the exercise of a power or to direct the exercise of a discretion in a particular way or to retraction or reversal of action already taken.

If the Kaduna State House of Assembly had hoped that the strain, the inconvenience and the consequent frustration of not having commissioners would bring the governor to his knees, curb his intransigence and make him compliant to its wishes, then, it was sadly mistaken. For the governor remained as belligerent as ever before, openly bluffing off the Assembly's refusal to approve commissioners for him. He asserted that he could not be coerced into surrender. The administration of government, he said, would go on without commissioners, notwithstanding the strain and inconvenience entailed.

It must have been quite unpalatable to the NPN-controlled House of Assembly that the rejection of the governor's four successive lists of nominees for ministerial appointment had not brought the expected result of making him compliant to its wishes. Governor Balarabe Musa's over-bold and defiant spirit had robbed the Assembly of the satisfaction of seeing him cringe before it under the weight of its superior power. The Assembly had now either to reconcile itself to the administration of government being carried on by the governor without commissioners or to invoke the ultimate weapon which the constitution placed at its disposal – namely, impeachment. The first alternative, which implied defeat and surrender, seemed too bitter and humiliating a pill to swallow in the circumstances. In a contest in which each side was determined to demonstrate its power against the other, it was perhaps too much to expect the House to accept the loss of pride and prestige which defeat and surrender would have entailed.

Not only the pride and prestige of the NPN legislators were at stake, but also their support among their followers outside the Assembly might be undermined if they were now to surrender. The assemblymen were under considerable pressure from their supporters, whom they could not afford to let down. The governor had therefore to be impeached and removed. That was the course dictated by the logic of the unyielding confrontation upon which the parties had embarked.

Intervention by the president, emirs, other eminent Nigerians and State Assemblies in an effort to. resolve the crisis and prevent impeachment was now to no avail given the governor's continued refusal to implement the terms of the Ikoku-Okadigbo peace agreement and his confrontational outpourings. To no avail too was the appeal by the governor for mutual co-existence and dialogue between him and the assemblymen. The Assembly had lost faith in the genuineness and sincerity of such appeal because of the governor's past record of recalcitrance and inconsistencies. It had now reached a point of no return.

Viewed as a course which the preservation of the assemblymen's pride, prestige and support among their followers dictated, the outcome of the impeachment was a foregone conclusion. It could not be allowed to fail, since its failure would harm their pride, prestige and public support more than would surrender to the governor carrying on the administration of government without commissioners. Once it was embarked upon, removal was predetermined, whether the governor was guilty of gross misconduct or not. Legality or constitutionality had to be subordinated to political interest in the impeachment process. The proceeding was political from beginning to end, though the façade of indictment, trial and conviction had to be put up just to satisfy the constitution. In so far as a verdict of guilty was already predetermined regardless of the merits, the impeachment may be said to have been a sham.

Without overburdening the reader with the details, it suffices to say that nearly everything about Governor Balarabe Musa's impeachment was marred by illegality or abuse – the composition of the investigating committee and its proceedings, the spurious charges, the superficial manner in which the committee conducted the investigation, the refusal to suspend the investigation to await the ruling of the court in the pending suits in which the legality of the composition and proceedings of the committee was challenged, the finding of the committee on the charges, and the politicisation of the entire impeachment process. With the adoption of the committee's report by more than a two-thirds majority, the speaker thereupon announced that Alhaji Balarabe Musa had thereby ceased to be governor of the state. He then sent a letter to the Kaduna State Commissioner of Police requesting that "all privileges and facilities accorded to the governor" be withdrawn.

The governor happened to be in Lagos at the time of his removal. According to him, he became aware of what had happened when the Kaduna State Guest House in Victoria Island, Lagos, where he was staying, was suddenly surrounded by more than a hundred mobile policemen who barred entry to all visitors including the Governor and Deputy Governor of Lagos State and some members of the National Assembly. When he realised that he had been put under house arrest, he telephoned the press to appraise them of the fact. The police explained that the ex-governor had to be restricted to the Guest House and prevented from returning to Kaduna for security reasons.

As the chairman of the investigating committee, Canon Mohammed, said after being sworn in, the impeachment was a "stigma" in the country's new experiment in constitutional democracy after fourteen years of military rule, one that every good and right-thinking Nigerian should regard as "very lamentable." It was indeed a tragedy that the confrontation should have been carried to the point of no return, when legality had to be sacrificed to crude political power. The whole stalemate in Kaduna State was indeed a sad reflection on Nigeria's and Africa's political maturity and its capacity to operate a constitutional democracy.

Sadder still, twenty years after the flagrant abuse of the

impeachment power in Kaduna State, nothing appears to have been learnt from it, as witness the several moves and the ever-recurrent talk in the National Assembly since the inception of the new democratic dispensation one year ago on 29 May, 1999 to remove President Obasanjo from office by impeachment. These moves and talks also show a lack of understanding on the part of the National Assembly members of the purpose for the Constitution bestowing the power on them. Impeachment, writes Clinton Rossiter in his admirable book, *The American Presidency* (2nd edn. 1960), "is not an 'inquest of office', a political process for turning out a president whom a majority of the House and two-thirds of the Senate simply cannot abide. It is certainly not, nor was it ever intended to be, an extraordinary device for registering a vote of no confidence."

Removal of the executive upon a vote of no confidence in the legislature pertains appropriately to a system where the former is made by the latter and owes its mandate of office to it. Not only is it wholly inapplicable in a system in which the executive is elected directly by, and derives its mandate of office from, the people, just like the legislature itself, but it is also manifestly antithetical to the co-equality of the two organs, which is a cardinal principle of the Nigerian constitutional system.

It is for the reasons above that the U.S. Constitution limits the grounds for the removal of the president upon an impeachment to "treason, bribery, or other high crimes and misdemeanours" (Article 2, sec. 3). Regrettably, not only are the grounds in the Nigerian Constitution not restricted to 'high crimes' like treason and bribery, but they are also unspecific and wide, *viz,* "gross misconduct in the performance of the functions of his office," defined as meaning "a grave violation or breach of the provisions of this Constitution or a misconduct of such nature as amounts in the opinion of the National Assembly to gross misconduct" (Section 143(2) & (11). Even as unspecific and wide as the grounds are, the provision is clear enough that impeachment under that constitution is not, nor is it intended to be, a political device for turning out of office a president elected directly by the whole people but who happens not to enjoy or to have lost the confidence of two-thirds of the National Assembly of 360 members.

Besides, misconduct, though not limited to criminal offences of a serious nature, has a definite, objective meaning in law. The Court of Appeal has adopted a definition of it in *Blacks Law Dictionary* as "an unlawful behaviour by a public officer in relation to the duties of his office, wilful in character" (*Anyah v. Att-Gen., Borno State & Another* (1982)). Misconduct in this objective legal sense must be first established before the discretion vested in the National Assembly to declare it to amount to a "gross" one can come into play. And "gross" is defined in the *New Webster's Dictionary* as "flagrant" or "enormous". Moreover, not every violation of the constitution is an impeachable offence; it has to be a "grave" one, such as amounts to a wilful subversion of, or treason against, the constitution. For, infractions of the constitution not of a too grievous nature are, in the government of a complex society, bound to be committed from time to time by both the executive and the legislature.

Restraining the Arrogance and Intolerance of State Power

Acting in excess of power or its abuse while keeping within its limits is often the result of an arrogant and intolerant attitude towards state power. The attitude is one that characterises government almost everywhere in Africa. The arrogance and intolerance of power in democratic Nigeria since May 29 1999 is nearly as great as under military rule, which is an indication that the spirit of democracy remains foreign to our new rulers in the legislative and executive arms of the government just as it was to their military predecessors in office. For, democracy requires in the rulers humility in the exercise of power. Democracy is preached and proclaimed simply as some abstract concept enshrined on the pages of the constitution, but it is not yet being lived in the utterances and behaviour of our rulers, as its spirit requires.

The arrogance and intolerance of state power exhibited almost daily in utterances and actions in democratic Nigeria is in turn the result of a failure on the part of the rulers to recognise that the power they exercise does not belong to them but is only entrusted to them as servants and trustees for the welfare of the people to whom the power properly belongs. Humility, courtesy, and devotion to the interests and service of the people, not arrogance and intolerance, are the attributes required of a servant or trustee, a public servant or trustee no less than a private one. An arrogant tyrannical public servant or one not devoted to the interests and service of the people is a contradiction of the very idea of public service or trusteeship.

Just few instances of such exhibition of the arrogance and intolerance of power in democratic Nigeria will suffice for our present purpose. The National Assembly may well be justified in allocating ₦27 billion to itself, though the justification is debatable. (Talking about harmonious partnership, it can readily be imagined the imbroglio that might ensue between the two organs if, as speculated in the newspapers, the allocation is to be slashed drastically by the president). But assuming that there is justification for the allocation, what democracy demands is that the justification be explained, with patience and humility, to the people, the owners of the money and who entrusted its care and management to the executive and legislators. To say to the very same people, millions and millions of whom are suffering untold privations in no way comparable to privations existing in the United States (the resources and amenities provided for members of the U.S. Congress were cited in justification of the allocation) that the National Assembly owes nobody any apology for allocating such a colossal amount of public money to itself is the language of an autocrat, not of a democrat, much less of a public servant and trustee. Paradoxically, this rather undemocratic statement was made at a "forum" supposed to inform and educate the people about democracy – about its principle and the standards of behaviour it requires.

The intolerance of power has manifested itself in an attitude that regards any interpretation of the constitution not favourable to the National Assembly as an attempt to mislead the nation, the National

Assembly being equated with the nation. In a dispute between it and the executive on the interpretation of the constitution, self-interest as a powerful factor conditioning the view of each organ tends to be overlooked. It is a mark of intolerance to regard the contrary opinion of a third party as having been influenced by the other side, and to deny it the weight due to it by his lack of self-interest in the subject-matter of the disputed issue.

As for President Obasanjo, the way he has carried on as civilian President has created the impression in the minds of the public that the arrogant, intolerant mentality of a former head of an oligarchic military autocracy has not altogether left him, despite his genuine efforts to be a democrat. Witness, for instance, the bombardment of the little community of Odi; the unwarranted threat to declare an emergency in Lagos State without regard to constitutional requirements (no emergency legislation is even extant in Nigeria today for emergency administration if so declared); the denunciation as treasonable, the call by the five South-East Governors for confederation following the killing of Igbos in the disturbances in Kaduna and some other parts of the North caused by the state enforcement of sharia law contrary to the secularity of the state proclaimed in Section 10 of the Constitution; the insufficient regard for the autonomy of the states as required by true federalism, with their governments being sometimes treated like mere instruments of the federal government, just as in the days of absolute military rule; the imposition of a minimum wage of ₦5,500 per month for state civil servants without the prior agreement of the state governments; his studied indifference to, or rather rebuff of, the demands for a national conference to negotiate the restructuring of the Nigerian federal union.

There have also been some actions of his, which were done, knowingly or unknowingly, somewhat in the fashion of a military autocrat, without complying with the constitution. Lastly, the management of his relations with the National Assembly, which is a vital index in measuring the success or failure of a president in a democratic setting, has a military-like style about it, no doubt a carry-over from his military past.

In fairness, no one should expect President Obasanjo to shed overnight habits and attitudes about the administration of affairs acquired over a long period of years as commander of a military unit, minister in, and later head of, a military government. In the nature of things they are bound from time to time to intrude, perhaps more often subconsciously than consciously, into his administration of public affairs as democratically elected civilian president. The important thing is that he has demonstrated a genuine effort and desire to be a democrat.

Intolerance is abhorrent to democracy. Democracy and civil liberties, said a great American jurist, Judge Learned Hand, lie in "habits, customs – conventions if you will – that tolerate dissent." They demand of Nigeria's new rulers in the legislative and executive arms of the government that they re-orient their attitude so as to imbibe the democratic spirit and habits of self-restraint, humility, courtesy, tolerance and selflessness.

Consultations and Dialogue

Consultations and dialogue hold the key to the fostering of a harmonious partnership between the legislature and the executive. The initiative for them must come from the president. The recent hike in fuel prices without prior consultations with the leadership of the National Assembly and the Nigerian Labour Congress is, as with the statement by the Speaker of the House of Representatives referred to above, the way of an autocrat, not of a democrat. It is an action that has aggravated the suffering of the people of this country. The reasons proffered for the increase do not justify it. To a non-economist like myself, the balance of advantages and disadvantages for the increase appears not to favour the individual members of society whose overall interests should be the deciding consideration in government measures of the kind.

Given the prevailing economic condition in the country, no gains accruing to the government and the **public** from the increase, no improvement in educational, health and infrastructural facilities likely to be effected with the additional revenue − even the likelihood of an improvement to a degree expected to improve significantly the conditions of life of the people is questionable − can completely offset the suffering and privations inflicted on the people as **individuals** − the increases in transport fares and in the prices of food and other necessaries of life. A government for the people should not embark upon an action which, on balance of advantages and disadvantages, is positively injurious to their well-being, considered as individuals.

We would like to see more of conversations over breakfast between the president and honourable members of the National Assembly. It is during such meetings that intimacy, confidence and mutual understanding needed for harmonious partnership can be cultivated. The establishment of confidence and understanding is expected to be facilitated by the fact that the federal executive and legislature in the present administration is controlled by the same party, the Peoples Democratic Party (PDP), of which Chief Olusegun Obasanjo is leader by virtue of being the president of the country − this is without prejudice to the position of the party chairman. The machinery of the party and the great influence which his leadership of it bestows upon the president should facilitate consultations and effective co-ordination of the work of the two arms of the government. Chief Obasanjo has tended to see himself more as Chief Executive of the Government than as president (with the primacy appertaining to the office) and party leader. He should do more to harness the vast resources of authority and influence afforded by those two latter positions.

CHAPTER 14

Limitations on Legislative and Executive Powers Arising from Constitutional Protection of the Liberty of the Individual

Whilst the limitations on the powers of the executive, the legislature and the judicature arising from the separation of powers under the constitution (discussed in Chapters 9-12 above) have as their underlying purpose, the safeguarding of the liberty of the people, they affect more directly the relations between those organs *inter se*. Though the operation of the limitations is designed for the protection of the people against governmental autocracy, yet they guarantee no rights to the individual. This chapter focuses on limitations on the powers of the executive and the legislature arising from the constitutional guarantee of the rights of the individual. As explained in Chapter 1, it is the legal protection of the rights and freedoms of the individual, not the safeguarding of the people as a whole against autocracy, that forms the core of the concept of limited government, and without which a democratic government (i.e., one freely elected by, and responsible to, the whole mass of the people) cannot be a constitutional democracy.

Limitations on Executive Power for the Protection of the Liberty of the Individual

The rule of law, perhaps the greatest of our inheritance from the English common law, ordains that, without specific authorisation by law, either the law of the constitution or one made by, or deemed to be made by, the legislative body, the executive cannot, on its own inherent authority, i.e., authority flowing from its power to execute the government, do anything that violates the rights or interests of the individual or which interferes with his freedom of action. It follows that, since most executive acts impinge directly or indirectly on the rights of individuals, the principle operates to limit quite severely what the executive can do in the execution of government without legal authorisation.

The limitation arising from this principle was affirmed by the Judicial Committee of the Privy Council in a case in 1931 (*Eshugbayi Eleko v. Government of Nigeria*) in which the colonial governor of Nigeria deported the traditional ruler of Lagos to another part of the country without authorisation by law, which he could have made by simply issuing an enabling ordinance or proclamation in his capacity as sole legislature for the colony. "In accordance with British jurisprudence," said the Judicial Committee speaking through the great Lord Atkin, "no member of the executive can interfere with the liberty or property of a British subject except on the condition that he can support the legality of his action before a court of justice." The deportation was accordingly declared unlawful and invalid. The colonial Constitution of Nigeria at the time had no guarantee of individual rights.

The limitation was given an even more historic affirmation by the U.S. Supreme Court in a landmark case (*Youngstown Sheet & Tube Co. v. Sawyer* (1951)). The case arose out of a nationwide strike call in the steel industry. The strike call had occurred at a time of national emergency formally proclaimed by the president because of a full-scale war in Korea in which the United States was involved. On the premise that, steel being an indispensable component of substantially

all of the weapons and materials needed for the war, a work stoppage
in the steel industry would immediately jeopardise and imperil national
defence, and endanger the armed forces fighting in the theatre of war
in Korea, the president, without express statutory authorisation, but
solely on his own independent authority under the U.S. Constitution
to preserve the security and safety of the nation, ordered the steel
factories to be seized and operated by government agents in order to
avert a national catastrophe.   But he immediately sent a message to
Congress informing it of his action, and inviting it to approve or revoke
it as it thought fit.   In an action by the owners of the factories
challenging the constitutionality of the seizure and praying that they
be returned to them, the U.S. Supreme Court, by a majority of six to
three, held that, without express statutory authorisation, the president
had, in the particular circumstances of the case, no independent power
under the Constitution to take possession of the steel mills and operate
them by his agents, on the ground that seizure of private property
requires legislative authorisation by Congress, to which alone the
Constitution has entrusted the law-making power in both good and
bad times.

It rejected the argument of the president based on his authority as
commander-in-chief of the armed forces, saying that

> even though 'theatre of war' be an expanding concept, we cannot
> with faithfulness to our constitutional system hold that the
> commander-in-chief of the armed forces has the ultimate power as
> such to take possession of private property in order to keep labour
> dispute from stopping production.

Mr. Justice Jackson in a separate concurring judgment said:

> No doctrine that the court would promulgate would seem to me
> more sinister and alarming than that a president ... can vastly enlarge
> his mastery over the internal affairs of the country by his own
> commitment of the Nation's armed forces to some foreign venture.
> (...) The constitution did not contemplate that the title Commander-
> in-Chief of the Army and Navy will constitute him also commander-
> in-chief of the country, its industries and its inhabitants.

The case shows that not even an emergency duly declared under the constitution justifies executive interference with individual rights without the backing of a law validly enacted by the legislative assembly.

The limitation became entrenched in the Constitution of the United States by the incorporation into it in 1791 of a guarantee of rights covering all rights, freedoms and interests of the individual, which guarantee can only be curtailed or interferred with by a constitutionally valid law, never by an executive act unbacked by a valid law made by the legislative body. Proclaiming the comprehensiveness of the guarantee in a 1897 case (*Allgeyer v. Louisiana*) in which it invalidated a statute that regulated marine insurance contracts, the U.S. Supreme Court said:

> The liberty mentioned in the (guarantee) means not only the right of the citizen to be free from the mere physical restraint of his person, as by incarceration, but the term is deemed to embrace the right of the citizen to be free in the enjoyment of all his faculties, to be free to use them in all lawful ways, to live and work where he will; to earn his livelihood by any lawful calling; to pursue any livelihood or a vocation; and for that purpose to enter into all contracts which may be proper, necessary or essential to his carrying out to a successful conclusion the purposes above mentioned.

The Nigerian Constitution also entrenches the limitation through the guarantee of fundamental rights and freedoms (Chapter IV), and by expressly making the power to execute the government subject to the guarantee (Section 5(1)), as well as by putting it beyond the competence of the executive to curtail or interfere with the guarantee by executive action unbacked by a constitutionally valid law made by the National Assembly. The guarantee of rights and freedoms in the Nigerian Constitution does not, however, unlike the American, cover all rights, freedoms and interests of the individual; yet that does not make rights, freedoms and interests not embraced in the guarantee any more amenable to interference by executive action not backed by a valid law. The scope of the guarantee of fundamental rights in the Nigerian Constitution, whether it embraces all the rights, freedoms and interests of the individual, is considered later.

With respect to rights not embraced in the constitutional guarantee, the principle of limitation, as embodied in the common law, still applies that the executive cannot, without authorisation by law, interfere with the liberty or property of the individual. The guarantee of rights in the Constitution does not abolish the common law as part of the law of Nigeria. There is no question here of *expressio unius est exclusio alterius*, though to avoid the possibility of such implication the Americans have expressly had to declare that "the enumeration in the constitution of certain rights shall not be construed to deny or disparage others retained by the people" (ixth Amendment).

In this connection, we may note the attempt by both the 1979 and 1999 Constitutions of Nigeria to qualify in favour of executive power, the freedom they guarantee to every person to "associate with other persons and in particular ... (to) form or belong to any political party, trade union or any other association for the protection of his interests" (Section 40, 1999). The attempt is in the form of a proviso, slipped in at the last minute by the Supreme Military Council, that the guarantee "shall not derogate from the powers conferred by this constitution on the Independent National Electoral Commission (INEC) with respect to political parties to which that Commission does not accord recognition" (S. 40). It is to be noted that only powers conferred by the Constitution for the recognition of political parties are relevant; powers conferred by any other law are irrelevant; furthermore the proviso itself grants no power to accord or not to accord recognition. The power has to be looked for in other provisions of the constitution. Part F of the Third Schedule to the Constitution provides that INEC "shall have power", among other things, to "register political parties **in accordance with the provisions of this Constitution** and an Act of the National Assembly." Like Section 40 this provision grants no power to INEC to register or not to register a political association as a political party. The Commission can only assume such power "in accordance with the provisions of this Constitution."

The only provision relevant for this purpose is that (S. 222) which states that no association by whatever name called shall function as a political party, unless:

(a)   the names and addresses of its national officers are registered with the Independent National Electoral Commission;

(b)   the membership of the association is open to every citizen of Nigeria irrespective of his place of origin, sex, religion or ethnic grouping;

(c)   a copy of its constitution is registered in the principal office of the Commission in such **form** as may be prescribed by the Commission;

(d)   any alteration in its registered constitution is also registered in the principal office of the Commission within 30 days of the making of such alteration;

(e)   the name of the association, its emblem or motto does not contain any ethnic or religious connotation or give the appearance that the activities of the association are confined to a part only of the geographical area of Nigeria; and

(f)   the headquarters of the association is situated in the capital of the Federation.

Three comments may be made on this provision. First, it does not prohibit the formation of a political association in the first instance. The conditions which it prescribes relate, not to the initial formation of a political association or to its formal or nominal existence thereafter, but to its operation as a political party. The distinction between incorporation of a company and commencement of business is familiar enough. Under the provision therefore the formation of a political association is a purely private act, but before it can begin to function as a political party and in particular to canvass for votes for any candidate at an election, it must satisfy the six conditions stipulated in the constitutional provision in Section 222.

Secondly, and more important, the provision gives no power to INEC to register or not to register, to recognise or not to recognise an association as a political party. Apart from the power granted to the Commission to prescribe the form of the party constitution, e.g., whether it should be typed or printed and whether it should be in bound form, the provision grants no power at all to the electoral commission. Its concern is to impose obligations on an association regarding the conditions it must satisfy before beginning to function as a political party. Only three of such obligations have any relation to the Commission (the other three make no reference at all to it), but they relate to it in the sense, not of conferring power, but rather of requiring identification particulars to be furnished to it. The requirement that the constitution of an association (and any amendments of it) as well as the names and addresses of its national officers should be "registered" with the Commission merely casts an obligation on the association to furnish the prescribed information and document to the Commission for identification purposes; no power is thereby created in favour of the Commission to grant or withhold recognition or registration. The Commission's role in the matter is the purely formal or ministerial one of taking the party constitution into its custody and recording the names and addresses of the party officers in its books. Of course the Commission can refuse to accept a party's constitution for filing or registration, but that confers no real discretion on it to grant or refuse recognition or registration.

The powers conferred on the Commission under Sections 223-226 of the 1999 Constitution relate and apply only to a political party, not to a political association that has not yet become a political party by complying with the requirements of Section 222 as set out above. Accordingly, until it has become a political party, a political association is not obliged to comply with Section 223 which provides that:

the constitution and rules of a **political party** shall provide:

(a) for the periodical election on a democratic basis of the principal officers and members of the executive committee or other governing body of the **political party**; and

(b) ensure that the members of the executive committee or other governing body of the **political party** reflect the federal character of Nigeria. (emphasis supplied).

This conclusion flows from the clear distinction drawn by the constitution between a political party and a political association.

The third comment concerns the question of how to ensure that an association complies with the constitutional requirements and how to enforce them should it begin to function as a political party without complying with them. Although the provision is couched in the form of a prohibition, no criminal offence is thereby created. At worst, the acts done in contravention of the prohibition may be unconstitutional and void. It is significant, however, that, even given the unconstitutionality of such acts, the electoral commission is granted no power directly by the constitution to ensure compliance – for example, by withholding recognition – or to enforce contraventions. Significantly too, the prohibition is not among the provisions for the contravention of which the National Assembly is empowered to prescribe punishment. The powers conferred on the National Assembly by Section 228 of the 1999 Constitution and Item 56 of the Exclusive Legislative List also relate and apply only to a political party, not to a political association that has not become a political party by complying with the requirements of Section 222. These requirements cannot be added to by the National Assembly by virtue of its power to regulate political parties.

It follows that the National Assembly cannot, in the exercise of its general power to regulate political parties, authorise the denial of recognition to any political association to function as a political party on grounds other than those stipulated in Section 222 above. That would amount to licensing which is unconstitutional. The unconstitutionality of a power of licensing in relation to the exercise or enjoyment of a guaranteed right is well stated by the U.S. Supreme Court as follows:

> It is settled by a long line of recent decisions of this court that an ordinance which, like this one, makes the peaceful enjoyment of freedom which the Constitution guarantees contingent upon the uncontrolled will of an official as by requiring a permit or licence which may be granted or withheld in the discretion of such official

– is an unconstitutional censorship or prior restraint upon the enjoyment of those freedoms. (*Staub v. Baxley* 335 U.S. 313 (1958)).

A political party, trade union, religious or other association may, however, justifiably be required to file certain information about itself which will enable it to be identified, provided that the information required is not more than is reasonably necessary for identification purposes. Thus, an order of a state court, issued in pursuance of a statute, compelling the National Association for the Advancement of Coloured People to produce a list of its members in the state was held unconstitutional and void, on the Association showing that on past occasions revelation of the identity of its rank-and-file members had exposed those members to economic reprisals, loss of employment, the calling-in or denial of bank loans, foreclosure of mortgages, threat of physical coercion, and other manifestations of public hostility. (*National Association for the Advancement of Coloured People v. Alabama* 357 U.S. 449 (1958); re-affirmed in *Bates v. Little Rock* 361 U.S. 516 (1960)). The court affirmed that disclosure in the circumstances would abridge the right of the members to engage in lawful association in support of their common beliefs, that effective advocacy of both public and private points of view, particularly controversial ones, is undeniably enhanced by group association, and that inviolability of privacy in group association may in many circumstances be indispensable to preservation of freedom of association, particularly where a group espouses dissident beliefs. It is not decisive therefore that no action had been taken by the state directly to restrict the ability of members of the Association to associate freely; indirect governmental actions such as that involved here could also have a highly restrictive effect on membership. The character of the Association as a lawful organisation engaged in the promotion of constitutional rights for all races on the basis of equality is of course an underlying premise of the decision. This decision was subsequently re-affirmed even against a city ordinance which required any organisation operating within the city to give certain information, including the names of all who paid dues, assessments or contributions.

In the view of the court there is no "relevant correlation" between the city's power to impose occupation licence taxes and the compulsory disclosure and publication of membership lists. (*Bates v. Little Rock*, ibid).

Compulsory disclosure of membership may be constitutionally justified in the case of an association which is formed for criminal purposes or engages in criminal conduct or which is a secret oath-bound society. (*Viereck v. United States* (1943) 318 U.S. 236; *Communist Party v. Subversive Activities Control Board* 351 U.S. 115 (1956); 361 U.S. 1 (1961); *Konigsberg v. State Bar of California* 366 U.S. 36 (1961); *New York ex rel Bryant v. Zimmerman* 278 U.S. 63 (1928)).

On the authority of these decisions, therefore, any law, whether an existing or future one, which purports to authorise INEC to grant or refuse registration or recognition to a political association to function as a political party on grounds other than those stipulated in Section 222 above is unconstitutional and void. Thus, the power conferred on the electoral commission by a Decree of 1977 to "register political parties and determine their eligibility to sponsor candidates for elections" is unconstitutional and void. Happily, the Decree expired by its own terms on 1 October, 1979. Equally the Guidelines for the Registration of Political Parties issued by INEC in May, 2002 and which purport to prescribe conditions and requirements outside those stipulated in section 222 of the 1999 Constitution are unconstitutional and void.

Limitations on Legislative Power for the Protection of the Liberty of the Individual

Limitations Arising from the Principle of the Rule of Law

The principle of the rule of law applies to and limits not only the executive but also the legislature as well: the former, by subjecting it to both the supreme law of the constitution and the laws made by the legislative body, and the latter, to the supreme law of the constitution. In exercising its power to make law regulating or interferring with the life, liberty or property of the individual, the legislature is legally bound to act in strict conformity with the supreme law of the constitution in regard to both the manner and form for exercising the power and to the substance of the law; any law made by it otherwise than in conformity with the law of the constitution in either or both of these respects is null and void.

The application of the principle in limiting the power of the legislature was again affirmed by the Judicial Committee of the Privy Council in an appeal from Ceylon (*The Bribery Commissioner v. Ranasingha* (1965)) where it was argued that the sovereignty of the legislature even under a written constitution, implies that any act purporting to have been passed by it is valid and effective, irrespective of any defect in procedure; because, if a legislature is sovereign, a mere defect in procedure cannot operate to invalidate an Act which is otherwise within the power of the legislature, and that the courts are bound to accept and act upon the official copy of the Act, and cannot go outside to ascertain whether it was passed in the manner and form prescribed by the constitution. On this view of sovereignty, a sovereign legislature operating under a written constitution is clearly above the constitution just like one operating under an unwritten constitution.

The Judicial Committee emphatically rejected this view, holding that under a written constitution which prescribed a procedure for law-making, the courts are not only entitled to go outside the official copy of the Act in order to enquire into the question of procedure, but have a duty to declare the Act invalid if in fact it was passed without due form. For where a legislature is given power subject to certain manner and form, whether it be a simple or special majority, or the requirement of presidential assent, that power does not exist unless and until the manner and form is complied with. The supremacy of the constitution demands that the court should hold void any exercise of power which does not comply with the prescribed manner and form or which is otherwise not "in accordance with the constitution from which the power derives." As the Committee observed, the proposition is not acceptable that:

a legislature, once established, has some inherent power derived from the mere fact of its establishment to make valid law by the resolution of a bare majority which its own constituent instrument has said shall not be a valid law unless made by a different type of majority or by a different legislative process. ...The minority are entitled under the Constitution of Ceylon to have no amendment of it which is not passed by a two-thirds majority.

But the main essence of the rule of law in relation to the legislature concerns, not the procedural requirements for law-making, binding though they are, but the limitations on legislative power by a constitutional guarantee of individual rights and freedoms. No conception of the rule of law is adequate unless the legislative power of the state is limited by a guarantee of individual rights and freedoms in the supreme law of the constitution. The absence of such a guarantee is indeed the very definition of arbitrary and repressive rule. So inseparably is the rule of law bound up with a constitutional guarantee of individual rights and freedoms that the concept cannot meaningfully exist or be defined without such a guarantee. This is considered later in this chapter.

Limitations Arising from the Separation of Powers

We are not here concerned with the usurpation of or interference with judicial power by the legislature which is indisputably unconstitutional and void, as by the use of legislation to condemn a named person of a criminal offence and to inflict punishment on him therefor (what is known as **legislative judgment**) or its use to authorise the executive or some other agency than the courts to exercise the power.

The issue here concerns the more general one whether the separation of powers requires that laws be made, not for particular, named persons (*ad hominem* laws), but for the generality of persons, i.e., that laws should be made to apply uniformly to all persons or classes of persons. It is indisputably desirable that this should be so. Making laws for individuals identified by name rather than for the generality of persons or classes of persons may create a lot of room for unfairness, arbitrariness and oppression, especially where such laws inflict punishment or disability on the persons affected. "Although the fact that a general measure has been adopted is not conclusive evidence that it is good or wise, it is strong presumptive evidence of its being so. In order to show that it is unfair in its bearing on any one individual, it is necessary to show that it is a measure which is quite unjustifiable, and which society could not have any good reason for imposing on itself." The greatest protection against the oppression of individuals by the use of legislation lies, therefore, in its generality of application.

But the issue is not about the undoubted undesirability of *ad hominem* laws, but rather about whether such laws are, as a necessary consequence of the separation of powers in the constitution, prohibited and invalid. Judicial opinions are divided upon the point. According to Chief Justice John Marshall, delivering the judgment of the U.S. Supreme Court in a case in which the Court declared invalid a statute which revoked a grant of land made by an earlier statute to an individual and reverted it to the state on the ground that "undue means" had been used to secure the grant (*Fletcher v. Peck* (1810)):

> To the legislature all legislative power is granted; but the question, whether the act of transferring the property of an individual to the public, be in the nature of the legislative power, is well worthy of serious reflection. It is the peculiar province of the legislature to prescribe general rules for the government of society; the application of those rules to individuals in society would seem to be the duty of other departments.

On the other hand, the Judicial Committee of the Privy Council has sustained the validity of a clearly *ad hominem* statute but one that did not constitute a usurpation of or interference with judicial power, saying that "a lack of generality in criminal legislation need not, of itself, involve the judicial function," and that "their Lordships are not prepared to hold that every enactment in this field which can be described as *ad hominem* and *ex post facto* must inevitably usurp or infringe the judicial function." (*Liyanage v. R.* (1967)). The decision implies that an *ad hominem* law is valid unless it usurps or infringes the judicial function. While upholding a statute by the colonial government of Swaziland which deported the traditional ruler to another part of the colony, the Court of Appeal in England castigated the statute as a *privilegium* which is something, it said, that "has never commended itself to English legislature" (*R. v. Earl of Crewe* (1910)). (There had been many *ad hominem* laws in England even as late as the 19th century.)

Limitations Resulting from the Guarantee of Individual Rights and Freedoms in the Constitution

The rights and freedoms of the individual are given enhanced protection by the limitation which their guarantee in the constitution imposes on legislative power. But the adequacy of the limitation on legislative power resulting from the guarantee of rights in the constitution depends on the scope of the guarantee, whether it embraces all rights and freedoms of the individual as well as on the qualifications on the guaranteed rights in favour of the legislative power. These two aspects will be considered in turn.

Range of Rights Covered by the Guarantee

The Constitution of Nigeria does not, like that of the United States, guarantee "liberty" in a generalised sense, as defined by the U.S. Supreme Court in the case mentioned above, but only specific rights and freedoms – life; dignity of the human person; personal liberty; fair hearing; family life and privacy; freedom of thought, conscience and religion; freedom of expression and press; peaceful assembly and association; freedom of movement; freedom from discrimination; and property – Chapter IV. The argument that "personal liberty" has the same amplitude of meaning as "liberty" in the American guarantee is clearly untenable; it is refuted by the context and wording of the provision in which it is guaranteed (Section 35), by the absence of appropriate qualifications that would have been necessary were it intended to have the same amplitude of meaning as liberty in a generalised sense, and by the limitation implied in the title of the chapter – **"fundamental rights"** – (emphasis supplied). We need not pursue the point further here.

The limited scope of the guarantee of rights in the Nigerian Constitution, the fact that only the specific rights mentioned above, and not liberty in the generalised American sense, are guaranteed has serious consequences as limiting the constitutional protection of individual rights against legislative encroachment. It means that freedom of choice and action in non-political and non-religious matters, i.e., freedom of choice and action in all other fields of human activity, in particular, freedom of contract and private enterprise, is not constitutionally guaranteed against legislative interference, except to the limited extent of freedom of choice and activity implied by the guarantee of certain specific rights – freedom of movement, freedom of speech and press, of association and family life, the right of property, and the **negative** freedom not to be compelled by law or by force to work for the government or for any other employer, which is guaranteed by the prohibition of servitude and forced or compulsory labour.

The guarantee of liberty in the U.S. Constitution has the effect of entrenching an economic philosophy based on private enterprise and private property and which, consequently, forbids **exclusive** state ownership of the means of production and distribution; the question of the government assuming total power of management over the economy is thereby ruled out. The state can enter into business in competition with private persons, but it cannot by law assume a monopoly of economic activities or any aspect of them, and exclude private persons therefrom. It cannot also impose unwarranted restriction on economic activity by private persons. To do either of these would infringe the constitutional guarantee of "liberty".

On the other hand, the omission of the Nigerian Constitution to guarantee freedom of choice and action (except to the limited extent noted above) has the constitutional implication that:

(i) the take-over by the state, with appropriate statutory backing, of all or most business activities and the prohibition of private enterprise will not be a violation of anyone's constitutional rights (except again to the limited extent noted above). In effect, therefore, the Bill of Rights in the Nigerian Constitution entrenches no particular brand of economic philosophy, whether capitalism or socialism. It leaves the government free to pursue the one or the other or a mixture of both as the changing circumstances of the society may demand, though at the moment the inherited tradition of free private enterprise still predominates to a considerable extent.

(ii) the state has full power (subject as aforesaid) to regulate by law business activities, as it sees fit, and in particular the making of contracts, whether or not such regulation has a real and substantial relation to the protection and promotion of the public welfare, and whether or not it is reasonable or arbitrary. Its regulatory power is thus not a mere police power, as in the United States. The idea of a police power implies that the government's power of control over a particular field is not general and unlimited but is restricted to the making of only such regulations as are necessary for the protection and promotion of the public health, safety, morality, general convenience, prosperity and welfare.

The Nigerian statute book abounds with laws regulating various aspects of the economic life of the country in a manner which no American government would dare to attempt: laws fixing minimum wages, prohibiting general wage increase, pegging income from dividends, fixing prices for various commodities, controlling fees and fares chargeable respectively by certain professionals and operators, controlling rent and the use and disposition of land, requiring a licence for or otherwise restricting the carrying on of certain professions, trades or industrial activities, etc. However unreasonable or arbitrary, and however unrelated to the public interest such regulations may be, no court can interfere. Nigeria's Bill of Rights recognises no such theory as is applied in the U.S. Supreme Court that prices may not normally be regulated, because "the public interest and private right are both adequately protected" when there is "free competition among buyers and sellers," and that state regulation is constitutionally permitted only when there exists "a situation or combination of circumstances materially restricting the regulative force of competition, so that buyers or sellers are placed at such a disadvantage in the bargaining struggle that serious economic consequences result to a very large number of members of the community." These observations were made in a case holding invalid a statute which limited the resale price of theatre tickets, and were repeated in another case invalidating a statute which regulated fees charged by employment agencies.

Qualifications on the Guaranteed Rights in Favour of the Legislative Power

The guarantee of rights in the Nigerian Constitution differs from the American as regards not only the range of rights covered but also the qualifications on the guaranteed rights in favour of the legislative power. The guarantee of rights in the U.S. Constitution is couched either as absolute prohibitions or in such "magnificent generalities" as "due process of law" or "equal protection of the laws." By the First Amendment "Congress shall make no law respecting an establishment of religion, prohibiting the free exercise thereof; or abridging the freedom of speech or of the press; or the right of the people peaceably to assemble, and to petition the government for a redress of grievance;" whilst by the Fifth, "no person shall be ... deprived of life, liberty, or property, without due process of law; nor shall private property be taken for public use without just compensation." These prohibitions are extended to the states by the Fourteenth Amendment, with the additional prohibition that no state shall "deny to any person within its jurisdiction the equal protection of the laws."

The absolute and sweeping language of the prohibitions means that it is for the courts to determine what qualifications, if any, are to be put on them. And the U.S. Supreme Court has laid it down in *Lockner v. New York* (1905) that:

> There are, however, certain powers, existing in the sovereignty of each State in the Union, somewhat vaguely termed police powers, the exact description and limitation of which have not been attempted by the courts. Those powers, broadly stated and without, at present, any attempt at a more specific limitation, relate to the safety, health, morals, and general welfare of the public. Both property and liberty are held on such reasonable conditions as may be imposed by the governing power of the State in the exercise of those powers.

For this purpose, the rights guaranteed in the Nigerian Constitution fall into three groups, *viz*,

(i) *Rights guaranteed absolutely without any qualifications in both normal times and during the period of a declared emergency:* Only two rights belong in this category: freedom from torture and other inhuman or degrading treatment; and freedom from slavery or servitude (Section 34(1)(a) and (b)).

(ii) *Rights guaranteed subject to specifically defined and narrowly circumscribed qualifications:* The rights in this category are life (Section 33); freedom from forced or compulsory labour (Section 34(1) and (2)); personal liberty (Section 35); fair hearing (Section 36); freedom from discrimination (Section 42); and right of property (Sections 43 and 44). A detailed discussion of the guarantee of these rights and the qualifications on them in favour of the legislative power will take us too far afield, but a few brief comments are called for.

First, the unlimited power permitted to the legislature to prescribe the death penalty for any criminal offence it deems fit is out of tune with developments in this field in other countries of the world. So is its power to authorise the arrest and detention of a person to "such extent as may be reasonably necessary to prevent his committing a criminal offence" (Section 35(1)(c)). No doubt, it is, as John Stuart Mill has said:

one of the undisputed functions of government is to take
precautions against crime before it has been committed, as well
as to detect and punish it afterwards. The preventive function
of government, however, is far more liable to be abused, to
the prejudice of liberty, than the punitory function; for there
is hardly any part of the legitimate freedom of action of a
human being which would not admit of being represented,
and fairly too, as increasing the facilities for some form or
other of delinquency.

The danger of abuse is real and great indeed. For while it may be
justifiable to detain a person in order to prevent him from committing
a criminal offence, which it is reasonably suspected he is about to
commit, the grounds on which it is believed that he may, if left at
large, commit a criminal offence may be filmsy and tenuous. The
belief may be based on activities which have no criminal tendencies
or intention at all but are simply offensive to the government or
inimical to its political interests. This is the cardinal danger of any
system of preventive detention. It is fraught with the tendency on
the part of government to equate activities that threaten its personal
political fortunes with a criminal threat to the security of the state.
Political opponents of government thus face the risk of being clamped
into detention, ostensibly to prevent them from committing
subversion or other criminal offences against the state, although no
shred of evidence exists of any preparations for it or of anyone having
contemplated it at all.

Of the rights in this group, life and personal liberty are, in addition
to the specifically defined qualifications on them, subject to derogation
in times of emergency declared in accordance with the stipulations of
the constitution, which are quite restrictive of the powers of the state
in that behalf (Section 11 and 305). But the derogation from the two
rights during an emergency validly and lawfully declared in accordance
with the constitution is limited to only such measures as are
"reasonably justifiable for the purpose of dealing with the situation
that exists during that period of emergency" (Section 45(2)).
Furthermore, an emergency does not justify the taking of life "except

in respect of death resulting from acts of war" (Section 45(2) proviso).

(iii) *Rights guaranteed subject to restrictions by law at all times in the interest of defence, public safety, public order, public morality, public health or for the purpose of protecting the rights and freedoms of other persons:* In this category fall the right to privacy, freedom of thought, conscience and religion, freedom to hold, receive and impart opinions and ideas, freedom of the press, right to peaceful assembly and association and freedom of movement (Sections 37, 38, 39, 40 and 41). Nothing in the guarantee of these rights, says the constitution, "shall invalidate any law that is reasonably justifiable in a democratic society (a) in the interest of defence, public safety, public order, public morality or public health; or (b) for the purpose of protecting the rights and freedom of other persons" (Section 45(1)). Four comments may be made on the qualification on these rights.

First, the wording of the qualification seems to shift the emphasis from liberty to the authority of the legislature to interfere with them, from protection of liberty to qualifications on it. It fails to emphasise as clearly as would be desired that liberty is the rule and governmental interference the exception. It seems to place on the individual the onus of showing that an interfering law is not reasonably justifiable in the specified public interests rather than on the state to show that it is. In short, it fails to strike the balance in favour of liberty which, says Lord Devlin, is "the true mark of a free society." Had the wording of the qualification read instead, "any law derogating from or interfering with a guaranteed right shall be invalid unless it is reasonably justifiable" etc, the onus of proving the reasonable justifiability of the law would have been cast unequivocally upon the authorities, and the guaranteed right would have been enhanced in value.

Secondly, while public morality (not just any morality) is rightly included as a legitimate ground of control by the state, it is an error to leave out economic well-being and general welfare, apparently because liberty as a generalised right is not guaranteed. (Some of the later

Commonwealth Bills of Rights, e.g., Zambia's, include economic well-being and development).

Thirdly, the provisions err in lumping freedoms of thought, opinion, feeling, conscience and religion together with their manifestation in speech, press, assembly, association, movement, religious practices or in other forms of action or overt ways. The former freedoms are, in their nature, absolute and beyond control by the state.

There is good reason for treating freedom of thought, opinion, feeling, conscience and religion not manifested in action or in other overt ways as absolute, and inviolable by the state. First because they constitute the essence of the sacredness, inherent dignity and the spiritual or moral integrity of the human person; they are, in other words, the elements or attributes of the human person that confer upon him sacredness, dignity and spiritual or moral integrity, and which therefore entitle it to inviolability. Man's endowment with reason, with the ability to think and reason, to judge between right and wrong, to form or hold opinions and beliefs, and to have feelings and emotions are the elements that distinguish him from non-human living things. The human physical body partakes, **to some extent,** of this sacredness, dignity and integrity because it encases those vital, spiritual elements.

Whereas a human person loses his integrity as a human being, whole and entire, if he is not able to think for himself, to feel or believe, his integrity or personality as a human being is not destroyed or lost because he is unable to move about, speak or act owing to the loss of his legs, tongue and hands, even eyes, unless such loss is deliberately inflicted by the state or another person as a punishment or a sheer act of brutalisation. His integrity or personality may well be adversely affected, but certainly not lost or destroyed because of such loss; he remains a human person with all the sacredness, dignity and moral integrity pertaining to the human person. A person disabled by the loss of his eyes, legs, hands or tongue not deliberately inflicted by others as punishment is as much a human being possessed of the same inherent dignity and integrity as one without such disability, and he may indeed be able to develop his human personality better than the latter, depending on the facilities and opportunities available to them both. But destroy his mind, his soul and his capacity to feel and judge, and he ceases to be a human person. He may still be living but he will have become an idiot, a robot or worse.

So when we speak of the human person as having an inherent dignity and integrity, and as entitled to inviolability, it is the elements of thought, conscience, the ability to form or hold opinions or beliefs and to feel that are primarily referred to as conferring sacredness, dignity and integrity on the human person. Torture, cruel, inhuman or degrading punishment or treatment, servitude, forced labour, arbitrary or wrongful detention or imprisonment, unfair discrimination on such grounds as race, colour, tribe or place of origin are derogatory of the dignity and integrity of the human person essentially because of their depressing and damaging effects on a man's mind, spirit, feelings and his entire psychology. The worst of all tyrannies, it has been truly said, is tyranny on men's minds. Few things depress the spirit as much as incarceration of a man, as by detention or imprisonment, for an offence he did not commit. Racial discrimination is so awfully damaging to the psychology of those subjected to it.

In the second place, it makes hardly any sense that the state should try to restrict human thought, opinion, conscience, beliefs and feelings, partly because they cannot, meaningfully, be controlled or restricted by the state, and partly because it serves no legitimate public interest for the state to try to control or restrict them. For, what a person thinks in his mind or feels or believes in his heart, but does not manifest in speech or action or in any other overt way (e.g., refusal, on conscientious grounds, to do something required by law), cannot be known to others so as to enable them to control or restrict it by legal punishment or otherwise. It is simply futile to prohibit a man by law from thinking certain thoughts, believing in certain things or from having certain feelings. Besides, mere thought, belief or feeling not

manifested in some overt way can have no disturbing effect on any
legitimate public interest which the state is entitled to protect, whether
it be public order, public security, public morality or public health.
Of course, as John Stuart Mill says, it is what men think, believe in or
feel that determines how they act, yet human thought, conscience,
belief or feeling is not for that reason to be controlled before and until
it is actually manifested in action or in some other overt way. A man;
said Justice William Douglas of the U.S. Supreme Court, may be
"punished for his acts, never for his thoughts or beliefs or creed."
Human thought, opinions, conscience, beliefs, feelings and emotions
require therefore to be put beyond the reach of governmental power;
no room should be given for their control by the state.

The absoluteness and inviolability of freedom of thought, opinion,
conscience, beliefs, feelings and emotions is accepted and enshrined in
the International Covenant on Civil and Political Rights (1966) of the
United Nations, which guarantees freedom of thought, conscience
and religion as well as the right to hold opinions free of any
qualifications whatsoever; only the guarantee of freedom to **manifest**
one's religion or beliefs and freedom of expression (including freedom
to seek, receive and impart information and ideas) is made subject to
such limitations as are prescribed by law and are necessary to protect
public security, public order, public health, morals and the rights and
freedoms of others (Arts 18 and 19). Similarly, under the European
Convention on Human Rights and Fundamental Freedoms (1954),
the guarantee of freedom of thought, conscience and religion is not
qualified at all except as it relates to freedom to **manifest** one's religion
or beliefs (Art. 9). However, under the European Convention freedom
to hold opinion, equally as freedom of expression with which it is
lumped, may be restricted by law to an extent necessary in a democratic
society in the interest of national security, territorial integrity, etc.
(Art. 10).

Fourthly, the provisions fail to specify in explicit terms the kind
of relations that must exist between an interfering law and the
prescribed public interests to make the interfering law reasonably

justifiable in a democratic society in those interests.

In a case before the High Court of Zambia, where the issue was whether the power given by the Exchange Control Regulations of the country to customs officers to open and search without warrant postal packets reasonably suspected of containing articles or currency notes being imported into or exported out of the country in contravention of the Regulations was an unconstitutional interference with the freedom of correspondence and expression guaranteed by the constitution, the High Court held that, to be reasonably required, the connection between a regulatory legislation and public order, public safety, etc., must be a proximate one; that is to say, its bearing on public order, public safety, etc., must be reasonably close and not too remote or far-fetched. It must also be reasonable and not arbitrary, as well as rational, in the sense that it must suggest itself to a reasonably intelligent mind.

Now, exchange control, being a very vital aspect of a country's development, has certainly some bearing on public order and safety. The question however is whether this bearing is sufficiently proximate and rational to make exchange control reasonably required in the interests of public order and safety and thereby to justify interference with the individual's freedom of expression. The Court held, rightly, that it was not. In the words of the learned judge:

> It could conceivably happen that complete financial anarchy might so weaken the economy that internal disaffection might be caused, leading to rioting and civil disturbance. So might widespread unemployment caused, say, by overpopulation. So might prolonged drought which disrupted agricultural production. One might think of many things which could, ultimately, affect the public safety. None of them would, however, have the quality of proximateness which would justify involving this exception. Nor do I think that exchange control is sufficiently proximate to public safety to warrant the present legislation being adopted in the interest of public safety.

The reasoning in this case is a gratifying repudiation of an earlier decision by another judge of the same Court. A regulation made by the government under the Education Act required children in government or government-aided schools to sing the national anthem and to salute the national flag on certain occasions. The requirement was challenged on the ground that it was an unconstitutional interference with the freedom of conscience guaranteed by the constitution. This depended on whether the regulation was reasonably required in the interest of public safety and public order. Chief Justice Blagden held that it was. His reasoning was that the singing of the national anthem and the saluting of the national flag were necessary to inculcate among the people, especially among children in their formative age, a love of nation, and a consciousness of common belonging. And the need for national unity, he further reasoned, was much greater in an emergent state like Zambia with its seventy-three distinct tribal groupings, divided not only by language and culture but also by economic and other interests.

All this must be admitted. Yet the question is whether the compulsion of children to sing the national anthem and salute the flag was reasonably required in the interests, not of national unity, which was not one of the specified public interests, but of national security. The Chief Justice had reasoned that since "national unity is the basis of national security" then, whatever was reasonably required in the interests of national unity must also be reasonably required in the interests of national security. But surely the connection between the singing of the national anthem or the saluting of the flag and national security is an ultimate, not a proximate, one. The danger to national security in school children not being made to sing the national anthem or salute the flag is rather remote. Indeed, the U.S. Supreme Court has held that it was not permissible under the U.S. Constitution to use compulsion to try to achieve national unity. "To believe that patriotism will not flourish if patriotic ceremonies are voluntary and spontaneous instead of a compulsory routine is to make an unflattering estimate of the appeal of our institutions to free minds." Accordingly, it held, reversing its earlier decision, that the compulsory flag salute and singing of the national anthem were unconstitutional.

The limitation thus imposed on governmental control of freedom is all the more remarkable because the "reasonableness of each regulation depends on the relevant facts," with the result that "a regulation valid for one sort of business, or in given circumstances, may be invalid for another sort, or for the same business under other circumstances." In upholding a building zone law which excluded from residential districts apartment houses, business houses, retail stores and shops, and other like establishments, the U.S. Supreme Court observed that "regulations, the wisdom, necessity and validity of which, as applied in existing conditions, are so apparent that they are uniformly sustained, a century ago or even half a century ago, probably would have been rejected as arbitrary and oppressive. Such regulations are sustained, under the complex conditions of our day, for reasons analogous to those which justify traffic regulations, which, before the advent of automobiles and rapid transit street railways, would have been condemned as fatally arbitrary and unreasonable .... A regulatory zoning ordinance, which would be clearly valid as applied to the great cities, might be clearly invalid as applied to rural communities." This approach to the matter has enabled the court to overrule the line of decisions which invalidated laws fixing minimum wages and maximum working hours or prices, as well as certain laws regulating business activities.

The U.S. Supreme Court has also laid it down that the test of substantial and rational connection applied in ordinary cases is not enough when freedom of political discussion, press and assembly is concerned. A restriction on these rights, the great political freedoms, is valid only if "the words used are in such circumstances and are of such a nature as to create a clear and present danger that they will bring about the substantive evils that congress has a right to prevent." This has become known as the "clear and present danger" test, but a discussion of it will again take us too far afield.

A Constitutional Guarantee of Liberty and the Open Society

The effect of a constitutional guarantee of liberty in terms of the U.S.

Bill of Rights and the Bills of Rights in the constitutions of some African countries, e.g., Ethiopia (1955), Liberia (1847), Burundi (1962), Congo (Leopoldville) (1964) and Equatorial Guinea (1982), is to establish an economic system, capitalism, which, because it is entrenched in the constitution, is not **open** to change. In the result, the American society, though unquestionably a free society, so far as concerns the protection of liberty against state interference, hardly qualifies to be called an open one. It is nearly as closed to change as the socialist system of the communist world was. The entrenchment of the system of capitalism has, for example, prevented the country from fully embracing social democracy and the welfare state.

Sir Ralf Dahrendorf has rightly cautioned that the collapse of socialism/communism in Eastern Europe and the former Soviet Union should not be seen as the triumph of capitalism as such, but rather as the triumph of freedom over system. He says: "The countries of East Central Europe have not shed their communist system in order to embrace the capitalist system; ... the road to freedom is not a road from one system to another, but one that leads into the open spaces of infinite futures, some of which compete with each other."[1]   For him,

> the battle of systems is an illiberal aberration. To drive the point home with the utmost force: if capitalism is a system, then it needs to be fought as hard as communism had to be fought. All systems mean serfdom, including the 'natural' system of a total 'market order' in which no one tries to do anything other than guard certain rules of the game discovered by a mysterious sect of economic advisers.[2]

It seems on the whole that the elasticity and openness permitted by the Nigerian-type Bill of Rights, which guarantees, not liberty in the comprehensive sense of the U.S. Bill of Rights, but only specific rights, are to be preferred to the rigid, systemic approach of the U.S.

---

1.   Ralf Dahrendorf, *Reflections on the Revolution in Europe* (1990), pp. 36-37.

2.   *ibid*, p. 37.

Bill of Rights. For, they permit the state, while keeping within the basic minimum framework of liberal democracy, to cater for the needs of the people for social services, social security and social justice generally, to operate, not an undiluted market order in the American systemic sense, but what has come to be known as a "social market economy."

The elasticity and openness of the Nigerian-type Bill of Rights create of course the problem of ensuring that the government will in fact keep within the basic minimum framework of liberal democracy, and will not pursue a policy of undue state involvement in economic activities as is indeed the trend in many of the countries of former British Africa whose economies would need to be considerably de-regulated and liberalised to qualify them as a free society in the fullest sense of the term. The question, then, is whether this tendency ought, desirably, to be guarded against by enshrining in the constitution, non-justiciable principles directing the state as to the broad line of economic policy to be pursued conformably with the principles of both liberal democracy and social democracy. Nigeria has set the example in its 1979 and 1999 Constitutions.

Directive Principles of State Policy

The Constitution of Nigeria 1999, as also the 1979 one, enshrines certain Directive Principles of State Policy. First, the National Assembly is directed, by resolution, to declare what areas of the economy are to be "major sectors" to be managed and operated exclusively by the federal government, but until a resolution to the contrary is made by the National Assembly all economic activities being operated exclusively by the federal government on the date immediately preceding the coming into force of the constitution shall be deemed to be major sectors. Secondly, within the context of the declared ideals and objectives the state is directed to –

    (a)   control the national economy in such manner as to secure the maximum welfare, freedom and happiness of every citizen on the basis of social justice and equality of status and opportunity;

(b) without prejudice to its right to operate or participate in areas of the economy other than the major sectors of the economy, manage and operate the major sectors of the economy;

(c) without prejudice to the right of any person to participate in areas of the economy within the major sector of the economy, protect the right of every citizen to engage in any economic activities outside the major sectors of the economy (S. 16(1)).

Perhaps the first point to notice about these directives concerns the constitutional protection which they bestow upon freedom of private enterprise as well as upon exclusive state monopoly. It is not clear however whether pending a resolution of the National Assembly, the exclusiveness of the government's operation of any economic activity needs to exist *de jure* or merely *de facto* in order to constitute the activity a major sector of the economy. For example, the railways are an exclusive monopoly of the federal government, but the monopoly merely exists *de facto* and does not rest upon a legal prohibition of private enterprise as in the case of postal, telegraphic and wireless communications. It seems that once an economic activity is being operated exclusively by the federal government, whether *de facto* or *de jure*, it is deemed a major sector by virtue of this provision.

A further doubt is as to whether the government operation of an economic activity needs to be **completely** exclusive. Electricity is a case in point. Not only is private enterprise not legally prohibited, but the federal government does not have, through the National Electric Power Authority, a complete *de facto* exclusive monopoly over the generation, distribution and supply of electricity. It may be that the constitutional provision envisages a state monopoly that does not completely exclude a measure of private enterprise. This seems to derive some support from the provision that the duty of the state to protect private enterprise outside the major sectors is "without prejudice to the right of any person to participate in areas of the economy within the major sector of the economy." The clear implication of this provision is that private persons are not completely excluded from the major sectors of the economy. On this view, exclusiveness has a special meaning under the constitutional provision. While a majority of the Court of Appeal in the private school case from Lagos State preferred to leave the point open, Mr. Justice Nnaemeka-Agu expressed the view that the phrase "without prejudice to the right of any person to participate in areas of the economy within the major sector of the economy" is a contradiction of the idea of exclusiveness and is therefore meaningless and ineffective.[3]

But a far more important point for consideration is the extent of the power of the National Assembly to declare areas of the economy to be major sectors. The assumption, which is widely shared, is that the Assembly has an unfettered discretion in the matter. This is not correct. The National Assembly cannot by its declaration exclude a person from an area of economic activity which he has a right to pursue under the Bill of Rights. The directive principles from which the National Assembly derives its power to declare areas of the economy to be major sectors are meant to define the duties of the state towards the individual, not to curtail the rights guaranteed to him by the Bill of Rights. As the Court of Appeal rightly observed in the private school case,[4] relying on a decision of the Supreme Court of India[5] and affirming the judge of first instance, "the Directive Principles of State Policy have to conform to and run subsidiary to the chapter on Fundamental Rights."

Furthermore, any declaration by the National Assembly has to be made within the context of the ideals and objectives ordained for the nation by the constitution. It must therefore conform with the declared **ideals** of freedom, equality, social justice and democracy; and within the declared **objectives** of a planned and balanced economic development; avoidance of concentration of wealth or the means of production and exchange in the hands of few individuals or of a group; the prevention of exploitation; provision of adequate means of

---

3. *Archbishop Okogie v. Att-Gen of Lagos State*, Suit No. FCA/L/74/80 decided on 30/9/90.

4. *Archbishop Okogie v. Att-Gen of Lagos State*, ibid.

5. *State of Madras v. Champaham* (1951) S.C.R. 252.

livelihood and employment opportunities; suitable and adequate shelter; suitable and adequate food; a reasonable national minimum living wage; old age care and pensions; and unemployment and sick benefits for all citizens.

The **objectives** of preventing exploitation and the concentration of wealth, and the **ideals** of equality and social justice, manifest a stand against capitalism in its pure, undiluted form, since "unlimited private enterprise generates inequality, concentration of wealth (through survival of the fittest in the cut-throat competition of capitalism), exploitation (because wealth accumulation involves private appropriation of profit which defines exploitation of labour) and is, therefore, inherently unegalitarian."[6] Equally, the ideals of freedom and participatory democracy point against thoroughgoing socialism. There would seem thus to be implied by the declared ideals and objectives a kind of half-way house between capitalism and socialism, a mixed kind of system that will permit of individual freedom of participation in the economy as well as optimum state participation and control, aimed at promoting social justice, the public welfare, and the minimisation of exploitation, inequality and concentration of wealth.

Granted this mixture of capitalist and socialist elements, the really crucial question is to determine the proportions in which the constitution has directed that these elements should be mixed, and whether the one or the other should predominate in the mixture. While the ideal of freedom of economic participation by the individual is matched against that of equality and social justice, all the declared objectives have a socialist orientation. Effective national planning, for example, has quite aptly been said to be incompatible with private enterprise having a dominant position. Taking the ideals and the objectives together, therefore, the emphasis is perhaps more on the side of socialism, but it is not socialism in the sense that the state should own and manage all or most of the means of production and

---

6.   B. Onimode and E. Osagie, "Economic Aspect of the Draft Constitution," in *The Great Debate*, a *Daily Times* publication, 424.

distribution. While the state may own and operate a limited number of business enterprises, the directives in Chapter 2 of the Constitution seem to contemplate more the use of the state's virtually unlimited regulatory power in a purposeful manner to bring about a socialist-oriented economy; that is to say, an economy that strives, by means of appropriate regulations, for the minimisation of exploitation and the concentration of wealth in a few hands; the securing of adequate means of livelihood and employment opportunities, suitable and adequate shelter, a reasonable minimum living wage, old age care and pensions, unemployment and sick benefits, etc. These objectives do not necessarily dictate state ownership and management of all or most of the means of production and distribution, since they can, without going to that extreme, be quite effectively pursued through purposeful regulation, as the indigenisation programme of the military government illustrates. The law which authorises the indigenisation of foreign enterprises operating in the country lays it down as a guideline that:

(a) Beneficial ownership of the affected enterprises should be as widespread as the circumstances of each case would justify, and deliberate efforts must be made to prevent the concentration of ownership in a few hands.

(b) Except in the case of owner-managers, no enterprise should be sold or transferred to a single individual and in no case is a single individual to be allowed to have control of more than one enterprise.

(c) As far as appropriate, the appropriate authorities must ensure that no individual is to have in any enterprise more than 5 per cent of the equity or more than 50,000 Naira nominal value of the equity whichever is the higher.[7]

The state's power to regulate private business activities under the constitution is not a mere police power, being unrestricted by any

---

7.   Nigerian Enterprises Promotion Act 1977, which repeals a 1972 Act of the same name and its amending Acts of 1973, 1974, and 1976.

constitutional guarantee of freedom of private enterprise, which will make it necessary for a regulation, in order to be constitutionally valid, to have a real and substantial relation to the protection and promotion of the public welfare, and not to be otherwise unreasonable, arbitrary or discriminatory. The directive principles in Chapter 2 require the state, as a matter not of discretion but of constitutional duty, to exercise this power to regulate the economy in a socialist-oriented direction to bring about greater social justice through a redistribution of the nation's wealth, the minimisation of exploitation and of the concentration of wealth. It is in this sense more than in the sense of a mere co-existence of public and private sectors that the constitution may be said to envisage a mixed economy. In the words of one commentator:

> A mixed economy combines the individual's enterprise and initiative which permit the best use of one's talents for a productive advantage with a state regulatory and redistribution interest. It contrasts with a capitalist system by the simple fact that the state regulations and guidelines are an important feature of the economy in order to direct the economy towards a particular pattern of behaviour and a social goal. It also contrasts with a socialist system because the individual initiative which is given a little consideration in the socialist system is encouraged and maximised in the ideal economy.[8]

It seems a little too doctrinaire to say that a modern industrial economy must be "either essentially capitalist or essentially socialist."[9] There should be no logical inconsistency in an economy being socialist-oriented without being "essentially" socialist. Admittedly, the socialist-oriented economy contemplated by the Constitution may be "partly exploitative, partly unfree, partly undemocratic, partly unequal, partly unjust,"[10] but there has to be only that amount of freedom of private enterprise that can acceptably be combined with the minimum of exploitation, inequality and social injustice.[11]

---

8.   E. C. Ndukwu, "Mixed Economy,: in *The Great Debate*, op. cit, p. 413.

9.   Eskor Toyo, "Mixed Economy: Is it a solution to Modern Socio-Economic Problems," in *The Great Debate*, op. cit., p. 452.

10. Eskor Toyo, *op. cit.,* p. 453.

11. Cf Nwosu, "Issues in the Nigerian Draft Constitution," in *The Great Debate, op. cit.,* pp. 25-26, 27.

Some judicial light has recently been shed on the mixed economy concept of the constitution. In the private school case already referred to, Justice Agoro of the Lagos State High Court observed that "the state is enjoined to protect the right of every citizen to engage in any economic activities outside the major sectors of the economy as may from time to time be declared by a resolution of each house of the national assembly." On the argument that the directive of equal and adequate educational opportunities, being a specific provision, overrides the general protection of the right to engage in any economic activities outside the major sectors of the economy, he observed:

> While it is true that fundamental objectives are ideals towards which the Nation is expected to strive whilst directive principles lay down the policies which are expected to be pursued in the efforts of the Nation to realise the national ideals, it seems to me that the provision of 'equal and adequate educational opportunities' under section 18 of the Constitution only means that the government should make provision for educational facilities throughout the administrative divisions or local government areas in the State. The requirement to provide equal and adequate educational opportunities would not be interpreted, in my view, to mean that only schools established and operated by the government or its agencies could exist in the State. The free education programme of the government could be implemented, in my view, without destroying the private primary or elementary schools which had been and are still regarded as useful and meritorious. The fundamental objectives and directive principles enunciated in Section 18 of the Constitution are, in my view, objectives required to be carried out by any government in the Federation without necessarily restricting the right of other persons or organisations to provide similar or different educational facilities at their own expense.[12]

This view of the meaning and effect of the provisions was affirmed by the court of appeal.[13]

12. *Archbishop Okogie v. Att-Gen of Lagos State*, Suit No. ID/17M/80 decided on 18 July, 1980.

13. *Archbishop Okogie v. Att-Gen of Lagos State*, Suit No. FCA/L/74/80 decided on 30/9/80.

Index

Abdication, 304-305

Aboyade Technical Committee on Revenue Allocation, 153

Absolute monarchy, 21-22, 27, 29, 44, 201-202, 246

Absolute power, 64

Absolutism, 19, 243

Abstract constitution and institutions, 13

Act of
– British Parliament, 63
– Congress, 279
– Parliament, 71, 331

Action Group, 71

Advance popular democracy, 41

African one-party state, 40-41

American
– Constitution, 10-11, 20, 32, 206, 223-224, 243, 259, 269, 334
– presidential system, 250, 268-269, 271
– prototype, 223
– Revolution, 188, 195
– revolutionaries, 60, 64
– system, 1

Apartheid South Africa, 327

Appropriation Bill, 263-267

Appropriation Law, 265, 270

Authoritarian rule, 15

Banda, Kamuzu, 30-31

Banking business, 95

Belgian Constitution, 1

Bicameral Assembly, 209-210

Bill of
– Attainder, 293-294
– Pains and Penalties, 294
– Rights, 27-28, 44, 202-203, 320-321, 328, 385-386, 396-397, 399

Black African Community, 187

Blackstone, William, 293

Boigny, Felix Houphonet, 30

Bokassa, Jean-Bedel, 31

Bongo, Omar, 30

Boundary adjustments, 348

Bourguiba, Habib, 30-31

Bribery and corruption, 91

British
– colonialism, 198
– constitution, 36, 269
– constitutional theory and practice, 206
– parliament, 313, 319, 327, 329
– parliamentary system, 250, 267-269, 271
– protectorate, 137

Centurial Assembly, 22-23, 26, 201, 246

Checks and balances, 18, 22, 26, 248, 252
– main forms of, 22-26

Christian principles, 51

Civil
– liberties, 241
– guarantee of, 17
– Service Commission, 228, 231, 288
– constitutional function of, 288

Clinton, President, 354

Code of Conduct
– Bureau, 228, 231
– Tribunal, 228, 231

Collective responsibility, 234

Collegium, 24

Comity of Nations, 142

Common law, 133, 137, 140, 142, 234, 238, 240, 371, 374

Commonwealth Bill of Rights, 390

Communist
– constitution, 4, 45
– Party, 4, 38, 40
– theory and practice, 4
– type totalitarianism, 50

Congolese Labour Party (Congo Brazzaville), 39
Consolidated Revenue Fund, 263-290
Constituent Assembly, 11, 151, 158-159, 195-198
Constitution
   – amendment of, 78-79
   – definition of, 36-37
   – Drafting Committee (CDC), 64, 151, 153, 155-156, 158-159, 234
   – execution of, 217-220
   – functions of, 36-58
   – meaning of, 60
Constitutional
   – amendment, 158, 324
   – Council, 314, 319
   – crisis, 327
   – democracy, 1-35, 241, 252, 313, 317, 320, 322, 363, 370
       – definition of, 8, 11-12
       – historical origins and evolution of. 21-35
       – relation to democratic government, 13-17
   – government, 2, 28, 203
       – concept of, 1-35
       – meaning of, 2-3
   – history, 252
   – limit, 143
   – limitations, 313, 319, 332
   – power, 46, 302
   – primacy, 334-338
   – protection, 398
   – right, 128, 158
Constitutionalism, 23, 44, 201, 207, 241-246, 313, 316, 326
Continental shelf, 124-126, 140-141, 144-145, 147-149
Corrupt practices and abuse of power, 115-116
Corruption and fraud, 114
Council of State, 228-229
Criminal
   – Code, 86, 106, 109-110, 114, 186
   – law, 237
   – legislation, 182
   – Procedure Code, 299-300
Cyprus Constitution, 54

Czechoslovak Federation, 58

Democracy Day Broadcast, 344
Democratic
   – and Industrial Age, 188
   – government
       – definition of, 15
   – Party of Guinea (PDG), 41
Democratisation
       – definition of, 16
Despotic government, 2
Dictatorial powers, 3
Diori, Hamani, 30
Directive Principles of State Policy, 397-403
Distributable Pool Account, 119
Dominant tradition, 10
Douglas-Home, Alec, 32

Emergency declaration
   – objective facts for, 73-74
Enforcement Machinery, 312-319
Estate tax, 96
Ethnic nationalities, 198
Exchange Control Regulations, 393
Exclusive Economic Zone, 124-126, 131-132, 134, 142
Executive power, 43-44, 65-66, 71, 73
   – nature and extent of, 211-240
Extra-territorial – laws, 131-133
       – legislation, 130
       – constitutionality of, 131-133
Eyadema, Gnassingbe, 30

Fatayi-Williams, Justice, 97, 310
Federal
   – character principle, 56-58
   – Civil Service Commission, 286-287, 292
   – offences, 107, 110
       – categories of, 107-108; 110·
   – Trade Commission, 283
Federalism, 59-62, 78, 80, 97-98, 149-150, 158-159
Federation Account, 83, 119, 128-129, 148
Finance bill, 193, 207, 276
Financial Legislation

– initiation of, 263-270
First World War, 44
Fraternity, 50
Freedom of
– expression, assembly and association, 6
– speech and press, 5, 350
FRELIMO (Mozambique), 39
French
– Constitutional Council, 315
– Parliament, 313, 319
– Revolution, 188
– System, 1, 259, 271-272, 274
Fundamental
– liberties and individual rights, 5
– rights and freedom, 103

Gaddafi, Muammar, 30, 39, 197
Gledhill, Alan, 213
Government bills, 275
Governmental
– autocracy, 370
– democracy, 247
Greek Age, 188
Guidance for the Registration of Political Parties, 379

Hamilton, Alexander, 9, 33, 313
House of
– Assembly Service Commission, 289
– Commons, 209
– Lords, 209

Ikoku-Okadigbo peace agreement, 362
Income Tax, 96
Independence
– Act, 138
– movements, 37
– Order-in-Council, 63
Independent
– Corrupt Practices and Related Offences Commission (ICPC), 90-91, 98, 116
– National Electoral Commission (INEC), 166, 352, 374
Industrial Revolution, 188
Inherent Power Theory, 221
Institutional government, 12

Instrument of Government, 60
International
– community, 134, 141
– conventious, 133
– law, 121-122, 124-125, 133-134, 136, 140, 144, 317
Interstate Commerce Commission, 283

Jackson, Andrew, 224
Jackson, Robert, 13
Jawara, Dauda, 30
Johnson, President, 254, 354
Jonathan, Lebua, 30
Judicial
– Committee of Privy Council, 8, 43, 61-62, 101, 108-110, 183, 193, 293-294, 298, 316, 335, 371, 380, 382
– Service Commission, 287, 289

Kaduna State Appropriation Law, 256
Kaunda, Kenneth, 30-31
Kenyan Constitution, 205
Kenyata, Jomo, 30
Khama, Seretse, 30

Land - locked nations, 125
Land title, 82
Legislation
– in modern government, 181-210
– initiation of, 258-263
Legislative
– act, 21
– authority, 23
– judgement, 293, 381
– list, 67, 71
– powers, 42-43, 75, 101, 105, 132, 163, 183, 193-194, 198, 204-206, 208-209, 212-213, 248, 253, 258-260, 281, 291, 295, 300-302, 308-310, 338, 381, 383, 386-387
Liberal democracy, 397
Life presidency, 31, 340
Lincoln, Abraham, 354
Littoral states, 119, 121-127, 141-147, 149
Local governments
– councils, 84
– Elections, 165-170

- reforms, 156
- Service Board, 345
Local governments
- finances, 174-175
- functions of, 170-174, 179

Macmillan, Harold, 32
Mariam, Menigstu Haile, 3
Mboya, Tom, 205
Mcllwain, Charles, 60, 201, 241, 245-246, 252
Medieval Age, 188
Military administration, 58
Mineral revenue, 127
Modern Age, 188
Money bill, 209-210
Moral responsibility, 326
Moslem countries, 51
MPLA – Workers' Party of Angola, 39
Municipal law, 217
Musa, Balarabe, 344, 361-363
Nasser, Abdel, 304

Nation
- definition of, 48
National Assembly, 43, 67, 74-75, 81-86, 90, 92, 106-107, 111-112, 115-117, 126, 128-129, 132-133, 148-154, 157-158, 165-166, 169, 173-175, 192-193, 198, 205-209, 213, 215-217, 221-222, 252-255, 258-259, 263-264, 266-271, 273-274, 276, 284-289, 291-292, 296, 306, 309, 311, 315-317, 346-350, 353, 363-364, 369
        - Service Commission, 287,
                - Bill, 289
National
- Association for the Advancement of Coloured People, 378
- character, 60
- Constitution, 47
- Defence Council, 228
- Economic Council, 228
- Electoral Commission, 231
- expenditure, 264
- Front for the Defence of the Revolution (Madagascar), 39

government, 66, 80
- Judicial Council, 290
- Liberation Front (FLN) Algeria, 39
- loyalty, 56
- Population Commission, 228, 231
- question, 58
- Security Council, 68, 228
Niger Delta Development Corporation, 284
Nigeria
- Police Council, 87, 231, 292
- Police Force, 84-86
Nigerian
- Constitution
    - rights guaranteed, 387-389
- Labour Congress, 368
Nkrumah, Kwame, 30-31, 198, 299
Nyerere, Julius, 30

Obasanjo, President, 193, 271, 344, 352, 364, 367-369
Official corruption, 342
Okigbo Presidential Commission on Revenue Allocation Report, 125
Oriental Empires, 188

Parliamentary
- bills, 275
- system, 176-177, 267
Paulus, Julius, 181
Penal Code, 86, 106, 109-110, 114
Peoples Democratic Party (PDP), 349, 369
Plural Society, 53, 55
Police
- Council, 228
- Service Commission, 88-89, 228, 231, 292
Political
- act, 10, 194
- association, 47, 374-375, 377, 379
- campaigning, 325
- camps, 340
- community, 10-11, 36-37, 194-195
- competition, 343
- control, 233, 240
- creation, 194
- education, 200
- expression, 155

- function, 343
- game, 13, 15
- groups, 15
- institutions, 28, 71, 313
  - definition of, 12
- line, 39
- objective, 6
- office, 15, 24
- organisation, 37
- organs, 255, 281, 314, 324, 344, 346
- orientation, 39
- party/parties, 15, 37-40, 81, 251, 317, 323, 343, 359, 374, 376-379
- power, 8, 137, 184, 363
- responsibility, 16
- retaliation, 359
- societies, 188
  - historical evolution of, 188
- theory, 195
Popular Movement for the Liberation of Angola (MPLA), 39
Popular Revolution Party of Benin (PRPB), 39
Power and jurisdiction, 137-140
President-in-Council, 70-71
Presidential System, 176-180, 244, 251, 272
Principle of derivation, 146-149
Private law, 22
Public
- affairs, 42
- expenditures, 263
- policy, 168
- rules and institutions, 13
- welfare, 50

Queen's Coronation oath, 218-219
Quota reservations, 55-56

Racial discrimination, 391
Regional governments, 62-63, 96, 150
Religious beliefs, 188
Religious rites, 24
Residual or Inherent Power Theory, 213
Resource control, 120
Revenue
- allocation commission, 152

- allocation formula and principles, 152
- Mobilisation Allocation and Fiscal Commission (RMAFC), 151, 153
- sharing formula, 129, 149
Revolutionary, 183, 186, 204
- concept of,
- movement, 40
- popular government, 41
- socialist Constitution of Russia, 1918
Roman
- Age, 188
- Law, 136, 182
Roosevelt, Franklin, 33-34, 224, 262, 272
Roosevelt, Theodore, 33, 213, 224, 262
Roseberg, Carl, 13
Rule of
- custom, 188
- law, 20, 50, 244, 313, 371, 379, 381

Saharawi Arab Republic (SADR), 39
Second Republic, 350
Second World War, 33, 48, 196
Seko, Mobutu Sese, 30
Self-government, 319-320, 351
Senghor, Leopold, 30
Separation of Powers, 18, 20-21, 44, 205, 213, 223, 349, 370, 381-382
- consequences flowing from, 278-311
- limits of, 258-277
- merits and demerits, 241-257, 285
Shagari, Shehu, 285
Sham democracy, 39
Sharia law, 367
Single Constitution
- execution and maintenance of, 65-79
Smith, Ian, 327
Social justice, 50, 52-53, 55-56
Socialist
- communist state, 5
- constitution, 3-4, 6-7
- constitution of Ethiopia, 3
- democratism, 5
- legality, 40
- oriented constitutions, 1
- party-state, 38

– Peoples' Libyan Arab Jamahiriya, 39
– Revolution, 5
– Society, 5
– states, 1, 3, 5-6, 39-41
Somali Revolutionary Socialist Party, 39
Sovereignty, 183, 186, 204, 329, 338, 380
– concept of, 133-144
Soyinka, Wole, 48
Specific Grant Theory, 213-214, 221
State
– Electoral Commission, 345
– Houses of Assembly, 43
– Independent Electoral Commission,
167
– of emergency, 69-70, 74, 347-348
Stewardship doctrine, 213
Supreme Military Council, 374
Sustainable democracy, 337-369

Territorial waters, 121-122, 124-125, 131-
132, 134, 140
Thatcher, Margaret, 32
Totalitarian regime, 2
Totalitarianism, 19, 243, 313
Toure, Sekou, 30, 41
Tribal
– Assembly, 22, 25-26, 201, 246
– loyalty, 56
Tubman, William, 30

Udoma, Udo, 98
Unitary Constitution for Federal System, 59-
89
United Nations Convention on the Law of
the Sea, (1982), 121-122, 124, 133,
140-141
Universal
– adult suffrage, 29, 203
– suffrage, 203
Unwritten constitution, 7-8

Von Hayek, Friedrich, 181

Washington, George, 32-33, 223, 273
Welfare state, 48
Westminster
– export model, 1
– parliamentary system, 204
– system, 20, 244
Williams, Rotimi, 132, 141
Wilson, Woodrow, 224, 273
Workers' Party, 40
– of Ethiopia (WPE), 39
Written
– constitution, 3, 9, 28, 36-37, 41-42,
44, 49, 183, 186, 189, 197, 278,
313, 335, 380
– functions of, 36